W9-ADI-900

Cover: Eugène Laermans,
'Exodus', central panel of
The Emigrants (detail).
1896. Canvas, 159 x 224
cm. Koninklijk Museum
voor Schone Kunsten,
Antwerp.

Published by the

The Low Countries

9

ARTS AND SOCIETY IN FLANDERS AND THE NETHERLANDS

Flemish-Netherlands Foundation 'Stichting Ons Erfdeel', 2001

ontents

Arts+Society

Gift

Low Countries, Host Countries?

10-14-01

Chronicle

Architecture

Cultural Policy

Visual Arts

Low Countries, Host Countries?

Foreword

The Geneva Convention on Refugees of 1951 for the first time included the 'right to asylum'. But now, fifty years on, more and more countries, including those of the European Union, are finding this humanitarian principle a nuisance. Fortress Europe opens its gates only to a fortunate few. And this despite demographic statistics which indicate that because of its ageing population Europe will need over 100 million new immigrants by about 2025.

In the Netherlands and Belgium, as elsewhere, restrictive measures have been introduced in an attempt to stem the flood of refugees. This attitude has caused some concern to the former United Nations High Commissioner for Refugees, Sadako Ogata; visiting the Netherlands in July 2000, she called for a new flowering of Europe's old humanitarian values.

After all, throughout the centuries the Low Countries have had a liberal tradition of offering refuge to the persecuted and oppressed. That is why the themed section of this yearbook is called 'Low Countries, Host Countries?'. It begins with a historical tour of the Low Countries as a refuge for the spirit, in the course of which we encounter René Descartes at his desk in Amsterdam, Charlotte and Emily Brontë at a Brussels boarding-school, Stefan Zweig and Joseph Roth on a café terrace in Ostend, Klaus Mann in his Amsterdam base and Karl Marx in a Belgian jail.

Gustave van de Woestijne,
Hospitality for Strangers.
1920.
Fresco, 66.7 x 74.3 cm.
Museum voor Schone
Kunsten, Ghent.

The last of the themed articles explains the question-mark in the title. It explores the boundaries of hospitality, discussing decolonisation, guest workers and the growing flood of refugees and showing how these factors have changed the Netherlands and Flanders over recent decades.

Between these two articles is a piece on 'intercultural authors', together with a group of texts in which a few of these authors speak for themselves. Intercultural authors? Like all labels, the term is convenient but restrictive. The choice of theme for the 2001 Netherlands Book Week – *Country of Origin: Writing between Two Cultures* – elicited from critics such words as 'parochialism', 'neo-colonialism' and 'apartheid mentality'. After all, don't all real writers work between different cultures, aren't they all in one way or another displaced persons? And some of the authors referred to above have already featured in this yearbook without any mention of their origins. The first yearbook in this series took as its motto Ralph Waldo Emerson's remark that '*The triumph of culture is to overpower nationality*'. And these writers vividly illustrate that.

The editors

Convenient Desert

The Low Countries as a Refuge for the Spirit

René Descartes first arrived in the Netherlands in 1618. An officer in the young Republic's army, which was more or less idle because of the Twelve Years' Truce, he stayed in Breda for about a year. Subsequently he spent a few years travelling round Central Europe and sampling salon society in Paris, before returning to the Republic in 1629. He was then 33.

In May 1648 he wrote to Chanut from Paris: '*The innocence of the desert from which I come pleased me much more, and I do not believe I can keep myself from returning in a little while.*' By that time the French philosopher had lived in the Netherlands for nearly twenty years. He wrote his great works there, and had a daughter whom he lost when she was five. He had chosen the country because people left him in peace there, and he could concentrate on his meditations. In France he felt he was the victim of superficial and time-consuming worldly obligations and an object of curiosity for bothersome visitors, so between the end of 1628 and September 1649 he went there only three times for a few months. In the Netherlands he sang the praises of the population's discretion and the pure, dry air that was so beneficial to the spirit: '*A stove and a great fire will keep you from being cold here*'.

At the end of part 3 of his *Discourse on Method* (Discours de la méthode, 1637) he wrote that he had retired to '*a country where the long duration of the war [had] established such well-ordered discipline that the armies quartered there seem to be there solely for the purpose of guaranteeing the enjoyment of the fruits of peace with even greater security, and where among the crowds of a great and very busy people and more concerned with their own affairs than curious about the affairs of others, I have been able to live as solitary and as retired a life as I could in the remotest deserts – but without lacking any of the amenities that are to be found in the most populous cities.*'

Descartes had indeed sought out a remarkable nation-in-the-making. The Republic was actually an administrative patchwork where, as a rule, the power of the authorities extended no further than the next town or province. The real power had been carved up between the States General, the Dutch Reformed Church and the stadtholder and his court. The States General, in

Anonymous portrait of
René Descartes.
Amsterdams Historisch
Museum.

which Holland dominated the other provinces, remained a colourful collection of ideologically divided provinces and towns that was condemned to reach consensus. The supremacy of the Calvinist Church continued to be challenged by strong minorities. The office of stadtholder never developed into that of an absolute monarchy and still had to contend with periodic vacancies and powerful opponents. Given the situation, constant compromise was required between flexibility and strictness, tolerance and purges.

In the framework of this complex organisation, which despite its economic and military successes was constantly under threat from outside, toleration was not a grand theoretical principle but rather a pleasant result of the circumstances, inspired by pragmatic and often opportunistic considerations and commercial good sense. The scope of negotiations as to what was or was not permissible was determined locally and continually redefined. The most important criterion was public order. This was how, in practical terms, people managed to live side by side and get on with each other. Perhaps, then, coexistence is a more accurate term than toleration. E.H. Kossman puts it rather nicely in his essay 'Republican Freedom against Monarchical Absolutism: The Dutch Experience in the Seventeenth Century': '*The point is that (the governmental system's) very complexity and the immense variety of customs, regulations and arrangements operating in the seven sovereign republics, their numerous towns and their countryside, all treasuring their old traditions (real or imagined), often prevented uniform legislation from being issued either on the federal or the provincial level or, if it was actually issued, from being effective. This created room for a form of pluralism decried by foreign absolutists as anarchy and disorder but cherished by the Dutch as liberty.*'

This being so, Descartes did encounter problems in the Netherlands with Calvinist theologians and academic pedants who considered that the new philosophy posed a threat to Aristotelian concepts, and that methodical and universal doubt was a licence for '*ongodisten*', unbelievers. In 1642 the University of Utrecht condemned the teaching of his philosophy. Descartes sought rehabilitation from the authorities and even went to the French Ambassador, who took it up with the stadtholder Frederick Henry. He made it clear to the authorities in Utrecht that they should leave Descartes in peace. In 1647, though, the University of Leiden did ban Cartesianism. But the French philosopher misjudged these administrative orders, which were never actually enforced. Although he praised Dutch tolerance in letters to his French friends, he does not seem to have understood how it really worked. He also underestimated the genuine success his ideas enjoyed in the Netherlands. Cartesians were appointed alongside Aristotelians in the universities, in a subtle balancing act intended to guarantee continuity and avoid excesses. They were often protected, even, as long as they left theology well alone.

The presses roll

In 1650 there were 265 printers, publishers and booksellers active in 38 different places in the Republic, twice as many as twenty years earlier. They supplied not only the domestic market, but the whole of Europe. The Republic's newspapers were considered to be the best informed and most reliable on the Continent. After all, traders need fast and reliable information. Press freedom was certainly not guaranteed there, but it was greater than anywhere else in Europe. It was the product of local political relations, enlightened economic self-interest, and a persistent testing of the limits by writers and printers, as well as of a considerable genuine religious pluralism. Most bans stemmed from the authorities' desire to maintain peace and order, and not to ruffle relations with foreign powers unnecessarily. In 1649, for example, following the execution of Charles I, the States of Holland, which were the most susceptible to foreign pressure, forbade preachers to express any opinions on the English question from the pulpit.

The only book Spinoza published under his own name was one on Descartes' ideas. Not for nothing was his motto '*caute*' ('cautiously'). His *Tractatus Theologico-Politicus* (1670) appeared anonymously. The book, which contained radical criticism of the Bible and a passionate plea for freedom of speech, provoked a storm of censure. No one doubted the author's identity, and the suspicion of atheism – the watershed in all press freedom – was not far away. In 1672, after the ghastly murder of the De Witt brothers who had

DICTIONAIRE
HISTORIQUE
ET
CRITIQUE:
Par Monsieur BAYLE
TOME PREMIER,
PREMIERE PARTIE.
A—B.

A ROTTERDAM,
Chez REINIER LEERS,
MDCXCVII.
AVEC PRIVILEGE.

TRACTATUS
THEOLOGICO-
POLITICUS

Continens
Differtationes aliquot,

Quibus oftenditur Libertatem Philofophandi non tantum
falva Pietate, & Reipublicæ Pace poffe concedi: fed
eandem nifi cum Pace Reipublicæ, ipfaque
Pietate tolli non poffe.

Johann: Epift: I. Cap: IV. verf: XIII.

*Per hoc cognofcimus quod in Deo manemus, & Deus manet
in nobis, quod de Spiritu fuo dedit nobis.*

HAMBURGI,
Apud *Henricum Künraht*. cIɔ Iɔ cLXX.

Title-page of Spinoza's *Tractatus Theologico-Politicus* (Hamburg (*sic*), 1670).

Title-page of the first edition of John Locke's *Epistola de Tolerantia* (Gouda, 1689).

Title-page of the first volume of Pierre Bayle's *Dictionaire historique et critique* (Rotterdam, 1697).

EPISTOLA
de
TOLERANTIA
ad
Clariffimum Virum
T. A. R. P. T. O. L. A.
Scripta à
P. A. P. O. I. L. A

GOUDÆ,
Apud JUSTUM AB HOEVE
cIɔ Iɔc Lxxxix.

probably protected Spinoza, it was banned. Wisely, Spinoza left his *Ethica* in the drawer. At any rate, one could get away with more in Latin than in Dutch, as Adriaan Koerbagh, a passionate Spinozist, was to discover in 1668. He was thrown into prison, where he died of his privations. All was not doom and gloom, though.

John Locke followed his disgraced friend, the Earl of Shaftesbury, into exile in Holland in 1683. He was to stay there for more than five years. It was a productive period in the philosopher's life, and he often looked back on his exile with affection. The air suited him, as it had Descartes. His health, which was always delicate, improved there. At last he had the time to organise his thoughts and his many notes, and he made friendships there that lasted a lifetime. When James II's envoy asked for his extradition, he went into hiding for a while in Amsterdam. Soon, though, he could move freely again and took the opportunity to travel throughout the country. In 1689 Locke returned to England in the retinue of Mary Stuart, the future Queen Mary, the daughter of the deposed James II and wife of William III of Orange.

Locke's *Epistola de Tolerantia* (Letter concerning Toleration), dedicated to the theologian Philip van Limborch, was published anonymously in Gouda in 1689, after his return to England. The topic was dealt with in the Netherlands by the French Huguenot exile Pierre Bayle, after the revocation of the Edict of Nantes in 1685. Locke and Bayle had met and respected each other, although Bayle held more radical opinions than the English philosopher. In his view atheism did not necessarily lead to moral corruption, but for Locke that was a bridge too far. In the Netherlands, Locke himself associated with Remonstrants, who were averse to imposing their convictions on others and opposed the Calvinist doctrine that met persecution with persecution.

Byron passed through Brussels in 1816, fleeing the scandal that surrounded his private life. The plaque on his lodgings near the park in Brussels says that his own country *'failed to recognise his genius'*. It is questionable whether Brussels, then part of the United Netherlands, recognised it either. He visited the brand new battlefield at Waterloo, of course, and told the story of the battle in the Third Canto of *Childe Harold.* Belgium became fashionable with travelling French writers, too, in the years following its creation in 1830. They came there to take the first trains on the Continent between Brussels and Antwerp and, like Victor Hugo, they were impressed with the artistic heritage of the Flemish cities.

Charlotte and Emily Brontë also descended on Brussels for several months in 1842, and went to boarding school there. The city had not yet acquired the evil reputation as a centre of the white slave trade and child prostitution that it would get after William Thomas Stead's investigative journalism in the 1880s. The Protestant sisters felt isolated in this Catholic milieu. They considered the locals as strange and inferior beings, and Emily was homesick for the rugged freedom of the moors. In 1843 Charlotte returned to Brussels alone to teach. She fell in love with the teacher and director of the school, Constantine Héger, the first erudite man she had met. Her unrequited love would result in the novels *Villette* (1853; 'Citylet', Brussels of course, in the country of *Labassecour,* 'The Farmyard') and the posthumous *The Professor* (1857).

Political refugees were attracted to Belgium by the reputation of the young country's modern, liberal constitution, but their choice was dominated by practical considerations. Above all Belgium was cheap, and one could easily get along in French. Since French was the *lingua franca* of the nineteenth-century European élite, this suited many political exiles, like the Poles after the failed revolt against their Russian occupiers in 1831. The country was centrally located between France, England and the German states, and communication was easy. Joachim Lelewel, the Polish historian and democratic leader, was to live in Brussels from 1833 until his death in 1861, and himself attracted many Polish exiles. But his choice of Belgium when he was expelled from France in 1833 was largely fortuitous, dictated by circumstances more than anything else. In the meantime, Lelewel, whose very name was banned in the Russian Empire, became the top attraction in Brussels for Russians travelling in Belgium.

Karl Marx arrived in Brussels in February 1845, after being expelled from France because of his revolutionary articles in the German newspaper *Vorwärts.* He had to sign an undertaking not to engage in any political activity in his new host country. Marx realised that his political activities could get him into trouble in Brussels. He renounced his Prussian citizenship in the hope of being left in peace and wrote a letter to King Leopold I requesting asylum, but got no reply. It later appeared from the archives that his request was refused. He moved frequently as he often had difficulties with the rent, but finally he, his wife and three children lived for two years in a street off the Avenue Louise, where he wrote the *Communist Manifesto* (1848). Ever loyal, Friedrich Engels, whom Marx had met in Paris, also came to Brussels at his behest. Policemen shadowed the bearded thinker as he dined in the

Title-page of the first part of Victor Hugo's *Les Misérables* (Brussels, 1862).

Karl Marx led away by two policemen in Brussels.

Swan on the Grand-Place, now an exclusive and expensive restaurant. But when it rains in Paris drops fall on Brussels. When an angry crowd stormed the Tuileries Palace in 1848 and threw the King's throne out of the window, they sang the Marseillaise and shouted *Vive la République* on the Grand-Place in Brussels. At this point liberal Belgians decided things had gone far enough. Marx was deported as a foreign agitator, after another brief spell in the Amigo prison in Brussels. Even his wife, '*Mme Jenny Marx, née Baroness de Westphalen*', ended up in the Amigo, though not in an ordinary cell. Belgium became a footnote in Marx' work. In *Das Kapital* (1867-1894) he refuted the idea current in England that Belgium was a 'workers' paradise'. Nothing was further from the truth, according to Marx. On the contrary, it was a capitalists' paradise.

But not everyone was a political exile. The colony of temporary émigrés often consisted of people on the run from their creditors, especially Frenchmen; Brussels was, after all, close to Paris.

In the first half of the nineteenth century there were many books in Brussels even if they were pirated editions that were sold at rock-bottom prices. In 1827 three thousand printers are said to have made their living out of pirated editions. Balzac's novels went for a tenth of the price they were sold for in France. '*I am 39 years old, I have debts of 150,000 francs and Belgium holds the 1 million francs I have earned*', the author complained. In 1834, Stendhal wrote to Sainte-Beuve that if he could get French literature in Rome it was only thanks to the Belgian editions. Clever entrepreneurial writers like Victor Hugo and Alexandre Dumas, with the motto '*If you can't beat them, join them*', managed to profit from the situation. Hugo

received large honoraria from the Brussels publisher Lacroix-Verboeck-hoven & Co, which had bought out a few pirate publishers. The successful and prolific Dumas also managed to off-load a serial that had been censored in Paris on a Brussels pirate publisher, as an unabridged edition.

On 11 December 1851 Victor Hugo crossed the Belgian border again, this time in the guise of a labourer, and went into self-imposed exile after the coup staged by the future Napoleon III. He rented a room on the Grand-Place in Brussels and installed his discarded but faithful mistress in a side passage of the Saint Hubert Galleries, one of the first covered shopping arcades in Europe. It was built in the famine year 1847 under the motto '*omnia om-*

The departure of Victor Hugo and Alexandre Dumas from Antwerp on 1 August 1852, drawn by F. Lix.

nibus' ('everything for everyone'). On 1 August 1852, the writer set off from Antwerp for London and Jersey, waved off by Dumas and cheered by Belgian democrats and exiles. He had promised the Mayor of Brussels not to disturb Franco-Belgian relations and only allowed his pamphlet *Napoléon le Petit* to appear on 5 August. Exiled from France, he was then expelled by the English after criticising Queen Victoria's state visit to Napoleon III, and withdrew to Guernsey. He returned to Belgium briefly in 1861 to do *'an autopsy on the catastrophe'* of Waterloo for the description of the battle in *Les Misérables*. The following year he launched his great novel at a banquet in Brussels, in front of the world's press. With a flair for literary marketing, he toasted the 'famous' Belgian freedom of the press. Hugo returned to Paris in triumph on 5 September 1870, after the debacle at Sedan and the proclamation of the Republic. But he spent the time of the Paris Commune (the revolutionary government of Paris) back in Brussels, where he had been summoned to settle his deceased son's debts. On 27 May 1871, after the Belgian Government had refused to give asylum to militants from the Commune, *L'Indépendance belge* published the writer's extraordinary declaration: *'I offer asylum, place des Barricades, no.4'*. The same evening, disturbances broke out under his window. Indignant young men, including a minister's son, came to shout abuse at him and sing the Brabançonne. Stones were thrown and windows broken. After a turbulent sitting, parliament had Hugo thrown out of the country. Only five socialist members had opposed the measure; Hugo sent them an emotional letter of thanks from Luxembourg.

Disturbances broke out under Victor Hugo's window, place des Barricades, no. 4, Brussels on 27 May 1871 (Print after a sketch by M. Von Elliot).

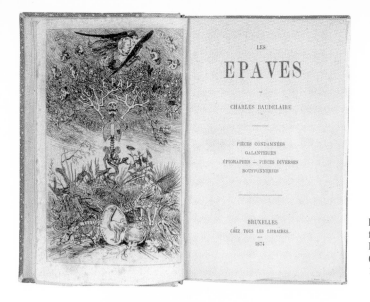

Félicien Rops' frontispiece for an edition of Charles Baudelaire's *Wreckage* (Les Epaves, Brussels, 1874).

The Saint Hubert Galleries in Brussels, built in 1847. Photo by Marc Boseret.

Charles Baudelaire arrived in Brussels in 1864, on the run from his creditors and frustrated in his artistic ambitions. He was 43 and was to remain in Brussels until two months before his death in 1867. Baudelaire hoped that Hugo's publisher, Lacroix, would publish his books and set up a lecture circuit, but nothing came of it. He met his Parisian publisher there, a fellow-exile who made a living publishing eighteenth-century French erotica and pamphlets against the Emperor of France. He published *Wreckage* (Les Epaves), Baudelaire's condemned poems from *The Flowers of Evil* (Les Fleurs du Mal), in Brussels in 1866. Very soon, though, the poet found in Brussels the same thing he had run away from in France, but in greater measure. As his syphilis spread he became more and more irritated with his country of exile. He began to collect all kinds of material for a monumental book, an inventory of his irritation with his host country. Its working title

Louis Ghémar, The 'Géant' hot-air balloon in Brussels. 1864. Musée Carnavalet, Paris.

was *Poor Belgium* (Pauvre Belgique). It was to be the most vicious work ever written about Belgium, a magnification of his hatred of life, a reversal of Nietzsche's exalted *Ecce Homo*, an *Ecce Belgica*. It was a frontal attack by a splenetic dandy on the mediocrity and materialism of the increasingly prosperous little country, and on Brussels – *Petit Paris* – in particular. Every afternoon, Baudelaire walked for half an hour in the Saint Hubert Galleries: '*I walk exactly two thousand measured paces and then I go back to my room. That is my only physical exercise. I have never been as far as the Park.*' A far cry from the *flâneur* in the urban 'passages' described by Walter Benjamin. When he did get out of the capital for a while he was, much to his own surprise, charmed by the Flemish towns and landscapes; but always had to imagine the Flemish themselves were not there. But Baudelaire could not get away from Belgium. In the end he could not even get off the ground in a balloon. When the photographer and journalist Nadar, at the Porte de Schaerbeek, invited him on a flight Baudelaire was forced, at the last minute, to stay on the ground as there was too much ballast. Austria and Turkey, where he had hoped to end up, remained inaccessible.

On 10 July 1873, Paul Verlaine fired two shots at Arthur Rimbaud with his revolver in the Hotel à la Ville de Courtray, in rue des Brasseurs, close to the Grand-Place in Brussels. Verlaine had left Rimbaud penniless in London, but his young demon had followed him to Brussels. Although Rimbaud later withdrew his charge, Verlaine still ended up in an ordinary cell in the nearby Amigo prison. Two months later Rimbaud was back in

Brussels to offer *A Season in Hell* (Une saison en enfer) to a publisher. The book, which was finally published at the author's expense, attracted absolutely no attention. Rimbaud kept a few author's copies of this, the only work he himself published during his lifetime. He personally brought one with a dedication to Verlaine in prison. In 1901 a bibliophile discovered the bulk of the edition sitting in a warehouse in Brussels. With a little goodwill, one might consider this accidental preservation of a masterpiece to be Brussels publishers' last contribution to French literature in exile.

Jef Rosman, *Arthur Rimbaud, July 1873*. Panel, 25 x 32 cm. Musée Arthur Rimbaud, Charleville-Mézières.

Götterdämmerung

On 30 January 1933, even before the official announcement of Hitler's appointment as Chancellor, Joseph Roth took the early train from Berlin to Paris. Roth saw all too clearly what was about to happen and knew that he had no future any more. From that moment on he was to drink himself slowly and methodically to death, in the midst of his admirers. Consider alcohol as his version of '*innere Emigration*'. In the meantime, he kept himself going for the six years he had left by writing half of his oeuvre. He continued his uncompromising battle against the Nazis, but realised that the writer in exile who warns his host country about the enemy goes unheeded and, worse still, that the host country does not want to be warned.

So France was Roth's one and only choice, but meanwhile it was little 'Holland' that published the German emigrants' work after the burning of books on 10 May 1933, and the publication ban on 250 Jewish and non-Jewish writers. In the space of seven years, forty-nine publishers brought out three hundred German books. It was not easy, though. Since the expulsion of the French in 1813 the Netherlands had basked in the cosy neutrality which had spared the country from the First World War. The German Kaiser Wilhelm II even found asylum there in 1918. He was to live and hunt there undisturbed until his death in 1941. Indeed, the Netherlands maintained the closest economic ties with its larger neighbour. Conservatives and many intellectuals were more afraid of communism than of Nazism. But between 1933 and 1940 tens of thousands would cross the Dutch border to escape their country, some passing through, others staying. Amongst them were about 7,000 political refugees and some fifty writers. If they stayed, or turned up regularly in Amsterdam, it was to see their publishers. From 1933 on, for example, nearly all Roth's books were first published in the Netherlands, by Querido Verlag, the German section of the Amsterdam publishing house of the same name, and by the German section of Allert de Lange and De Gemeenschap (Bilthoven). Emanuel Querido, '*a small, white-haired man with a lot of temperament*' (Klaus Mann), was a Dutchman of Portuguese-Jewish origin, a social democrat who hated fascism in all its forms. During the German occupation the Nazis were to deport him and his wife to Poland and murder them. Querido published, amongst others, Klaus and Heinrich Mann, Erich-Maria Remarque, Alfred Döblin, Ludwig Marcuse, Vicki Baum and Bruno Frank. But Roth was one of the stars of the *Exil-Literatur*. He could demand exorbitant advances and, with a tumbler full of geneva in hand, amaze the Dutch press with his theory that only the House of Habsburg could save Europe.

For him a day in Amsterdam went as follows: he used to take the ferry from the Eden Hotel in Warmoesstraat across Damrak, then, armed with

Joseph Roth (l.) and friends in Café Reynders, Amsterdam, 1936. Joseph Roth Collection, New York.

Stefan Zweig and Joseph Roth in Ostend, 1930s. Library of Congress (Ben Huebsch Collection, Manuscript Division), Washington, DC.

bottles of Bols, he would write his books in a bay window in the Hotel de Pool. He could also be seen writing in Café Scheltema, Nieuwezijds Voorburgwal. The evening he would spend with friends in Café Reynders on the Leidseplein. Roth, too, respected Amsterdam for its toleration, but he did not settle there because most of the German-speaking emigrants were socialists, and he continued to rave about God and old imperial Austria. According to Anton van Duinkerken, his closest Dutch friend, he used to introduce himself in cafés as '*Joseph Roth, officer of the Imperial and Royal Austro-Hungarian Army*'. Van Duinkerken, essayist, historian, poet and brilliant Catholic polemicist, was himself a charming *bon vivant* and a heavy drinker. Roth, the former officer, stood to attention at military parades in the Grand-Place in Brussels, and went several times to Steenokkerzeel Castle, near Brussels, where Otto, the pretender to the Austrian throne, lived from 1930 to 1938. '*I have seen my Emperor*', he would say then ceremoniously. When Stefan Zweig bought him a desperately-needed pair of trousers, one day in Ostend, the tailor's price was high because the legs had to be very narrow at the bottom, in the style of the old Austrian military uniform.

Zweig had written to Roth on 4 July 1936 that he should come to Ostend where there were hundreds of cheap hotels. He himself had arrived there via 'boring' Brussels, where he found it impossible to work. Roth accepted the invitation because he could always get money from the generous Zweig. He soon established himself there in the Hôtel de la Couronne with the stranded German writer Irmgard Keun, who would follow him round for a year and a half. In the worldly but waning resort they worked during the day, and in the evening Zweig took Roth out to smart restaurants. Zweig wanted to get Roth to walk and swim, but Roth used to retort: '*Jews belong in coffee-houses*' and '*Fish don't go to coffee-houses, do they*?' There is still a photo of the two of them on a pavement café in Ostend. Zweig, a rather smooth man of the world, looks caringly and admiringly at the surly, resigned, distrustful and inaccessible Roth. Roth is just 42, but already in full physical decline. Roth went by tram to Bredene along the coast, where his friend the '*raging reporter*' Egon Erwin Kisch lived. During his exile Kisch, a communist, made documentaries about the mines in the Borinage and the lunatics in Geel. Roth got on well with Kisch, though he had little time for the German communists who hung around him. He continued to hanker forlornly after a world that was lost and gone, and which he had evoked with such monumental nostalgia in *The Radetzky March* (Radetzkymarsch, 1932).

Roth visited Amsterdam for the last time in the late autumn of 1938. At the time he was working on his *Legend of the Holy Drinker* (Die Legende vom Heiligen Trinker, 1939), and mislaid his manuscript. Panic. Drink. His hotelier had to advance him the money for the journey back to Paris. His friend the art historian Hans Hannema got him a first class ticket. On the platform of Amsterdam Central Station they embraced. Roth had tears in his eyes. He did not look out of the window.

Klaus Mann, Thomas Mann's eldest son, also fled Germany in 1933. One of the most dynamic of the German emigrants, he knew almost all the others and set up his 'headquarters' in Amsterdam until 1936. Five months of the year he stayed there, the rest he spent in Zürich, Paris, the French Riviera and Vienna. In Amsterdam he founded *Die Sammlung*, a literary journal strongly opposed to the Nazis. It was published monthly from September 1933 till August 1935 by Querido. André Gide, Aldous Huxley and Heinrich Mann supported it. Almost all the German emigrant writers published in it, and so did Romain Rolland, Jean Cocteau, Ignazio Silone, Stephen Spender, Christopher Isherwood (who settled in Amsterdam for a while), Ernest Hemingway and Boris Pasternak. Within two years the paper had gone to the wall; it was too expensive and too literary at a time when things were looking increasingly grim.

Klaus' father, the more aloof Thomas Mann, the 'magician', liked to spend the summer in Noordwijk. In 1933, the morally committed Dutch crit-

Menno ter Braak (l.) and Thomas Mann (r.) on the steps of the Mauritshuis in The Hague, 1930s. Collection Letterkundig Museum, The Hague.

ic Nico Rost had already asked him during a lecture tour in the Netherlands to speak out clearly against the Hitler regime. He would do it in 1936. In Noordwijk Thomas Mann met the essayist and polemicist Menno ter Braak. Ter Braak stuck to the *honnête homme* principle and clear thinking without dogma or illusion. He had opposed Hitler consistently since 1933 and would commit suicide, just as consistently, on 15 May 1940, five days after the German invasion of the Netherlands. Thomas Mann, safe in Brentwood, CA, would not learn of it until 1 October. Ter Braak supported the emigrant writers in the 1930s, but he was hard on them too. He expected them to take moral positions against the Nazi regime in their work, but most of them were glad to have escaped, and just wanted to carry on working on their historical novels or biographies. Ter Braak felt the writer should be a *'vent'* (a 'real man', a 'bloke' i.e. his ideas and personality should be foremost in his work) and not disappear behind *'vorm'* ('form'); but the emigrants did not understand this distinction, which had become notorious in Dutch literary polemic during the thirties.

The Netherlands gave Klaus Mann, son of a famous father, a *laissez-passer* which gave him as a stateless person a certain freedom of movement. But most émigrés quickly found that the world was constructed of passports, residence permits and stamps. 'A visa is something that runs out', Irmgard Keun would have the daughter of an émigré writer (for whom Roth was clearly the model) remark laconically in *Child of all Nations* (Kind aller Länder, 1938). Much of the exiles' energy went into obtaining the right papers. That is why W.H. Auden married Erika Mann: to give her British nationality. Looking at the *Exil* scene in the Low Countries between 1933 and 1940, one cannot escape the impression that the Netherlands and Belgium were above all else a beach, a hotel room, a pavement café, with heated conversations that contained 'much wit' but 'no joy'. Waiting rooms. The two small countries thought that by withdrawing into themselves they could escape the worst. The Belgian King, Albert I, visited Einstein personally in De Haan aan Zee in 1933, to urge him to abandon his pacifist propaganda because it was endangering Belgium's neutrality. King Leopold III, too, consistently maintained the policy of neutrality.

Antwerp under the socialist mayor Camille Huysmans actually had a rather liberal asylum policy for leftist German exiles. But in 1938 the Germans managed to force Huysmans to tighten up by pulling three of North German Lloyd's ships out of the harbour. They also had authority over the emigrants removed from the city police, who came under the Mayor's jurisdiction. The Netherlands too was quick to tighten up its asylum policy after Hitler came to power. The writer Heinz Liepmann, for example, was arrested in Amsterdam in 1934 and sentenced to a month in prison for insulting a friendly head of state – Hindenburg – in his novel *The Fatherland* (Das Vaterland, 1934). Ter Braak protested loudly. Liepmann had travelled from France to Amsterdam with a valid German passport to negotiate the Dutch translation of his book, which had already been published in German in Amsterdam, and had also been translated into French and English. After serving his sentence, the writer was put across the border into Belgium; the Dutch translation was published without the offending passage.

Though some writers were able to find a publisher in Amsterdam, prospects for artists and actors were almost non-existent. The *'Pfeffermühle'*,

Erika Mann's political cabaret, which dealt constantly with Hitler and Germany without naming them, was banned in 1936. Again, Ter Braak protested strongly. Klaus and Erika Mann left for America on a Dutch steamship in September that year. Europe still tolerated them, but for how much longer? A bigger, more stable safe haven awaited them. Klaus Mann's *Journey into Freedom* had appeared in the US. He was to become an American citizen and, in the end, fight against Germany in an American uniform.

The turning point

Then came the war, and the end of an era. Cleveringa, Dean of the Faculty of Law at Leiden made a courageous speech opposing the dismissal of the Jewish professors from his faculty. The occupying forces closed the university. With a perfect sense of timing Roth had already organised his end in Paris. Zweig, who wanted to perish with yesterday's world, would commit suicide with his wife in Brazil in 1942. Ter Braak's suicide and E. du Perron's heart attack on the same day, 15 May 1940, devastated Dutch literature. The poet Marsman, fleeing to England, would drown in the North Sea in June 1940, torpedoed by a U-boat. Klaus Mann took longer to succumb to this turning point in his life. He committed suicide in 1949.

Sometimes things turned out differently. The German writer, director and cineast Ludwig Berger came to Amsterdam in 1936 to film G.B. Shaw's *Pygmalion.* When England declared war on Germany he left London in great haste to avoid being interned. At the airport he met Thomas and Erika Mann, on their way to America. On the day that Berger was due to drive to Antwerp for the première of his film *Somewhere in Holland,* war broke out. By this time he had learnt Dutch and assumed a Dutch name, so during the

Albert Einstein (l.) and James Ensor (r.) in De Haan (Belgium), 2 August 1933. Photo courtesy of Jacques van der Heyde, Librairie Fl. Tulkens, Brussels

occupation he lived quietly in his house by Vondel Park, hidden behind the necessary papers and stamps. In 1944 he put on Shakespeare's *A Midsummer Night's Dream* in English. The interior of his house formed the décor and the actors performed in their ordinary clothes. Drawn by the suspiciously large number of bicycles in front of the house, the Gestapo burst in during the seventh performance. Berger escaped by pretending to be crazy like Hamlet; after the war he returned to Germany. Irmgard Keun, who had left the US and returned to Amsterdam before the war broke out, went back to Germany illegally during the occupation and survived the war there. She remained in Germany until her death in 1969.

The young writer Konrad Merz had left Germany in 1934. Ter Braak thought highly of his autobiographical epistolary novel *A Man Falls from Germany* (Ein Mann fällt aus Deutschland, published by Querido Verlag in 1936), translated into Dutch as *Duitscher aangespoeld*, though Klaus Mann did not. He went into hiding in 1940 and after the war remained in the Netherlands until his death in 1999. Not until 1972 did Merz, who was by now completely assimilated and had not spoken German for forty years, write another book – in German.

In 1939 the Jewish Austrian Hans Maier fled to Belgium with his young bride and ended up in Antwerp. When the Germans invaded he was arrested as an enemy and put on a train to the Pyrenees. He returned to Belgium and joined the resistance. Picked up again and tortured, he was able to conceal his Jewish identity for a while, but still finished up in Auschwitz. After the war Maier belonged nowhere, not in Austria and not in Belgium, where he was still a foreigner, though he settled in Brussels and made his living there as a journalist. His wife had died in 1944. This intellectual, whose whole humanist culture had become meaningless in the camp, could only hit back by constantly reminding the Germans of their crimes. After 1955 he did so under a French pseudonym, Jean Améry. Eventually, in 1978, he killed himself in Salzburg. He had long ago found that for him there were no safe havens any more.

But for all that the Flemish writer, Willem Elsschot, still took three Afghan coolies on a tour of his city, Antwerp, in search of a woman's warm embrace, which becomes less attainable by the line. *Will-o'-the-Wisp* (Het Dwaallicht) is Elsschot's last novella. He finished the manuscript in 1946, but the story is set in 1938. Melancholy, bourgeois Laarmans, the writer's alter ego, drags his coloured friends around like an unwilling host who starts to believe in his role and surpasses himself. The three kings will never reach the star, but the quest they have embarked on together leads to mutual understanding and affection. For a while Laarmans offers a safe haven all on his own.

Another battle

In a world changed by the Second World War, the Low Countries ceased to be a safe haven. If this particular stroll through the history of intellectual hospitality has taught us anything, it is that the concept of a safe haven must in the end be put into perspective. Because of their favourable political setup, circumstances were right in the Netherlands in the seventeenth century, and in nineteenth-century Belgium, for foreign writers and intellectual and / or political refugees to stay there for longer or shorter periods. The presses rolled freely. Chance and their advantageous geographical location, in particular, took care of the rest. In the final analysis the Low Countries are just two small countries, more or less squeezed between superpowers. In the thirties they seem really to have been transit countries, waiting rooms for a bigger – new – world. Since the sixties the Netherlands, and especially Amsterdam, have again acquired a reputation as a haven – for permissiveness this time. But that is another story.

There are no privileged safe havens any more in the Western world. Thomas Mann tells of a German emigrant on his way back to Europe in 1950. In mid-Atlantic he passes a friend who is steaming in the opposite direction. As their ships pass they shout to each other, '*Are you crazy?*' Mann died in Switzerland, the cradle of democracy and the cuckoo clock. In the Low Countries Europe dictates the law more and more. On the outer limits of the fortress, with its many weak spots, another battle is now being fought.

LUC DEVOLDERE
Translated by Lindsay Edwards.

Extracts and Poems

I could spend my entire life without seeing a single person
by René Descartes, 1631

Letter to Balzac, Amsterdam, 5 May 1631

Sir,
When I read in your letter that you were planning to come here, I had to rub my eyes to make sure that I wasn't still asleep. Even now I hardly dare to rejoice at the news any more than if I had in fact dreamed it. Anyway, I do not find it particularly strange that a broad-minded and generous spirit like yours should no longer be able to tolerate the servile constraints that the Court imposes. And since you assure me in good faith that God has inspired you to withdraw from the world, I should regard it a sin against the Holy Spirit to attempt to dissuade you from such a holy resolve.

But you must excuse my zeal if I urge you to choose Amsterdam for your retirement and to prefer it not only above all the Capuchin and Carthusian monasteries to which many good people retire, but also above the most beautiful residences in France and Italy, even the famous Hermitage where you were last year. However well appointed a house in the countryside might be, it will always lack an infinite number of those conveniences that one can only find in towns. Even the solitude that one hopes to find is never entirely perfect. I truly hope that you find there that canal which causes even the most talkative to dream and a valley so solitary that it would inspire in them ecstasy and joy.[1] But I have an uneasy feeling that you may also have a number of neighbours who will at times importune you and whose visits will be even more inconvenient than those you now receive in Paris. Here, on the other hand, in this great city where I live and where everyone but myself is engaged in trade, each person is so concerned with making a profit that I could spend my entire life without seeing a single person.

Every day I take a walk amongst the confusion of large crowds with as much freedom and tranquillity as you might do along your forest paths, and I regard the people whom I see in the same way as I would the trees in your forests or the animals that live there. Even the fretful noise of their little worries interrupts my musings no more than would the sound of some stream. If I ever do reflect on their activities, it gives me the same pleasure as you would have in observing the peasants tilling your fields. For I see that all their work serves to embellish my place of residence and ensure that I lack for nothing. If you can find pleasure in watching the fruit swell in your orchards and in being up to your eyes in abundance, do you not think that you could enjoy equally the sight of vessels arriving here bearing an abundance of all that the Indies produce and of rarities from all over Europe? Where else in the world but here is it so easy to find all the conveniences of life and all the curiosities that one could wish for? Is there any other country where one can enjoy such complete liberty, where one can sleep with less worry, where there are always armies ready to protect us, where poisonings, treachery and calumny are little known, and where so much of our ancestors' innocence has survived? I do not know how you can love the air of Italy so much, in which all too often one breathes in the plague, where the heat during the day is unbearable, where the evening chill is unhealthy, and where the darkness of night offers a cover for larceny and murder. If you are afraid of our northern winters, tell me what shade, what fan, what fountains can protect you from the discomfort of Rome's heat as effectively as a stove and a big fire would preserve you from getting cold here?

For the rest, I can say that I await you with a little volume of musings that I hope you will not find disagreeable. And whether you come or not, I shall always be affectionately etc.

From *Descartes' Works* (Oeuvres de Descartes, eds. Charles Adam & Paul Tannery). Paris, 1996. *Translated by Chris Emery.*

1. *Lettres de Balzac* (7th edition, Paris, 1628), vol. I, p. 123-128. In this letter of 4 September 1622 to M. de la Motte-Aigron, one reads 'a *canal* that makes the most talkative dream as soon as they approach it, on the banks of which I am contented, whether I am happy or sad ... This *valley*, which is the most secret part of my desert and has never been known by anyone else.' (Oeuvres de Balzac, 1665, vol. I, p. 250)

An Ode to Amsterdam
by Benedictus de Spinoza, 1670

In order to prove that from such freedom no inconvenience arises, which cannot easily be checked by the exercise of the sovereign power, and that men's actions can easily be kept in bounds, though their opinions be at open variance, it will be well to cite an example. Such an one is not very far to seek. The city of Amsterdam reaps the fruit of this freedom in its own great prosperity and in the admiration of all other people. For in this most flourishing state, and most splendid city, men of every nation and religion live together in the greatest harmony, and ask no questions before trusting their goods to a fellow-citizen, save whether he be rich or poor, and whether he generally acts honestly, or the reverse. His religion and sect is considered of no importance: for it has no effect before the judges in gaining or losing a cause, and there is no sect so despised that its followers, provided that they harm no one, pay every man his due, and live uprightly, are deprived of the protection of the magisterial authority.

On the other hand, when the religious controversy between Remonstrants and Counter-Remonstrants began to be taken up by politicians and the States, it grew into a schism, and abundantly showed that laws dealing with religion and seeking to settle its controversies are much more calculated to irritate than to reform, and that they give rise to extreme licence: further, it was seen that schisms do not originate in a love of truth, which is a source of courtesy and gentleness, but rather in an inordinate desire for supremacy. From all these considerations it is clearer than the sun at noonday, that the true schismatics are those who condemn other men's writings, and seditiously stir up the quarrelsome masses against their authors, rather than those authors themselves, who generally write only for the learned, and appeal solely to reason. In fact, the real disturbers of the peace are those who, in a free state, seek to curtail the liberty of judgment which they are unable to tyrannize over.

From *Tractatus Theologico-politicus*. Amsterdam, 1670.
Translated by R.H.M. Elwes (in: 'The Chief Works of Benedictus de Spinoza'. London, 1883).

A Complete Schoolgirl
by Charlotte Brontë, 1842

Letter to Ellen Nussey, Brussels, May 1842

Dear Ellen,
It is the fashion now a days for persons to send sheets of blank paper instead of letters to their friends in foreign parts –

I was twenty-six years old a week or two since – and at that ripe time of life I am a schoolgirl – a complete school-girl and on the whole very happy in that capacity It felt very strange at first to 'submit to' authority instead of exercising it – to obey orders instead of giving them – but I like that state of things – I returned to it with the 'same' avidity that a cow that has long been kept on dry hay returns to fresh grass – don't laugh at my simile – it is natural to me to submit and very unnatural to command.

This is a large school in which there are about 40 externes or day-pupils and 12 pensionnaires or boarders – Madame Heger the head is a lady of precisely the same cast of mind degree of cultivation & quality of character as Miss Catherine Wooler – I think the severe points are a little softened because she has not been disappointed & consequently soured – in a word – she is a married instead of a maiden lady – there are 3 teachers in the school Mademoiselle Blanche – mademoiselle Sophie & Mademoiselle Marie – The two first have no particular character – one is an old maid & the other will be one – Mademoiselle Marie is talented & original – but of repulsive & arbitrary manners which have made the whole school except myself and Emily her bitter enemies – no less than seven masters attend to teach the different branches of education – French drawing – music, singing, writing, arithmetic, and German.

All in the house are Catholics except ourselves one other girl and the gouvernante of Madam's children – an Englishwoman in rank something between a

Portrait of Charlotte Brontë.
National Portrait Gallery,
London.

lady's maid and a nursery governess the difference in Country & religion makes a broad line of demarcation between us & all the rest we are completely isolated in the midst of numbers – yet I think I am never unhappy – my present life is so delightful so congenial to my (own) nature compared to that of a Governess – my time constantly occupied passes too rapidly – hitherto both Emily and I have had good health & therefore we have been able to work well. There is one individual of whom I have not yet spoken Monsieur Heger the husband of Madame – he is professor of Rhetoric a man of power as to mind but very choleric & irritable in temperament – a little, black, ugly being with 'a face' that varies in expression, sometimes he borrows the lineaments of an insane Tom-cat – sometimes those of a delirious Hyena – occasionally – but very seldom he discards these perilous attractions and assumes an air not above a hundred degrees removed from what you would call mild & gentleman-like he is very angry with me just at present because I have written a translation which he chose to stigmatize as *peu-correct* – not because it was particularly so in reality but because he happened to be in a bad humour when he read it – he did not tell me so – but wrote the accusation in the margin of my book and asked in brief stern phrase how it happened that my compositions were always better than my translations – adding that the thing seemed to him inexplicable the fact is some weeks ago in a high-flown humour he forbade me to use either dictionary or grammar – in translating the most difficult English compositions into French this makes the task rather arduous – & compels me every now and then to introduce an English word which nearly plucks the eyes out of his head when he sees it.

Emily and he don't draw well together at all – when he is very ferocious with me I cry – & that sets all things straight.

Emily works like a horse and she has had great difficulties 'to contend with' – far greater than I have had indeed those who come to a French school for instruction ought previously to have acquired a considerable knowledge of the French language – otherwise they will lose a great deal of time for the course of instruction is adapted to natives & not to foreigners and in these large establishments they will not change their ordinary course for one or two strangers – the few private lessons that monsieur Heger has vouchsafed to give us are I suppose to be considered a great favour & I can perceive they have already excited much spite & jealousy in the school –.

You will abuse this letter for being short I daresay, and there are a hundred things which I wish to tell you but I have not time. Do write to me and cherish Christian charity in your heart!' Brussels is a beautiful city – the Belgians hate the English – their external morality is more rigid than ours – to lace the stays without any handkerchief on the neck is considered a disgusting piece of indelicacy – Remember me to Mercy & your Mother, and believe me, my dear Ellen – Yours, sundered by the Sea,

C. Brontë

Roman Catholicism beats them all

by Charlotte Brontë, 1842

Letter to Ellen Nussey, Brussels, ? July 1842.

Dear Ellen,

I began seriously to think you had no particular intention of writing to me again – however let us have no reproaches, thank you for your letter.

I consider it doubtful whether I shall come home in September or not – Madame Heger has made a proposal for both me and Emily to stay another half year – offering to dismiss her English master and take me as English teacher – also to employ Emily some part of each day in teaching music to a certain number of pupils – for these services we are to be allowed to continue our 'studies' in French and German – and to have board & c without paying for it – no salaries however are offered – the proposal is kind and in a great selfish city like Brussels and a great selfish school containing nearly ninety pupils (boarders & day-pupils included) implies a degree of interest which demands gratitude in return – I am inclined to accept it – what think you?

Your letter set my teeth on edge – I can but half divine the signification of a great part of it but what I guess makes me wish to know all you must speedily write again and explain yourself –

I don't deny that I sometimes wish to be in England or that I have brief attacks of home-sickness – but on the whole I have borne a very valiant heart so far – and I have been happy in Brussels because I have always been fully occupied with the employments that I like – Emily is making rapid progresse in French, German, Music and Drawing – Monsieur & Madame Heger begin to recognise the valuable points of her character under her singularities.

If the national character of the Belgians is to be measured by the character of most of the girls in this school, it is a character singularly cold, selfish, animal and inferior – they are besides very mutinous and difficult for the teachers to manage – and their principles are rotten to the core – we avoid them – which is not difficult to do – as we have the brand of Protestantism and Anglicism upon us.

People talk of the danger which protestants expose themselves to in going to reside in Catholic countries – and thereby running the chance of changing their faith – my advice to all protestants who are tempted to do anything so besotted as turn Catholic – is to walk over the sea on to the continent – to attend mass sedulously for a time – to note well the mum(m)eries thereof – also the idiotic, mercenary, aspect of <u>all</u> the priests – & <u>then</u> if they are still disposed to consider Papistry in any other light than a most feeble childish piece of humbug let them turn papists at once that's all – I consider Methodism, Quakerism & the extremes of high & low Churchism foolish but Roman Catholicism beats them all.

At the same time allow me to tell you that there are some Catholics – who are as good as any christians can be to whom the bible is a sealed book and much better than scores of Protestants.

Give my love to your Mother & Mercy – believe me present occasionally in spirit when absent in flesh.

C. Brontë

From *The Letters of Charlotte Brontë* (ed. Margaret Smith). Oxford, 1995.

The Arrival and Observations of an Exile

by Victor Hugo, 1852

Brussels, 8 January

Unusual manners. The Flemish middle-class has something of the uncomplicated, crude *bourgeoisie* of the past. Rabelais would have laughed at their sayings. Instead of *It never rains but it pours*, here they say *It never rains but it pees*. The most popular monument in Brussels is a small boy 'peeing'; another famous fountain depicts a little fellow throwing up.

There is something jovial, obscene and patriarchal about it.

Senators here go to the pub. In the evening you see them at tables in bars in a brown fug in which everyone has to find their way almost by touch, the mayors sitting drinking their glass of *faro* (a sweet, heavy Brussels beer) and the judges smoking their pipes. No one makes any secret of the fact that they frequently visit the rue des Crombras. There is a renowned brothel in this street – one of the many – whose salon is adorned by a full-length portrait of the former King of the Netherlands, William I, which he presented to the establishment himself. He visited it every day; the madam sheds sentimental tears on hearing his name.

Faider, a prosecutor-general at the Supreme Court, never goes home in the evenings; he spends every night in the rue des Crombras. When the court session starts in the morning and the prosecutor-general keeps them all waiting, the judge says, 'Will you go and fetch him from Trinette's.'

Brussels, 12 January

I have been officially banished.

Now I shall remain outside France as long as it pleases God, but I feel unassailable; I have right entirely on my side and my conscience is clear. One day the people will awaken, and on that day everyone will be back where they belong; I in my house and Louis Bonaparte in the pillory.

From Things Seen 1849-1885 *(Choses vues 1849-1885). Paris, 1972.*
Translated by Gregory Ball.

Photo of Charles Baudelaire by Charles Neyts, c.1865. The inscriptions read: '*Ridentem ferient Ruinae*' and '*To My Friend Auguste Malassis, the only being whose laughter has alleviated my Sadness in Belgium. C.B.*'

Belgian Hospitality
by Charles Baudelaire, 1866

A short chapter on Belgian hospitality. (Rents in Belgium). How this falsehood came into being among the Belgians and the French. Political exiles. Adventures that have come to my ears. People have talked so much about their hospitality that the Belgians themselves have started to believe it. Belgian hospitality consists in picking up poor, starved Frenchmen and immediately shipping them to England. Or in the muzzling of journalists, grievously insulting them and throwing them over the border somewhere; after that they ask the Emperor for their reward, even though he had not asked them to do anything. But when they see that a Frenchman has money, they take care to hold on to him so as to bleed him dry. And then, when he is ruined, they throw him roughly into prison for his debts, where new attempts at exploitation are made (the bed, the table, the chairs, etc.). So in fact Belgian hospitality (a word that applies to all travellers) consists of systematic greed and cannibalism.

From *Poor Belgium* (Pauvre Belgique). Paris, 1953.
Translated by Gregory Ball.

Idyllic Exile
by Klaus Mann, 1930s

In the meantime we are still here, but I shan't commit myself as to whether that is a good or a bad thing. Recently we were in Amsterdam, on the terrace of the Hotel Américain. I was talking about Gemütlichkeit. This was by no means restricted to the German emigrant milieu. We made Dutch friends; my closest friendships were with the literary philosopher and essayist Menno ter Braak, a passionate, pure spirit and a highly original imagination; with the writer Jef Last, who had just published one of his best books, *Zuiderzee,* and with whom I shared a friendly admiration for André Gide; and with the painters Karin and Ernst van Leyden, a hard-working artist couple who were remarkably well-educated cosmopolitans with good taste and a broad intellectual interest. Moreover, they were friendly and hospitable people whose idyllically situated country house was an excellent place to rest and work.

René Crevel came to visit from Paris, perhaps accompanied by our mutual friend Thea 'Mopsa' Sternheim, or alone, or accompanied by an elegant South American lady with whom he was associating at the time. He swore, complained, made jokes, got drunk, read extracts from his new work, was mild-mannered, intolerant, helpful, and sometimes cruel. And he could be cruel – to himself and to others. The flame that burned in his wide-open eyes with their explosive gaze showed no trace of compromise or compassion.

Visitors came from London, too. My oldest English friend, Brian Howard, appeared with his familiar temperament and obligatory coterie, and the young novelist Christopher Isherwood, a stylist and psychologist of extraordinary qualities, settled for a time in Amsterdam. I already knew him from Berlin. There was always something going on in Berlin and consequently we had no time for each other, but in the more peaceful atmosphere of Amsterdam there was no shortage of time for becoming better acquainted with someone if it seemed worth the trouble.

In Christopher's case it was certainly worth the trouble, and the genuine friendship that developed has become more and more valuable to me over the years.

Christopher's presence attracted other English visitors to Amsterdam. Stephen Spender came; warm, dynamic, extrovert, always full of high-minded ideas and projects, a typical militant dreamer and activist poet, aggressive yet a dreamer, a young poet with unshakeable principles, an Ariel who had read Karl Marx. W.H. Auden, my new brother-in-law Wystan, visited too. He was still in his activist-revolutionary period. Already his élan seemed less naive than the rhetorical sentimentality or the pedantic dogmatism of most radical left-wing bards. With Auden, everything is more complex, has more substance, and is quieter, more mysterious, more intelligent. Someone who is so complex will never become completely absorbed by a school of thought or a conviction. He leads his comrades along a certain path and commits them to a certain dogma, while he himself continues to have ironic reservations. It was curious watching W.H. among his friends and disciples. What a complex young master he was, with a character open to many interpretations! I recall with great fondness the day which we – Landshoff, Isherwood, myself and a few friends – spent in Zandvoort aan Zee with E.M. Forster. The writer of *A Passage to India*, a novel generally acknowledged as a 'classic' in the English-speaking world, indeed belongs to a somewhat older generation, but he enjoys extraordinary popularity among the intellectual *avant garde*, the next generation represented at the time by Auden, Spender and Isherwood. Of all the literary figures I have come to know more or less intimately over the years (and God knows there have been enough of them – more than enough!), Forster is one of the most charming, precisely because he appears to be wholly unaware of his charm and the effect of his personality. He is good-humoured, harbours no pretensions, and is sublimely tactful as a person and as a writer. Everything about him is, to use an untranslatable English expression, characterised by 'understatement', there are no piercing tones, no arrogant or coquettish gestures. In his company one can be cheerful and enjoy oneself. On that summer's day in Zandvoort – it could have been in 1935 – we *were* cheerful and we *did* enjoy ourselves. We swam, then raced along the beach, and then we lay and lazed in the sun and told each other silly stories, at which we laughed for far too long. It was a real holiday. We did not think about Hitler. We forgot that there were concentration camps; that there would probably be a war and that, all things considered, the situation in the world was nothing to laugh about.

From *The Turning Point* (Der Wendepunkt). München, 1976.
Translated by Yvette Mead.

Two Poems
by W.H. Auden, 1930s

Brussels in the Winter

Wandering through cold streets tangled like old string,
Coming on fountains rigid in the frost,
Its formula escapes you; it has lost
The certainty that constitutes a thing.

Only the old, the hungry and the humbled
Keep at this temperature a sense of place,
And in their misery are all assembled;
The winter holds them like an Opera-House.

Ridges of rich apartments loom to-night
Where isolated windows glow like farms,
A phrase goes packed with meaning like a van,

A look contains the history of man,
And fifty francs will earn a stranger right
To take the shuddering city in his arms.

Gare du Midi

A nondescript express in from the South,
Crowds round the ticket barrier, a face
To welcome which the mayor has not contrived
Bugles or braid: something about the mouth
Distracts the stray look with alarm and pity.
Snow is falling. Clutching a little case,
He walks out briskly to infect a city
Whose terrible future may have just arrived.

From *Collected Shorter Poems 1927-1957*. London, 1966.

Gare du Midi, Brussels,
c.1930. Photo by Leonard
Misonne / © SABAM
Belgium 2001.

On Visas and Borders

by Irmgard Keun, 1938

My mother and I always used to walk for an hour before lunch; now we just walk, so at least we get some fresh air. My mother says it's almost as healthy as eating.

Every day we go down the rue Neuve to the Grand-Place, because my father liked it so much. And it is very beautiful there. In the sun the great mansions seem to be made of silver and gold, and there are lots of flower stalls with the most colourful flowers in the world. My mother wants to look at all the flowers. She says it's much nicer to look at so many flowers than to buy a few of them. But when we have money, we buy a few anyway, since the flower-sellers always shout at us and beckon us so frantically.

My mother walks sadly beside me. She's frightened that I'm hungry, and she's frightened that something has happened to my father. We can't write to him, we can't send a telegram or telephone him – we don't even have an address for him.

I say to my mother, 'I don't think anything's happened to him', and my mother breathes a little more easily.

But she doesn't know what will become of us. As we walk slowly along, she doesn't teach me about Barbarossa but about all our perils.

We have so many perils and they are hard to understand.

First of all I have to learn what a visa is. We have a German passport, given to us by the police in Frankfurt. A passport is a little book with stamps in it and the proof of one's existence. If one loses the passport, one is dead as far as the world is concerned. One can't get into any country any longer. One has to leave one country and can't get into the other. But God in his wisdom has ordained that people should only be able to live on land. Now I pray secretly every evening that God in his wisdom will ordain that people can swim for years in the sea or suddenly fly into the air.

My mother read to me from the Bible, and it clearly says there that God created the world, but borders he did not create.

One can't cross a border if one has no passport or visa. I always wanted to see a border properly, but I don't think it's possible. My mother can't explain it to me either. She says, 'A border is what separates two countries.' At first I thought borders were garden fences, as high as the sky. But that was stupid of me, because then no trains would be able to cross. A border is not earth either, otherwise one could simply position oneself in the middle of the border or walk around on it, if one has to leave one country and is not allowed into the other. In that case one would stay exactly astride the border and build a hut for oneself and stick out one's tongue at the countries to left and right. But a border consists of nothing at all that one can walk on. It's something that happens in the middle of the train with the help of men who are officials.

If you have a visa, the officials let you stay on the train and travel on. Because our passport was issued in Frankfurt, we can really only get a visa in Frankfurt. But Frankfurt is in Germany and we can't go back to Germany, because if we do the government will lock us up, as my father has written in the French and other newspapers that he can't stand the government, and he's written a book about it too.

A visa is a stamp that is stamped into one's passport. You have to ask every country you want to go to for a stamp in advance. For that you have to go to a consulate. A consulate is an office, in which you have to wait for a long time and be very quiet and nice. A consulate is the piece of a border in the middle of a foreign country and the consul is the king of the border.

A visa is also something that runs out. At first we are always terribly happy that we have been given a visa and can go to another country. But then the visa immediately starts running out, it runs out more every day – and suddenly it's run out completely and we have to leave the country again.

I have to learn all that. My mother cries about it a lot and says everything was easier in the past. Well, I wasn't alive in the past, when everything was so easy. I find everything quite easy and don't need to cry. When I'm grown up, I'll have a husband and a child too and perhaps everything will be easy again then.

I'm not afraid of policemen in uniform either or officials on the train.

When we were travelling from Poland, a customs man first wanted to confiscate my doll's kitchen and not let in my two tortoises, and afterwards he wiped my nose with his own handkerchief.

And here in Brussels a traffic policeman was going to arrest me in the Place Rogier, because I crossed in front of the cars at the wrong moment, and looked at the policeman, as he had such a wonderful place on a white throne in the middle of the action and directed everything. Green and red lights come on in turn, I love to see that.

One is only allowed to cross the street when the green light is on, but I often forget, as I like the red light better.

When I looked at the policeman the traffic got stuck and could no longer be directed, since it so happened that these cars didn't want to run me over, only one of them almost did, but its driver was able to restrain it in time.

Cars are much more dangerous than lions, and must be kept under very strict control, as they constantly long to roar towards people. I'm not at all frightened of lions. I have seen some at the zoo and in the circus. I think, though, that I would be a little frightened if a hungry lion came roaring up to me. But perhaps I would stand my ground and speak to it and stroke it. You can't do that with a car, when it comes roaring up, and that's why I always walk away from roaring cars. Because cars like that just want to kill you and aren't hungry and don't even want to eat you.

As I stood in the middle of the traffic and was hemmed in by trams and hostile cars, the beautiful policeman got down from his throne and roared towards me like a lion anxious to eat me.

I couldn't run away.

The policeman took my arm, and his mouth was fierce and open. I really thought he was a lion, snorting cars surrounded me, headlights gleamed like eyes, the houses were so big, and the sky was so far away that misty clouds fell on me. And since the policeman was a lion, I treated him like a lion. I stroked his hand, and said to him in French that he mustn't hurt me and not keep me prisoner and eat me up, if he wasn't hungry, because, 'mon père n'est pas chez nous et ma mère ne peut pas rester sans moi. Excusez-moi, monsieur – je vous ai regardé – vous êtes si beau.'

Then the lion stopped growling and turned back into a beautiful traffic policeman, who no longer wanted to arrest me, but became a prince who carried me across to the other side of the street to the woman who sits on rails.

The woman is fat and sells nuts from two big blond baskets. And no more trams travel over these rails, though one used to.

The prince set me down in front of the fat woman. Before he did I was just able to give him a quick kiss, and he bought me ten fat walnuts from the fat ginger woman. Then he went off and remounted his throne and controlled the traffic again and was no longer transformed, but just as he was when I had to look at him in amazement and as a result the traffic stopped.

Now I pass him every day and always wink at him, and he smiles down at me. Sometimes I have a terrible urge to wave my hand too. But I prefer not to. It might stop the traffic again.

From *Child of All Nations* (Kind aller Länder). Amsterdam, 1938.
Translated by Paul Vincent.

The Spark into the Powder Keg
by L.P.J. Braat, 1930s

He would not be the last emigrant to wind up at our table. The fact that these feverish years became so important was with hindsight to a large extent due to the numerous emigrants, who through their reports of the horrors in other countries and their often great, exotic gifts, forced us into surprising initiatives. Around their frequently tragic figures blew the wind of countries infinitely larger and more exciting than the Netherlands, which apparently cannot get very far without 'foreign blood'. At least not much further than the oppressive burden of bourgeois consciousness and self-indulgent navel-gazing. Without doubt the *Chronicle* came into being in the climate generated by the emigrants. They sent the spark into the powder keg, which without them would fairly certainly have been damp and impossible to detonate. Empty talk and no action were in the air of the Netherlands – the fact that we had valuable qualities, that there was a great deal of talent about, was something that all the German, Austrian, Italian and later Czech Jews and other anarchists rubbed our noses in, believing – how wrong they were – that they had found a safe place to live and work in the Netherlands.

From *Wreathed Lacunae, Memories* (Omkranste hiaten, levensherinneringen). Amsterdam, 1966.
Translated by Paul Vincent.

Arrival in Antwerp
by Jean Améry, 1939

The traveller from Central Europe, arriving rather late in the evening, with the rear lights of the city's cars (most of them American) shining like benevolent, sparkling eyes, is struck by the wealth of this city. He had imagined Antwerp differently, not so elegant, not so extravagantly illuminated by neon signs. Something of the 'fortress Antwerp' of the First World War had vaguely implanted itself in his memory, and he had formed an image of a grey and inhospitable city – rainy, dark, a city where taciturn people earn their daily bread amongst citadels and harbour sheds.

But they're not at all reserved, these large and mostly heavy-set men, these voluptuous and (at least to German eyes) excessively made-up women. The stranger – or should we say 'intruder', this man who made his getaway yesterday – sees these men and women walking down De Keyserlei, the main street running from the station to the harbour, sees them in cafés eating fragrant, warm, butter-fried waffles that are enough to make a hungry man's mouth water. Bruegel. Wash the make-up from the woman's face, dress the men in peasant smocks, and they look just like the plain folk painted by the master. They do business together despite the crisis in which the industrial world has been floundering since 1929. They feel good about themselves, at least if you can believe their smacking lips and good-natured, gullible eyes, nestled in fat. They feel good about this city, too, which they call the 'metropolis' and which they all know was Europe's mightiest commercial centre in the time of Charles V, richer in silver, gold and magnificent houses than London or Paris.

How vigorous is the pulse of life here, thinks the intruder, much more vigorous than in Cologne, the city he just left, and even than in Vienna, which sinks deeper and deeper into the mists of his fading memory. The stranger will learn soon enough that not all the people of Antwerp go carousing every Sunday like Bruegel's peasants; not all of them are satisfied with their city, country and government. For the time being, however, he'll find that what stands between him and the city's 600,000 inhabitants is a language – an anti-language, he was tempted to say at first, because there's hardly anything in it that doesn't gurgle, cough, roll its r's and only occasionally break free into vowels that slide from A to O! Call that a language? But you get used to it, as you get used to so many other things that seemed intolerable at first. The stranger learns the language. He learns it with relative ease, in fact, by listening carefully and reading the newspapers, although the latter tend to pose some deeply mysterious riddles for him. He reads about *taalwetten* – language laws – and for a long time he associates this with cross-country skiing competitions in some valley or other. (The Dutch word for 'language' – 'taal' – reminds the German speaker of 'Tal', the German word for 'valley'; 'laws' – 'wetten' in Dutch – makes him think of the German 'wetten' – to wager – and of 'Wettbewerb' – competition.) But he figures it all out soon enough, even the surprising fact that the *te huur* signs (meaning 'to let') posted on some of the houses have nothing to do with the world's oldest profession. (The German word for prostitute is 'Hure'.) No, the Dutch language is something you quickly get the hang of more or less, and then it loses its painful cacophony, because what you yourself speak is never ugly.

The undesirable (he reads about *undesirables* every day in the newspaper whenever the topic turns to people of his kind) must find shelter. With the few francs and cents in his pocket that Antwerp's tirelessly attentive Jewish community makes available to its refugees, he walks to the city centre in increasingly shabby footwear in search of a room that is both *te huur* and affordable. There are plenty of souls in the same predicament in Antwerp who are willing to give him advice, but all of them direct him to *de joodse wijk*, the Jewish quarter. And that's exactly where he doesn't want to go. He knows a thing or two about Antwerp's social milieu, and he's also read that there are a considerable number of rich diamond dealers living in impressive new flats on the edge of the city. They've escaped from the *joodse wijk*, because climbing the rungs of the social ladder seems to go hand in hand with extricating onself, at least superficially, from one's fated human origins. These people – these gentlemen and their good, often smartly dressed and usually French-speaking ladies, who've gained entrée into every corner of European culture (not by birth, certainly, but by virtue of their husbands' diamond wealth) – these are not the people whom the intruder is likely to visit. He has yet to attain such heights. They stand up for him being given the minimum means of subsistence out of their sense of duty to the national government, but for obvious reasons they want as little as possible to do with these insufficiently avaricious wretches whose ethnic origins and physiognomy are the same as theirs, but whose national backgrounds are totally different. Anyone who nevertheless manages to look these people in the eye is told, at the very most, 'Well, you're safe here, thank God! But why didn't you people organise a revolt against that Hitler?' Not a very promising door to knock on.

And the old *joodse wijk*, dwelling place of poor Jews, diamond cutters, small-time merchants and factory workers – that's a district the stranger avoids with the instinct of someone who knows that the unfamiliar isn't really offensive until it starts huddling together. And so the search continues.

Almost automatically, his path leads him to one of those hostelries in the harbour district – they call themselves hotels – where you can rent a room for a song. There he finds shelter for about a year and a half in accommodation that can hardly be called genteel. His next-door neighbours are not exactly people of quality. There's one who leaves the building each morning with a small suitcase filled with combs, cheap cosmetics and other assorted junk that he hopes to sell. Another, who slinks through the corridors, always in his dressing gown, seems to be entertaining ambitions as a pimp on the lookout for whores. The undesirable, who in the eyes of the authorities is as suspect as a young girl, quickly makes the acquaintance of the large-bosomed lady who seems to have a pleasant manner and is very helpful. She comes from Liège, which is called Lüttich in German and Luik in Dutch. She only speaks French and she hates the Flemish people of Antwerp, who happen to form her clientele. They're not real Belgians, she says. They're already making eyes at the Germans and they're going to sell us down the river. The newcomer doesn't want to believe her. Wasn't it a Flemish labourer who assured him yesterday that Hitler was a *smeerlap* – a filthy bastard? He gets on pretty well with the Flemings now that he's half-mastered their language. It makes no difference to him that every now and then when they're in a euphoric mood they like to sing nationalistic songs like '*Vliegt de Blauwvoet*', which was the title of a novel by the National-Socialist writer Otto Brües ('*Fliegt der Blaufuss?*').

All he knows is that this is a democracy. This city has a socialist mayor, and one of the most popular politicians in the country, Paul-Henri Spaak, is also a socialist. It will take a little more time before he's able to see through the façade of Belgian democracy and discover the two nations locked in a death grip that lie behind it. For the time being he just tries to discover the city. Not as an ordinary tourist or a cultural tourist! He never enters the beautiful Late Gothic Cathedral of Our Lady, which he passes every day, not even when Rubens' paintings are being displayed for the art crowd. And he hasn't got enough money for the Flemish opera or the Flemish theatre (where Lessing's *Nathan der Weise* is often performed). The harbour district is where the stranger mostly hangs out. The brothels right behind the Great Market, with its magnificent Renaissance city hall, are what interest him. He's never seen anything like it: glass doors, like in a little shop, with modest but clean rooms behind them containing wide beds, embroidered table cloths and bouquets of artificial flowers. They're display windows, and the items on display are women between the ages of seventeen and fifty in low-cut dresses and heavy make-up, women with mask-like faces who flash their eternally frozen smiles whenever someone passes by, hoping for a customer. Sometimes they beckon to him to come closer, or they make come-hither gestures like the witch in Hansel and Gretel. He never tires of it, pondering their mysterious way of life. Besides, he feels like a kindred soul. A few steps away from this web of narrow streets and alleys where they've pitched their camp is the town hall, the location of the supreme authority – the police. The unwanted guest is fully aware that the police look at him with the same cold stare that they fix on the local girls. What he doesn't have any way of knowing is how much more comfortable than his the situation of these poor whores will be a year from now. They'll find customers, men in short, black boots – beetle-crushers, they call them. And him ... what about him? We'll soon see.

The time has come to speak of this, too. Right now he's content to roam the alleyways with a rather serene trust in the world, dropping down to the quay where the Salvation Army dishes out dirt-cheap meals to all and sundry. Horse steak is very high on the menu here. During the late afternoon he might walk through the narrow streets past the lovely gabled houses, looking for the city library. There he finds a well-stocked section of German books where he can pursue his constantly interrupted course of study under his own steam – still the best method. The librarians are helpful and polite. For them, one well-bred foreigner is just a reader, like any other. They obligingly drag out Thomas Mann's 'Joseph' novels, or an entire volume of the magazine *Mass und Wert*, or *Der Logische Aufbau der Welt*, a massive tome by Rudolf Carnap. Every now and then he has a shot at a Dutch book – by Felix Timmermans or Ernest Claes, for instance, in which the world of the Flemish farmer is contrasted, and not without malicious undertones, with that of the filth and the so-called corruption of the Walloon industrial areas. (He doesn't pick up on these undertones, though, unfamiliar as he still is with the contours of Belgian political, social and economic life.)

Sometimes, while taking a cigarette break in front of the small library, so idyllic in the North Sea light, he strikes up a conversation with Flemish library visitors, students, intellectuals. That's when he learns that Flanders is finally waking up and is about to capture a place in the sun in this country, and that this Belgium is nothing but a despicable state that has oppressed the Flemings for an entire century and kept them staggering under the yoke of a totally foreign culture and a hated language. The French-speakers – the Walloons and the people of Brussels – are only interested in Paris, according to his interlocutors. To them, Dutch is mere gibberish and the Flemings a bunch of stupid peasants. And – would you believe it? – even in Antwerp, the metropolis, there are traitors to their race: Flemings who only speak French, a disgraceful bourgeoisie! Those people will get what's coming to them soon enough. And if it ever comes to war, France is bound to lose to the new Germany and the French-speakers will have to surrender their privileged position.

The guest, suddenly feeling more undesirable than ever, doesn't dare answer and shyly backs away in silence. The new Germany! My God! He could tell them a thing or two about that. But anyone who is there on sufferance, who has to go begging for his residence permit every three months, always afraid that this unsightly bit of paper will be withheld from him, is wise to keep quiet. So he flees upstairs, back to the library's nicely warmed interior, so much more hospitable than his gloomy room in that disreputable hotel. He seeks shelter with Thomas Mann, but is sadly unsuccessful. Yes, he even detects a bit of jealousy and resentment in himself when he thinks of the beloved writer: 'You, sir, it was easy enough for you, writing away in Küsnacht-Zürich with all your money and fame and an awareness of how incomparable you were! Why not come here for a change, and listen to the obnoxious drivel of these blockheads who don't know what they're talking about, which doesn't make them any less guilty. Ah, you'd rather not, would you? You'd sooner write noble letters full of noble words to noble individuals.'

The intruder hurries back to his residence, a tall, drab, almost black structure with a tavern on the ground floor. He looks for Denise the whore and invites her for a glass of beer, which is just about as far as his money will take him. Denise from Liège, the frumpy, heavy-breasted yet not unattractive Denise – at least Denise tells him that if there's a war, the Huns will be defeated. France. The Maginot Line. Just let those eastern barbarians try to knock their skulls against that! Even Belgium is armed to the teeth. *La Belgique*: for Denise, the sanctified native soil that must be defended at all costs is an ally of invincible superpowers, France and England. When push comes to shove, King Leopold III's declaration of neutrality won't stand a chance. Denise found that out from one of her best customers, an officer. The uninvited guest feels so moved by this lady's anti-Nazi, Belgian patriotism that he takes her up on her much-repeated offer. She's got sympathy for the plight of a refugee. Didn't her own father have to flee from the German conqueror during the First World War?

Denise's body is soft and warm, and very maternal. With her he feels at home. Secure in her abundance, his thoughts are far from Antwerp. But if war ever comes, says Denise afterwards, then...

From *Localities* (Örtlichkeiten). Stuttgart, 1980.
Translated by Nancy Forest-Flier.

A Dean Steps into the Breach
By R.P. Cleveringa, 1940

Address given on 26 November 1940 on the occasion of the dismissal of Professor E.M. Meijers from his position at the University of Leiden.

I stand before you today when you were expecting to see someone else: your, and my, learned teacher Professor Meijers. The reason for this is a letter he received this morning from the Department of Education, Arts and Sciences, which reads as follows: '*In accordance with the instructions of the Reichscommissar for the Occupied Netherlands relating to non-Arian civil servants and other persons of similar status, I hereby inform you that, with effect from today, you are dismissed from the office of Professor of the University of Leiden. The Reichscommissar has decreed that the persons concerned shall for the present be entitled to retain their salary and allowances etc.*'

I convey this news to you as it was written, in all its naked bluntness, and shall not attempt to interpret it further. I fear that the words I should use in doing so, however carefully chosen, would in no way do justice to the bitterness and grief felt by myself and my colleagues and also, I am convinced, by yourselves and countless others in this country and abroad who learn of this news. I believe that I can dispense with any attempt to voice those feelings, since I sense that our thoughts and emotions are at this moment hovering soundlessly, but perfectly recognisably, among and around us all.

It is not to talk about feelings that I wish to address you now. If that had been my only purpose here today, there would be no better way of emphasising our mood than to end my speech here, and leave you in the stony oppression of the horrifying silence which would immediately envelop us.

Neither shall I attempt to guide your thoughts towards those who wrote the letter I have just reported to you. Their actions speak for themselves. My only desire is to banish them from our thoughts to the depths where they belong, and to direct our gaze upward to the shining figure who is the reason we are here today. Because it seems to me that we should take this opportunity to remind ourselves who he is; this person who has been pushed aside, after thirty years of service, by a power supported by nothing other than itself; this person whose work has been so cruelly curtailed.

(…)

This Dutchman, this true and noble son of our nation, this human being, this student father-figure, this scholar, has been *dismissed from his position* by the alien, the hostile force that now occupies our country! I have said that I would not speak of my feelings. I shall keep my word, although my feelings threaten to burst like boiling lava through all the cracks that I fear will tear apart my head and my heart.

Yet I believe that, in a Faculty dedicated to furthering the cause of justice, the following points must be made. In accordance with the tradition of the Netherlands, the Constitution states that all subjects of the Netherlands shall have the right to serve their country, to be appointed to public office and to be admitted to any honour or rank. Furthermore, the Constitution states that every subject shall be entitled to the same civil rights and rights of citizenship, irrespective of their religion. According to Article 43 of the laws of war, the Occupier shall observe the law of the country he occupies 'sauf empêchement absolu'. We can only conclude that there was nothing whatsoever to prevent the Occupier from allowing Meijers to remain in office. The way in which he has been dismissed, as I have reported, and the similar measures inflicted upon others (I think in the first place of our friend and colleague David), can only be regarded as unjust.

We had believed that we were – and would remain – protected from such injustice. This is not so. Without lapsing into acts of futile stupidity, which I would strongly discourage, we have no alternative but to submit to superior force. In the meantime we shall continue our work to the best of our ability. I and my colleagues Telders and Kollewijn shall attempt to fill the void which has arisen, knowing only too well that neither we nor anyone else could be more than an inferior substitute. My colleagues Kollewijn and Telders will take up their new duties on Tuesday 3 December at 10 o'clock and 11 o'clock respectively, and I myself shall do so on Thursday at 10 o'clock.

In the meantime we shall wait and trust and hope, and keep in our hearts and in our minds the image and figure of the person whose rightful place we will always believe this to be and to which, God willing, he will return.

From *Shocking Speeches* (Schokkende redevoeringen, ed. J.P. Guépin). Amsterdam, 1990.
Translated by Yvette Mead.

Two Extracts from *Will-o'-the-Wisp*

by Willem Elsschot, 1946

It must have been written in the stars, because my tram stood waiting a long time. I don't know what came over me, but I felt somehow uneasy, as if I had something on my conscience. I was standing in the back compartment staring vacantly at the rain, which had slackened off a little, when I caught sight of my three blackies just as they came out of Jonkheer's the baker, each of them gnawing eagerly at a roll while they glanced round to get their bearings. They seemed to be hesitating between Reyndersstraat, which was the first lap on the good road, and the Oude Koornmarkt, which was the maw of a labyrinth of back-streets where they would wander hopelessly up and down until they had to go back to their ship at the break of dawn and turn to for another day's toil. No, they'd never find Kloosterstraat. And even if they did find it, how could they pick out number fifteen, because our figures must be like hieroglyphics to them.

Suddenly I had a vision of myself trudging through the heart of Bombay, forlorn and weary. It is night, and a chilly mist soaks through my thin cotton jacket. I am going from one street to the other, through slums and past bazaars, searching for Fathma who sits waiting for me by the light of a red lamp in a house that is somewhere at the end of a trek along the thirty-seventh street on the right, the fifteenth on the left, the ninth on the right, the seventh on the left, and then a winding alley that I'll never find. I am holding in my hand a pathetic piece of cardboard that no one will look at in that crowd of thousands that streams past like a living Ganges without even giving me a glance. I started out bright-eyed and with a heart full of hope, and now I'm standing on the same corner for the third or fourth time. It is an endless, futile circle with no way out, and I know now that I'll never find Fathma, that I'll never hold her in my arms and press her close. By the first light of the new day she'll put out her lamp and throw herself on her couch sobbing because the faithless white man hasn't kept his promise.

I had to admit to myself that I hadn't done much to help those three fellows, and that my sign language must have looked silly, especially the zigzag, because it was hardly likely they had understood what I meant. Then this Maria Van Dam, this name they bore like some proud motto on their cardboard scutcheon, who was she? She would be the sort of wench who'd belong in this area. I couldn't imagine that three coolies would be looking for a countess round the docks at night. But in a district like this you come across fine-looking girls who don't suffer from inhibitions. Besides, Maria is a name I like more than any other. That wasn't important, though. It was these three wandering pilgrims who had to see her, not me.

Without reflecting any more I jumped off the tram and went over to my three blackies. They recognised me and greeted me with smiles as broad as daybreak.

'A strange city,' Ali said, 'all the streets look the same.' But I held up my hand reassuringly and announced that I would guide them to the girl on the cigarette packet. I stepped out resolutely towards the third on the right, Ali walking next to me and his two dark, silent companions following behind.

So there I was walking along with three strangers who were different in every way from the people I was doomed to live out my days with – three strangers who had another colour of skin, who walked differently and laughed and greeted differently, and maybe loved differently and hated differently, strangers who had never heard of the foremost pillars of our state and cared naught for our princes and prelates, so they would most likely be men after my own heart. Now that these three had happened to cross my path I should try to make the most of the chance while I could, for our encounter would only be a brief and passing interlude.

I had to find something to start the conversation, so I asked Ali if he had met Maria. After all, I didn't know how he'd got hold of that homemade visiting-card, and I wanted to be sure that she was real flesh-and-blood and not just a fancy.

Yes, he had met her.

Was she a nice girl?

'Very nice,' Ali assured me with conviction.

Young? It would be a let-down if she turned out to be some old crone.

Ali confirmed in a rather guarded tone that she was young.

'About fifteen or so?' I asked. Our ideas of old and young might be worlds apart, but I didn't imagine that these blackies would take our moral strictures very seriously. I wouldn't have bothered if I'd thought they did. I'm not the sort to take a lot of trouble to uphold all the prudish taboos of our Western lexicon.

'Oh, no,' he said, laughing and making a gesture of denial. He turned his head and said something in his own tongue that made his two companions laugh like children.

'Fourteen, then?'

This time he raised his brown index finger to reprimand me, and he confided that she must be about twenty.

'Well, so much the better,' I said paternally, though I was disappointed.

'Better for the white man's law,' Ali pointed out.

So there was no prudery. It was only out of necessity that he was toeing the line of our conventions.

We had reached the second on the left, and the goal would soon be in sight. If only the rain would stop, everything would be fine, for after all we were on our way to a wedding. I was thinking that we actually ought to have a bouquet so that we wouldn't arrive empty-handed, but at that time of the year there isn't much besides chrysanthemums, and I wasn't sure, whether that would strike the right note since it has become the fashion to use them to give tone to funerals. For years there had been a florist's shop across the street next to the butcher's, and I guessed it couldn't do any harm to have a look. The window was full of ornamental plants, but finally I saw at the back a basket filled with some flowers I didn't know the name of. At least their fiery red colour certainly matched the mood of my companions. But then there was no knowing whether a bouquet would impress Maria van Dam, and in any case I hadn't the slightest idea if Indian etiquette called for saying it with flowers. Flowers or no flowers. It was a delicate problem.

'Some flowers for the girl?' I asked Ali. After all it was their affair, and it was only right that they should have the last word.

Ali consulted his companions and said that it would be all right.

All right! That wasn't any sort of answer at all. It didn't matter a damn to me whether they had flowers or not, it wasn't my party. So I asked him if they really thought it was a good idea.

'In every country the stranger must do whatever is the custom,' he insisted, and would I buy the flowers for them because they got mixed up with our money and they'd been gypped a couple of times already.

The bouquet looked fine, and it was small enough not to attract too much attention from an awkward landlady or anyone else they might have to get past to see Maria. Ali immediately asked me how much it cost, and he wouldn't move a step until I accepted the money from him. Then he took the flowers and we were able to go on.

I asked if they had known Maria very long.

No, only since that morning. She had come on board to mend the bags, and they had given her a scarf, a pot of ginger, and six packets of cigarettes. After she had accepted all these tokens of esteem they had made an appointment for the evening, and when the first packet of cigarettes was empty she had written her name and address on the back. So it wasn't just a casual pick-up. It sounded fairly genuine.

But which of them was in love with Maria, I asked him. Was it he himself or one of his two friends.

'All three of us,' he affirmed.

I looked at him sharply, not sure whether he was joking or not, but his face was a picture of earnestness and truthfulness. I couldn't restrain my crude Western inquisitiveness. Was he sure she had really invited them all, I asked. If she had, she was, for a girl of only twenty, unusually enterprising.

'Oh, yes,' he assured me, 'all three.' She had accepted a gift from each of them, and she hadn't shown any preference for the one or the other, so they took it for granted that she could cope with the lot of them.

That seemed to open up possibilities. It was a promising beginning, anyway. 'Do you think she'll be there waiting for you?'

'Of course,' Ali said. 'She wouldn't have taken the presents if she wasn't going to be there, would she, sir?'

His optimism was so infectious that I began to be convinced of Maria's noble altruism myself. 'This is the street,' I told him, 'and number fifteen is over there. She won't have to wait much longer!' We crossed over to inspect the trysting place.

Now I could say good-bye and leave them to it. I had fulfilled my Christian duty and they wouldn't be needing any help or guidance from me for the apotheosis. Yet why not stay? Where there was room for three there was room for four. But I resolutely thrust aside this unseemly thought. My three companions were all smiles, and I had the impression that they wouldn't mind sharing Maria with me like a cake. No, that wouldn't be right. I'd just wait to watch the welcoming of my three Romeos, give them my blessing, then go off home with my paper and my aching feet and the consolation of knowing my mission had been crowned with success. (…)

By this time we had reached the dock. If they kept straight on they'd soon be back on the *Delhi Castle* and in their hammocks. They couldn't get lost now, the way was marked out for them by a row of slumbering mammoths moored along the quayside.

Now that the hour of parting had come, my thoughts went back to the police station and the reproach in Ali's eyes when he looked up at me, and, as though we were going to go on seeing each other for years to come, I expressed the hope that he would never doubt me again. He meditated and seemed to be examining his conscience so he could give a true and honest answer.

'No,' he said, 'I didn't doubt you. My thoughts were uncertain, but my heart was sure.'

Then I wished him a safe and speedy voyage, and to ease the solemnity of the parting I said that his married friend shouldn't talk too much about the girl when he got home. That wasn't the sort of thing to tell a wife he'd had to leave behind to go to sea. 'No, he won't do that,' Ali said. 'Even if he is soft in the head, he has a prudent tongue.'

There was a silence for a few moments, because I had nothing more to say. Then Ali spoke again. 'Just as the time comes for each of us when we must die, sir,' he said, 'now it is the time for us to leave you, I wish you happiness and health in this misty land, and I hope that you will be blessed with still more sons, for then you will not be forgotten when you are dead. We went with you and watched you carefully, because a stranger in a strange land must be as cautious as the animals in the jungle, and we saw that you treated us like brothers, even though we are not of your own people. You would not take a reward from us, and you paid for the water and the fiery drink, and I had to argue with you before you would let us give you the money for the flowers. You helped us just because you knew we couldn't find our way in your city. We have understood it all. I am grateful to you, and so are my two friends who cannot tell you. If you ever go to a far-off land, sir, I hope that your man on the cross sends someone to guide you who will walk with you as far as you have walked with us, never complaining of the rain, because a helpful stranger is like a beacon in the night.

'And if you meet the girl, sir, tell her that we went to the shop with the cages where the man threw her letter on the ground and wouldn't speak to us, and to the big police officer who laughed and picked up the flowers, and to the man who washed glasses and sang songs, and that we did everything we could to try and find her. And tell her to watch out for the *Delhi Castle*, because our ship will surely come back again if it is spared, and if she isn't sent on board to mend the bags she should come anyway, and one of us will be there by the hatch waiting for her. We'll have more presents, even though the first ones we gave her didn't help. But be careful, because it's not easy to resist her. So it would be better to speak to her without touching her.'

I reminded him once again that, much to my regret, I hadn't even seen her.

'But you know the words that were on the paper, sir, so you can ask about her. It won't be hard to find her, because none of the others who mend the bags could be like her. That is as certain as Allah is the one true almighty God.'

He stood still, staring at the ground as if he was debating with himself, then he fumbled inside his long jacket and offered me the packet of cigarettes again.

'Now that our ways are parting, you can't refuse it,' he said.

I accepted the gift, and I promised him that I would keep it to remember them by.

'No,' he protested, 'you must smoke them or they will go dry. True friends don't need souvenirs to remember.' These words, the last that were spoken, sealed the bond of our short-lived brotherhood.

Another round of handshakes and they started off, walking in file with Ali in the lead. At the first street-light they stopped, as if they knew I'd be watching. They waved a last farewell, and soon they had shrunk to ants in the endless stretch of the dockside.

To get home from here I had to go along Lange Ridderstraat, and it would have been an admission of guilt to make a detour. After all, I was no criminal, so why shouldn't I go along Lange Ridderstraat, even if I broke my neck doing it? I turned the next corner and there it was, one side a streak of moonlight, the other side a dark, solid shadow. How late would it be, I wondered.

There couldn't be a drearier and sadder street than this in all the centre of the city. Generation after generation had huddled and stunk and survived here in tumbledown hovels that somehow or other still managed to stay upright. There wasn't a sound or sight of anyone at that ungodly hour. A stench that made me sick seeped out of the old sewers.

Number seventy-one was a grimy front with the plaster hanging in strips. The door was crooked and battered, and the window was half boarded up. A leaky drainpipe stuck out like a gallows, and through the holes trickled the last drops of the downpour that had stopped me from going to the bar I drank at every night.

Should I risk it and knock, and ask in Ali's name for Maria who had been on the *Delhi Castle* that morning to mend the bags? It was here, this must be the place. I was certain of it.

No, old satyr, enough is enough. Leave her in peace to enjoy her last cigarette and dream of her scarf and her pot of ginger. Keep going, and maybe the lechery that sent you off on this nocturnal wench-hunt won't be counted against you. Forget all about Bombay and Fathma and go home. Yes, back home with my paper, back to the family circle, back to the ties that bind and bore me, utterly and endlessly.

I thought of Ali again, and the words of an old song came back to me:

Adieu, adieu, kind friends, adieu, adieu, adieu,
I can no longer stay with you.
I'll hang my harp on a weeping willow tree,
And may the world go well with thee.

Yes, comrades, may all go well with you. May Allah smooth your way and watch over you at sea, and when the time has come bring you safely home to your village in the mountains. And Maria and Fathma, ah, there's always hope, for how incomprehensible are the judgments of the Lord, and his ways unsearchable.

From *Will-o'-the-Wisp* (Het dwaallicht). Amsterdam: Querido, 1946.
Translated by Alex Brotherton (in: 'Three Novels'. Leiden / London / New York, 1965).

Another Ode to Amsterdam
by György Konrád, 1999

This city is striking for its ability to be an ant during the day and a cricket at night. Amsterdam is less than averagely violent, but it is exceptionally strong: all manner of authorities are indeed on hand here and they turn out quickly and are well-organised. If the citizens of Amsterdam are efficient in commerce, why should they not be so in keeping order? The maintaining of public order does not bring with it any threatening, unfriendly behaviour by the police. They will not torment the inhabitants with an excessive show of strength. The only purpose of that sort of thing is to disguise corrupt aimlessness. The behaviour of the authorities corresponds to the prevailing views of the citizens. When one's basic principle is respect for others, for one's neighbour, and as part of this, respect for his decisions, tolerance comes naturally.

The adult consciousness is patient, but the immature, conversely, is impatient, hostile, volatile, hot-headed, pugnacious, easily offended, gloomy and distrustful, tends to self-pity, will try to camouflage reprehensibility with something sublime, and aggressively interferes in everything. Immature public opinion sticks its nose into things that do not concern it. I do not accuse Amsterdammers of being angels, far from it, I do not even expect to come across Spinoza, Erasmus or Grotius on the terraces of the coffee shops, but believe me, I know quite a few cities whose people have bigger mouths but are much less civilised. Amsterdammers are not angels, but they are realists regarding mankind, other people and, let's say, their neighbour. They try to domesticate, guide and legalise differences of inclination against the background of the reasonableness of the community.

We are just like a teacher on a school trip with his class: we try to keep divergent inclinations together. Keep them together? We call this imposing the law. An adult citizen weighs up his freedoms and obligations himself. This independent contemplation, and its naturalness, the natural smile with which it is elevated to the status of a habit, is a virtue for which the inhabitants of this city, probably because the oldest democracy in Europe is rooted here, would be rewarded with good marks by any imaginary group of teachers.

The toleration of the coffee shops is part of Amsterdam's worldly wisdom. As long as someone does not harm or pose a threat to others, he cannot be punished: he has committed no crime.

By using grass as a stimulant, just another stimulant like tobacco or the fermented juice of grapes and other fruit and the alcoholic derivatives of certain types of grain, visitors to the coffee shops are not harming anyone in any way at all, and the difference between this and the establishments where alcoholic drinks are served is that the patrons of coffee shops are usually calmer and quieter. These shops sell coffee, tea and orange juice in addition to hashish and marijuana. Their range does not include hard drugs, but they have brought about a refined cannabis culture. What he believes in, what he reads and consumes and with what sort of one-sided consumption he harms himself is a matter for the individual's own free choice. There is none of the demonisation that comes from putting the non-addictive cannabis on the same level as addictive opiates. The reason for this is probably the realisation that if the same prohibition applied to both categories, grass smokers, having experienced no ill effects, would also give heroin a try, on the assumption that it was also harmless. A rigid outlook that pays no heed to the differences can easily lead to youngsters ending up as addicts.

Respect for one's fellow men, freedom of religion and freedom of consumption presuppose each other. This city has decided to tolerate a variety of human desires. The differing manifestations of human nature that are tolerated here, and what goods or services are considered acceptable in everyday trading is in fact a question of the philosophy of the boundaries of tolerance. This tolerance towards life, the odd and the aberrant goes quite far here. Do what you feel like, in everything: eating, drinking, smoking, reading, listening, watching. Allow the possibility, if you want to spend money on it, of buying sexual pleasure and physical contact. Visitors come here to enjoy themselves, and the museums, coffee shops and the red-light district are all, in combination, sources of income. Together they are the response to the tourist's various desires.

However, there is one particular desire which Amsterdam satisfies in an exceptionally agreeable way: the passion for walking, wandering, drifting round an unfamiliar city. Sauntering along the canals in the old city is made possible by deliberate restrictions on traffic. Where cars rule, the joy of walking suffers. It is a question of making choices: in this city the authorities have voted for walking, strolling, using one's legs. Where people go for long walks along the waterside, they are more inclined to ponder deeply, and are probably more intelligent.

From *Amsterdam* (Tr. from the Hungarian by Györgyi Dandoy). Amsterdam: Van Gennep, 1999. *Translated by Gregory Ball.*

Jan Toorop, *Café Mille Colonnes, Brussels.* 1885. Canvas, 99 x 89 cm. Private collection.

We Are a Hospitable People

by Josse de Pauw, 2000

Ladies and gentlemen, dear friends, John, Joanna and Nigel,
chers compatriotes, mesdames, messieurs, we are a hospitable people.
This is written in blood in the books that tell of our past.
We are a hospitable people.
We are a helpful people.
The man in the house on the hill leaps out of bed at the first knock on the door in the night.
He will switch on the light and lay a fire.
He will feed the hungry, refresh the thirsty, care for the wounded.
He will do what he can to ease his fellow man's suffering.
He will do what he can!
He has been taught to do so.
His parents impressed this upon him,
as their parents impressed it upon them,
having learnt it from their parents, and so on and so on...
We have ever been a hospitable and helpful people.
But if they loom up out of the desert in their hordes to settle here in our oasis, if they cross the great waters in their rickety ships to pitch their tents here on our shores, if, like Icarus, they start to sew on wings and flap them wildly about, to fly up towards our sun...
Then we should not stand silently looking on!
No god demands our downfall!
We have moved forward step by step for millions of years,
step by step we have left the apes behind us.
For millions of years we have been born and have died,
we have fought and struggled for the place where we now stand.
We shall never leave this place!
We shall not allow ourselves to be forced out!
It is not our fault that others appear incapable of shaking off the ape!
They must realise one thing,
THEY
THEY
THEY
THEY
THEY

From *Larf*. In: *Work* (Werk). Antwerp, 2000.
Translated by Gregory Ball.

Between

Descent and Destiny

Intercultural Authors in the Netherlands

The symposium *Language on the Move: New Writing by New Europeans*, held in Amsterdam in September 2000, focused on a number of authors who could be called 'newcomers' to the regions where French, German, English or Dutch is spoken. The objective of the symposium's organisers, the Foundation for the Production and Translation of Dutch Literature, was to bring together these writers, their public and their translators. Among the questions discussed during the workshops, discussion sessions and open evenings were: '*Does this literature call for a new and different type of literary criticism? Why are publishers prompted to publish the work of these authors? Do translators play a greater role in the production process? Does the emergence of new intercultural literature signal the demise of national literature?*' In organising this symposium, the Foundation benefited not only from the attention (and financial support) given by the current Dutch Secretary of State for Culture, Rik van der Ploeg, to the work of migrant artists but also from the fact that the Netherlands is experiencing (later than its neighbours) an upsurge in the number of 'new European' authors writing in Dutch.

Astrid Roemer (1947-).
Photo by Willy Dee.

For some years now it has been generally accepted that literature from the larger language areas – such as the French-, English- and German-speaking countries – is renewed by the fringe, by those authors who come from outside and breathe new life into the literary establishment. Salman Rushdie, of course, is the pre-eminent example of this trend in English literature, but V.S. Naipaul and Ben Okri are also worthy of mention here. Their counterpart in Dutch literature is Astrid Roemer (of Surinamese descent). Like her 'New Dutch' colleagues Hafid Bouazza and Mustafa Stitou, she adopts an easy, playful approach to language, displaying a particular penchant for 'antiquated' Dutch and using words in an expressive and poetic way. In Germany, Sevgi Özdamar and Herta Müller (originally Turkish and Rumanian, respectively) are opening up new vistas in the German language, and in France the Algerian writers Malika Mokeddem and Assia Djebar – to name only two – have given French a new lustre. Fouad Laroui, a Moroccan who lives in the Netherlands and writes in French, is another example of such cultural globalisation. He left his native village at an early age to attend first the French school and then the prestigious 'Ecole des mines', going on to work in America and finally to settle in Amsterdam, where he writes satirical novels set either in his native country or in Paris. Laroui has been translated into Dutch.

The joy of writing

The emergence of these so-called second-generation authors in the Netherlands is closely linked to initiatives taken by such institutions as El Hizjra, a centre for the promotion of Arabic culture in Amsterdam that sponsors an annual writing competition for authors with an Arabic background, thus providing guidance and encouragement to talented writers. In 1998 the centre compiled a book from work submitted to one of its competitions. Some of the contributions were translated from the Arabic, but most of the stories and poems had been written directly in Dutch. Many of these young authors have lived in the Netherlands since childhood, and one thing these incipient writers all have in common is a touching desire to write, to express themselves. They also feel a need to reflect on their cultural background, as did the Morocco-born Halima Benaissa when she wrote '*Not torn between two cultures, but two cultures united in me*'.

Past winners of the El Hizjra competition include the highly successful Abdelkader Benali, Mustafa Stitou and the nineteen-year-old Rashid Novaire, whose debut *Herons in Cairo* (Reigers in Caïro) was published in 1999. *My Shapes* (Mijn vormen, 1994) by Mustafa Stitou was the first volume of poetry to be published in Dutch by a writer of Moroccan origin. The year 1998 saw the publication of another volume by this talented author: *My Poems* (Mijn gedichten). The huge success of this whimsical work must have made other publishers realise how lucrative it can be to publish young writers who commute, as it were, between various cultures, carrying things foreign as a permanent part of their baggage. In *My Shapes* Stitou observes

Photo used for the 2000 Literary Award of El Hizjra, a centre for the promotion of Arabic culture in Amsterdam. Photo courtesy of El Hizjra, Amsterdam.

Mustafa Stitou (1974-). Photo by Klaas Koppe.

Hafid Bouazza (1970-).
Photo by Klaas Koppe.

both cultures with marked detachment. Typical of his poems are a certain irony and a Dutch matter-of-factness. He plays around with clichés about Moroccans, poking fun in his poem 'Great men' ('Grote mannen'), for example, at Berbers and Moroccan mountain-dwellers living in the Netherlands and fighting for Dutch subsidies to fund a place of worship. His poems also have a cosmopolitan feel to them: their 'stories' take place in cafés or are set against the backdrop of Paris or Amsterdam. The poet conjures up the sound of Charlie Parker, the images of Pasolini. Although the Koran prohibits the consumption of alcohol, the first-person narrator drinks beer at an outdoor café in Amsterdam. The basic threads of the culture that, with that of the Netherlands, forms the fabric of his background mingle with the culture in which he writes: '*a Koran of memories / of a mosque / poetry?*' Stitou is inspired not so much by Arabic tradition as by Western cosmopolitanism. Like other authors of Moroccan descent, such as Abdelkader Benali and Hafid Bouazza, Stitou has so much fun with the Dutch language that the joy of writing practically leaps out at you from the page.

Hafid Bouazza is an elegant writer who seems to take pleasure in both stripping down and dressing up the Dutch language, showing a predilection for ceremonious or old Dutch words. In *De voeten van Abdullah* (1996), published in 2000 in English as *Abdullah's Feet*, he describes his native village and its people in delightfully ironic terms, poking fun at imams and making all the men drink themselves under the table and commit every sin imaginable. Sexuality is a leitmotiv in this novel. In his most recent book, *Momo* (1998) – about a couple living in Herfsthoven (a takeoff on the quiet, boring Dutch town of Schoonhoven) who produce a son late in life – the writer stays closer to home. In this zany novella Bouazza uses the most delicious Dutch, with a detached irony reminiscent of the work of Simon Carmiggelt and Remco Campert. The latter writer in particular has been a great source of inspiration for Stitou.

Abdelkader Benali is another writer who is attracted to a world that traditional and religious Moroccans want nothing to do with. In his book *Bruiloft aan zee* (1996; published in English in 1999 as *Wedding by the Sea*), the pro-

Abdelkader Benali (facing the camera)(1975-). Photo by Klaas Koppe.

Naima El Bezaz (1974-). Photo by Klaas Koppe.

tagonist ends up in a whorehouse called 'Lolita', where he finds his uncle in a drunken stupor.

What this younger generation of authors – who not only write in Dutch but have also received their education within the context of Dutch culture – have in common, besides their playful use of language, is their refusal to have the label 'immigrant author' pinned on them. Naima El Bezaz says it's better to think in terms of trends and not of countries. Her first book, *The Road North* (De weg naar het Noorden, 1995), was published when she was twenty-one. In clipped, unadorned phrases – almost like a black-and-white documentary making sparing use of poignant images, the young writer tells of a man who wants to leave M. because there is no future for him there. El Bezaz gives a heart-rending account of an existence with no prospect of work and no possibility of building a life of one's own. We read about the enticements of the West with its get-rich-quick mentality, about young Moroccans falling under the spell of mafia bosses who make vast fortunes as drug dealers. A clear picture emerges of the hope felt by a young man who goes to try his luck elsewhere, the same hope cherished by millions of migrants. In the Netherlands his dreams come to nothing, and in Paris his luck is no better. He is pushed around simply because he is an illegal immigrant. This book's merits lie not in its use of language but in its content. El Bezaz is not a stylist; instead she tries to evoke sympathy with the fate of her protagonist, putting the plight of an illegal immigrant in its proper perspective and bringing him to life as an individual. Ghali is smuggled into Europe by money-hungry compatriots, traffickers in human beings. Tragically, he sinks into total isolation, gradually realising there is no bright future in store for him. He is even beaten up somewhere on the outskirts of town. Naima El Bezaz paints a disconcerting picture of the treatment to which illegal immigrants are subjected.

The year 2000 saw the publication of *The Days of Shaitan* (De dagen van sjaitan) by Said El Haji, in which he describes the Berber community in the fictitious Dutch town of Berkerode. In the authoritative newspaper *NRC Handelsblad* the author received high praise as the Islamic counterpart of

Maarten 't Hart, because he writes about the struggles of young Dutch Moroccans against the religious authorities, just as 't Hart takes to task his own strict Dutch Reformed upbringing.

Diverted like the course of a river

In addition to these second-generation Dutch authors, a number of 'in-between figures' have made their appearance in the Netherlands in the past ten years, writers who have emerged between two cultures, whose work cannot be interpreted within the context of a single homogeneous culture. Their mother country continues to reverberate in their work; their words often reveal the deep sorrow caused by their uprooting and alienation. These writers have lost something for good, and they are seeking to make their new home in language: the ultimate exile. New writers in Dutch include the Beijing-born Lulu Wang, who has lived for more than 25 years in the Netherlands and achieved success with her first novel, *Het lelietheater* (1997) – published in England in 2000 as *The Lily Theatre*; Nausicaa Marbe from Bucharest, a resident of the Netherlands since 1982, who won the Charlotte Köhler grant 'for promising artists aged under thirty-five' for her first book, *Mândraga* (1998), which also earned her the epithet of '*the Rumanian Isabel Allende*'; and finally, the highly gifted Yasmine Allas of Somalia, whose novel *Idil, a Girl* (Idil, een meisje) was published in 1998, followed in 2001 by *The General with Six Fingers* (De generaal met zes vingers). In Allas' words, '*There is nothing worse than people without a country. They're always in transit.*' The Czech Jan Stavinoha, who has lived in the Netherlands since the 1970s, started writing in Dutch after the publication of his first book, *Prague Dixieland* (Praagse Dixieland). His Dutch is imbued with a 'typically Czech' brand of humour. In contrast to his earlier writings, his latest book is set entirely in his old homeland.

Stavinoha's compatriot Jana Beranová has written a novel and two volumes of poetry – the most recent appeared in 1999 and is called *Between the Rivers* (Tussen de rivieren). She has now been in the Netherlands for forty years, and has learned – as a poet, novelist and translator (of Kundera and Seifert) – how to look at Dutch from the outside: '*my path is paved with foreign sounds*', her poetry discloses. A writer's diary published in the literary magazine *Lust & Gratie* (no. 62, 1999) reveals how very much alive the writer's past still is: '*Saturday, Sunday. Things have turned out well for me. No comparison with Kosovo. Yet pictures of the past keep thrusting themselves on me. I relive them, I can't get rid of them. I reflect on how the past is anchored in me. A child doesn't easily admit to being sad. Should I just stop and take stock? Leaving with a child's backpack and a school travel pass, first by train, then on foot through the mountains. Father led the way, he had skied there since he was a little boy. All three of us had, in fact. No goodbyes to friends at school. I was attending a gymnasium in Prague. A year in a refugee camp in Germany. Not too bad. I didn't see any dead bodies. We heard dogs barking at the border and lay on the cold ground for a long time, afraid of their sniffing noses. We've stayed together: my father, my mother and I. I've learned new languages. "Everything has two sides, darling, the sunny side and the other one." Things have turned out very well for me.*'

The consequences of fleeing – always crying over a nameless sorrow, because from one day to the next you have to put down roots somewhere else – is also described by Vera Illés, originally from Hungary. In her autobiography, *Child of Another Time* (Kind van een andere tijd, 1992), she tells how, as a ten-year-old girl in Budapest, she stumbled into the revolution carrying two bottles of soda water. She had gone to do some shopping for her neighbour, and, not realising what was happening, she ran into demonstrating crowds who surrounded her on all sides, forcing her farther and farther away from home, towards the River Danube. Six weeks after the uprising, this Jewish girl fled at night with her parents and sister over the border to Austria. Like Jana Beranová, Vera Illés has lived in the Netherlands for forty years, having come to her adoptive country as a child. Her book deals with such fundamental questions as: As a child, how do you manage to fit in when you're clearly different from the others, even though you don't want to be different? What happens to your mother tongue when you're forced to learn a new language as a matter of survival? What happens to an 'I' that is diverted like the course of a river? What is your relationship to the past? In a foreign country, Illés writes, you can't allow yourself to have pleasant memories; in order to survive you have to learn to forget. Only when you are writing can memories be allowed to take on concrete shapes.

Vera Illés (1946-). Photo by Wout Jan Balhuizen.

Fresh views

Nasser Fakhteh is an Iranian exile who has lived in the Netherlands since 1988. He started out writing prose and poetry in Persian. In his volume of short stories, *Someone Else* (Iemand anders, 1996), he draws a poignant picture of how intolerable life was under the regimes of two tyrants, first the Shah and later the Ayatollahs. Twice he was jailed, each time for several

Yasmine Allas (1968-).
Photo by Klaas Koppe.

years. His stories are about exiles living in desolate centres for political refugees or in gloomy blocks of flats. In the first story, an Iranian immigrant with a residence permit helps a Polish woman, who has entered the Netherlands illegally and has no place to live, by letting her live for a while in his two-room flat. This is a subtly told tale of the blind leading the blind. These uprooted people acquire a face and a voice. Fakhteh confronts the reader with the hopeless existence and heart-rending fate of exiles.

In 1993 the writer Kader Abdolah (see p.66), also originally from Iran, first appeared on the Dutch literary scene with the publication of his book of short stories, *The Eagles* (De adelaars, 1993). The story which gave the volume its name, 'Eagles', was published in the literary magazine *Icarus* (1994, no. 15). Abdolah, who now occupies a unique place in the field of Dutch literature, writes sparse, sober prose full of powerful images. The simplicity of his stories is pure magic. In all his books Abdolah's inimitable style drives home to the reader what it feels like to be a refugee who has lost everything most dear to him.

The most productive contribution made by intercultural authors stems from their ability to revitalise the Dutch language, to see Dutch customs and traditions from a new angle, to shed new light on Dutch literature. Hafid Bouazza is inspired by the work of nineteenth-century Dutch poets, for example, and Kader Abdolah describes how an Iranian exile looks at his homosexual neighbour. Moreover, native Dutch readers appear to like these intercultural authors, as is clear from the success enjoyed by the writers mentioned in this article. For the literary critic things really start to get exciting when an intercultural author is translated into another language (and therefore into another culture). How Dutch does he or she still seem in French, for example? A case in point: in France, Benali's Moroccan surname has caused him to be thought of as 'just another French-Moroccan writer'. More remarkably, the Ugandan Moses Isegawa (see p.89) delivered his manuscript of *Abyssinian Chronicles* in English to a Dutch publisher. The manuscript was translated into Dutch and edited, subsequently appearing in the Netherlands in 1998 as *Abessijnse Kronieken*. The author then reworked his original manuscript, basing it on the Dutch edition, and in 2000 an English publisher put it on the market simply as a work by an English-African writer, with no mention of the important role played by the intervening Dutch translation. Clearly, these new European writers have brought us not only a new brand of literature but also a new way of marketing the exotic.

Kader Abdolah (1954-).
Photo by Harry Pierck.

DÉSIRÉE SCHYNS
Translated by Diane L. Webb.

LIST OF TRANSLATIONS

BENALI, ABDELKADER, *Wedding by the Sea* (Tr. Susan Massotty). London: Phoenix House / Weidenfeld & Nicolson, 1999.

BOUAZZA, HAFID, *Abdullah's Feet* (Tr. Ina Rilke). London: Headline Book Publishing, 2000.

ISEGAWA, MOSES, *Abyssinian Chronicles*. New York: Knopf, 2000.

WANG, LULU, *The Lily Theatre* (Tr. Hester Velmans). London: Little Brown, 2000.

Extract from *Abdullah's Feet*
by Hafid Bouazza

I can no longer recall my first impression of Amsterdam, grafted as I am on to the vertebrae of her cobbles, the wooden wombs of her bars and weathered loins of her seedy neighbourhoods. I moved into a bedsit in Eglantine Street: a cavity in a row of decaying teeth. It was a room with all the poetry of a solitary life: dented saucepan, unmade bed, dusty window panes. Single-handed solace in the tedious gloom, love at a price on Fridays. It was not long before I met Apolline.

Taller than I, blonde, high-cheekboned, bushy-lashed, full-hipped, she was the perfect embodiment of my first, lonely golden summer in Vondel Park. She had an airy self-confidence that was unassailable. She sat at the table resting a cheek on her rosy palm, collarbones bare, smiling faintly. She shot me a glance from under her eyebrows, drew back her shoulders, jutted her round breasts, uncrossed her legs.

Soon Apolline detached herself from the framework of my shallow reverence. Her personality began to dominate my world.

For one thing, she would not have me perform my prayer duties in her presence. My devotion and loyalty to a religion were meaningless to her. She scoffed, wishing to divest me of what was to me my identity but to her merely the beads and henna tracery of folklore. She wasn't having it, she was imperious, she was all woman.

She showed me Amsterdam, a naked, omnivorous, much-loved overbearing city. She was proud to walk with me at her side: those were the days when we emigrants still had a certain exotic appeal. Each walk began with a drink in a small cafe in a nameless alley, an oasis of bicycles and bin liners and urinated writing on the wall. (The infinitely feminine gesture of feeling for her purse in her shoulder bag.)

The Amsterdam of blue jeans, tight shirts, canals: my memory sees the city of that time in the muted shades of an eight-millimetre film. The canals dimpled and swayed with our reflections in dun-coloured water, transforming us and the city and the sky into lugubrious ghosts.

She paused by a fountain and said pensively: 'Funny how water always sounds so inviting. But you'd know all about that wouldn't you, son of the dead desert?' I wonder if the last bit was a quotation.

I can still remember the briny sweetness of my first taste of pork, the acrid shudder of my first sip of wine. I remember my first drunkenness when I broke down and wept in anonymous remorse and she consoled me in her own way: my snivelling, tearful thrusting in her luxurious confines drove her to outermost abandon.

She believed I was in need of sexual re-education. Not that I was wholly inexperienced in the world's oldest rhythm and ritual, but the way Apolline saw it I came from a country where sex served for procreation and where aphrodisiac contortions prior to penetration were not on the cards. These are her words. She could be so hurtful in her frivolous intelligence and breezy cynicism.

I often watched her reading magazines in which women complained and cooed unashamedly over debacles and delights in bed. She read them with conspicuous amusement and approval – purely, so I thought, to hurt my feelings. My boyfriend wants us to get into all sorts of weird positions. Is it all right if I swallow it? Apolline made me read them all. My boyfriend has never touched me there (Apolline: 'Get this – their advice is:') Tell your boyfriend this is the twentieth century we're living in; you must stand up for your rights.

She always threatened (in jest, I hope) to send off a detailed letter if I proved unwilling to satisfy her whims (what else can I call them?) and forswear my ethnic pride and primitive principles. Adjusting to a new homeland, she said, had to start, rather literally, from the bottom. She wouldn't take no for an answer: she was so domineering, so uncontradictable, so vibrant, so womanly. So I gave myself up – reluctant, dragging my feet, with dark circles under my eyes.

From *Abdullah's Feet* (De voeten van Abdullah). Amsterdam: Arena, 1996.
Translated by Ina Rilke (in: 'Abdullah's Feet'. London: Review, 2000).

Three Poems
by Mustafa Stitou

The Goat

	De geit
when I was born	toen ik werd geboren
there was a feast	was het feest
the goat that they slaughtered	de geit die werd geslacht
proved pregnant	bleek zwanger
here you'd say that's killing	hier noem je dat
two birds with one stone	twee vliegen in één klap
I was born	ik werd geboren
in a frugal house	in een sober huis
during the feast	tijdens het feest
a man came by	kwam er een man langs
he was a tramp	hij was zwerver
did some begging too	en deels bedelaar
from a sister he got	van een zus kreeg hij
a loaf	een brood
wrapped in a cloth	gewikkeld in een doek
he said if the child's a boy	hij zei is het een jongetje
call him Mrizak	noem hem Mrizak
Put bluntly I know	simpelgezegd weet ik
I am a possibility	ik ben een mogelijkheid
I am actuated	ik word bewogen
by my idea	door mijn voorstelling
of Mrizak and the others	van Mrizak en de anderen

From *My Shapes* (Mijn vormen). Amsterdam: Arena, 1994.
Translated by Tanis Guest.

This poem has no enduring value

Heart of darkness a ruler stamps
(formerly immortal, fat and photogenic)
dying (but with the leopard cap immovably
upon his head) in nappies through the palace

yelping: rebels are coming, fast and furious.
Would the earth but lay on a more relentless upheaval!
Some arms-dealers go on with their hand of cards,
Wrinkle their brows, swig their whisky

But his generals, future ministers
of National Reconstruction, think this is neither
fury nor strategy: this is incompetence
and beat it. What should Stabilising Factor

(massacres here have never smacked
of Failure; Humanity lives in Europe),
what should Great Warrior do now?
Phone up an agency for mercenaries,

order some paratroops (in a fine Flemish
accent)? There's no time. France, then?
Is deeply, diplomatically asleep
and Ronald has Alzheimer's.

Oh private airplane-pilot
is there in the world
in the wide world still a country
one can escape to?

That there is: Morocco.

From *My Poems* (Mijn gedichten). Amsterdam: Vassalluci, 1998.
Translated by Tanis Guest.

Dit gedicht heeft geen eeuwigheidswaarde

Hartje duisternis stampvoet een vorst
(voormalig onsterfelijk, vet & fotogeniek)
stervende (maar de luipaardmuts onverzettelijk
op zijn hoofd) in luiers door het paleis

jankend: rebellen naderen niet schoorvoetend.
Zorgde de aarde maar voor onverbiddelijker opschudding!
Wat wapenhandelaars leggen nog een kaartje
fronsen de wenkbrauwen, drinken whisky

maar zijn generaals, toekomstige ministers
van Nationale Wederopbouw, denken dit is furie
noch strategie: dit is onbeholpenheid
en smeren 'm. – Wat moet Stabiliserende Factor

(massaslachtingen hebben hier nooit
iets van Failliet gehad: de Mensheid ligt in Europa),
wat moet Grote Krijger nu?
Een huurlingenuitzendbureau bellen,

paracommando's (met mooi Vlaams accent)
bestellen? Te kort dag. Frankrijk?
Verkeert in diepe diplomatieke slaap
en Ronald heeft Alzheimer.

O privé-vliegtuigpiloot
is er in de wereld
in de wereld nog een land
om naar uit te wijken?

Dat is er: Marokko.

On a saucer shimmers honey	Op een schoteltje schittert honing
diluted with water	met water verdund
round it astonishingly neatly ranged	verbazingwekkend keurig eromheen
a necklace of strung-tight-together ants,	een kettinkje aaneengeregen mieren,
their heads sunk in the sweet	hun kopjes in de zoete
and sun-drenched sea	zonovergoten zee
– The reckless drink themselves to death,	– Verzuipen zich de dolzinnigen,
the moderate drinkers lift	die met mate drinken heffen
their heads again, give Mother	hun kopjes weer op, knikken
a nod of approbation	Moeder instemmend toe
and primly leave the house	en verlaten vroom het huis

From *My Poems* (Mijn gedichten). Amsterdam: Vassalluci, 1998.
Translated by Tanis Guest.

Extract from *Child of Another Time*
by Vera Illés

Dutch had become the language I was growing up with, the language in which I was learning to express myself precisely and with subtlety. My Dutch kept pace with my development, grew along with my need to put feelings and ideas into words and to comprehend them. I spoke the kind of Dutch that was appropriate to my age, to my education, to my needs and talents, and also to the social and intellectual ambitions I had acquired.

My Hungarian got stuck at a child's level, but even so, I've preserved a mysterious intimacy with Hungarian. Words I've never consciously come across I can usually place without difficulty. Turns of phrase that I would never be able to use myself I can understand the first time I hear them. Reading or listening to Hungarian, I detect the jokes, the irony, the double entendre. I can even guess the cultural background of the speaker.

But when I speak or write Hungarian I find myself out of my depth. I utter Hungarian words, my sentences are even grammatically correct, but it's as though it's not me speaking. It's like losing control of the steering wheel, or trying to stand on a foot that's gone to sleep. I don't have such problems in Dutch. I feel I'm on firm ground when I'm writing or speaking. But no matter how skilfully I've learned to use Dutch, it's still not my mother tongue.

With some regularity I experience a flash of insight, a momentary vision of what it must be like to live with a language that is completely infused into all your senses, into every cell of your brain. An example: Walking through the Vondel-park, I see a thrush. *Sárgarigó*. Its name in Hungarian springs to mind, immediately followed by a nursery rhyme about the thrush, a rhyme full of r-sounds that I was taught as a child to practice pronouncing the hard Hungarian *r*.

Such flashes of recognition of almost sensual intensity – when I experience total perception of the connotations of one single word – come to me frequently when I see certain animals, trees or flowers.

Strange that it's the words that have to do with nature that are so deeply root-ed in my subconscious. I can't remember my parents or grandparents ever trying to instil in us an appreciation of nature. They didn't know much about it them-selves, and as a child I seldom spent time in the countryside. The city parks of Pest and the hills of Buda were where we took our walks. That's where I learned the names of the oak, the chestnut tree, the blackbird and the sparrow, the pigeon and the swallow.

My grandmother grew petunias and geraniums on her windowsills, and she was the one who taught me that you shouldn't water the plants until the sun goes down. That's when these unpretentious beautifiers of city balconies begin to give off their scent. One whiff of it, and I see the large, sombre inner courtyard of the block of flats where my grandparents lived.

My knowledge of nature is limited to those few trees, plants and birds. Know-ing their names in such a profound, self-evident way must have something to do with those songs and fairy tales, those proverbs and pieces of conventional wis-dom I learned when I was very young, all of which contain a lot more nature than I ever saw in real life. My notion of the 'old oak tree', the 'stork with its red feet' or the 'birch sapling bent by the wind' is based not on any observed reality but on images conjured up by the words the moment their meaning first became clear to me.

I cherish this intimacy with the language of my childhood. It gets to me when-ever a Hungarian word pops into my head, accompanied by something that seems like recollection but is actually much deeper, often calling to mind frag-ments of a song, a rhyme, an expression we used to use at home.

From *Child of Another Time* (Kind van een andere tijd). Amsterdam: Prometheus, 1992, pp. 108-110. *Translated by Diane L. Webb.*

And
then in that Low Country

Kader Abdolah (1954-) is an Iranian physicist who combined his literary activities with his job as manager of a packaging factory.

He had already published two volumes of stories when he had to flee the country in 1985 after the authorities discovered his involvement in the opposition to Khomeini. He had previously also been an opponent of the Shah's regime. Abdolah took as his pseudonym the name of a friend killed in the resistance. He came to the Netherlands in 1988 as a political refugee.

As a child Abdolah had wanted to be a writer, and as an exile he was determined to continue writing. It took him a scant five years to master Dutch, and in 1993 he published his first Dutch book, *The Eagles* (De adelaars). Only the title story is set in his native country; the others concern his life as a foreigner in a different culture and give a penetrating picture of the anxiety and discomfort of life in border hostels and reception centres. The volume won the prize for the best-selling first book of its year, and his subsequent books – among

them *The Journey of the Empty Bottles* (De reis van de lege flessen, 1997) and *Cuneiform* (Spijkerschrift, 2000) – were received with equal enthusiasm.

In an interview Abdolah said: *'If you love a language, you start to love a people. Now the IJssel flows through my thoughts, now I have a thousand cows in my head. Now I see green landscapes. The Netherlands is not just a country to me, I have made the Netherlands into a world, Abdolah's world, and I love it.'*

(Tr. Tanis Guest)

For the attention of the editors.
With best wishes from Kader Abdolah.

Five years ago you asked me to write something about the Dutch language. And it was about Dutch as my second homeland. Now you have asked me to write something about the Netherlands. Okay, I'll do my best.

In those past five years I have learnt a lot, done a lot and seen a lot in Dutch society. And Dutch society has changed me together with the Dutch language.

Here are a couple of texts on my experiences with the Dutch.
First a story about a sad Dutch woman.

A sad woman

If I were able to decide who could enter my dreams, I would have admitted a different Dutch woman. But she comes. She disturbs my sleep.

I'd prefer not to hear from her. Not bump into her in the street either, but I can't escape her, she's inside me.

When I came to the Netherlands, like everyone else I had to attend a sort of integration course. Our teacher was a thirty-eight-year-old woman. She had a thin face and dark bags under her eyes. She seemed to be starving. A Dutch woman starving?

She taught us where we ought to shop and also that shopping trolleys were free. Every day she brought in a new list telling us where we ought to get meat from and where potatoes tasted reasonable and were cheap. She brought scissors with her and an empty milk carton and taught us how we ought to save stamps.

Shopping had become a difficult subject. On a copied map we made a scratch where Wibra was and where in town the Zeeman discount store was located.

We made notes, notes and more notes and remembered where we could get flannels with stamps. But we didn't manage to put the lessons into practice. At the end of the course, just to spell it out, she wrote on the board: 'Never to Albert Heijn, but to Aldi' (the latter being much cheaper).

Thanks to her efforts we knew where we could get second-hand clothes. Because with so much poverty in the world, something that we, refugees, knew only too well, why should we have to buy new clothes? It wasn't necessary to look at those greedy Dutch. She was convinced, absolutely convinced that we had brought our brains with us. We had all survived a war, a dictator, a famine. So we knew that life wasn't about clothes, or about Albert Heijn.

She came into class looking pathetic and tearful. Her face never wore a smile. Her 1950s dress had never felt the warmth of an iron. Her long greasy

Photo by Martin Kers.

Iranian refugee in a Dutch second-hand clothes shop. 1992. Photo by Sake Rijpkema / HH.

hair never had the chance to bob cheerfully like a tail.

She was the one who destroyed my first fantasy of Dutch women. She even treacherously usurped the place of another Dutch woman in my sleep.

She frightened us with a long ghostly Dutch word. 'The bailiff.'

Suppose you couldn't pay 'the property tax'. Suppose you stayed under the shower too long. And then couldn't pay the bill. Suddenly the man would come, the bailiff. He would take your bed. Just when your Dutch women neighbours were standing peering out of their windows: 'Look! That man, that foreigner stayed too long under the shower'.

She bored into my soul and tried to settle somewhere in my unconscious.

In the break she deliberately came and sat with us. She would take a wrinkled apple out of her bag and eat. No, she didn't eat it. She mourned for the apple. She held it upside down and devoured it core and every last scrap and all. Then she placed the stalk proudly on the table under the astonished dark foreign eyes.

After eight years she still won't leave me. Whenever I eat something greasy and cheap, she appears in my sleep. Last Sunday, late at night I ate a couple of cheap croquettes from an automat near Zwolle station. That night I dreamed I was getting married to her. My real wife shook me awake. 'Why are you crying in your sleep?'

I'm frightened that if I'm ever allowed to go home, she'll come too.

Later I had a problem with a ladder that I had taken home with me and didn't know how to return. This is the story:

A ladder

Finally the time has come to tell the story of the Dutch ladder. I don't know how to explain it. I see the ladder every day.

In my parents' home we had a ladder too, a big long wooden ladder. But I paid it no attention. Always standing there against the wall.

The story of the Dutch ladder is as old as my Dutch existence.

Seven and a half years.

I had been offered a house. When you've left everything behind and know few Dutch words you start by painting your still empty house. And I had no ladder.

I wasn't allowed to bring home a ladder from town on the bus. I didn't have a bike yet.

How had my father brought that great wooden ladder home from town? I had forgotten about the ladder from my parents' home for years. In my new home, it suddenly appeared. You needed at least three men to move a ladder like that.

Painting the ceiling without a ladder is a terrible job. It gave me a stiff neck. Towards evening I went for a walk in the neighbourhood. After walking a little way I came to a pond. That intrigued me. I'd never seen a pond in a residential area. There was a house with a thatched roof on the bank. In front of the house was a skip and a pile of building waste. 'Look! A ladder too! What a waste of that ladder.'

I was about to grab it. But I had not fled my country to take Dutch people's rubbish home with me. 'The new resident is taking our rubbish,' everyone would say.

It was dark. How would they be able to see that the person carrying the ladder was a foreigner? So I put the ladder on my shoulder, bent my head into my chest and strode home through unfamiliar streets.

Once in the living room I put on the light. 'How terrible, really terrible of those Dutch. A new ladder like that, why do they throw new things like that away?'

That was their business. I climbed up the ladder.

It took a little while before I understood their customs a little. Suddenly I broke out in a sweat. Wrong, wrong, wrong. I made a mistake. The ladder wasn't rubbish.

I didn't dare take the ladder back. I would have to wait until I'd mastered the language a bit better.

When the moment had come when I could explain my action, I put my smart suit on, combed my hair and went to the house where the ladder had stood.

'Excuse me, sir, I wasn't allowed to take a ladder on the bus. I put it on my shoulder. Your ladder. Shall I…?'

The man thought I wanted to borrow a ladder from him. He gestured with his hand to indicate that that was impossible and that he didn't want to give any ladders away.

I must improve my command of the language. A few months later I knocked on his door again.

'Excuse me, sir. The ladder, that long one. I didn't know the rules at the time. So I put it on my shoulder. Do you follow me?'

He thought I must be off my head. An idiotic chap who was always talking about ladders.

A little later, when I felt I could speak reasonable Dutch, I knocked confidently. 'That ladder again', cried the man. 'For Christ's sake, I haven't got a ladder.'

Seven times the pond froze. Seven times it thawed.

This evening I shall go to his house with the ladder on my shoulder and this text in my hand.

The ladder is still in my shed and it's become mine now. The ladder has even acquired a Persian name: Nardebam.

When the ladder was dry in the shed, I had to go running in the rain with Dutch people in order to get to know them. Here is the story:

The weather and the word

You asked me recently if I would write about Holland for you now and then. Now that everyone is happily occupied with the budget, I'll make some space and write to you about two completely different matters. The weather and the Dutch language.

You still climb in the mountains I take it. I don't. When I came here, I put on a pair of trainers. For seven and a half solid years I have run with the village jogging group in the rain, in the cold and in the sun. Long tracksuit bottoms with a top? Without a top? A sports shirt underneath? A thick one? A thin one? No, you never learn. It's weird. I listen to the weather forecast, even go outside. 'Good weather. No wind. Right, I'll put shorts on.' I run to the start, but I see that everyone has tracksuit bottoms and windproof tops. On the way a cold wind gets up. Once I'm home I crawl straight into bed.

I don't need to tell you that if I put on tracksuit bottoms and a top, everyone turns up in shorts. I rarely guess right. One time when there was a mass of dark cloud in the sky, I really didn't know what to put on. Because I didn't want to stick out like a sore thumb in the group, I went outside first and looked to see what the others were putting on. A fellow-jogger ran past. He had a tracksuit top and bottom on.

'Aren't you running tonight?' he shouted.

'Oh yes. I'm just going to change.'

Properly dressed I ran to the start. Everyone had wrapped up against the cold like me. But as soon as the trainer whistled for the start, everyone took off their tracksuit and began running in shorts. I didn't. I couldn't. I had no shorts on under my tracksuit bottoms.

'Aren't you hot?' asked the trainer.

'No,' I lied. 'I'm used to it. I can take it.'

I don't have that uncertainty just with the weather. It happens with the language too. Dutch is linguistically unique anyway. You have to imbibe it with your mother's milk, otherwise you'll never learn it perfectly. As a foreigner you can go shopping after a few weeks.

'A kilo of potatoes, please.'

'AZC Werkboek': a Dutch course used in reception centres. Photo by Werry Crone / HH.

And you get them. Or you can read a children's book after a year with a dictionary. You understand the story, but you don't really feel it. After you've lived for eight years in the Netherlands you still keep your words in your mouth and speak them hesitantly one by one. You're always frightened of using a wrong article, of putting the stress on the wrong part of the word. Of making the long 'ij' sound short. And making a short 'o' too long. And 'ui' is still a problem. I still can't pronounce the word '*schreeuwen*' ('to scream'). Instead of screaming I cry in my pronunciation. The Dutch also have a troublesome little word, '*er*'. If you have thirteen '*er*'s, you can put six in the right place, but you're stuck with the rest. The Dutch language belongs to the Dutch. If you disguise yourself as a Dutchman, everyone knows that you've got no shorts on under your tracksuit bottoms the moment you open your mouth.

I must go on learning, reading and writing the rest until I get better acquainted with this special people who live in this low country.

Yours, Kader Abdolah

KADER ABDOLAH
Translated by Paul Vincent.

Half

a Century of Belgium

Rudolf Boehm (1927-) was born in Berlin and studied philosophy, physics and mathematics in Leipzig and Rostock. In 1952 he came to Belgium, where he set to work in the Husserl Archive in Louvain. In 1967 he began teaching philosophy at the University of Ghent. There he was not only a foreigner – he has always retained his German nationality – but also an odd-man-out in his own field: a phenome-nologist in a climate of positivism and scientism. Despite his different academic style and orientation, however, he was able to win himself a place in the intellectual and cultural life of Flanders. He published a number of books – among them *Critique of the Foundations of Our Time* (Kritiek der grond-slagen van onze tijd, 1973; also published in French and German) – as well as writing numerous articles for Flemish daily and weekly papers and cultural journals.

Although Boehm has long been a 'naturalised citizen of Ghent', he has also remained an 'East German' emigrant. As an expert on Marxism he has kept an eagle eye on the new carving-up of Europe following the fall of the Berlin Wall and urges continuing critical reflection on the causes and consequences of that upheaval.

(Tr. Tanis Guest)

Having been born and brought up in Berlin, then lived successively in Leipzig (with a break for military service), Rostock, Cologne and the Belgian city of Leuven, I have now dwelt for over thirty years in Ghent, in the heart of Flanders. Strangely enough, this means that I have ended up exactly where I always wanted to be, ever since I was quite young. As early as the 1940s, during the war, I had been impressed by what happened in the Low Countries in the sixteenth century, and drawn parallels with the murderous conflict of which I was myself then an eye-witness. I was enthralled by Schiller's masterly history of the Dutch Revolt, by his *Don Carlos*, by Goethe's *Egmont* and Beethoven's overture to it; fascinated, too, by Emperor Charles v (himself born in Ghent) whom I saw as a tragic figure. So that even then I knew more about Flanders, and specifically about Ghent, than most of the city's inhabitants probably know today.

Even so: when I first arrived in Leuven in the spring of 1952, aged just twenty-four, I had no idea that I would be staying in this country, in Belgium, for the rest of my life. But it was not pure chance that brought me here; I had made a considered decision to come and work, and so also live, in this country. I came to Leuven because I had studied philosophy, because I found my work as a research assistant at Cologne University unsatisfying, because I was still wondering whether to start on a doctoral thesis, because I had become fascinated by the philosophy of Edmund Husserl and Leuven was where the papers of this German-Austrian-Jewish thinker were housed, because I liked the idea of spending some time helping to sort out his literary estate, and because I had just been invited to do exactly that by the founder of Leuven's Husserl Archive (Herman Leo van Breda, the man who rescued Husserl's manuscripts from the Nazis). Even more clearly, it was by my own choice that I spent the next fifteen years in Leuven doing this work (and gaining my doctorate). And in 1967 I chose even more decisively in favour of Belgium when I opted for a chair at the University of Ghent even though I also had offers of teaching posts in Germany, the Netherlands and America (as well as one in Wallonia). True, during my early years in Ghent I still assumed that sooner or later I should return to Germany. But when there seemed to be a real prospect of this, I suddenly realised: I just don't want to leave here. I had grown too attached to this country, its people (Flemings as well as Walloons), their languages (Dutch as well as French) and the way they lived, thought, and behaved. Why? Let me try to explain by recounting three anecdotes from my early years in Belgium.

In 1952 Belgium, like other European countries, had by no means come to terms with, let alone forgotten, the horrors of the war and the German occupation. Even at that time, though, I was to discover that the Belgians, Flemings and Walloons alike, are a magnanimous race. At that time, in other European countries subjected to Nazi occupation, you were – quite understandably – regarded with hostility or at least suspicion simply because you were German. But not in Belgium. The Belgians are individualists, but in their case individualism means not only having a sharp eye for their own interests but also, and equally, acknowledging the individuality of others. As a result, the Belgians did not automatically equate being German with being a Nazi; you were always given the chance to show for yourself where you stood, what you were for or against. With a few rare exceptions, the fact that I happen to be German has never caused me any problems in this country. (Please note: I have never associated with those who collaborated with the German occupation). One of those rare incidents was particularly striking. I shall never forget it. For various (purely practical) reasons, the director of the Husserl Archive and another professor from the Leuven Institute of Philosophy wanted me to meet the housekeeper of a former president of the Institute who had recently died. When they introduced me as a colleague from Germany, the lady withdrew her already outstretched hand with the words 'Moi je n'aime pas les boches' ('I don't like Huns'). I made a slight bow and left the house, but waited outside. A few minutes later the two professors also emerged, full of apologies for their 'blunder'. It turned out that the lady's father had been one of some hundred and fifty citizens of Leuven shot by the Germans in 1914 for their supposed involvement in a popular uprising against the invaders. In a strange and complex solidarity all of us, my Belgian friends as well as myself, had to accept this irrevocable historical fact. In any case, this experience made me resolve that under no circumstances would I exchange my German nationality for Belgian. Some years later the Institute of Criminology at Ghent University, with which I was then closely involved, was planning a trip to Poland, including a visit to Auschwitz. I couldn't go around there with them as a 'Belgian', could I? In this

Freedom begins at home: the author's garden house. Photo by Rudolf Boehm.

day and age, if you're a German there's no escaping the fact.

About the same time I had another experience which was in a way analogous – less morally and politically sensitive, but for me still significant. I had arrived in Belgium on a three-month visa, with no residence permit, no work permit, no health insurance, nothing. The one possible justification for my presence was that the Husserl Archive received a modest subsidy from UNESCO, and this could at a pinch be regarded as the source of my salary. So I had to report to the local authorities in Koorbeek-Lo, the village near Leuven where I was living at the time. At the town hall they told me 'The burgomaster is in his fields' and showed me how to get there. The burgomaster was busy ploughing, and signalled that he would be with me in a minute. I decided to tell him the truth. And in French quite as bad as mine he said, 'Tout celà est très bien, mon fils, mais on ne va pas raconter celà aux autorités, on n'aura que des ennuis' ('That's all well and good, my son, but don't go telling the authorities that, you'll have nothing but trouble'). And then my burgomaster proceeded to cook up a tale that would make my presence in the country reasonably acceptable to the 'authorities' – thus showing the same respect for the individual and his story as in the earlier incident.

These two stories come together, so to speak, in my third anecdote. 1968: the year of student protest. In Ghent this did not reach its peak until early 1969. The students occupied my faculty building. I was on their side; not that I necessarily agreed with all their ideas, but I strongly believed that they had the right, and should have the opportunity, to express them. Alone among my colleagues, incidentally, I continued to teach, in my room, during the occupation – something the students appreciated. After a few days the building was forcibly cleared by the gendarmerie, and I was hauled over the coals by the university's governing body. (I had put my office at the students' disposal, and had other rooms opened for them, giving them access to duplicators and so on, thus preventing a deal of criminal damage.) Some of the

Governors suspected me of having instigated the whole student revolt; after all, I did come from what was then Communist East Germany. However, the Rector invited me to justify my actions, and asked the other members of the Council to listen to my account without interrupting. I said that, in my view, as a teacher I had only done my duty to my pupils: letting them have their say and listening to them. 'According to you,' the rather conservative-minded Rector replied, 'we should really give you a vote of thanks.' And with that the matter was settled, with true Belgian magnanimity (though some friends among my colleagues had feared that as a foreigner I would be thrown out of the country for engaging in unacceptable political activity).

Generally speaking, the great majority of Belgians are reasonably well-disposed to the (peaceful) presence of foreigners and/or strangers in their midst, except when they feel (usually wrongly) that they are being cheated in some way. Even then, though, their reactions are no more violent than in the well-known bickering between Flemings and Francophones. Belgium is actually a very 'European' country. In two ways: on the one hand I don't find Belgium particularly globally-minded; on the other, it is very much involved, particularly on a cultural level, with events in its neighbouring countries: in the Netherlands, Germany and especially, and this goes for the Flemings as well, in France (unlike larger countries, which sometimes seem to be interested only in what is going on within their own borders). It is typical of this attitude that Husserl's philosophical legacy – which brought me here in the first place – should have found a home in this country; but also that French twentieth-century thinkers, in particular, such as Maurice Merleau-Ponty, Emmanuel Levinas and Jacques Lacan made their names here. Where culture is concerned, Belgium is a quite exceptionally welcoming land. And is not this very quality, this openness to ideas from outside, a better hallmark of true culture than a desire to impose one's own culture on others? A cultured individual is someone who reads books, not someone who writes them; though one may hope that the latter will read before he writes.

There is no denying that this Belgian individualism (which also shows itself in the country's privileged relationship with its immediate neighbours) also has a less attractive side. Any form of public institution or authority is guaranteed to be regarded by the people with an often irritating indifference or even contempt. Even after nearly two centuries of independence, everything that smacks of 'authority' is still distrusted. Public works, such as the restoration of monuments from the country's rich cultural past, still proceed at a snail's pace. But many Belgian railway stations too are in a lamentable state. This reluctance to spend money on public works and institutions must have its roots in the fact that for centuries this country was ruled by foreign powers: the Burgundians, Charles v, Spain, Austria, France and the Northern Netherlands too; the 'authorities' were exploiters and oppressors, or were at least perceived as such. Anything they planned, the populace felt it had to sabotage; and this became an instinctive reaction. (An attitude which in Europe the Belgians probably share only with the Czechs and Slovaks and the peoples of former Yugoslavia, from Slovenia to Kosovo, with the proud Serbs as the one exception.) It has even been said that after 1944 Belgium was the first country to repair its war damage simply because at the end of the war the government forbade any reconstruction work; the people then

immediately understood that in their own interest they should defy the ban.

As this shows, the Belgians' attitude to authority had – and still has – its advantages; and I must conclude by confessing that my attachment to this country is partly due to my discovery that everyday life here is decidedly comfortable. Here in Ghent I live, as I never could in Germany or elsewhere, for a reasonable price, in a somewhat scruffy 'residence' with seven spacious rooms, on a street lined with old plane-trees that runs beside a watercourse, with a little garden at the back and a view over two ancient abbeys and a beguinage. (Note, too, that this is no up-market academic area; my neighbours are an electrician and a nurse.). My house is within easy walking distance of the town centre and the railway station; I can still do all my day-to-day shopping without needing a car. That's what I call freedom. At present, this is still a free country. Here I am still free to do what I want, what I feel I have to do.

RUDOLF BOEHM
Translated by Tanis Guest.

The author's view over an ancient Ghent abbey from his backyard. Photo by Rudolf Boehm.

The

Enigma of Arrival

Anil Ramdas, of Hindustani descent, was born in Surinam in 1958 and came to Amsterdam to study social geography. This was the beginning of a career as an essayist, columnist and maker of TV programmes. Among his books are: *The Parrot, the Bull and the Climbing Bougainvillea* (De papegaai, de stier en de klimmende bougainvillea, 1992), *The Professional Rememberer and Other Stories* (De beroepsherinneraar en andere verhalen, 1996) and *The Town Has a Memory: Stories* (Het geheugen van de stad: verhalen, 2000). In 1997 he received the E. du Perron Prize, an award given to persons or institutions who by their active contribution to culture have promoted mutual understanding and good relations between different population groups in the Netherlands.

Much of Ramdas' work displays the powerful influence of the writers V.S. Naipaul and Salman Rushdie, like him children of the Indian diaspora. Rushdie's view that the past is a country from which we all emigrate, in particular, plays a key role. In his books Ramdas homes in on 'identity', and the effect on that identity of living between different cultures. In the Netherlands he has sometimes been called a 'professional immigrant' because he has taken a stand on all manner of minority-related issues, whether invited to or not.

In Autumn 2000 Ramdas moved to India, where he works as a correspondent for the *NRC Handelsblad*.

(Tr. Tanis Guest)

As I increase speed and join the turbulent stream of the A2 motorway in order to leave Amsterdam, I realise that I know at least a hundred stories about coming to the city, but none about leaving for the countryside. Even V.S. Naipaul's great novel *The Enigma of Arrival*, which begins as a journey to a remote village, is in fact a story of something else: a boy leaves his colonial island to establish himself in the metropolis. He succeeds, he recreates himself as a free human being, but remains burdened by the restlessness of the traveller, constantly on the move and forever experiencing everything as new and strange. He never becomes a resident, never becomes assimilated, every contact with the world around him feels raw.

In order to overcome his inner turmoil and the constant nervousness, he sets out in search of the origin of everything, the beginning of modern history, which he supposes can be found outside the city, in the landscape of peasant life, where everything is static and unchanging. But he is wrong. Here too nothing is original, everything comes from elsewhere, nothing has always been there, everything is new and in motion. And so he discovers

that motion is our lot, we travel on and on, sometimes towards the centre, sometimes towards the periphery, sometimes to the effervescent energy of the city, sometimes to the quiet of the countryside. But ultimately we have a common destination: death.

Photo by Aad Schenk.

It is a beautiful, gloomy narrative, the most melancholy novel Naipaul ever wrote, but it did not provide an answer to my own trivial, concrete problems.

You could even say that I'm leaving Amsterdam with the opposite aim and with the same feeling of excitement that country people experience when they move into town, as Toni Morrison described in *Jazz*. This incomparable ode to urban life presents the city as the place where you find yourself, because you are left to your own devices; where individuality is possible, where you can ignore your surroundings for as long as possible and where you have the chance of making something of your life and ending up with more than you were born with. The city, so full of tensions, opportunities and… strangers. For that is the essence of arriving in the city: giving up what you know and are familiar with. Leaving all certainties behind you. Forcing yourself to stand up for yourself, without the help of relatives.

In fact, you could say that all social science is based on this fascination: the transition from countryside to city, when peasants become modern citizens. When cousins and brothers-in-law lose their axiomatic links and are suddenly faced with non-committal friends and unpredictable enemies. Once upon a time the question of why anonymous people are prepared to do or own something together was of no interest. Everyone was a fellow-villager or a relation and strangers were chased off with sticks and stones. Then great cities suddenly emerged where there were only strangers.

So it is understandable that so many writers should see coming to the city as a definitive, essential rift, but now I am driving along the A2, the transition from town to countryside strikes me as just as drastic. The great grey swathes that cut through the meadows like motionless rivers, the drivers who keep a sharp watch on each other's behaviour but avoid all eye contact, the bewildered cows that good-naturedly let the roar pass over them, the weird electricity pylons that shoot out of the ground like extraterrestrial locusts – it has never struck me before how quickly you find yourself leaving the big city. The road slices further and further into the polders, following an inexorable hierarchy from motorway to dual carriageway, to two-lane road and finally the little street through this unknown village, whose history I know nothing of.

I know the history of Amsterdam only too well. The romantic stories of the first settlement, the old part with its dark, narrow streets that muffled the horses' hooves and through which policemen now ride on sporty mountain bikes in search of the new owners of the territory, the junkies, dealers and mugged tourists. The imposing gables along the canals in the newer section, the mansions with Persian rugs on long solid wooden tables... Sometimes I imagine that it was on those tables that the decision was taken that directly influenced my life. That it was there that the accounts of slave capitalism were kept, of the proceeds of sugar and cotton, the writing off of human beings, abducted, branded and tortured.

It must have been a silent decision, with the documents being slid across the soft rugs to the accompaniment of faint muttering, with signatures establishing that they, the black slaves, were now free and that new workers must be brought from other continents. In those mansions they talked about and determined the fate of my forebears and before you knew it, after less than a hundred years, I was strolling past those houses with their solid tables and sumptuous rugs, as the result of an unexpected twist of history. If the directors of the West India Company and the shareholders of the once so profitable plantations had known, if they had had an inkling of the surprising turn that their bookkeeping calculations would take and that a hundred years later they would have migrants on their doorstep desperately trying to arrive somewhere and gain citizenship, would they have taken a different decision?

When I think of those canal-side mansions and the luxurious rugs on the tables, I occasionally have the strange sense that in some way I am a co-owner. But it is a strictly theoretical sense. I have never really got used to Amsterdam. Never felt truly at home, at ease, really. I had a roof over my head, I lived there, but always with the guilty feeling of the outsider.

Using an odd expression I could call the road to this village my 'trajectory of assimilation'. A cumbersome term dreamt up by civil servants to give politicians the feeling that it enabled them to pursue a policy, and a contradiction in terms. One must cover the trajectory oneself, but the assimilation, being absorbed into one's new environment, is something determined by others. It is like joining a motorway: you flash your indicator, signalling what you wish and have to do, in the hope that other road-users will make room for you and prevent you from colliding with the last post in the merging lane.

'*I know the history of Amsterdam only too well. (...) The imposing gables along the canals in the newer section, the mansions with Persian rugs on long solid wooden tables... Sometimes I imagine that it was on those tables that the decision was taken that directly influenced my life.*'
Photo by Piet van der Meer.

But why did I choose this village rather than another? It was pure coincidence. A good female friend who heard me talking about the desire finally to settle down somewhere, in a spot where I would be able to exercise my citizenship in peace, cried spontaneously: buy my place! The next moment I was in her living room and fell in love with the way the light entered through a small, useless-looking side window, which gave the deep room the atmosphere that I still remembered from the darkened library in Paramaribo, where, long ago, my 'trajectory of assimilation' must have begun. But now I'm chasing too far ahead, or backwards – I want to dwell on the house a little longer. It was a charming, bourgeois house, in the tradition of the 1960s. Without ornament, without fussy touches and without the alienating abstraction of modern building on the new estates, with prefabricated boxes shoved together. This house was old enough to have been really made of bricks laid by builders with a heart, though the one frivolity they had allowed themselves was that single side window. And with my back to the light of that side window I asked the question that revealed my vulnerability. 'Are there any other coloured people in the village?'

'No,' said my friend, 'why?'

Why did that alarm me so? It could have been a conspiracy, said a foolish voice inside me, the village had wilfully kept itself pure, there were forces barring admission to coloured people. But I must stay sensible: it was, of course, coincidence. If you had lived in Amsterdam you could scarcely imagine the Netherlands as a non-coloured society. The idea of a homogenous society belongs to the past, it seems, but that is wrong. It is not the Netherlands, but the big cities that are multicultural. In the villages foreigners are still rare and strange. I knew that from the statistics, but had never been so keenly aware of it. And now it was happening, I felt unsafe in an odd sort of way. Why? On the assumption that in a racial emergency coloured people rush to assist each other? Or that, simply by virtue of their numbers, they managed to suppress feelings of aversion in others? Or because, since they were an everyday phenomenon, people became in some way conditioned?

No, I think that the unsafe feeling was created by the fact that the people in this village had never before had the chance to decide for themselves what they thought of coloured people. I was the guinea pig and that made me nervous.

So it wasn't exactly with head held high that I entered the solicitor's office, especially because things weren't that simple. My friend had explained to him on the telephone that the housing corporation had offered the house for sale to her, on condition that she did not immediately sell it on. That could be arranged, the solicitor had said, there were legal ways of getting round these things, no problem. But perhaps my friend should have told him more about the potential purchaser. She had talked of 'a friend' and that friend turned out to be, well, coloured.

The solicitor shook hands with me and apart from that addressed himself solely to my friend. Two sets of conveyancing charges, first transfer, second transfer, commission, 'I don't think the gentleman can handle all that,' said the solicitor to my friend. And he was right, but not in the way that he meant.

The solicitor's office was soberly furnished. In the corner stood an old-fashioned desk, at the window a low wooden table with unassuming chairs on a green carpet, and on the wall, as the only sign of formality, hung a large portrait of the Queen. It emanated some kind of magic, the portrait not only legitimated his special competence to do what he did, more especially it demonstrated the confidence of the highest authority in the land. It confirmed his unimpeachable honesty, his integrity, his respectability.

For that precise reason the solicitor was a very ordinary man, with an ordinary sports jacket and an ordinary tie, an ordinary Opel Vectra outside an ordinary house, an ordinary yearly income in the bank and an ordinary family that went on an ordinary holiday to the most ordinary little village in the South of France. Not the least flamboyance, no outward show, no colour. That is what this man stood for, he guarded the entrance to the bourgeois world.

'On the wall, as the only sign of formality, hung a large portrait of the Queen. It emanated some kind of magic'.
Painting by Sierk Schröder.

As I walked through the village, still somewhat hurt by the humiliation in the solicitor's office, I realised that until recently I had cherished a completely different view of life. I was a migrant, I had maintained, a restless traveller who crossed frontiers and explored new worlds. A migrant is enterprising and adventurous, courageous and stylish. I had once even compared the migrant to Madame Bovary, since she was also looking for adventure, in the tension of romantic adultery, in the sensation of melodramatic betrayal. Emma had freed herself from her bourgeois prison, just as the migrant frees himself from his native land and his community. And now it suddenly struck me that that was untrue, or at least only half true. Of course adventurousness demands that you leave your own world, but you do so in the unexpressed hope of arriving in another world. And that hope, it now seemed, was vain.

I walked past the front gardens with their clipped hedges, and here and there a knee-high gnome, a windmill, and I realised to my astonishment that this was what I wanted to be: a bourgeois. I wanted precisely one of these single-family dwellings, with the same light net curtains and velour curtains, I wanted a three-seater sofa, and a rug on the floor, a wall cabinet, I wanted exactly the kind of piano for my children that the blonde girl was now tinkling on, I wanted a pull-out dining table and a vacuum cleaner and a washing machine and a television set with a china dog or cat on it.

I wanted children's rooms with cloud wallpaper and blue-and-red children's desks, a solid parental bed, on which the children could romp to their heart's content on Sunday mornings, I wanted a loft, yes, I also wanted a loft

to store things in that you will never need again, but that you keep for the sake of family history. That was it: I wanted a real family history.

The history I have is rather fragmented: I don't even know where my grandparents come from. A village in Bihar, or Uttar Pradesh, but a hundred million people live there. What village, where do their brothers and sisters live; how many cousins do I have? An uncle on my father's side once tried, in a burst of nostalgia, to trace the genealogy of his grandparents, but got no further than the shocking fact that their names were probably different to those they gave the authorities. Only the contract number is certain: 742085. That was my great-grandfather. It cannot have been a serial number, because that many Hindustanis were never brought to Surinam. So there must be a code, the figures have a meaning, an administrative content, but what is it?

One day I intend writing down carefully all the motives I myself had for leaving Surinam. Because one day my children will ask me about it and the truth won't convince them: that I came to the Netherlands because I wanted to become a bourgeois.

It had all seemed so simple: my friend would buy the house from the corporation and sell it on to me, with a bridging period of a few months, since the property, according to the deeds, must not change hands directly, to prevent speculation. But there was no question of speculation; she would earn nothing from the transaction, and I would simply have avoided buying a house on the open market, which would assign me to a long queue, right at the back.

That is simply the disadvantage that migrants are under; they are always late, and hence often the last, and they have a chronic lack of 'social capital', as sociologists say: a lack of contacts and connections. Now I had such a connection, but still couldn't capitalise on it, because the solicitor put a spanner in the works, with greater passion than I had expected.

Two weeks after my visit to his office he rang up with the announcement that he did not wish to be involved in the matter.

Why not?

Because such agreements were usual, but not between unusual parties.

Unusual parties?

'You see, it remains an informal agreement, during the period that the house remains in the name of the first purchaser, and if the corporation gets wind of the fact that the purchaser wished to sell the property on from the outset, then in a purely formal sense there is, er, an infringement, and that carries a penalty of twenty percent or more of the purchase price.'

But how is the corporation to get wind of the purchaser's intentions?

'Normally it doesn't interest them, unless there is heightened interest in the transaction.'

Heightened interest?

Now the solicitor lost his patience: 'Listen: surely you can understand that the neighbours will start chattering if they suddenly see strange people living in the house?'

Yes, I understood. I am strange; my strangeness is even visible, which I can't help. But that makes me an unusual party and there is heightened interest in me. Normally I would take this as a compliment, but now I hung up in a state of confusion.

Was the solicitor a racist? Was he trying to keep me out of the village, was he trying to keep his village white, could he not tolerate any coloured people around him? But perhaps he wasn't a racist and was actually doing me a favour, by protecting me from the possible wrath of the villagers. The neighbours would chatter, so the fault lay with them, not with him.

It was an annoying dilemma. The world is simply not divided up neatly between good and bad people, whom you can distinguish, catch out, reward and punish. But what was I to do now? Walk around the neighbourhood and ask who had anything against me? Was this actually the village where I wanted to 'assimilate'? It was as if ordinary citizenship was not in prospect for me and I would always retain the status that the solicitor had casually referred to: an unusual party.

I went to see my friend and told her I was backing out. She flew into a rage and accused me of cowardice, allowing myself to be intimidated by a bastard like that. I accused her of naivety, because it might not be just one bastard but a whole neighbourhood full of them. And the moment I said it, it sounded to me as it was: improbable.

She paced the room, ranting and cursing belligerently. She's like that, her charming and motherly nature can unexpectedly turn into furious militancy when she feels attacked, and she felt attacked now. But obviously not just by the solicitor, whom she had dismissed as a sneaky racist. No, she felt attacked mainly by my doubt. She had known the people in the neighbourhood for twenty years, she knew where they worked, how many grandchildren they had, what things they argued about, what garage they took their cars to, what they earned and what they spent it on. And now I was suddenly making them suspect. Of course they weren't saints, they had their fair share of vices. The neighbour across the road was a divorced kleptomaniac, the neighbour on the right was a plumber who had got himself declared unfit for work so that he could do odd jobs for cash, the people two doors down had the habit of depositing their bulky rubbish outside other people's doors, the girl further down was being threatened by her boyfriend, who should be put away, but on balance, in general, they were ordinary Dutch folk. Simple souls, with a smaller or larger nugget of gold deep in their hearts.

My friend could not be talked out of the notion that people were essentially good. All their failings could be explained: the divorcée stole earrings from Woolworth's because she was lonely and wanted attention. The plumber had had a terrible boss, whereupon he had gone to the doctor with back problems. They were understandable, small failings; there was nothing diabolical about them. That was why she did not accept my indirect accusation: that they were secret racists who would try to keep me out of their neighbourhood.

It turned into an inextricable misunderstanding. I said that I was not in any way trying to say that the whole village was xenophobic. But what was I saying then, she shouted grumpily, why was I suddenly hesitating about buying the house, after one phone call like that from someone who was no good?

If only I could explain. If only I could say that the sore point was not the solicitor or the neighbours, but me. That it was really a point that was too sore to be captured in a big and easily condemnable word like xenophobia.

It's more like the feeling you have when you arrive late for a party: the slight feeling that you're no longer welcome. A strange and indefinable uneasiness that you've forfeited your place, that all the goodwill and hospitality has been dispensed. That in your absence a mystical bond has been formed between those already there, a mood of unanimity based on a shared sense of being in the right: they were on time, that unites them in their rightness, and you are late, which makes you a transgressor and hence an outsider. The latecomer is faced with an accusation, that he must first overcome before joining the company. He encounters an obstacle, an invisible barrier, and it is not so much that barrier as the sense that it is aimed at him that makes him nervous. And the silent triumph of those around, who are savouring in anticipation the possibility that he will be unable to take the hurdle and that his excuse will not be accepted.

Because that is the problem of the migrant, he has no valid excuse. He can shout about something like 'historical right' or 'basic freedom of movement', but doesn't believe that himself. That is the source of the feeling of superfluity, dispensability.

I can imagine that my great-grandparents did not have that problem, when they arrived in Surinam from India. They found an undeveloped country, useless woods that they were free to use. But when I reached Holland, the land was already full and built-up, without my tangible help. I might maintain that part of the prosperity belonged to me, because of colonialism and so on, but it sounded abstract.

To a certain extent I agreed with the villagers, because in fact I didn't have a good reason for wanting to be here, in this country, let alone in their village. Perhaps that is precisely why migrants opt for anonymous cities. In a big city no one has a special link with their surroundings and precisely because of that they are accessible to all.

But I had taken the moral decision to appropriate this country, in a more direct and confident way than hitherto. I had been reasonably content with my status of migrant. I had told moving stories about the 'uprootedness', the inner emptiness one acquires in the diaspora, the crisis of identity that the stranger undergoes and never gets over. Because migrants are always dying to tell you where they're from, but they never answer the question where they are going. They can wax lyrical about departure, but about arrival they say nothing. They never want to be reminded of the gain. No, I wanted to be honest and talk not just of the pain of leaving, but also about the joy of arriving. And that house in that village had come to symbolise my definitive arrival, my first attempt to give a sincere and clear answer to the question where I belonged and where I wanted to be: here.

As I joined the A2, in the direction of Amsterdam, I looked back on my failed 'trajectory of assimilation' in the rear-view mirror. The term suddenly sounded ridiculous to me: why did I want to assimilate anywhere, why couldn't I just remain the fluttering, wandering, roaming migrant, with that eternal sense of grievance, blackmailing the world with the loss of his native land, in which he was rooted? Rooted, like a cactus. Who I wonder dreamt up that stupid metaphor?

Why did we act as if we were cactuses, when we wanted to be sparrows? Flying and singing and mating and just nesting anywhere, laying and hatching eggs, to leave the nest and again fly and sing and mate. Chaotic birds without policy or plan. Quite ordinary, inconspicuous and promiscuous, always hanging round the inhabited world setting up home in other people's houses.

But that image too was untrue and all that flapping and flying was mainly totally exhausting and utterly boring. I wanted a place where my little ones could return and where in the oddest corners they would find old toys and clothes that they had known, which evoked memories that were hung round with stories.

Everything around me is new and scarcely worn, nothing is older than a human lifetime, nothing has any history. The oldest object I possess is as old as the number of years I have been in Holland: an eraser that I bought in a department store in Leiden and made dirty smudges and so remained unused. In a strange way it has attached itself to me, by going everywhere with me, from student room to student room, from flat to flat. No teddy bears worn out with hugging or sketchbooks full of mysterious child's doodles, but a stupid thing like that eraser, which anyway I had bought myself when I was already grown up. Sometimes I look at it with forced tenderness, based on the feeling that it says something about a beginning. But I don't want to inflict that on my children. The beginning of their presence must be axiomatic and natural, without feelings of guilt and vagueness. I want to spare them the enigma of arrival.

In Surinam we had a wooden cupboard in which all our school exercise books, reports, readers and trinkets were kept. I can still remember the arrival of that cupboard, which was so large and heavy that it took six men an afternoon of lifting, turning and pushing to put in place. But the day before he left for Holland my father emptied the cupboard. Everything went onto the bonfire: he threw one exercise book at a time into the fire, fair-copy books, rough books, revision books full of sums and dictations. 'Here,' said my father, his eyes watering from the smoke, 'a whole family history is being lost.'

Many years later I read the essay by the German thinker Hans Marius Enzensberger 'On the Irrepressibility of the Petite Bourgeoisie', in which he said that the bourgeoisie and proletariat have the great history of heroism and revolution, but that the lower middle classes become adept precisely at small stories of insignificant events. That would mean that assimilation meant something like wanting to belong to the class of rememberers of normal, day-to-day life.

After about two months I had put the matter out of my mind. No house in that village for me. And then the telephone rang. Breathless with excitement, my friend told me that the sale could go ahead. She had taken the impudent liberty of going straight to the corporation and simply confessing our intention: I was a good friend and in the last twenty years that she had lived there as a tenant she had become so attached to the house that she would prefer not to see it pass into strange hands. The man from the corporation took her feelings seriously. Officially she was not allowed to do what she intended, but oh well, in practice, just you go ahead.

Was she sure? Did she have it in black and white? My friend got irritated. You funny foreigner, she said. You come from a country where everything is done with a nod and a wink and here you suddenly want it in black and white!

What about the solicitor then? She had rung him at once and he in turn had asked the corporation if it was true and so now it was all fine, OK, agreed. More importantly, she had told the neighbours and the kleptomaniac woman neighbour had set up a welcoming committee with a few other residents to prove that the solicitor had been wrong to cast aspersions.

Funny, sentimental Dutch folk.

Now one rainy day I am again driving along my assimilation trajectory on the A2, with my expensive pen in my breast pocket, for the momentous signature that I am allowed to write in the solicitor's office. My arrival is within reach, nothing can go wrong now, everyone welcomes me and forgives my impoliteness in bursting in so late when I had no longer been expected. The feeling of euphoria is unmistakable, but so is the doubt, the silent fear, the slight panic. I have known that contradictory emotion ever since I left, as the plane taxied slowly over the wet runway of Zanderij airport and my family stood waving from the roof of the departures hall. Excitement, pain, nervousness and happiness, all in small quantities, all mixed up. That is the enigma of arrival: it's like the memory of leaving.

ANIL RAMDAS
Translated by Paul Vincent.

This essay originally appeared in *The Professional Rememberer and Other Stories* (De beroepsherinneraar en andere verhalen). Amsterdam: De Bezige Bij, 1996. pp. 45-57.

Jackfruit

and Dry Mushrooms

Moses Isegawa (pseudonym of Sey Wava) was born in 1963 in Kawemte in Uganda. He was a history teacher in a secondary school when in 1984 he started writing a column for the Third World journal *Bijeen* – a chance procured for him by a Dutch pen-friend. One of the paper's editors made it possible for him to come to the Netherlands on a tourist visa. Since 1990 he has lived in Beverwijk, not far from Amsterdam. In March 1998 an Amsterdam publisher brought out his *Abyssinian Chronicles* (Abessijnse Kronieken), which he wrote in English. In this family epic a certain Mugezi tells of his struggles to free himself from constricting family ties in a strife-torn Uganda. The book became a best-seller and the translation rights of the Dutch version were sold to a number of foreign publishers. In 2001 he published *Two Chimpanzees* (Twee chimpansees).

Isegawa himself said of his voluntary exile: *'I left as soon as I realised that I couldn't write in Uganda'.* So is he a refugee? *'Not according to Dutch law. But I left Uganda to make something of myself; in a sense, I ran away because I could not achieve my potential there. I've never had to go through the asylum process, but in a deeper sense I am a refugee. (…) I made my own decision to go elsewhere to live and work.'*

(Tr. Tanis Guest)

Home is where your heart is. Home is where they have to take you in. Home is everywhere and nowhere. I think of home mostly in terms of a place where I can work and achieve my goals as opposed to a place where one feels comfortable. This might have to do with my secondary school days which I spent in boarding school, a seminary for that matter. In boarding school you live in your suitcase, you spend most of the year with boys your own age or older, you are policed by teachers, who take over the role of parents. You get another way of thinking and seeing the world and seeing yourself. You leave your siblings and parents and commit yourself to your education and goals. Everything else is subsidiary: the present, the pains, the pleasures. In my case I was working towards a profession that in its own nature is centred on rootlessness: a priest can be transferred from place A to B to C all in the same year. In that case home was everywhere and nowhere and one had little choice in the matter; it came with the territory. The first thing one learns in boarding school is to wean oneself from the safe concepts of home: parents and siblings and the supposed coziness of it all. Acquiring a mercenary frame of mind is a *sine qua non* in surviving and prospering. Duty before pleasure. If the umbilical cord with home is not cut properly, if

Moses Isegawa in the Netherlands. Photo by Klaas Koppe.

one is unsuccessfully weaned, the studies would suffer, homesickness would torture that unfortunate person to senselessness; it would be a disaster. I was weaned when I was thirteen and I remained in the system for thirteen years. The process started in late primary school, the last two years of which I spent in boarding school. At the end of it I transferred to secondary school in a different area. At the end of four years I had to move again. The process went on till I completed teacher training in the same environment of sharing a dormitory with guys. It is too late for me to unwean myself from this way of life; I can never properly return home. I expect change; I anticipate change; I can only resist change by staying in a certain place without travelling much in order to achieve a certain goal. After achieving my goal I start itching to move.

I knew clearly from the eighties on that I would ultimately leave Uganda. It was a feeling that started slowly and grew and pressed almost with physical force. It had to do with writing and with the fact that books were luxury items people no longer bought or read and I knew that in order to write I had to be in a place where books were readily available. All the foreign publishers had left Uganda in the seventies and bookshops were empty, selling magazines or United Nations reports instead of fiction. I also knew that in order to learn more about Europe I had to live among Europeans where I could observe them properly and make up my own mind. I wanted to explore new horizons, test myself and see if I had it in me to write a book. I was hankering for a place to unfold my wings and fly and experience other ways of living or being as opposed to the predictable ones I had grown up with in Uganda. I longed to be in a place where nobody knew me, a throwback to my secondary school days, where I could be whatever I wanted to be. Such a place would be home. For the last ten years Beverwijk has been my home. It is a place suitable for working as it has few attractions, few distractions. It gave me the space to hide and hatch plans, and think out my coup d'états. It was perfect guerrilla territory for me, a place offering little comfort, a place reminding me every day that I was there to do a job and that there was little room for laziness or despair or lack of discipline or commitment. It was a place that did not give a damn about me, the perfect training

Moses Isegawa in Kampala, Uganda. Photo by Peter Vermaas.

ground. It took me eight years to accomplish my mission and declare my presence. Those years made me a writer and it is now after achieving my goal that I am thinking and wondering whether I should stay in the same place. I think I might look for another theatre of endeavour and try my luck there and see what I can extract from it. I did not travel at all in the first eight years because I did not want to be distracted by the beauty and seductions of other potential homes. Now I am travelling and I am enjoying it. I have been to Austria, Germany, Finland, Spain, I have been to the United States, I have gone back to Uganda and also visited South Africa. I am planning to go to Italy, France, Denmark, Norway...

In the course of the last ten years people have asked me regularly where I came from. Some even had answers in their heads before they put me the question: Nigeria, Ghana, somebody even said India. Now, now, now. It is a question that used to bother me because I wanted to hide, I wanted to disappear in the greenery and do my job unmolested. It is a question that no longer bothers me. If in the papers they say I come from Nigeria I just laugh. I don't bother to correct them. I am who I am. I have finally become African and that happened here in Europe. In Uganda I was Ugandan. When I left I inherited a whole continent because nobody sees me on the street and says, 'There goes a Ugandan'. 'There goes an African' is the most likely comment. I have taken that in my stride. My vision has become larger, more inclusive. I can now stand on my two feet and declare I come from Africa and say things about Africa with confidence and pride. The last three years have swept away any anxiety I had at the beginning. My anxiety had to do with the fact that I had been taken in but felt that there was only one way to justify my stay in the new home: writing a book. I wanted to have my own voice, set my own terms. I was afraid of rejection. I wanted to be seen in the light of my new home, as a worthy member. I had cut my roots and the tree was floating in unfulfilled ambition. In those days hell was being told I did not belong. As long as I had no book I felt useless, powerless. Having no security, no voice meant that I was staying because of the goodwill of others, which goodwill the government could withdraw without my being able to defend myself, meaning a premature end to my mission. One day I dreamed of being proud of my stay in Beverwijk; I dreamed of dominating the town in my chosen profession; I dreamed of putting my stamp on the place – enough reason to make one anxious if it would all come to pass. The day I finished my book, the day my book came out clothed in Dutch, was the day I felt at home in Beverwijk, in Holland. I could now stick up my head and say, 'I did this'. My book was my second passport, life's passport opening doors which had been firmly shut in my face a few years before. It enabled me to dream, to live where I wanted, to loosen up a little bit. It enabled me to see the back of my anxiety. It wasn't the end of the fight; it was a cessation of conflict.

In the last ten years I have heard incessant stories of people, exiles, wracked by the pangs of nostalgia, homesickness, a craving for the past, a wish to revisit the past. Many have spent thousands in efforts to return home for a few weeks. I didn't move a muscle. If it hadn't been for my English publisher my return to Uganda would have been postponed for a little longer. But with the changes in Uganda and especially the return of Macmillan the time was ripe. The book had done well abroad; it was time to send it home. News had reached me that people were watching out for it, waiting for it to hit the bookshops. I had been booked into a good hotel from where I could explore the landscape unencumbered by family or friends. I would be like an eagle coasting on thermals. I would be like a pasha dispensing goodwill and largesse at will. Suddenly it was exciting to be back.

My arrival in Uganda signified the end of a period and the beginning of a new one: my definition of home depended totally on me. Belatedly, I experienced a bit of anxiety as the plane touched down, dramatising the possibility of rejection which was infinitesimal. I walked the tarmac I had walked ten years ago and smelled the air. I could see banana trees and little houses in the distance. Some things had not changed; they had become just a little older. The journey to the city was smooth and assured me that ten years is a long time but not long enough to change everything. I could recognise every little town, remembered the fruit stands, the curve of the hills. I sighed with relief. The city centre had changed in parts, a new building here and there, but the chipped side walks, the crowded taxi parks were still the same. Many people on the street looked thin, very thin compared to the Dutch, and there were many street children lying on the sidewalks. The suburbs had changed most, becoming very overcrowded while the rural areas looked relatively empty. A few hours after arrival I tucked into Ugandan fare: *matooke na nyama*. It was delicious. I listened to stories of who had emigrated, who had graduated and was still looking for a job, who had started a school here and there, who was in the financial doldrums, who had made a killing in the last decade. I felt near to it all but at the same time I was detached in a way. It was one of those situations where one wanted somebody to come to the punch line of the story quickly. I was itching to go the village I had made famous. I directed the driver past the path that led into the swamp and the village. We doubled back and started the climb. I was impressed by the order, by the space, the calm. I could not recognise my grandfather's house because it had been rebuilt. I kept arguing that we were still some way off. We again doubled back and parked in the yard. I walked about examining the trees which I used to climb daily. They looked different, older. I went to the burial ground where my grandfather had been lying for almost a year. He had been cemented into his grave and an iron cross stood where his head had to be. I had a photo taken of me leaning on it. I walked about the village looking for former playmates. I found them peeling bananas to make beer; the village had claimed them totally. We were miles apart; deep conversation was almost impossible. I took a few pictures and drove away. Visits to other places transpired in the same vein: the roots had been cut. In one place a cousin had come to commiserate with my relatives after hearing that I had died. She greeted me without recognising me. I introduced myself and she squirmed with embarrassment. I just laughed. On my last day in Uganda I went round Kampala shopping for things I wanted to take back to Holland. I was on the front page of a big daily newspaper, the story of the book launch splashed with the dust of pedestrians. I kept seeing myself on the sidewalk where most news sellers ply their business. I had walked the same streets a decade ago, heard the music coming from the same shop entrances, saw hawkers carrying their shops in their arms, visited the crowded markets and also had a haircut. This time though a friend carried my shopping, guiding me to where dry mushrooms were sold, where a certain book could be bought. We had my last lunch together: *matooke na nyama*. We ate with our fingers. In a few hours pictures of me on the street would be gone and mark the end of my stay. Off I would go. I wasn't sorry I was leaving. It was like end of holidays with my suitcase packed ready for school. I had come with the burning desire to stuff myself sick with jackfruit but in all my eight days there I didn't taste a single piece of jackfruit. My favourite tree in the village was out of season, and the one jackfruit I got from the neighbours was not yet ripe. Now and then I saw jackfruits on fruit stands but usually there was no time to stop because of an appointment or because I had already eaten food. So much for homecomings.

As a voluntary exile I carry my home with me wherever I go, meaning the fond memories, the important bits and pieces. I could live in America, in Zimbabwe, or in Spain or somewhere else. I am already formed, I only have to transplant my views into new soil. I contemplate living in two homes, say one in Holland, one in America. It doesn't really matter. Home for me is the place where you can live and work, the physicality of it is a matter of detail.

In the last ten years I have missed little about Uganda, except jackfruit and the smell of dry mushrooms floating in thick groundnut soup. Maybe now and then I have had pangs of tender feeling when the name of a faraway village came across my consciousness or when a piece of music touched off a chord somewhere in the crevices of body or mind. Uganda is so near yet so far; home is always within sight but elusive. It is like devil water shimmering on the hot tarmac but whenever you reach it it recedes; it is only meant to be touched by the heart not greasy fingers. It is as much between the ears as between the ribs. It is the way I like it. I have always loved the possibility of walking away. I want to feel at home but I also want to miss home.

MOSES ISEGAWA

This essay was originally published in Dutch translation in *Vrij Nederland,* 8 August 2000.

orders

of Hospitality

The Difficult Birth of a Multicultural Society

Large-scale migrations have always been a feature of the Low Countries, with Belgium and the Netherlands in turn receiving and sending out various groups of migrants. After the King of Spain regained military control of the Southern Netherlands (the present-day Belgium) in the second half of the sixteenth century, it is estimated that more than 100,000 refugees fled to the independent North. There they not only found shelter from the violence of the Spanish army, but were also free to practice their Protestant religion. The departure of such a large group of refugees was a massive drain on the Southern Netherlands, and heralded economic stagnation for cities such as Antwerp, Ghent and Leuven. The North, on the other hand, benefited considerably from the spirit of enterprise that the refugees brought with them: when the United East India Company was founded in 1602, about a third of the start-up capital came from immigrants from the Southern Netherlands. Later migrations too were often due to religious reasons: after the King of France revoked the Edict of Nantes in 1685, more than 50,000 Huguenots fled to the Netherlands.

As we have said, though, there are also examples of the migratory movement going in the opposite direction. In the years immediately following the Second World War almost half a million Dutch people left their country to settle in Australia, Canada, the United States and New Zealand. The general feeling at the time was that the Netherlands, one of the most densely populated countries in the world, had become too 'full' and in any case did not offer sufficient prospects of success in, for instance, the agricultural sector. On the whole, these emigrants integrated successfully into their new communities, although they maintained their own cultural identity to a large extent. This explains why, at the height of the Australian summer, the Dutch community still sticks to its traditional Sinterklaas celebrations on the eve of the sixth of December. However, the children of these emigrants do seem to be fully assimilated into Australian or New Zealand society.

In the nineteenth century Flanders especially faced severe economic problems, and this too triggered a wave of migration. Some of these migrants headed for the United States, but most of the destitute Flemings sought a better life in the large cities and newly developing industrial areas of

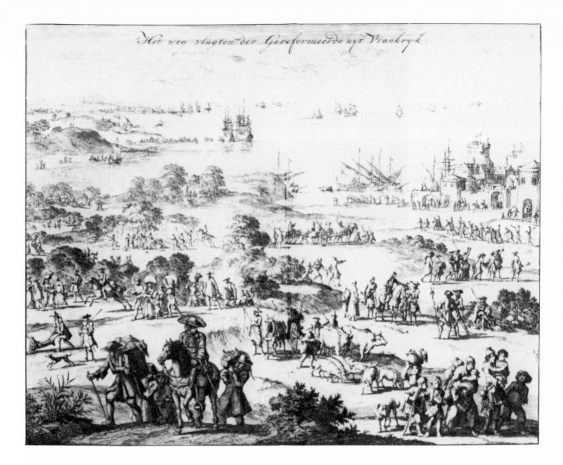

Het weg vlugten der Gereformeerde uyt Vrankryk.

French Huguenots taking refuge in Holland, as shown in a 1695 print by Jan Luiken.

Wallonia. The Walloon mines attracted Flemish workers in large numbers, and in the course of one generation most of them became completely gallicised. The economic backwardness of Flanders also resulted in seasonal migration: Flemings went to work for a few months in the industrial centres in Wallonia, or the agricultural areas of Northern France, without settling permanently in these areas.

Since the 1960s, however, there has been no more mass emigration, and the Low Countries have become recipient countries, absorbing relatively large groups of foreigners into their own societies. This has led to tensions in the past, and still does, although only in a few instances have these tensions given rise to open conflict. For both Flanders and the Netherlands this influx of newcomers was a relatively new phenomenon that required some degree of adjustment. Although some researchers argue, correctly, that in the sixteenth and seventeenth centuries the Low Countries had a much more diverse population, the circumstances of most of that population were then so fundamentally different that the two situations can hardly be compared. In spite of the cosmopolitan nature of a city such as Amsterdam, until 1950 the Low Countries were in ethnic terms relatively homogeneous communities, with little experience of living with people of other cultures. In 1947 no more than 4 per cent of the Belgian population was of foreign origin, and in the period immediately following the Second World War even the Netherlands had not much more than 2 per cent of ethnic minorities. Roughly half

Kwakoe Festival: an annual event held by Dutch Surinamers.

a century later, however, that has changed drastically, and one can now say that for both countries almost 10 per cent of the population belongs to an ethnic or cultural minority. In the course of fifty years the Low Countries have de facto become multicultural societies, and, as in other countries, the process has not always gone smoothly.

Decolonisation

In the migrations of the past six decades we can distinguish three different motives: a) the aftermath of colonisation; b) the deliberate attraction of 'guest workers' and c) the 'spontaneous' influx of new groups.

In the decades following the Second World War both the Netherlands and Belgium lost their former colonies and mandates. (The Netherlands lost Indonesia, Surinam, the Antilles; Belgium lost the Congo, Rwanda, Burundi.) This process gave rise to relatively large-scale shifts of population. Indonesia's difficult transition to independence (1949) set in motion a massive migratory movement, in the first instance of the roughly 300,000 Dutch colonials who returned home, but also of people of mixed descent or of Indonesian origin. The former soldiers from the South Moluccas caused a particular problem. This Christian area in the east of the Indonesian archipelago was used by the Dutch as a recruiting base for an army of occupation, and naturally these ex-soldiers were not welcome in the newly-independent and for the main part Islamic Indonesia. They and their families therefore opted to emigrate to the Netherlands, where they were housed in refugee camps. Their integration into Dutch society was not particularly successful, however, and as late as the 1970s a few small groups of Moluccans were still carrying out terrorist actions because they thought their community had been let down by the Dutch government. The independence of Surinam (1975) was no more of a success story: huge numbers of this colony's inhabitants exercised their right to settle in their former mother country, on account of the rapidly deteriorating economic and political situation in Surinam. It is now thought that the Surinamese community in the Netherlands numbers some 300,000 people, with no more than 400,000 remaining in Surinam itself.

In 1960 Belgium lost control of its African colonies and mandates (the Congo, Rwanda, Burundi), but their independence provided far less scope for large-scale population movements, partly because of a much more restrictive entry policy. The white colonials came back in huge numbers, particularly after the violent incidents in the Congo, but the strong economic growth of the Sixties meant that this group could be relatively quickly integrated into the labour market and the machinery of government. The influx of Congolese subjects remained limited; even today Belgium has no more than 12,000 inhabitants of Congolese nationality, and many of these have only temporary student visas. It was only in Brussels that a fully fledged Congolese community established itself, and the composition of this has changed several times in recent decades as a result of the successive changes of government in Kinshasa.

Employment-driven migration

A second important reason for migration was the systematic recruitment of foreign labour by Dutch and Belgian industry. As early as June 1946 Belgium and Italy signed a bilateral agreement, in which Italy promised to 'de-

Distribution of emergency rations among the families of the victims of the great Marcinelle mine disaster of August 1956. More than half of the casualties were Italian migrant workers. These people were living as second-class citizens in temporary wooden sheds.

liver' 50,000 workers for the Belgian coal mines. In exchange Italy was assured of a steady supply of Belgian coal. Eventually some 80,000 Italians were to work in the Belgian coal mines, a migration which did not end until 1956. In the great Marcinelle mine disaster of August 1956 232 mineworkers lost their lives; 136 of them were Italians. This disaster made such an impression in Italy that migration from that country ceased abruptly. However, the Italians who were already in Belgium stayed there, and this led to the formation of a relatively large Italian community. Even today, the 203,000 Italians still make up the largest group of foreigners in Belgium, and that despite the fact that a great many of them have acquired Belgian citizenship in the intervening period. About 80 per cent of the Italians live in Brussels or Wallonia, which, given the relationship between French and Italian, has made their integration easier. One noteworthy example is the politician Elio di Rupo, whose father worked as a guest worker in a coal mine, but who himself rose to be vice-premier of Belgium and chairman of the powerful French-language socialist party. Integration of the Italian community seems unlikely to give rise to systematic conflicts. At the same time, this community has succeeded in preserving much of its cultural identity. When there is a football match between Belgium and Italy, in some of the former mining areas one still sees more Italian flags than Belgian.

After the Marcinelle disaster however, and because the standard of living in Italy had risen, industry was obliged to recruit its workers from even further afield. In 1964 Belgium made bilateral agreements with Morocco and Turkey that gave guest workers access to the Belgian labour market. The Netherlands also made similar agreements with countries such as Portugal, Turkey, Greece, Morocco and Tunisia. These agreements introduced a whole new category of foreigners into Belgian and Dutch society. While the Italians at least shared the same religion and a related language, this was much less true for the new workforce. Moreover, the Dutch and the Belgians had little experience in dealing with such differences in culture. Whereas in

Palestinians in the Noordoostpolder, 1988. Photo by Marcel Molle.

The Taibah Mosque in Bijlmermeer, Amsterdam.

A Moroccan man in a Belgian street. Photo by Edgard Alsteens.

1961 Belgian had a total of 461 inhabitants of Moroccan nationality, twenty years later there were 105,000. In the Sixties, certainly, no attempt was made to develop an integration policy for these 'guest workers'. The governments of the time assumed that such people would stay for a few years, leaving their wives or children at home. The underlying idea was that the guest workers would get together a certain amount of start-up capital, and return with it to their country of origin. Many of them did indeed return, but an equally large proportion decided to settle here for good. From 1974 on both the Netherlands and Belgium officially closed their frontiers to this form of employment-driven migration, due to the economic crisis and the resultant fall in the demand for labour; but those who were already there naturally had the right to be joined by members of their family. In addition, people who later married someone from their country of origin were allowed to bring their wife or husband into the country. This creating and reuniting of families meant that even after 1974 the Turkish and Moroccan presence in the Low Countries went on increasing. If we also take into account the 'second generation' (the children of former immigrants who were born here), we are looking at a total of some 800,000 people for the Netherlands and Belgium together.

The third wave

In the last few years both Belgium and the Netherlands have been confronted with what one might call a third wave of migrants. Officially the 1974 freeze on immigration still applies, so there is no longer any question of entry for workers. This means that those who wish to come have to find other ways of gaining entry to the country, and most of them apply for asylum as political refugees. Both countries are signatories to the Geneva Convention of 28 July 1951 regarding the status of refugees, and have developed procedures for granting asylum to those who are persecuted for political reasons in their homeland. For more than thirty years this was a matter of a few thousand cases a year at most. In the last few years, however, the number of requests has rocketed: whereas in 1996 Belgium and the Netherlands together dealt with some 40,000 asylum seekers, in 2000 that number doubled to more than 80,000. There are various reasons for this growth in numbers. For some years now we have seen a considerable world-wide increase in migratory movements, and, compared to this the number of newcomers to Belgium and the Netherlands remains relatively modest. The political and economic collapse of the former Soviet Union has led to mass immigration, while the conflicts in the Balkans also increased the number of refugees. Moreover, the abolition of internal border controls in the European Union

Extradition of Somalis
in Wassenaar
(The Netherlands), 1996.
Photo by Guus Dubbelman.

A Saturday afternoon in
Rotterdam, Summer 2000.

'Regularisati(e)(on)': waiting at the office window of the Brussels Immigration Services.

made it relatively easy for these refugees to move from one EU country to another. Belgium and the Netherlands were clearly unprepared for this massive influx: in both countries the appropriate services were accustomed to dealing thoroughly with a relatively small number of cases. Despite sizeable increases in staff, the services proved unable to cope with ten times as many requests as they had been used to, and the whole process can now easily take two to three years. During this time those seeking asylum can legally remain in the country. In the vast majority of cases, however, there are insufficient grounds for granting political asylum; over ninety per cent of applications are turned down. We can therefore assume that the great majority of applicants are actually economic migrants trying to escape the difficult economic situation in such countries as the Ukraine, Russia or Romania. Only when the whole procedure has been gone through are rejected applicants ordered to leave the country, but one gets the strong impression that such orders are not systematically followed up in either the Netherlands or Belgium. On the contrary, the feeling is that some at least of those who have been refused entry stay in the country, but go underground. Naturally no one knows exactly how many people are living illegally in the Low Countries, but most estimates assume it to be at least a few tens of thousands. The strong economic growth of the last few years means that there is a clear demand for cheap illegal labourers in areas like agriculture and horticulture and in the construction industry. Thus most of the illegal immigrants can disappear fairly easily into the black economy. Since the scandals concerning various prostitution networks a few years ago, controls in this area have been tightened considerably, but it is still thought that a relatively large number of women end up as prostitutes. The tragic death in June 2000 of 58 illegal refugees from China who suffocated in a Dutch container lorry carrying them from the Belgian port of Zeebrugge to Dover in the UK demonstrates that some of this traffic is in the hands of criminal networks with few scruples. Certainly in the last few years the European Union has introduced a great many measures to restrict illegal immigration; but with the continuing economic dislocation in some Eastern European countries and the tensions in the Balkans a considerable number of people are still trying to get to rich Western Europe.

Fuzzy figures

These successive waves of immigration mean that nowadays Belgium and the Netherlands give the impression of having far more 'coloured' people than forty years ago. The irony is, though, that there are no reliable or comparative statistics on the proportion of ethnic and cultural minorities in the total population. The reason for this is that many of the newcomers from the Sixties and Seventies have in the meantime acquired Belgian or Dutch citizenship. The children born since that time almost all have Belgian or Dutch nationality. However, the population statistics are almost entirely nationality-based, making it difficult to assess the exact size of this 'second generation'. The Dutch Minister for the Conurbations and Integration Policy works on the assumption that more than 9 per cent of the current Dutch population belongs to an ethnic minority. The chief countries of origin are Surinam and Turkey (each 300,000), Morocco (250,000), the Antilles (100,000), ex-Yugoslavia (60,000), Italy and Spain (each 30,000), Somalia, Iran and Iraq and the former Soviet Union (each around 20,000). However, the concentration of non-indigenous people is far higher in the large cities. For instance, it is thought that nearly 40 per cent of the population of Amsterdam is of non-western origin. Moreover, the minister expects that by the year 2020 about one-fifth of the Dutch population will be of foreign origin.

As far as Belgium is concerned, we must make do with official statistics based on the inhabitants' nationality. Some 900,000 Belgian residents do not have Belgian citizenship (9 per cent of the population, 5 per cent in Flanders, 29 per cent in the Brussels region). In the majority of cases, though, these are citizens of other member states of the European Union, such as France, the Netherlands, Germany, Italy and Spain. On the whole these groups have a healthy socio-economic position, and consequently these EU subjects pose no real problems of integration. Such problems do arise, though, with people from outside the European Union, and primarily with countries such as Morocco, Turkey, the former Yugoslavia and the former Soviet Union. The number of non-Europeans in the total population is far smaller, amounting to 330,000 people in the whole of Belgium (3 per cent of the population, 2 per cent in Flanders and Wallonia, 14 per cent in Brussels). However, this figure is an *underestimate*, since the statistics do not show people who have acquired Belgian nationality since their arrival. At a conservative estimate, perhaps 5 to 7 per cent of the Belgian population belongs to an ethnic/cultural minority.

The multicultural arena

People living in countries which traditionally had a much greater degree of ethnic diversity may find it somewhat strange that the presence of relative-

Turkish women in Brussels.
Photo by Tim Dirven.

ly small groups of ethnic minorities has become a major political issue in the Low Countries. In Flanders the Vlaams Blok far-right party, which campaigns mainly against the presence of ethnic minorities, polls some 15 per cent of the vote. In the latest local elections (October 2000) it took as much as 33 per cent of the vote in the port city of Antwerp. Although no similar anti-immigration party has ever really got off the ground in the Netherlands, there too the co-existence of different cultures sometimes leads to heated debate.

There are a number of reasons why the presence of ethnic minorities has given rise to tensions and conflicts. To begin with, there is the fact that they make up a rapidly increasing proportion of the total population, and certainly the massive Eastern European influx in recent years has contributed to this. As far as the indigenous population is concerned, it is perhaps not the total number of immigrants that is important so much as the rate at which that number is increasing. It is precisely this increase that can lead to them

feeling that the existence of their own culture is under threat.

Secondly, there is the fact that the figure of between 5 and 10 per cent ethnic minorities conceals significant local differences. In the large cities such as Amsterdam, Rotterdam, Antwerp and Brussels these minorities make up something like a third of the population. From the 1960s onwards Belgium and the Netherlands have seen an exodus from the cities, with large numbers of well-off indigenous people vacating the inner cities for the greener suburbs. The often run-down housing in the inner cities was then rapidly taken over by the newcomers, and because of this concentration the indigenous people consistently tend to overestimate the percentage of ethnic minorities. This perception is reinforced by the fact that, due to the ageing of the indigenous population, among younger people the percentage of non-indigenous people is far higher than in the total population, and because they spend more time out and about these younger people are naturally a more conspicuous presence on the streets.

In the past, run-down housing in the inner cities was rapidly taken over by the newcomers: Turkish children in an old working-class neighbourhood in Ghent. Photo by Lieve Colruyt.

Thirdly, one must remember that Belgium and the Netherlands are highly complex societies, which impinge upon the daily lives of their citizens in a great many areas. Not only do they have exceptionally highly developed education and health systems, there is also an exceptionally wide range of provisions for social security, housing, culture, welfare, and the environment. All of these, however, contain the potential for clashes between the indigenous population and newcomers, whereas in countries where such services are less well developed, they will be less likely to provoke friction.

Indeed, the last few years particularly there seems to have been an increasing awareness that the Netherlands and Belgium are in fact multicultural societies, but that in practice there are still enormous problems of integration. So far there have been no incidents of extreme violence such as we have seen in Germany, for instance, but that is not to say that the various cultures co-exist peacefully. In Flanders the continuing electoral success of the far-right Vlaams Blok demonstrates that there are still a number of problems with integration. Indeed, it is typical that a separate commissionership for integration policy was established in Belgium only after the first far-right election victory in 1988. In the Netherlands it was the conservative-liberal politician Frits Bolkestein who was the prime mover in kindling the debate.

In 1991 he argued that progressive circles in the Netherlands were too ready to assume that the intended integration was proceeding successfully, and that we were all being assimilated into one large, multicultural society. In actual fact, according to Bolkestein, there was still a considerable degree of apartheid. Dutch people and newcomers were to a great extent living separate lives, and as far as housing, employment, education and health care were concerned, the newcomers held the least enviable positions in society, and had become a sort of socio-cultural underclass. Bolkestein also wondered to what extent the traditional values of openness, fairness and pluralism, to which the Dutch attached so much importance, were compatible in practice with the values of, in particular, some of the Islamic minorities. While this sparked a passionate debate in the Netherlands, we see that in Flanders there has never been any real discussion of the desirability of a multicultural society. That, of course, was entirely due to the electoral success of the Vlaams Blok: the slightest critical reflection on the integration of ethnic minorities was almost automatically equated with support for the Blok, so that there was little opportunity for an open dialogue on the matter.

Bolkestein's remarks, together with those of a number of other commentators (such as Herman Vuijsje in 1986 and Paul Scheffer early in 2000, see p. 122) led to a heated debate in which accusations of covert racism and naïvety flew back and forth. But this polemic cannot hide the fact that in practice there are still very real differences, with education probably the most significant example simply because one's level of education is so vital to one's prospects of social integration. Both Flanders and the Netherlands are faced with the existence of 'white' and 'black' schools. Implicit in the concentration of ethnic minorities in the inner cities is the fact that schools in these areas will be attended primarily by children of a different ethnic origin, which often means a lowered standard of education, if only because of the language problem. Both countries have in the past tried to prevent the development of such ethnic concentrations in schools, but with little success. Traditionally both Belgium and the Netherlands have attached great importance to freedom of education, which also means that parents are free to choose their children's school. Government therefore has few legal means of ensuring that non-Dutch-speaking children are spread over a great number of schools. Moreover, the parents of white children display an extremely stubborn and predictable pattern of behaviour, a pattern found also in other countries. As soon as the percentage of non-indigenous children in their children's school gets too high, they shift their children *en masse* to a more purely white school. Thus it is precisely in education that we find what is almost the strongest form of apartheid: children from ethnic minorities systematically end up in worse schools, and in the weakest classes in those schools. For instance, in the Netherlands the drop-out rate is at least four times higher among children of Turkish origin than among indigenous Dutch children. This means that a generation which hasn't even grown up yet already has its chances of integration severely prejudiced. Indeed, the unemployment rate in the non-indigenous community is a good deal higher than in the indigenous population, partly due to lack of education and negative prejudices among employers. Even so, there are significant differences between communities. It appears that Turkish immigrants and their children do relatively better than, for instance, Moroccans or Antilleans, both at school and in the labour market.

Integration and curtailment

In recent years considerable emphasis has been placed on trying to achieve better integration in both countries. Thus in 1998 an Immigrants Assimilation Act was introduced in the Netherlands, under which immigrants are expected to attend assimilation courses so as to become acquainted with the Dutch language, the Dutch political and economic system and the prevailing standards of behaviour. In Belgium this is not general policy to the same extent, and this is largely due to the country's complicated political structure. Entry to Belgium is a matter for the federal authorities, all decisions relating to asylum, immigration and nationality being made by the national government. The implementation of anti-discrimination legislation is also a federal responsibility and is carried out, among other things, by the Centre for Equal Opportunities and the Eradication of Racialism (Centrum voor Gelijkheid van Kansen en Racismebestrijding). Yet everything that has to do with the actual integration of new arrivals, from language courses, through education, to integration into the labour market, is the responsibility of the regions (Flanders, Brussels and Wallonia). In the past one could not always rely on uniformly good co-ordination between the different policy levels. The differences of opinion were partly due to the fact that the situation differed considerably between the three regions. Its thriving economy and the attendant demand for cheap labour make Flanders a far more attractive destination for newcomers than, for instance, Wallonia. Largely because of pressure from the Flemish political parties, in 2000 the Belgian government introduced various measures in a drastic attempt to reduce the number of asylum seekers, among other things by withdrawing financial assistance while applications were being processed and only giving practical help. In the Netherlands too there was a new Aliens Act in 2000 (which came into effect in April 2001) with more or less the same objective: the procedure for obtaining political refugee status has been considerably simplified and shortened, the number of grounds for appeal has been limited, and the government has greater powers to deport those who have been turned down. Thus Belgium and the Netherlands are both facing the same phenomenon: strict legislation in large neighbouring countries such as Germany and France has made the Low Countries an attractive area for immigrants, especially for economic refugees from the Balkans and Eastern Europe. Thanks to the complicated procedure and the slow functioning of the services concerned, these refugees could count on being able to stay in the country for a couple of years or so, even if they clearly had no valid claim to political refugee status. By tightening procedures as from 2001 both countries hope to stem the flow. However, human rights organisations are concerned as to whether these new, rapid, procedures will still provide sufficient guarantees that the applications of genuine political refugees will be assessed with expertise and objectivity. In addition, certainly in progressive quarters, the question is increasingly being asked as to how far it is right to restrict entry to the territory to political refugees, while closing the door on those fleeing from difficult economic circumstances.

Although the number of new asylum seekers has indeed declined during the first months of 2001, it seems unlikely that these new measures will effectively reverse the trend. The whole world over we are finding that eco-

Pupils at the Erasmiaans Gymnasium in Rotterdam, posing in front of a statue of Erasmus. Photo by Bert Nienhuis.

nomic polarisation (the growing gap between rich and poor) and the greater availability of means of communication are leading to an increase in migration. Thus far the Low Countries have taken in only a very limited number of people, compared with the millions of refugees in Africa or Asia, for example, who have been driven to seek new homes. Furthermore, the whole issue of whether or not a multicultural society is something to be desired has been somewhat overtaken by economic and demographic facts. In economic circles it is already assumed that in the coming decades the European Union will have to admit several million economic migrants to supply the demands of the labour market, which cannot be met by the rapidly ageing population. In the Netherlands and in Flanders the average number of children per family is hovering around 1.5, yet actually 2.1 children per family are needed to maintain the level of population. The most likely outcome, then, is that in the coming decades we shall see a revised edition of the 1960s policy: the deliberate attraction of foreign workers. Despite all the cultural and political considerations, it appears to be yet again the case that it is economic requirements, and especially the situation in the labour market, that determine where the borders of hospitality are set in the Low Countries.

MARC HOOGHE
1 May 2001
Translated by Sheila M. Dale.

pace

Light, Order

The Paintings of Pieter de Hooch

Pieter de Hooch's paintings offer a remarkable vision of domestic life in seventeenth-century Holland. Working first in Delft and later in Amsterdam, De Hooch specialised in depictions of family life, domestic tasks, flirtations and musicmaking. His pictures radiate a quiet composure; their tonalities favour luminous reds and yellows and deep browns, while their composition is often stunningly complex. He was particularly drawn to the expressive possibilities of architecture. The beautifully appointed houses he used as settings demonstrate his notable fondness for intricate interior spaces, meticulously ordered and further enriched by the effects of sunlight penetrating dark rooms. Few Dutch painters were as skilled at organising space or at teasing out its social and psychological nuances.

Rooms with a view

Born in 1629, De Hooch began his career in about 1650, painting scenes of soldiers and peasants in dimly lit inns and stables. In 1652 he arrived in Delft from his native Rotterdam; by 1658 he had shifted his subject matter to domestic life, and at the same time started to articulate and clarify his interior spaces with a more developed use of perspective. He also added more light: these Delft pictures were the most brightly-toned of his career. Around 1660, he moved to Amsterdam to better his professional fortunes; he remained there, in ever more precarious financial circumstances, until his death in 1684. By the time of his move he had established his signature formula, which he used for both genre scenes and commissioned portraits: scenes of leisure or domestic work, the exteriors set either in courtyards or gardens, the interiors generally lit from a side window at the left and a doorway on the back wall. From the mid-1660s on his interiors darkened considerably, penetrated by windows and rear doorways revealing the most brightly lit areas of the picture: the street, garden or canal beyond the house.

From the late 1640s onward Dutch painters, especially in Delft, were experimenting with the analytical description of architectural space. While there is a lack of documentation that proves any specific connections be-

Pieter de Hooch, *Interior with a Linen Chest*. 1663. Canvas, 72 x 77.5 cm. Rijksmuseum, Amsterdam.

tween local artists and De Hooch, who had arrived in Delft from Rotterdam by 1650, his pictures show a powerful response to their experiments. Like Carel Fabritius, he opted for a bright, light-toned palette, and broad brushstrokes. Like the architectural painter Emanuel de Witte, he organised his scenes with a deep perspective scheme. Indeed, his work displays especially strong affinities with that of De Witte and the other Delft architectural specialists, who depicted both real and imaginary church interiors, usually with people strolling through them or listening to sermons. He borrowed their preference for altering pre-existing architecture and their technique of painting the complete setting first, then adding the figures.

Far more than any of his fellow genre painters, De Hooch made the complexity of architectural space his special project. He rarely leaves the background of a picture unexplored, or a back wall unpenetrated. Of the one hundred and sixty-odd paintings currently attributed to De Hooch, only about a dozen do not feature a view to a back room, a courtyard, a garden, or a street. A compelling subplot of his harmonious yet pleasingly complex images is the relation between the house and its immediate environment, the city. De Hooch's pictures represent the intersection of urban and domestic experience.

In the typical *Interior with a Linen Chest*, from his early Amsterdam

Pieter de Hooch, *Family Group in a Courtyard.* c.1657-1660. Canvas, 112.5 x 97 cm. Gemäldegalerie der Akademie der bildenden Künste, Vienna.

years, two women are calmly putting linen away in a large cabinet, while a little girl runs indoors with her *kolf* club. Significant here is the distinction between the sunlit exterior and the somewhat dimly lit house, where the women hold sway. The child is silhouetted in the doorway, with a *contre-jour* effect that was one of De Hooch's specialties. Behind her is a seductive glimpse of houses across the canal, a Mondrian-like series of white, yellow and vermilion oblongs forming the most brightly lit area of the picture. The rectangle of the doorway is echoed in the tiles on the polished floor, the treads and risers of the staircase, the picture on the wall, the window to the outer room, and the windows and shutters of the distant houses. Such near-abstract matrices of rectilinear shapes are a foil for his commonplace subjects.

While many Dutch painters at midcentury were depicting scenes of family life, De Hooch was the first artist to use the courtyard as a setting. A mainstay of seventeenth-century Dutch vernacular architecture, it was used both for entertaining and for basic household tasks, and to admit more light into the house. In De Hooch's imaginative adaptations of the Delft and Amsterdam neighbourhoods where he lived, these outdoor areas mediate between the enclave of the household and its public, urban setting. In an unusual family portrait, apparently the first to be set in a courtyard, the scene is bounded on the right by the old town wall of Delft. Meanwhile, glimpsed through the open door in the wall behind, a solitary figure goes down the path toward a second wall opening to a garden. Looming above is the tower of Delft's Nieuwe Kerk, on which all the orthogonals (the town wall, the paving on the floor, the top edge of the open door in the wall behind the family) converge, while the retreating man in grey echoes its colour and vertical shape. While the fruit-laden table and the little dog evoke the comfortable intimacy associated with interiors, the plunging perspective leads our eyes to this family's outer environment: the town.

Women and children first

De Hooch's genre scenes are nearly all portrayals of women, often accompanied by children, usually little girls. The men are often absent, while those who do appear are more or less transient: indoors, their coats are slung over chairs to suggest they are visitors; outside, they are reduced to small figures in the distance. This is very much in keeping with the writings of popular moralists. In the ideal Calvinist marriage, the wife was to oversee the household while the husband roamed the professional arena of the city. In *Interior with a Linen Chest* the women and child are all indoors. A statue of Perseus over the doorway (copied from Cellini's famous statue in Florence) functions as a surrogate for the missing man of the household. Placed just above access to the street, this male figure is visually linked with the world beyond the house door.

Quite apart from instructional literature, the association of women with houses (and that of men with the environment outside the house) has a long tradition in the art of the Low Countries. As early as the fifteenth century, the *Mérode Altarpiece* visualised the traditional Annunciation chamber as a bourgeois home. Similarly, Petrus Christus' *Holy Family in a Domestic Interior* shows the use of architecture to reinforce distinctions between the sacred virgin dominating the middle-class house and her mortal environment, that is, the town glimpsed through the door through which Joseph enters.

De Hooch's *Woman and a Maid in a Courtyard* strikes us as a modern, secular version of Christus' picture, set outdoors under grey autumnal skies. A maid crouches on the ground, preparing to cook fish in a pot. She is framed by the tall water-pump to the right, the piece of tan fabric hanging over the back wall, and the diagonal gutter along the ground that cuts her off from her mistress. The housewife, seen only from behind, stands solidly and imperiously over her servant. De Hooch balances the housewife's figure with the water pump and aligns her with the tall wooden gate at the left, fixing her – as well as her maid – firmly in place. Meanwhile, in the distance, a man comes down the path, entering this geometrically precise, feminine

Petrus Christus, *Holy Family in an Interior.* 15th century. Panel, 69.5 x 51 cm. Spencer Museum of Art, Kansas City.

Pieter de Hooch, *Woman
and a Maid in a Courtyard.*
c.1660-1661 or 1663.
Canvas, 73.7 x 62.6 cm.
National Gallery, London.

ménage from the unseen city beyond the gate. The man's tiny figure is
framed by the series of rectangles from the archway of the courtyard gate to
the doorway to the street behind him, and juxtaposed almost directly with
the housewife's head. While he is easily overlooked, his presence anchors
the entire picture, just as he is apparently necessary to the establishment of
this household despite his isolation from it.

Yet these architectural gender divisions, which also occur in his images
of courtship, are curiously mitigated by the remarkable fluidity of De
Hooch's spaces. The two environments are different, but linked and mutu-
ally accessible. The interior, feminine space of the domestic world is rarely
isolated or hermetic, but open to the surrounding skies, buildings, streets,
and canals. Windows give on to distant views. Gables and church spires appear in the background. Doors and gates remain open; the sunlight streams
in across the gleaming floors.

Public and private space

In fact, the interaction between the domestic sphere and the surrounding town described in De Hooch's contiguous spaces is an intriguing variation on the emerging concept of privacy in early modern urban society. At the middle of the seventeenth century the distinction between private and public life was still in flux. The issue of privacy was beginning to be addressed in Dutch house design through demarcating functional from recreational spaces, or servants from employers. Yet the Dutch household was not yet a fully intimate sphere. Instead, it was a nexus of domestic and professional activity: many professionals – including painters – worked at home, and rooms usually had multiple uses. During this period, Dutch painters of interior scenes began to use elements of home design as allusions to the world outside the house walls. Pictures of landscapes and seascapes, maps, views

Pieter de Hooch, *The Interior of the Burgo-masters' Council Chamber in the Amsterdam Town Hall with Visitors.* c.1663-1665. Canvas, 112.5 x 99 cm. Fundación Colección Thyssen-Bornemisza, Madrid.

Pieter de Hooch,
A Musical Party in a Hall.
c.1663-1665. Canvas,
81 x 68.3 cm. Museum der
bildenden Künste, Leipzig.

out of windows and doors, became conventional devices in all manner of interiors, whether portraits or domestic and courtship scenes. Family groups were often posed in front of an open window, revealing a local townscape.

De Hooch's particular interest in the merging of public and private environments found a unique, poetic expression in a handful of pictures set in the Amsterdam Town Hall. This renowned neoclassical structure, today the Royal Palace, was one of the largest and grandest public buildings in Europe. Not only a famous landmark, the Town Hall was also a particularly resonant image in the city's culture and a source of considerable pride to its citizens. Three scenes take place in recognisable areas of the building, while several others are free adaptations of the interior, borrowing some of its neoclassical details. These scenes are populated with the same types we often see in his genre scenes: in *A Musical Party in a Hall*, a group of flirting couples is seated around a table laden with fruit; they are dressed in slightly antiquated costume, playing instruments and drinking as if they were at home. These elegant, rather theatrical types are essentially close-ups of the anonymous figures in church interiors, large enough for their social identities, and even their personalities, to emerge. Such pictures are fantasies of private interactions within Holland's most authoritative, ornate and forbidding public space. Along with the courtyard scenes, they are De Hooch's most significant inventions.

Let there be light... but not too much

Many of De Hooch's contemporaries were influenced by his art. Other Delft painters such as Cornelis de Man, Hendrick van der Burch and Pieter Janssens Elinga responded to his fondness for contrasting light and shade, his insistently ordered spaces, and his masterful use of perspective. He was probably the single most important influence on Vermeer, who adopted for his own interiors De Hooch's side-window format and expanses of tiled floor. (He also took up, then quickly abandoned, the motif of the open door, which De Hooch exploited so superbly.) This legacy continued into the eighteenth century, when his works were widely copied and collected.

Interestingly, some twentieth-century critics harshly decried his later Amsterdam work, viewing the darker tonalities and grander settings as a decline from the high-keyed, somewhat humbler scenes of his Delft years. This bias arises in part from a modernist aesthetic, coloured further, ironically, by an appreciation for Vermeer. In fact, the darker tone and richer appointments of these later interiors are, in part, calculated to suit the more sophisticated tastes of Amsterdam's wealthy elite. De Hooch was not alone; during the early 1660s many genre painters in Amsterdam, such as Gerard ter Borch and Frans van Mieris, went in for darker palettes in response to new aristocratic fashions.

Yet there is no denying the contrast between the limpid freshness of the work prior to 1660 and the sombre quality of his later interiors. Even his rare courtyard scenes from this period, while still scrupulously arranged and detailed, are quite dark; the only brightly lit area is framed by the doorway to the street. The backlit doorway, and patches of sunshine along the walls of rooms, offer the only illumination. Repeated endlessly throughout the 1670s, they are among De Hooch's trademarks. The late works are also quite different in mood from the more inventive and audacious Town Hall interiors, where De Hooch alters Holland's most important building according to his whim. As his productivity increased, he settled into repetition and modishness in keeping with the new aesthetic; his figures became more stylised as their surroundings become grander. Yet this new manner makes a fitting close to the arc of his career: having begun with shadowy inns and taverns, he progressed to the pale outdoor colours of the mid-1650s and returned, a decade or so later, to a velvety gloom, pierced with the jewel-like light of the world beyond the threshold.

MARTHA HOLLANDER

FURTHER READING

HOLLANDER, MARTHA, 'Public and Private Life in the Art of Pieter De Hooch'. In: Nederlands Kunsthistorisch Jaarboek 51 (ed. Jan de Jong et. al.). Zwolle, 2001, pp. 273-293.

HOLLANDER, MARTHA, 'Pieter De Hooch's Revisions of the Amsterdam Town Hall'. In: The Built Surface: Architecture and Pictures from Antiquity to the Millennium. (ed. Christy Anderson and Karen Koehler). London, 2001.

KERSTEN, M. C. C. and D. H. A. C. LOKIN, Delft Masters, Vermeer's Contemporaries. Zwolle, 1996.

SUTTON, PETER C., Pieter De Hooch. Oxford, 1980.

SUTTON, PETER C., Pieter De Hooch 1629-1684. London / Hartford, CT / New Haven, CT, 1998.

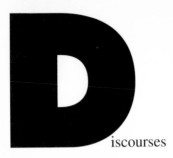

Discourses

on Dutchness

'A people who do not respect their own culture and don't know how to make sacrifices for it will in the long term go to the dogs. The danger of a psychological invasion from the East or West is not in the least hypothetical: we must mount an intellectual, cultural defence against it.'

With these militant words shortly after the Second World War the folklorist Jop Pollmann warned against what he saw as the lax attitude of the Dutch towards foreign cultural influences. Culture pessimists of various persuasions shared Pollman's defensive position and worried about threats to Dutch cultural individuality. Nor was this position new. Since intellectuals at the end of the eighteenth century began to articulate what characterised the Dutch, they have shown themselves fearful of alien influences.

During the nineteenth and twentieth centuries the characteristic features of Dutch culture and identity have been written about and debated with

Photo by Paul Huf.

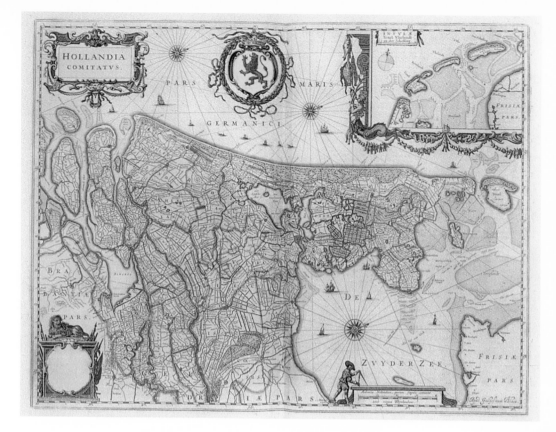

Map of the Netherlands from J. Blaeu's *Grooten Atlas* (1664). Royal Library, The Hague.

varying intensity by people from a wide range of social groups. Intellectuals discussed among themselves the essence of Dutchness and then tried to mobilise the emotions of the Dutch people. Driven by questions like: who are we, what are our historic roots, what binds or divides us and what distinguishes us from other nations, they have put forward various views of Dutch culture and identity, views that are connected with their political, religious and regional background. The concept of Dutchness is therefore far from unambiguous. Different groupings have interpreted the same symbols and cultural expressions in their own way, and as a result no consensus has been reached on a national identity.

This essay focuses on the Dutch identity debate and on the attempts of intellectuals to promote national cohesion. A nation that wants to strengthen its coherence has to suppress internal historical and socio-cultural differences. Nation-formation therefore implies cultural colonisation. At the same time a nation needs to distinguish itself from other nations. Nationality and identity are thus not given, but won, not inherited but acquired.

The rise of a 'national' culture

The birth in 1648 of the Republic of the Seven United Netherlands was the result of military and political contingencies. The central authority was weak; the regions were to a large extent sovereign and local power centres

Rembrandt H. van Rijn, *The Oath of Claudius Civilis*. c.1661-1662. Canvas, 196 x 309 cm. Nationalmuseum, Stockholm. According to a nationalist myth, Civilis was the leader of a 'Dutch' (Batavian) revolt against the Romans in 69 AD.

dominated the provincial authority. Notions about the Dutch as a separate people did indeed exist, but the circles in which these ideas circulated, mostly supported by myths of origin and images of enemies, were small and exclusive. There was as yet no question of a nationalistic ambition in which state and nation would coincide.

The unified state only started to appear on the political agenda around 1780. Then too, a national consciousness manifested itself in various publications on the characteristic nature, morals and customs of the Dutch. Thus, in 1797 the patriot Willem Anthonie Ockerse published an essay in which he characterised the Dutch as phlegmatic, bourgeois, reserved, indifferent and cautious, which put them, according to him, in between the '*frivolous liveliness*' of the French and the '*proud dreariness*' of the English.

In his view, this typical character had been eroded through '*the mixing of blood*' and the imitation of things coming from elsewhere, by which the Dutch in effect ranked as '*the Apes of Europe*' and had reached the '*most dangerous degree of national bastardisation*'. He therefore pleaded for the restoration of the Dutch national character, patriotism and '*national passion*'. The characteristics cited by Ockerse would subsequently be repeated many times and formed the basis of a carefully nourished myth of individuality in values and nature.

The creation of the Kingdom of the United Netherlands in 1813, the result of agreements between the European great powers, gave a new stimulus to the process of state- and nation-formation. However, King William I's pursuit of integration evoked reactions from local elites who feared losing their influence to higher government bodies. The separation from Belgium in 1830 brought about a crisis in the northern Netherlands, plunging the country into a lengthy search for its own place amongst the nations and its own identity. Not until around 1848 did the crisis abate and the Dutch position as a small nation state amongst the larger powers become accepted. The idea gained ground that Dutch culture was essentially different from other cultures, especially from those of France and Germany – a view which was interpreted in two ways. One saw the individuality of Dutch culture as a result of a 'moderate eclecticism' in which the best foreign cultural elements were incorporated. The other claimed that the Netherlands adapted these elements and then passed them on again to foreign countries.

The process of national integration gained momentum in the Netherlands in the second half of the nineteenth century. In the middle of the nineteenth century the whole of the Dutch countryside was a mosaic of regions and communities with their own customs, habits, traditional costumes and other cultural characteristics. They had limited horizons, centred first and foremost on the individual village and its surrounding area. Through the development of the infrastructure, transport and communication, language standardisation, unifying legislation, education, compulsory military service, increase in scale of production, growth in trade and the involvement of ever larger groups in national politics, local and regional cultures made way for a national culture. Dutch people came into contact with each other more often and more intensively, they became dependent upon each other and became in a socio-cultural sense more like each other.

'National' feeling therefore came about in competition not only with other national cultural traditions but also with regional ones and, as will presently be apparent, with 'Weltanschauung'. Also of importance for cultural unification were the cultivation of a national past in historiography, festivals and commemorations, monuments and national museums, the promotion of national education, national development and national songs. In addition, seventeenth-century painting came to be stamped as 'typically Dutch', whilst an age-long tradition was attributed to the national culture which was then held up as a valid model of 'true' national culture. Everywhere in Europe cultural and political elites were bending over backwards to elevate their fellow-countrymen into citizens whose thoughts and actions were governed by national feeling. The curious thing about the initiatives towards cultural homogenisation, the broadening of national consciousness and nationalist expression in the Netherlands, is that often it was the bourgeois elite of liberal persuasion – and not the state – that took the lead in this.

Unity in diversity

With the political polarisation that emerged after 1870 the connection between liberalism and national identity was no longer obvious. Historic sources of inspiration led not to unity but on the contrary to discord; with the rise of the confessional parties the identity of the nation became controversial. The arguments centred on claims regarding the nature of the nation. Protestants emphasised its Protestant character, liberals did so less firmly, but Catholics strongly disputed this view. The result was that every political movement had its own interpretation of history, so that the past and with it national remembrance days and monuments became issues of confrontation. Thus Protestants considered the Revolt a religious war, whilst Catholics saw it as a fight for freedom. Catholic leaders fought against the anti-papist feelings with which commemorative occasions were sometimes associated. They used the (Catholic) Middle Ages to create a distinct profile, to claim a place in the nineteenth-century fatherland for themselves and cultivate a personal identity within the nation.

Despite this, liberals, Catholics and Protestants alike wanted to maintain the impression of a national community so they put on a conciliatory face. Their cultivation of a national consciousness was above all an alliance against socialism. The pillarised subcultures were well aware of the national bond that existed alongside the bond to their own pillar. This awareness was evident, for example in demonstrations of loyalty to and celebrations connected with the royal house. Their international orientation meant that social democrats had difficulty with the nation and nationalism; for them the country's past served no ideological purpose. But it was not so much the nation as such that they opposed, but the position of power of the liberals and confessional parties within it. Additionally, the international idea was undermined by events during the First World War and worker's movements developed that were first and foremost national. In the third decade of the twentieth century social democratic leaders in the Netherlands pledged their loyalty to the fatherland and abandoned their reservations regarding the monarchy.

A certain measure of regionalism, especially in the provinces of Friesland, South Limburg and North Brabant, also appeared to undermine national unity. Frisian, Limburg and Brabant regionalisms differed strongly from each other however; they never achieved a mass following and there was never any question of separatist aspirations. In fact, several regionalist leaders played an important role in the Greater-Netherlands ideal and in the quest for national unity that emerged in the thirties. Followers of the national unity idea supported a pluriform Netherlands, but one in which the national consciousness would be dominant. The wide range of ideas and interpretations of what was 'national' and pillarisation were a thorn in their flesh.

Queen's Day in Marken, North Holland in 1989. Photo by Martin Kers.

They berated the alleged discord in the nation and strove for greater unity, even though this was to be a unity in diversity. Driven by cultural pessimism, they sought to put an end to what they saw as Dutch narrow-mindedness. There were numerous attempts both within and outside these circles to define the Dutch 'national character'. These descriptions were invariably also prescriptive: that is to say they argued not only how the Dutch were, but also how they should be.

This very emphasis on national solidarity, sense of belonging and resistance to rationalisation and modernisation brought some supporters of national unity dangerously close to fascist and national socialist views and terminology. All too soon the occupation in 1940 forced people to take a clear position with regard to the preservation of a Dutch national identity. The politico-cultural aim of the German occupiers was clear: they wanted to germanise the Dutch. A number of people – including quite a few folklore experts – let themselves be seduced into affirming the 'Germanic' origin of Dutch culture. Others emphasised the contrary, that the Dutch were different from the Germans.

The post-war period produced an abundance of publications stressing Dutch individuality. It was a period par excellence of reflection on the essence and value of Dutchness, in which nationalistic rhetoric dominated. The topic of national characteristics was once again brought to the fore, as if ritual repetition would confirm these presumed Dutch characteristics and avert their possible loss. The authors were reacting not only against the German influences that the Netherlands had inevitably been subjected to in five years of occupation, but also against Americanisation. The opening quotation of this essay is an example of this. Intellectuals expressed concern about the moral decline that would afflict the country. The Dutch would, in their eyes, have to be re-educated to be Dutch. '*Being Dutch*', so Gerardus van der Leeuw, the first post-war Minister of Education, Arts and Sciences, maintained, '*is not a condition but a task, (…) an ideal, and a conviction*'.

A continuous dialogue

The desire for a society founded upon a sense of national unity could not however be translated into political terms within the pluralism of parliamentary democracy and modern society. Intellectuals who discussed nationhood resigned themselves to this fact. From the end of the 1940s we find a marked change in work on the nature of Dutch society and culture. Where previously politico-ideological connotations had been inherent in views of the nation and things national, the thinking now became more detached, reflective and conciliatory. The negative experience with virulent nationalism, the international Atlantic Alliance as a response to tense East-West relations and a growing trend towards European co-operation played an important role in this. The debate on national identity and national consciousness was not entirely extinguished, but it was pushed onto the back burner. The same thing happened with regionalism. Many nationalists and regionalists even began to propagate the concept of Europe. In the sixties and seventies the national community idea lost still more ground. The image of Dutchness became more and more diffuse and as a result of de-pillarisation, secularisation and political pragmatism was less bound up with politics and philosophical convictions. At the same time, people in scholarly circles were becoming ever more critical of nationalism and static, psychological, generalised and homogenised concepts such as 'national character', though such essentialist views did not disappear entirely. The result of this criticism was indifference rather than any clearer definition of concepts.

In the early eighties and after, the discussion gained a new lease of life with the arrival of and debate on ethnic minorities. In this context some authors expressed fears of an erosion of Dutch cultural identity, giving rise to sometimes violent polemics. The issue was whether citizenship rather than membership of the Dutch cultural community should be the frame of reference. Since the late eighties many people see globalisation, and especially European unification, as a threat to Dutch individuality. Some fear that unification will lead to a decline of the Dutch language, culture and identity. Recently a few intellectuals have even argued for a deepening and dissemination of national awareness and protection of Dutch cultural identity, both in relation to the presence of ethnic minorities and to European unification. Anyone venturing to express such opinions can bank on vehement reactions, and certainly when these touch upon the relationships between indigenous and non-native Dutch people.

One recent example is the furore caused by the essay 'The Multicultural Drama' by the social democrat intellectual Paul Scheffer in *NRC Handelsblad* of 29 January 2000. Scheffer, a long time advocate of reflection on the *minima moralia* of Dutch cultural identity, opined that the integration of ethnic minorities into Dutch society left much to be desired and threatened to create an ethnic underclass. He rebuked the lax attitude of politicians and intelligentsia for this: '*An easy-going multiculturalism is gathering a following because we fail to put into words what holds our society together. We say too little about our boundaries, cherish no relationship with our own past and treat the language in a nonchalant manner. A society that renounces itself has nothing to offer newcomers. A majority that denies it is a majority, doesn't have an eye on the "heavy-handedness" of integration that also always means a loss of one's own traditions.*' The culture and education policy, according to Scheffer, should also be more strongly directed at integration. The many reactions to the essay, from ethnic minority circles and academics amongst others, were predominantly piqued. Yet it did not fundamentally challenge the benefits of integration, though opinions differ about the ways in which these can be achieved. In a response to the reactions Scheffer suggested (*NRC Handelsblad* of 27 March 2000) that his plea for inclusion was confused by many of his critics with a plea for exclusion. He stressed that what was at stake was actually full citizenship for ethnic minorities. This message had however been misunderstood by many.

In conclusion it should be observed that discussion about Dutch individuality is always fed by fear on the one hand of a dilution of character by influences from outside and on the other hand of threats from within as a consequence of Weltanschauung, political, regional and – recently – ethnic differentiation. The debate is therefore always driven by the construction of boundaries between 'us' and 'them', by cultural in- and exclusion and by myth formation. Consensus about what Dutch individuality currently in-

Dutch football supporters.
Photo Belga.

cludes was, and is, miles away. The best indication that the Netherlands possesses, creates and recreates that individuality is the continuing discussion about it in its own Dutch language, even though the terminology has been constantly subject to change

ROB VAN GINKEL
Translated by Derek Denné.

BIBLIOGRAPHY

LEEUW, G. VAN DER, 'De toekomst van de Nederlandsche beschaving'. In: *Commentaar* I (26), 1945, pp.5-6.

OCKERSE, W.A., *Ontwerp tot eene algemeene characterkunde. Dl. III. Het nationaal characterter der Nederlanderen.* Amsterdam, 1797.

POLLMANN, J., 'Na één jaar: voor volkszáng tot onze gehele volkscultuur'. In: *Binding* II, 17 February 1947, pp. 4-5.

SCHEFFER, P., 'Het multiculturele drama'. In: *NRC Handelsblad*, 29 January 2000.

SCHEFFER, P., 'Het multiculturele drama: een repliek'. In: *NRC Handelsblad*, 27 March 2000.

ast
Imperfect, Present Continuous

Belgian Current Affairs in Flemish Literature

The political and social upheavals of Belgium's recent troubled past have not left Flemish literature untouched. In the literary world they gave rise to a brief but vigorous debate about politics and literature, social commitment and *belles-lettres*. However, the creative fall-out of all this has been rather meagre.

In the autumn of 1996 it seemed for a time that the ghost of the turbulent 1960s was walking again. The immediate occasion for this was the Dutroux affair, a case of serial child-abuse and murder that attracted international interest. The case, which led to an unprecedented demonstration of over half a million citizens in the streets of Brussels (the so-called White March), was a catalyst for the airing of general, if often extremely vague, social and political disquiet and criticism (see *The Low Countries* 1999-2000: pp. 65-72). In Belgium, as in other European states, the institutions of administration, justice and politics had for some time been suffering a crisis of public confidence.

For writers, this period had the attraction of a 'twilight zone'. If the ordinary citizen could become *engagé* – committed to a cause – and take to the streets, why not the artist? From every corner the question re-echoed again: *quoi faire?* – at a time when the citizen was demanding justice on the steps of the law courts.

And with the onrushing millennium as a backdrop, is it any wonder that writers got itchy fingers? They wanted to capture their time. Flanders has a tradition of authors who, as the Flemish author Louis Paul Boon often expressed it, want to be the 'seismograph' of their age and their society. This gave rise, especially in the 1960s and 1970s, to some literary monstrosities: books in which social and political *engagement*– in the form of a 'message' – was rammed home with a sledge-hammer at the expense of aesthetics and even of literature itself. But other writers, like Boon or Hugo Claus, who realised that literary commitment automatically implied social commitment (because form and content are always one) avoided that pitfall. Their work was what good literature ought always to be: an integrated testimony to their time and to the people and society of that time.

When Ivo Michiels, in whose books language becomes both the medium and the message, was asked why his work did not reflect any *engagement*, he referred to Kafka '*who, though he did not describe industrial disputes, nevertheless provided one of the most profound testimonies of his turbulent age*'. And Michiels is right: his own so-called 'other prose' – brimful of experimental language and form – reflects a high level of social commitment. He has defined that commitment himself: '*What counts is not the anecdotal, but the spirit of the time.*' He has even described literature that explicitly aims to change the world as a form of fraud.

By 1996, artistic Flanders had already spent several years in heated debate about the pressing question: 'Can art save the world?'. It is no accident that the question, though first asked when Antwerp became the 1993 European City of Culture, came after the successes of the far right-wing Vlaams Blok in 1991 had begun to pose a real threat to democracy.

So in the autumn of 1996 the old fallacies from the 1960s and 70s concerning social and political commitment in literature surfaced again, in public debates and lofty declarations of intent. Once again one heard echoes of the spirit of the Dutch writer Harry Mulisch who during the Vietnam War said that it was not a time for '*writing stories*'. It was a time for '*doing something*'. The young Flemish writer Jeroen Olyslaegers seemed in 1996 to be a poor copy of Mulisch. He talked about '*horror show Belgium*' and suggested that the newspaper reports on the Dutroux affair could be turned straight into a novel. Indeed, a few years later he tried it, in a novel whose title was a reference to Louis Paul Boon: *Open Like a Mouth* (Open gelijk een mond, 1999). It was an instructive failure. It gave a vague impression of the uncomfortable atmosphere then prevailing in the Kingdom of Belgium, larded with many references to actual events. It was a fashionable book, with much youthful idiom and hip braggadocio. But all that did not make it either a great book or a modern one.

On balance, the four years of Flemish literature between 1996 and 2000 have, with few exceptions, produced disappointingly little. Writers either got bogged down in unconvincing, over-stated 'messages' – as in the 1960s – with the clamour and media attention surrounding the writer often overshadowing the book itself. Or references to actual events from social and political reality were reduced to the status of décor, a backdrop.

The power of the implicit

The writer who was most explicitly inspired by Belgian current affairs was Tom Lanoye. It shows in his political columns, in an essay/address/performance, *Splintered and Soiled* (Gespleten en bescheten, 1998), in a cycle of plays, *To War* (Ten oorlog, 1997), and in a trilogy of novels, *The Divine Monster* (Het goddelijke monster, 1997-1999). Lanoye is a many-sided and refined artist. He is conscious of his position in the tradition of 'seismographic' writers such as Gerard Walschap, Louis Paul Boon and Walter van den Broeck. At the same time he is a modern artist with his finger on the pulse of the time. He is perfectly aware of the pitfalls of socially *engagé* literature, which is why he was so upset when his trilogy of novels was once described as '*a glorified press review*'.

In *The Divine Monster* every Flemish reader will instantly recognise actual persons and events from Belgium's recent past. They are 'used' by Lanoye as material for the life and times of a Flemish family, of a generation. Perhaps the anecdotal element does distract somewhat from the larger, literary purpose. Nevertheless, it is an undeniably enjoyable and compelling game for readers to try to identify the references to current events in Belgium in the 1990s.

Ironically, Lanoye says more about the spirit of the times and about Belgian society in his cycle of plays *To War* where there are fewer – or even no – references to actual events. His reworking of Shakespeare's history plays is clearly politics as art. While writing them, Lanoye paid particularly close attention to the questions of power and powerlessness, the cold war and the hot peace as they made their daily appearance even in Belgian politics. *To War* does not deal directly with Belgian politics or current affairs, and the reader/viewer is therefore not 'distracted'; but at the same time it does provide the reader/viewer with powerful glasses through which to view that time and its events. It is art.

This was also true of his explicitly political columns, a genre in which he is not only a master but also the only practising Flemish author. The *quoi faire* question finally led Lanoye himself into active political commitment: he confessed to being a member of the ecology renewal party, Agalev.

That was a step which Hugo Claus, the man who once designated Lanoye as his spiritual son, rejected. In recent years, Claus has twice been the unwitting illustration (or should it be caricature?) of the epigram that poets are prophets. His novel *Rumours* (De geruchten, 1996) was already at the printer's when some of the events that he described cropped up in reality in the Dutroux affair. And when its successor, *Past Imperfect* (Onvoltooid verleden, 1997), was translated into Swedish, its Swedish readers promptly associated the book with the paedophile scandal that had just erupted in their own country.

Yet the strength of Claus' most recent novels does not lie in their direct link with current affairs. Like Lanoye, but more powerfully and with more epic tension, any reminders of or allusions to Belgian affairs, whether or not deliberate, are there to serve the larger themes of Claus' work: guilt and punishment, Eros and Thanatos. Claus works on an immense psychological canvas, which is already present in his earlier work: mystery, the obscure essence of humanity, or more specifically of the Fleming, with his many taboos and hidden lives, the cellars of the psyche. Claus' ambitions do not extend beyond that: he has no pretensions to comprehend Belgium politically: '*Ach, how does that go exactly, creation, so much has been written about it. One thing I can say for sure: it never begins with an idea. It is never anything like: "what shall we do about the approaching dust cloud of the Vlaams Blok".*'

Like *To War*, Claus' diptych *Rumours* and *Past Imperfect* does offer the reader a pair of glasses that enable him to see events more clearly than the reading of newspapers here and now could ever do. Claus himself sees it thus: '*Don't expect rational political analysis from me. However, from a symbolic and allegorical point of view I am capable of seeing ahead.*'

A nice detail: *Past Imperfect* was commissioned by the national newspaper *De Morgen* and was published at the very moment that the 'real' reports on the Dutroux affair were coming to a head.

Finally, there is also Walter van den Broeck who, again with direct reference to the Dutroux affair, published the novel *Lost in the Post* (Verdwaalde post, 1998). Van den Broeck comes across in this book as one who despairs of civilisation, who regards the mendacious language of politics, advertising and the media as responsible for the dislocation in society. He draws a contrast between them and a timeless love story. Just like Louis Paul Boon, Van den Broeck combines historical concerns with the urge to experiment with form.

Possibly the events of Belgium's recent history are too recent, too fresh, to give direct rise to good literature. The past is incomplete; the present still unprocessed. There is no novel that encapsulates, that 'captures' contemporary Belgium. As yet no-one has produced a proper socio-political analysis of the (post)modern *zeitgeist*. There is still too much curiosity and too little real understanding of politics and society, and as a result in most novels Belgium remains mere décor. Ironically, writers get closer to Belgium's past and present in those parts of their work that stay a reasonable distance from current events, or at least from the actual facts and personages of those events.

Furthermore, in the most recent Flemish literature there is a growing interest in and appreciation of a generation of young writers who distance themselves from current affairs, and therefore, it would seem, from any *engagement*: authors such as Peter Verhelst (*Tonguecat* (Tongkat) and *Swelling Fruit* (Zwellend fruit, 2000); see p. 197) and Erwin Mortier (*Marcel* (1999) and *My Other Skin* (Mijn tweede huid, 2000); see p. 284). The critic Frank Hellemans once labelled them '*the new aesthetes*'. But perhaps such labels and the need to distinguish between different sorts of writing are now too dated, rooted as they are in the literary-critical fault-line of the 1960s and 1970s: the fault-line between *engagement*, socially committed writing, and *belles-lettres*.

Verhelst himself denies, as does Ivo Michiels, the accusation that his work is 'uncommitted' and that it is 'art for art's sake': '*In "Tonguecat", among other things, I merged style and structure with the content. There is a duality in the work that is also clearly detectable in our time: that of fragmentation on the one hand and the urge towards greater unity on the other: two movements that are not only socially, politically and economically highly visible but which also have extremely far-reaching consequences.*'

Verhelst therefore also delights in saying the almost unsayable; he avoids the lies of actual reality (non-fiction) and, as an artist, searches for a Grand Narrative, which is best captured in fairy tales, in poetry. Like Boon, who 'retold' the old allegorical fable of Reynard the Fox, and thereby cast a clearer light on his own (Belgian) time than any non-fictional or explicitly committed book could have done. And are not Lanoye's Shakespearean historical plays also fairy tales?

Seismography, in the sense that Boon used the term, means more than the registering and 'translation' of events, the facts of true happenings. It is rather a question of capturing the spirit of the time, of trends and movements, of real social evolution. At the time they are happening such trends do not lend themselves to neatly rounded stories (*mimesis*); they belong rather to what lingers in the sphere of the still-unsayable. And that makes them all the more challenging to artists. It was no accident that the colour of the White March was white. Nor that it is also the colour of poetry. Precisely in that lies or can lie the power of artists.

Other paradigms please!

The Grand Narrative with '*extremely far-reaching consequences*' obviously takes us beyond events in Flanders or Belgium. Part of that narrative in the twenty-first century is the lightning-fast development of science. Together with globalisation, it has led to entirely new questions, new paradigms of humanity, environment, life and death. What is striking is the total absence of such 'modernity' from Flemish literature (and not only Flemish, as is apparent from a recent complaint by George Steiner).

In this too, Boon is the lonely exception in Flanders and the Netherlands. As an artist, he stood at the centre of the politics, economics and science of his age. Long before modern chaos theory, modern times vibrated through his prose. In the early 1950s Boon was already viewing the world through the eyes of later modern science. In English-language literature you find the same 'modernity' in the work of Jenny Diski (*Monkey's Uncle*) and Jeanette Winterson. In contemporary Flemish literature, on the other hand, one looks in vain for a writer who uses modern scientific insights to observe the course of the world and humanity.

So anyone wanting to learn about present-day Flanders and Belgium through its literature should read *To War* by Tom Lanoye. Or he should read the literary-journalistic book that became a best seller in 2000 in both the fiction and non-fiction categories: *The Breach* (De bres) by Chris de Stoop. It is about the polder village of Doel and its farming community, who are faced with extinction through the expansion of Antwerp's port and industry. An 'old' story for these modern times.

Or better still, one should read a good poem such as 'Sémira' by the young Flemish poet Peter Theunynck. It is 'about' a Nigerian asylum seeker who, while being repatriated from Belgium to her native land, dies when the policemen escorting her smother her with a cushion because she resists them. The poem is not just about that one girl; it is about Belgium and, by extension, Fortress Europe in the year 2000. It is about life and death at the end of the twentieth century. And at the same time it creates a bridge to life and death in earlier times. So much in so few words. It cannot be coincidence that this is poetry and not a novel. It cannot be anything else than *engagement*. It is art.

Sémira

Somewhere in this throwaway land
A track of dolomite on which
A girl is sitting, quite alone.
Below her arms, her lower body

A broken white. Too little
Time, too little linen to
Wrap her in.

In men doors slam
Shut, humanity drops away,
The ovens have been lit.

But does that touch her
Beauty? No. A swan
With wings shot full of lead remains
A swan, still floating after death.

FILIP ROGIERS
Translated by Chris Emery.

Marcel Broodthaers,
Thighbone of a Belgian.
1964-1965. Femur painted
black, red and yellow,
8 x 47 x 10 cm. Sylvio
Perlstein Collection,
Antwerp / © SABAM
Belgium 2001.

Extracts

Extract from *Rumours*
by Hugo Claus

In the early 1960s René Catrijsse, an army deserter in a colonial war in Black Africa, returns to the West Flemish village where he was born. With him comes the Sickness. His arrival marks the beginning of a series of mysterious incidents and rumours. 'We have to be careful with rumours. They so easily turn into truth, a kind of truth', says Father Lamantijn. In this excerpt he gives, without knowing it, his last sermon.

REV. FR.

Father Lamantijn stood in the late-eighteenth-century pulpit before his most faithful parishioners, some twenty empty seats and at the back a little troop of boy scouts, eight lumpish hairy youths. You could see the priest's breath coming out of his mouth.

And this is what he said: 'Dearly beloved, a country boy was walking along the road that led to his parents' farmstead. For two years he had seen neither his father nor his mother because he had been in prison for involuntary manslaughter. Beside him walked an invisible man, or perhaps it was not a man but a mysterious force which would once have been called an angel or a devil, and that force whispered to the young farm-boy: 'What in God's name will you do in your father's house? You're scum, there's no place for you in your father's house. Do us all a favour, go and hang yourself on yonder pear-tree'. – 'If you're ordering me to do that, then I'll do it,' said the youth and he threw a rope over a branch of the pear-tree, forgetting that killing oneself is one of the worst sins that can plague humanity, because you are throwing the gift God has given you, the most beautiful gift, the gift of life, back in His face. As if by a miracle, however, the boy suddenly thought of his mother. He saw her in front of him and she looked so sad that the boy immediately untied the rope and ran home. In the end he was running so fast that as he came to the farm he tripped and landed in the dungheap. His mother the farmer's wife, who was on her way to the well with her pitcher to fetch water, saw her son. And he saw her, and he was shocked for in those two calamitous years her hair and her face had turned white as snow. Heartrendingly he cries, 'Oh mother mine, what have I done to you in the reckless folly of my youth?'

'Don't say such things,' she stammers and she puts her old arms round his neck. All is forgotten and forgiven. 'Oh my boy, I'm so very happy you've found your way back here to our farm, for while you were away father died. He sees us from behind the clouds, and there is nothing he'd like better than for you to take the running of our property upon yourself. You mustn't go out into the dangerous world again, you can work here in our fields and make a good life for yourself in our village.'

This pastoral parable, dearly beloved, belongs to a time which is now, alas, behind us, and will never return.

And you there, at the back, you scouts, take that chewing-gum out of your mouths! For the new parable I am about to tell you is certainly meant for you in these new times. Listen. A farmer's son returned to his parents' place after two years in jail. No supernatural force, good or evil, accompanied him. He came into the farmhouse, saw his mother and said, 'Mother, I have a sickness whose nature cannot be spoken of in your presence, but it is deadly dangerous. But I am so happy that I shall still embrace you. Come into my arms, and you too, little sister, embrace and kiss me and you too grandmother, and you too, faithful farmdog who chases away strangers with your barking, and you, the youngest of our clan, my brother's child in your little crib.' For, dearly beloved, even into the sweet face of that most innocent child he blew the infected breath from his lungs. Two days later that farmstead was filled with the dead and the groans of the dying. Now the question is this: What should the mother do? Is the monster to be allowed to go on blowing his lethal breath over his fellow-men until the destruction spreads country-wide, world-wide, planet-wide? Or should one discreetly, as hygienically and efficiently as possible, destroy the source of the calamity, nip the evil in the bud? I will go further. Should not the mother herself, who in a sense brought this disaster on the world in the person of her son, should not she take the decision that hurls him into eternal darkness?

The question is, then, should one listen to Romans twelve, twenty-one: 'Be not overcome of evil, but overcome evil with good'? or should one resolve to make an end, a drastic, irrevocable, if need be cruel and inhuman end of him who has brought all this about?'

Turmoil erupted among the scouts. The other members of the congregation turned to stare at the young people. Their leader, who had a nasty case of acne, asked if he might say something.

'Go on,' said Fr Lamantijn, clutching the edge of the pulpit convulsively. The knuckles of both hands went white as snow.

The leader said, 'We think, as young people, and looking to the future, that that man must be put to death, after he has first confessed where the origin of that filthy sickness is to be found. It is not definite that it comes from the Third World.'

'That I leave to your sense of honour and your conscience,' said the priest. Whether he was feeling unwell, or he meant to descend from the pulpit and more democratically join his hearers down below and discuss predestination and free will with them there, or whether he got a sudden sharp cramp, at any event the

Reverend Father Lamantijn took a step back and slipped on the late-eighteenth-century steps which our Diana had waxed to a high polish and by sheer bad luck landed on a bluestone tomb-slab and did not get up again.

US

'That does it,' said Notary Albrecht. We murmured assent. We were in the Café Riviera when we heard what had happened from the excited scouts. The scouts were having a beer to recover. Their leader kept saying that it was a damned shame because the Reverend was about to have a thoroughgoing man-to-man discussion with him about the current position of the Church.

When the ambulance took off with the dead man, siren wailing, a group of women also came into the Café Riviera. So far as we could make out, for the women were all talking at once, the priest had been on top form. And it's true that he was a fine storyteller, our Reverend Father. In no time at all he could make a fable or a parable out of the smallest thing.

'Yes, well, that's so, but,' said Hedwige, Rombouts' wife, 'in among those parables like the one about the Prodigal Son, he did get across what he wanted to say.'

We don't much care for Hedwige Rombouts. Her two daughters, Julia and Alice, are all right, but their mother... She can't stand getting old, that's the trouble. But however much perfumed muck she plasters on her face, her age and especially her envious nature show through it, like cracks in a dried-up river bed. No, I wouldn't fancy lying under Hedwige Rombouts.

While we are playing darts we can hear her going on at the youngsters' spotty chief.

How is it possible for people to be so vicious, that's what they're talking about. 'It's very strange,' Hedwige Rombouts says, 'that someone who has never done anybody any harm should have to suffer like that. I'm thinking of Our Holy Father who died of the hiccups. And my young niece who's got fibroids.' The scout purses his lips and says that the existence of omnipresent evil makes it impossible to believe in an all-powerful god but that we should not therefore neglect to pursue what is good in us, that we have to fight evil even though there is nothing at all up there in the sky.

'Well,' says Hedwige Rombouts, 'you can start by fighting René Catrijsse.'

'Who's he?'

'The prodigal son our unfortunate priest was talking about. The one with some disease in him that can't be cured. The Father said it straight out, without mincing words. It's René Catrijsse that's the sickness.'

'And where is the guy?'

'In the woods. Or with his mother.'

Leipe Nietje, who can never quite keep up with the conversation, says, 'I don't trust God any more. He's clever and wise and I have the feeling that he's there to help us, but he never tells us when.'

That, more or less, is what we overheard in the Café Riviera, so named by our mayor and the establishment's owner when he had a sweetheart in Italy who lived by a river, that's right, by a *riviera*, that's river in Italian.

From *Rumours* (De geruchten). Amsterdam: De Bezige Bij, 1996, pp. 140-145.
Translated by Tanis Guest.

Extract from *The Breach*
by Chris de Stoop

Farmers against containers and birds

The polder would long remember that evening. About a dozen young farmers, the last generation, were gathered at the Driewieler. A select group that included the sons of the biggest farmers of the polder. Their fathers had themselves been young during the bitter demonstrations against the first wave of dispossession.

The desperation and bitterness of the sons was great. They felt they were losing control over their farms and their lives. Their acres produced twice as much grain, their cows twice as much milk, their beef herds twice as much meat as a generation ago – and yet they faced financial disaster. They craved new prospects. Again there was talk of emigration, to Eastern Europe. There was now a 'green' Minister of Agriculture, who had brought them the bleak message that there was no longer any future for their kind of agriculture. A flood of directives had come their way: less manure, fewer cattle, less pesticide, fewer antibiotics, fewer poultry batteries, fewer subsidies. More and more regulations, more control, more paperwork. But did anyone ever mention their right to exist? There were even some who talked of simply abolishing agriculture and importing all foodstuffs.

The little group that set off from the Driewieler was led by André, a young poultry farmer from Prosperpolder who on a previous occasion had forced the Prime Minister off the road. His debts ran into millions and now he faced losing much of his land. He prided himself on being one of the few 'free farmers' in the poultry sector and he'd refused to submit to the industry. But during the previous year he had lost a great deal of money on his chickens and his potatoes. And working hard in order to lose money is doubly hard. He had also invested a lot in making his farm environmentally friendly and he deeply resented the fact that he was still being branded an eco-criminal.

When André was with the other lads he often said that they should not take things lying down. That they should smash everything up. That if things got worse a terrorist group like the IRA would emerge on the polder. There was much extremist talk, born out of anger against the bureaucracy, the Farmers Union, the greens, against the whole of the society that had driven them into their isolation.

'They want to replace us with containers and birds. We've got to show them that we're still here', said André.

Enthroned on their heavy tractors, in their cockpits full of knobs and levers, they drove from the Driewieler to the container village where the engineers and contractors had set up their offices. There everything was silent and dim.
The farmer's sons rammed the barbed wire fence that surrounded the offices.
They crushed the big sign in front of the Deurganck dock into scrap.
They demolished all the traffic signs on the dikes.

With their tractors they battered the high voltage cabin that supplied the entire dock with electricity. The cables crackled and then the whole thing blew up. The explosion could easily have killed them all.

The lights went out in the Hooghuis, in the church, in the mill at Doel, in the whole village and in the surrounding polder.

One evening, Ossaart lay asleep in the road to the mill. He was snoring like a Turk. He lay with his head against a thorn bush. Everyone who saw him made a detour to avoid having to pass him.

But that evening the miller's lad came down that road on his way to the mill. His cart was heavily laden with rye and wheat, and the mill hand – a particularly strong fellow with knock-knees – was leading the horse on foot. As he approached Ossaart he noticed in the light of his lantern who it was. He called to him to get out of the way.

He got no reply. Then he shook Ossaart to and fro. But still there was no answer and Ossaart didn't move. Then the mill hand became impatient. He grabbed Ossaart by the neck and lower back and hurled him violently into the thorn hedge so that he howled like a stuck pig. Ossaart was bleeding from his nose and mouth and chose the wisest course of action. He took to his heels.

'Good' she says, as we drive towards the motorway. 'Resistance is a sign of self-respect.'

'A few days after the explosion there were raids and a whole lot of tractors were impounded.'

'And now what?'

'If the offenders are found guilty, they'll have to pay tens of millions', I say. 'It can only lead to the farmers becoming even more extreme.'

'Doel will be uninhabitable.'

'The village has been condemned twice; it'll just have to wait a bit before dying.'

God ... again all that scheming and time-wasting by the bureaucrats, the council, the harbour bosses. The official enquiry into living conditions concluded that the village was, after all, inhabitable. Nevertheless, it has now been definitely decided to issue a compulsory purchase order. After that, those wishing to do so may rent their own houses back for a number of years.

That is, until another container dock has to be dug. The dock on the hidden agenda. The dock in the insidious decision-making process.

The future would bring millions of containers. The whole world in containers. Containers with agricultural produce, genetically modified or not. Containers with refugees, dead or alive.

A 'permanent harbour policy' was promised, extending as far as the front gardens of Kieldrecht and Verrebroek. For after Doel, the other polder communities would also come under pressure.

For years, the people of Doel had quarrelled over the question of whether it was possible to live next to the Deurganck dock. Now suddenly a second dock loomed up out of nothing.

The Saeftinghe dock.

Slap on top of the village.

Ships would sail and eels would swim over the Hooghuis, just as I had heard tell as a child.

Once again the village saw red.

Old Albert got his wish and died just in time. His placards protesting against the 'prosperity' for which he had been forced out of his property long remained hanging in his window.

Jo, my neighbour opposite, requested an interview with the Commissioner for Compulsory Purchase. His wife invoked Brother Isidoor.

Brother Isidoor, who had been beatified, remained the patron saint of the young farmers until the young farmers were no more.

'And now all at once the dike warden is also dead,' I end my story. 'Ach, all those chocolate-box polders. In a few years' time who will even remember their names?'

That would make a good quiz, I think to myself on the way back to Antwerp.

Where was the Sint-Annahof?
Under the incinerator.
Where was the Lindenhof?
Under the power station.
Where was the Ketelhof?
Under Bayer's poison.

Where was the Geslecht?
Under the Deurganck dock.
Where was Sint-Antoniushoek?
Under the Doel dock.
Where the Blikken?
Under the Verrebroek dock.

Where is Remi Bogaert?
In the churchyard.
What about the Arenberg polder?
Under the sand.
What about the Hedwige polder?
Under water.
What about the Zaligem polder?

Or perhaps better still: material for surfers of the World Wide Web. For the government has proclaimed the new welfare state. The active welfare state. The polder model, actually. And now it's no longer a question of beef steaks, as in the previous welfare state, but computers.

Everybody's working.
Each one on the Web.

Search on: Countryside
Click on: Polderland
Doubleclick: Submerged Land
Save in memory: Zaligem

Delete Doel
Delete the polder
Delete the farmers

Close window

From *The Breach* (De bres). Amsterdam: De Bezige Bij, 2000, pp. 221-226.
Translated by Chris Emery.

'Auntie Yet'

and Humanity

The Internationalism of Henriette Roland Holst

Henriette Roland Holst-van der Schalk (1869-1952), poetess, writer and socialist, is one of the most revered women in the history of the Netherlands. Her contemporaries hailed her as '*our greatest poet*' and saw her as a prophetess; the proclaimer of a beautiful, pure and righteous future. The historian Johan Huizinga compared her work as a poet to that of Vondel and, following the publication of her anthology *Between Time and Eternity* (Tusschen tijd en eeuwigheid, 1934), predicted that people would learn Dutch in order to read her poetry. That prediction has not yet come true. Although she became a great international figure, Henriette Roland Holst's renown was due to her international political activism rather than her poetry.

The daughter of a wealthy notary, Roland Holst supported the Marxist labour movement from an early age and became one of its international leaders. Rosa Luxemburg, Karl Kautsky, Trotsky and Lenin were among her friends. Her most famous text is a translation into Dutch of the Internationale, the socialist anthem. Roland Holst's interests had always extended beyond the Netherlands. Her governess taught her to speak French fluently when she was a child and at 14 she went to a German boarding school near Arnhem, where lessons were also given in English and Italian. After leaving boarding school, she lived for some time with a family in Liège. In 1888 she wrote her first love poem in French to a young baritone at the Liège opera company: '*Et quand vous reviendrez, je ne serai plus là*'.

She met her husband, the painter Richard Roland Holst, in 1892 during Paul Verlaine's visit to the Netherlands. She was introduced to the French poet as the '*jeune poète hollandaise*'. Six months later she made her debut with six sonnets published in *De Nieuwe Gids*, the journal of the Men of the 'Eighties ('*Tachtigers*') that breathed new life into Dutch literature.

Discovering Marx

At the end of the nineteenth century, many Dutch artists turned to socialism under the influence of the British social reformer and artist William Morris, who perceived socialism as an improved version of medieval religious society. Henriette Roland Holst and her husband, a personal friend of Morris, were among them. They shared his belief that artistic renewal was impossible without social renewal in the socialist sense.

Towards the end of 1896, the poet Herman Gorter recommended Karl Marx's *Das Kapital* to Henriette. According to Gorter, the book was '*the key to understanding society*'. Gorter held that '*without that understanding it is impossible to write great poetry*'. Henriette was moved by Marx's conviction that the international working class would seize power and implement socialist methods of production. A year later, together with her husband and Gorter, she joined the Social Democratic Labour Party (SDAP; Sociaal Democratische Arbeiders Partij) in the Netherlands, which had been founded in 1894. They quickly became the party's leading propagandists. Henriette and Gorter became editors of the theoretical journal *De Nieuwe Tijd*. She practised Marxist literary criticism and spoke at meetings. In 1900 Henriette attended the International Socialist Congress in Paris. This was the fifth congress of the Second International (successor to the First International in which Marx played a prominent role). Here she met leading international social democrats such as Karl Kautsky, Clara Zetkin, Rosa Luxemburg and Jean Jaurès. She spent many days attending meetings with international figures, and enjoyed the atmosphere of passionate intellectual debate.

In addition to poetry and political propaganda, Henriette published influential theoretical works during this period, including the much-praised *Capital and Labour in the Netherlands* (Kapitaal en Arbeid in Nederland, 1902). At Kautsky's request she wrote – in German – *General Strike and Social Democracy* (Generalstreik und Sozialdemokratie, 1905), a book that was translated into many languages. So too were the articles she wrote for the influential German journal *Die Neue Zeit*. Influenced by her international circle of Marxist friends, she took a stand against reformism and revisionism

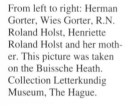

From left to right: Herman Gorter, Wies Gorter, R.N. Roland Holst, Henriette Roland Holst and her mother. This picture was taken on the Buissche Heath. Collection Letterkundig Museum, The Hague.

in social democracy. This led to dramatic conflicts of principle that were serious enough to result in a schism within the SDAP in 1909. The Marxist
wing split from the party and called itself the SDP (Social Democratic Party).
Initially Henriette remained a member of the SDAP, but found herself in a
somewhat isolated position. Despite the support she received from Kautsky,
she suffered a nervous breakdown and left the SDAP in 1912. The anguish
she felt as a result of her isolation and her inability to make a political choice
found its expression in the anthology *The Woman in the Wood* (De vrouw
in het woud, 1912), the drama *Thomas More* (1912) and a biography of
Jacques Rousseau.

Henriette did not become politically active again until the beginning of
the First World War. Strongly influenced by the ideas of Rosa Luxemburg,
she founded the Revolutionary Socialist Party (RSV; Revolutionair Socialis-
tisch Verbond), an organisation of radical Marxists from within and outside
existing parties. She also founded the journal *De Internationale*. In 1915 she
was the only Dutch delegate to attend the Zimmerwald Conference, a secret
international gathering of radical socialists – including Lenin and Trotsky –
held in Switzerland. At the Zimmerwald Conference the foundations were
laid for the Third International, or Comintern. Roland Holst's meeting with
Trotsky inspired a devotion that bordered on love.

In 1916 Henriette and her Revolutionary Socialist Party joined the SDP –
which Gorter had joined when it was founded. This move was instigated by
Lenin, who gave Henriette the leadership of the international Marxist publication *Vorbote*. In the same year, the SDP organ *De Tribune* became a daily newspaper. Roland Holst became one of its chief editors and helped to finance the publication.

Henriette Roland Holst in
Stuttgart, 1907. She was
a speaker at a conference
there, during which she met
Trotsky. Collection
Letterkundig Museum,
The Hague.

'The Revolutionary Hangover', a cartoon by Joh. Braakensiek in *De Amsterdammer* of 23 November 1918. Henriette Roland Holst is on the right.

At the barricades

From 1917 to 1927, Henriette Roland Holst was a communist. After the Russian Revolution in 1917 the SDP joined the Comintern and called itself the Dutch Communist Party (CPH; Communistische Partij Holland, later CPN). During the unsuccessful Dutch 'revolution' of November 1918 Roland Holst led workers and soldiers in a demonstration in Amsterdam – an action that she almost paid for with her life. Months later, Rosa Luxemburg and Karl Liebknecht were murdered in Berlin during the Spartacus Revolt. Although Roland Holst began to criticise Marxism during the war, her critical powers were not yet equal to those of Luxemburg, who, in a visionary article published shortly before her death, warned against Lenin's Marxist dictatorship. Against her husband's will, Henriette travelled to Russia illegally in 1921 to attend the third Comintern congress. But she returned disillusioned and incensed at the bloody suppression of the Kronstadt Rebellion, the sailors' uprising she had been informed about by Aleksandra Kollontaj, a minister in Lenin's first government. Yet she remained loyal to Moscow, subjecting herself to communist discipline and, initially, defending the terror that was being perpetrated in the name of revolution.

During the 1920s Roland Holst several times came into conflict with the CPH leadership. In numerous publications, of which her book *Communism and Morals* (Communisme en moraal, 1925) is the best known, her criticism of Marxism grew increasingly radical. Like her Belgian sympathiser Hendrik de Man, she championed a new form of socialism, '*Gesinnungs-socialisme*', that was based on a change in mentality brought about through education and training. Henriette's political texts and poetry reflect her spiritual development during the 1920s. Her contacts with religious socialists eased her break with communism. She left the CPH following Stalin's campaign against Trotsky, who was ejected from the Communist Party of the Soviet Union (CPSU) at the end of 1927. Roland Holst campaigned in vain for Trotsky for many years: first against his exile, and later for political asylum in the Netherlands. Other victims of political terror world-wide, such as the Indonesian nationalists, could also count on her support. She was one of the first human rights activists in the Netherlands, and established numerous protest and support committees.

At the end of the 1920s Roland Holst joined the religious socialists. This brought her into close contact with Leonhard Ragaz, the Swiss theorist of religious socialism, and he became a close friend. In the years that followed she wrote biographies of international figures such as Tolstoy, Rosa Luxemburg, the Flemish poet and priest Guido Gezelle, and Gustav Landauer (one of the founders of the German Socialist Party). She also continued to publish poetry and wrote numerous mystery plays at the request of Christian-Socialist youth and student organisations.

Even before Hitler came to power in 1933, Roland Holst opposed fascism and National Socialism. She championed the cause of Indonesian independence and, on the occasion of Princess Juliana's wedding to Prince Bernhard in 1937, she wrote a letter to Juliana requesting amnesty for imprisoned Indonesian nationalists such as Sukarno, Hatta and Shahrir. During the German occupation she worked for the resistance – as far as her advanced age would allow. She refused to join the Chamber of Culture and her calls for support for the Jews led to the founding of the illegal newspaper *De Vonk*, to which she contributed from early 1941. She took Jews into hiding at her country house in Brabant and wrote resistance poetry under the pseudonym '*In Liefde Bloeiende*' ('Blossoming in Love'). She also worked on biographies of international figures such as Victor Hugo (not published), Gandhi and Romain Rolland.

Conscience of the nation

After the war Roland Holst, widowed since 1938, settled in Amsterdam.

Henriette Roland Holst and Mohammed Hatta (in the middle of the second row) at a Youth Peace Action conference, Haarlem, 21 April 1929. Collection Letterkundig Museum, The Hague.

Known affectionately as '*Tante Jet*' ('Auntie Yet') she had become a living legend; the conscience of a nation. She remained politically active up to her death. In the radical-socialist publication *De Vlam* she opposed the death penalty for war criminals and wartime collaborators. She also supported Indonesian independence, which came about in 1949. Vice President Hatta of Indonesia honoured her with a visit to show his gratitude for her work.

On her death in 1952, Henriette Roland Holst was hailed as the greatest poet in the Netherlands. Yet her poems, contrary to prevailing opinion at the time, have not become classic works. The poetry which won her so much acclaim as a socialist, communist and later a religious socialist, is largely characterised by her presumption to speak for 'humanity', which found its expression in high-flown language. Yet her oeuvre is strewn with works that express doubt and uncertainty, in stark contrast to the certainty she desired. These verses, which she wrote without the 'prophet's cloak' about her shoulders, still move those that read them today.

The question is whether Roland Holst's urge to prophesy destroyed her as a poet, as her mentor, the poet Albert Verwey, believed. He considered her aspirations a danger to her work. In the long term he was proved right: her tendency to use her poetry as a vehicle for her political views was detrimental to her work. At the same time, her contemporaries were so inspired by her ambition to change the world – literally to re-create it – that they proclaimed her a national poet.

Henriette Roland Holst monument in Katwijk. Photo by Jan Stegeman.

From a young age, Roland Holst needed an all-embracing ideal to work towards and live for. Without such an ideal, which soon came to be embodied in international socialism, she could not develop as a poet. Conversely, her social influence and authority are inextricably linked to her inspired and prophetic work as a poet. For Roland Holst, poetry was the servant of her ideals, to which she devoted herself in countless other ways too. She was acclaimed as a poet because, in her work, she searched for answers to man's existential questions – and this was precisely what was expected of artists at that time. Her search for existential meaning lead her to explore various all-encompassing ideals, which, although formulated in different ways, were essentially the same: brotherly love, justice, community spirit, becoming completely absorbed into a greater whole and, finally, subjection to something that she could hardly define but eventually came to call God. Although she was apparently attracted by dogma, Roland Holst's views changed constantly. This made her unpredictable as a politician, but as a poet the doubts she so openly experienced were the driving force behind her work. Her idealism and spirit of sacrifice appealed not only to her political sympathisers – an ever-changing group – but also to a much broader audience.

A believer

But what Verwey deplored in Roland Holst's poetry – aspiration – was also true of her political life. She proudly took it upon herself to change society, striving at the same time to keep her hands clean and her conscience clear. In practice this problem – depicted in her poetry as the conflict between 'dream and deed' – amounted to the impossibility of combining purity and pragmatism. Her constant attempts to resolve that conflict made her into an eternal dissident, much maligned by opportunistic party supporters and venerated by idealists seeking to perform conscientious and uncompromising acts. Eventually she found her spiritual home among the religious socialists. The combination of ethics and socialism in their movement appealed to her more than its religious aspects.

Henriette Roland Holst came to religion late in life. Precisely how and when, she herself could not say, although she acknowledged that it was largely a reaction to her disillusionment with communism. Her poetry had always tended towards the religious; her early work was clearly inspired by mysticism. It is not difficult to prove that, in her politics too, Henriette Roland Holst had always been a believer. She experienced socialism and communism as religions. Her political passion, particularly in her communist period, stemmed from the desire to be absorbed into a greater whole and bear the burden of human suffering, so that she herself could find redemption. Roland Holst was aware of her duality, yet she tried to perceive her life as an entity. She drew a circuitous comparison between herself and Tolstoy in this respect. In her biography of Tolstoy, she wrote that he had undergone a terrible struggle '*to find harmony in his inner world*'. The unity in his life, she wrote, came from the fact that he '*pursued the goal of attaining that which, at a given moment, he perceived as being his highest self, and subjecting all things to that goal*'. Roland Holst was largely successful in attaining self-realisation. As she grew older, the significance attributed to her work became more and more indistinguishable from her own ideal: prophetess, international pioneer, inspiring example and mythical figure.

The voice of the individual conscience

Roland Holst's significance derives not only from the image that she and her followers created, but also from the way in which she struggled to overcome her inner conflict. As a writer and poet she publicly testified to her crises of conscience, her changing beliefs, the splits with former political sympathisers, and the ethical questions with which she struggled. She thus came to personify the political and moral dilemmas of the twentieth century. Her *engagement* in the history of that period is the very source of her poetic art. She was involved in all the important events and developments of her time, and she made choices she regretted and mistakes that she acknowledged. That experience enabled her to develop independent beliefs that still command respect today. As a communist she condemned Stalin's dictatorship early on. In the 1920s and 1930s she warned against the dangers of fascism and National Socialism. She was one of the first human rights activists. During the German occupation, while illegal words flowed from her pen, she called upon her compatriots not to lapse into hatred and revenge. In old age her hatred of colonialism led her to support the Indonesian republic. Although she always strove to speak for a party or a majority, for the proletariat or humanity, the voice that was ultimately heard was that of the individual conscience.

ELSBETH ETTY
Translated by Yvette Mead.

A Poem
by Henriette Roland Holst

On the comforting certainty I found

People are mired in uncertainty,
the face of a god has bleached the time white,
now I come to comfort them with songs
of what never changes and in nothing falls short.
I can be encouragement to the fearful,
the clear voice always reasonable and calm,
because my heart that knows no frantic clinging
to clouds, sees what through clouds does break.

I was born with a nature which instinctively
goes straight to the heart of every matter
but much there was that held me from my work.
Growing, I put all of that aside:
the light spread, every darkness split asunder,
and I saw love as the one law of life.

From *An Anthology of Poems by Henriette Roland Holst-
Van der Schalk* (Bloemlezing van gedichten van Henriette
Roland Holst-Van der Schalk). Rotterdam: W.L. & J. Brusse, 1951.
Translated by Tanis Guest.

Over rustigende vastheid die ik vond

De mensen zijn in getwijfel gevangen,
't gezicht van een god heeft de tijd gebleekt,
nu kom ik ze vertroosten met gezangen
van wat nooit wisselt en in niets ontbreekt.
Ik kan bemoediging zijn voor de bangen,
de klare stem die altijd rustig spreekt,
omdat mijn hart dat geen angstvallig hangen
aan wolken kent, ziet wat door wolken breekt.

Ik werd geboren met een aard die sterk
van zelf gaat naar de kern van alle zaken
maar veel stond tussen mij in en mijn werk.
Groeiend, heb ik dat op zij gezet:
het werd al lichter, alle duisters braken
en ik zag liefde als de levenswet.

Dick Broos, *Portrait of
Henriette Roland Holst*.
1944. Crayon, 76 x 43 cm.
Collection Letterkundig
Museum, The Hague.

essalina

or Salomé?

The Life and Times of Mata Hari,

International Woman of Mystery

Olga Pulloffski, the beautiful spy!
The gay continental rascallion!
Some say she's Russian and some say she's French
But her accent is Gin and Italian.
Shame on you! Shame on you! Oh fie fie!
Olga Pulloffski you beautiful spy!

R.P. Weston & Bert Lee (1935)

In October 1964 the Frisian poet Douwe Tamminga held a whip-around at that year's Frisian Bookweek Ball as part of a personal campaign to raise a statue in Leeuwarden to Margaretha Geertruida Zelle, Friesland's most famous woman. But the project foundered on the municipal powers that were. The trouble, Tamminga was informed politely, was not that Ms Zelle fell short on fame, but that as long as her international press image remained *'both positive and negative in equal measure'*, such a mark of recognition from her native city would not be opportune.

This reticence in official quarters was understandable, for Mata Hari, to give Margaretha Zelle her more familiar stage name, then as now remains an icon of controversy. As Raphael Gould, the Director of the American Library Service, put it in 1954, Mata Hari was so notorious throughout the world that her name was synonymous with 'spy'. So much so, in fact, that after 1919 the CIA used to refer to certain female agents by the code-name 'Mata Hari'.

Today, in 2001, an Internet search for Mata Hari brings up some unexpected results, of which a good number lead to the webtool Mata Mari Pro V2.01: *'If you need information for research, job, fun or profit, let Mata Hari be your personal agent to unlock the Web's secrets.'* Next we hit a site selling fine French lingerie, including a Mata Hari outfit *'ideal for secret...missions'*, as exemplified by a kneeling model whose flimsy attire is clearly designed to divert attention from the pistol clutched behind her back. On yet another site we come across news about a piece of cinetrash by Curtis Har-

A portrait of Margaretha Zelle by Isaac Israëls. Kröller-Müller Museum, Otterlo.

Margaretha Geertruida Zelle and Rudolph 'John' MacLeod in April 1897, just before they set sail for the Netherlands Indies. Mata Hari Collection, Fries Museum, Leeuwarden.

rington, *Mata Hari* (1985), with Sylvia 'Emmanuelle' Kristel in the protagonist's role. No great hit at the time, the film is now available on video and is promoted in terms such as '*Mata Hari weaves her spell between enemy camps and between satin sheets leaving behind her broken hearts...and lifeless bodies*'. In a similar vein we find the otherwise highly respectable A&E Biography Series commending the documentary *Mata Hari, The Seductive Spy* for its evocation of '*mystery, seduction, betrayal and duplicity*', '*deadly pillow talk*', and '*the beauty who captivated a continent*'.

Notorious, deceitful, and a voluptuary...not on the face of it precisely the kind of reputation that merits a statue. But for all that it has stood in pride of place in Leeuwarden since 1978.

'A single orchid amidst a thousand dandelions'

Margaretha was born in Leeuwarden on 7 August 1876 to Antje van der Meulen and Adam Zelle, a well-to-do dealer in hats and caps. A cherished firstborn, nothing was too good for her. She was always dressed in the prettiest of clothes, and for her sixth birthday was given a miniature goat-cart in which she created quite a stir in town. As she grew up her tall, slender frame, challenging eyes, and melodious voice set her apart from her fellows. Her general bearing made most of the other girls think her brazen, yet at least one classmate betrayed a secret admiration with her inscription '*a single orchid amidst a thousand dandelions*' in Margaretha's autograph album.

Adam Zelle was a vain and ambitious man, but a series of misfortunes on the stock exchange eventually bankrupted him. Rather than attempt to re-build his business, he ran out on his family and moved to Amsterdam. In 1890 the couple were formally separated, and Antje van der Meulen died shortly after. Margaretha was placed with an uncle, who sent her off to Leiden to be trained as a kindergarten teacher. This, however, was put paid to after she was caught reclining half-naked in the lap of the headmaster, a certain Wijnbrandus Haanstra. Next she moved to another uncle in The Hague where, in 1894, she came across this interesting announcement in *Het Nieuws van de Dag*: '*Officer on leave from the Indies seeks amiable young lady with a view to marriage*'. A few months later 38 year-old Rudolph 'John' MacLeod and Margaretha had their first meeting at the Rijksmuseum in Amsterdam. Six days later they were affianced. MacLeod was much taken with the youthful beauty, while she, for her part, was not in-sensible to the somewhat crude admiration she evoked. In one of her letters she writes: '*Do I like being naughty? you ask. Well, Johnnie dear, ten times over rather than once. How fortunate that we both have the same fiery na-ture.*' After an engagement of barely four months their marriage was solem-nised in the town hall of Amsterdam.

But it did not take long for the rot to set into the pair's initially passion-ate but never balanced relationship. In 1897 they had gone out to the Dutch Indies with their son Norman John. MacLeod was promoted to Major and posted to Malang; a daughter, Louise Jeanne, followed in 1898. Meanwhile tension between the two was mounting. Malang was a social centre where Margaretha could live out her yearnings for glamour in an endless round of balls and theatre-going. MacLeod resented his wife's expensive shopping habits and flirtatiousness, and frequented local prostitutes. When their son died in 1899 under suspicious circumstances – poisoned, rumour had it, by an Indonesian in revenge for some brutality of MacLeod's – there was a brief rapprochement. But Margaretha could not reconcile herself with her husband's stinginess, brutishness, alcoholism, and infidelity. As for him, he could not stand her free-spiritedness, and charged her with being a bad mother. Writing to his sister he calls her a '*stinking bitch*', a '*leech*', and mentions that '*I can't help laughing when I think of her remarrying one day, and how this fellow, once it's too late, will just like me discover that he's been plunged from heaven into hell.*'

In October 1900 John retired from the army and took his family to Sindanglaja, a quiet backwater. To the life-loving Margaretha it was un-thinkable that she should sit out her youth in such a hole of a place. After two years of persistent arguing she won the day and in March 1902 they re-turned to Amsterdam to live. However, the marriage had deteriorated be-yond all salvage, and at the end of August of the same year they were di-vorced. John moved away, taking their daughter with him. He was never to pay a penny in alimony. Margaretha, left with no means whatsoever, took off for Paris to seek her fortune.

The Eastern high priestess of the Belle Epoque

Margaretha opted for the French capital because '*all divorced women look for refuge in Paris*'. Paris promised a world of possibilities after nine years of a stifling marriage. Initially the new life was disappointingly hard. She tried to establish herself as an artists' model, but when this failed was forced to return to the Netherlands. In 1904 she tried again, and this time struck lucky, managing to join the Molier Circus as an 'amazon'. On Monsieur Molier's advice she now turned her energies to dance. Although her expertise was limited to the basic ballroom repertory, during her years in the Dutch Indies she had been exposed to traditional court and temple dance. Using this as a model she created an act of her own. At the beginning of 1905 she made her debut as an Eastern dancer at the *salon* of Madame Kiréevsky, a singer whose charity entertainment events were frequented by Parisian high society. Present that evening was Emile Guimet, industrialist, art collector and founder of the great Musée des Arts Orientales in the Place d'Iéna, who immediately determined to treat his friends to a special display of 'genuine' Eastern dance at the Museum. 'Lady MacLeod', as she called herself, agreed, and was invited to array herself for the occasion from the Museum's costumes and jewellery collections. Guimet also suggested she pick herself an stage name more in harmony with her exotic art.

Mata Hari, Paris, 1905. Mata Hari Collection, Fries Museum, Leeuwarden.

Mata Hari as an icon of the Orient, Paris, 1905. Mata Hari Collection, Fries Museum, Leeuwarden.

The result was Mata Hari, Malay for 'Eye of the Day', in a sheer sarong and a jewel-encrusted brassiere, flanked by a quartet of black-garbed female dancers, performing the Dance of the Veil for which she became famous. She followed this with a tribute to Shiva, at the climax of which she subsided, near-naked, in ecstasy before a statue of the god. The critics went wild with joy. *La Presse*, on 18 October 1905, spoke of her as a '*sister to the nymphs*', who from the burning earth of Java itself had drawn an unbelievable suppleness of body and magical dramatic power, together with a strength of upper torso for which she was indebted to her native Netherlands. *Le Journal*, one of the most influential morning papers, thought her

'Lady MacLeod' at the 'Steeple Militaire' in Paris, November 1911. Mata Hari Collection, Fries Museum, Leeuwarden.

the personification of the poetic, mystic and opulent charm of the Indies. Margaretha herself did not fail to add fuel to the fire by adopting a persona in keeping. She was, she put about, in reality a mixed-blood temple dancer from India, though she sometimes also claimed to have acquired her art in Java. Incoherent though her personal mythology was, this did not matter to her admirers, for whom she embodied – and very literally so – every dream image of the hidden, untainted sensuality of the East. Highly erotic, her act was also finely attuned to the reigning French intellectual elite's obsession with the Oriental *femme fatale* as portrayed by writers and artists ranging from Swinburne to Baudelaire, Huysmans, and Moreau.

Mata Hari was now a fixture on the Paris cultural agenda. As the Belle Epoque's acknowledged high priestess of the mysterious East she made thousands of francs per performance. Soon she was ready for a wider audience. Under the auspices of the seasoned impresario Gabriel Astruc, she played the famous Olympia Theatre as the launch-pad to a tour of Europe's most important theatres. She appeared in the Madrid Kurzaal, glittered on the Monte Carlo Opera stage in Jules Massenet's *Le Roi de Lahore*, and showed off her arts at the Wiener Secession before an exclusive audience of artists that included Gustav Klimt. The highpoint of her career came early in 1911, when she appeared at la Scala in Milan to perform the ballet interlude 'The Princess and the Magic Flower' in Gluck's opera *Aramide*. Shortly after, la Scala invited her back as 'Black Venus' in Romualdo Morenco's *Bacchus and Cambrinus*.

'Serious' artistic recognition mattered greatly to Mata Hari. The more mortifying, thus, when French writer Colette bitchily observed in print: '*She hardly danced... confining herself to progressively disrobing and swaying that long swarthy body of hers, slender and proud.*' Close to the bone, no doubt, for Mata Hari herself knew only too well to what she owed her success. In an interview she gallantly admitted as much: '*With every veil I shed my success increased. On the pretext of finding my dancing highly artistic and expressive, that is praising my art, it was nudity they really came to see (...) I play on sensuality (...) But the artistic gloss with which I imbue everything I do preserves me from vulgarity*'. Nor, for the record, did Mata Hari ever go the full monty, for the trademark metal bustier always remained firmly in place. For this, too, she concocted a good story, namely that her erstwhile spouse had in a fit of rage bitten off her left nipple. However in the *Souvenirs d'un Médicin* by Dr Léon Bizard, who more than once had occasion to examine her thoroughly, we read that her breasts were perfectly intact, though extremely small and with unattractively large, colourless nipples, which she had no interest in displaying.

Margaretha Zelle as 'La Habanera', Paris, 1913. Mata Hari Collection, Fries Museum, Leeuwarden.

Margaretha Zelle, right after her very last performance in the Netherlands, March 1915. Mata Hari Collection, Fries Museum, Leeuwarden.

When in 1912 Mata Hari lamentably failed an audition for Diaghilev's Ballets Russes, she did her best to boost her sense of self-respect and professional integrity by taking ballet lessons, but she never really developed into more than a moderately gifted dancer. When eventually she found herself seriously challenged by other, often more talented, 'Eastern' dancers such as Maud Allen and Ruth St. Denis, and besides began to feel the competitive threat of dozens of less artistically-concerned nude dancers on the Paris circuit, her riposte, published in an interview with the British magazine *The Era*, was that the performances of ladies of this ilk were anything but accurate or aesthetically justifiable. In the same breath she also asserted her 'birthright': by dint of having herself been born and bred in Java and having absorbed the deeper significance of this kind of dance in her earliest youth, she was in a position to know that none but the chosen few who were born and raised there, in the heart of the tropics, were able to perform these dances properly.

Partly on account of this mounting competition, but also because interest in orientalism was on the wane, Mata Hari saw her market value decline. Characteristically, her response was to reinvent herself afresh. Thus, in 1907, she travelled to Egypt to look for inspiration in the traditional dance

Margaretha Zelle as a prisoner, photographed the day after her arrest in 1917. Mata Hari Collection, Fries Museum, Leeuwarden.

Margaretha Zelle in the uniform of Lt Hallaure, one of her many lovers. This picture was taken in Normandy during World War I. Mata Hari Collection, Fries Museum, Leeuwarden.

of the Nile villages. In 1912, before a select, invited audience in the garden of her home in Neuilly, she staged a private performance accompanied by the 'Royal Hindu Musicians' led by the revered musician Inayat Khan, who had recently set up the Sufi movement in the West – a collaboration which considerably enhanced the credibility of her 'Indian' dances. A year later she was engaged to open the Folies Bergère summer season in the role of a Spanish dancer, La Habanera. But in spite of her multiple attempts to reinvent and diversify her image, Mata Hari was never to find a more successful act than the Shiva Dances.

A grande horizontale

Summer 1914 found Mata Hari ensconced in Berlin with her latest lover, Alfred Kiepert, a wealthy landowner and lieutenant in the 11th Regiment of Westphalian Hussars. She had been formally divorced from 'Johnnie'

MacLeod in 1906 and had since then conducted her artistic career in tandem with a highly public private life. As a *grande horizontale* she had had liaisons with a string of prominent men, while preserving her independence. Most of her lovers were wealthy, married, and undemanding. As the public's interest in her as a performer declined these lovers became increasingly important to the maintenance of her standard of living.

This time, though, it was more than the enjoyment of Kiepert's company and purse that had brought her to Berlin. From September onwards she was booked to appear at the Metropol Theatre in the opera *Der Millionendieb*, which promised to open up a new artistic lease of life for her. All this fizzled out before her eyes after 28 June 1914, when the assassination in Sarajevo of Archduke Franz Ferdinand by the Serbian nationalist Gavrilo Prinzip set in motion the chain of events leading to the outbreak of the First World War. Mata Hari had to leave Germany pell-mell, briefly noting in her still-extant scrapbook: '*la guerre... partie de Berlin... théâtre fermé.*'

Her destination was the neutral Netherlands where, arriving without a penny in her pocket, she briefly reverted to being Margaretha Zelle. Soon, however, she tracked down Baron Eduard Willem van der Capellen, a sometime lover, with whom she proceeded to take The Hague society by storm. She even trod the boards for the first time in her native country, but after the second night's performance at the Municipal Theatre of Arnhem her compatriots lost interest. Meanwhile the local paper published an interview with MacLeod, who when queried as to his possible presence at his ex-wife's show had in characteristically coarse vein replied: '*I've seen her from every angle, and that's more than enough for me.*'

Margaretha for her part had had it with the Netherlands. She felt gradually strangled in the close-knit, petit bourgeois atmosphere of The Hague and determined to make her way back to Paris by way of England and the crossing from Dover to Dieppe. This decision turned out to be a fatal one. Mata Hari was never again to dance, nor even to live out the Great War.

A sinister Salomé

On 13 February 1917, almost two years to the day since her departure from The Hague in quest of fresh adventure, five officers of the Paris police inspectorate entered Room 131 of the Elysée Palace Hôtel where Maya Hari was then staying. In command was Commissioner André Priolet, who read out aloud to her the following notice of arrest: '*Female, Zelle, Margaretha, also known as Mata Hari, residing in the Palace Hôtel, religion Protestant, an alien national, born in the Netherlands on 7 August 1876, height 1.75 m, and able to both write and read is hereby charged with espionage and attempted collaboration with and the supply of information to the enemy with a view to aiding the latter in his activities.*' She was forthwith conducted to the office of Captain Pierre Bouchardon, where over the succeeding four months and more she was to be questioned on fourteen separate occasions. Eduard Clunet, her legal adviser, was present at no more than two of these sessions. Except for these interrogation sessions she was throughout this period unremittingly confined to a filthy cell in Saint-Lazare prison.

To this day Mata Hari's role as a spy remains a subject of controversy.

Early in 1999 MI5, the British Secret Service, released archive material from which it appears that there was scant evidence of guilt. This, though, was but the umpteenth turn in a did-she-or-didn't-she see-saw debate that has dragged on for decades. In 1964 Sam Wagenaar published the Mata Hari biography *par excellence*, which he entitled *The Murder of Mata Hari* and in which he completely exculpates her from espionage for Germany. But later, after having access to a secret German file of 1940, Wagenaar began to question his earlier view, amended his book and republished it in 1976 as *Mata Hari. Not Quite so Guiltless*.

Exactly what happened before and during the trial is not entirely clear. Nor is it likely that the official French documents relating to the case, which are due for release in 2017, will provide a conclusive answer. Gerk Koopmans, head of the Resistance Museum and curator of the Mata Hari Collection of the Fries Museum in Leeuwarden, probably hit the nail on the head when he suggested that Margaretha Zelle had out of sheer naivety manoeuvred herself into a hornets' nest; she did not realise how suspicious her comings and goings might look, or indeed that a bird of passage like herself was bound to arouse intelligence interest.

Between March 1915 and late 1916 Margaretha had travelled extensively through the war zone. A sophisticated cosmopolitan at a time when nationalism was the order of the day, this provoked suspicion. On top of that she simply adored men in uniform, and was never too picky about what nationality went with whoever parked his boots beside her bed. During her interrogations and trial she defended this proclivity in these words: '*In my eyes officers are a race apart (...). I never paid any attention to whether they were Germans, Italians, or French.*' To this she added that she never discussed the war with them, and that they were invariably '*very happy*' when they departed her bedroom.

At this time Margaretha was also chronically short of cash. Kiepert had given her considerable sums, and in 1916 she had also accepted money from Karl Cramer, the German consul in Amsterdam. She admitted that Cramer wanted her to spy for him and that she had acceded to his proposal for the sake of the pay. But this she had regarded as a kind of compensation for the seizure of her personal belongings after her precipitate departure from Berlin at the outbreak of the war. At no time, however, had she provided him with any of the information requested. What she did concede was that she had passed on information to Arnold von Kalle, the German naval attaché in Madrid, but only to win his confidence so that she would be able to spy for her beloved France. For shortly before she had by chance made the acquaintance of Captain Georges Ladoux, the head of French counter-espionage, who had recognised the ideal agent in this *femme galante* with her extensive international contacts and exceptional mobility. He had promised her a million francs for her co-operation. Margaretha accepted, but waited in vain for further instructions. But soon after, when Scotland Yard took her off the ss Hollandia in Falmouth harbour for questioning at Cannon Row and she referred them to him, Ladoux sent them a telegram denying that Margaretha was in his employ. The British had suspected her of being Clara Benedix, a notorious German spy, but they quickly realised their mistake and returned this fish to the water. Subsequently, in Madrid, she had on her own initiative set about seducing and trying to get information from Von

Kalle, hoping in this way to obtain money from Ladoux. Money that she needed to marry Vladimir de Massloff, a young Russian officer with whom she had fallen passionately in love in Paris.

After Margaretha's arrest Ladoux claimed that he had always known her to be a double agent and that his proposal had been intended as a trap. He also produced a number of German telegrams which referred to an agent known as H21. The movements of this agent displayed striking similarities with the peregrinations of Mata Hari. While Bouchardon avidly seized on this point as evidence for the prosecution, everyone conveniently ignored the fact that the Germans had transmitted these messages in a code which they well knew the French had cracked.

Romance galore: Ramon Navarro and Greta Garbo in *Mata Hari* (1932). Photo Metro Goldwyn Mayer.

What above all finished off poor Margaretha was her self-constructed image. In the course of her interrogations she was continually making conflicting statements because she herself could scarcely distinguish any more between fact and fiction, fantasy and reality. Worse still, her interrogator also increasingly came to believe in her myth of the fatal, exotic female. Even on their first encounter he had perceived her as a '*born spy*', and he thereafter blithely continued to let himself be guided by prejudice: '*I saw before me a tall woman with thick lips, a swarthy skin, and artificial pearls in her ears. She had something of the savage about her*'. In his memoirs he recollects the accused as a once celebrated dancer who could no longer rely on her physical charms and was hence obliged to look for an alternative source of income: she had '*a lumpy nose, cleft chin, thick lips like a Negro's, enormously large teeth, dyed hair, and the corners of her mouth reached to her ears.*'

Through her performances she had redefined the accepted limits of sensuality, and trampled down the conventional contemporary perceptions of femininity. She had resolutely broken with the image of woman as a passive, nurturing mother figure, and for this she was now to do penance. What had in the Belle Epoque been seen as the exciting amorous adventures of a public idol were now magically transformed into the immoral excesses of a degenerate foreigner, a tawdry *femme internationale*. 1917 was a disaster year for the French, with major defeats, countless instances of mutiny and desertion, and spy phobia of hysterical proportions. There was an urgent need to clear the air and restore order and authority. Mata Hari was a public sore to be excised from French society.

The trial in July 1917 was conducted before a closed court and lasted barely two days. The public prosecutor, Lieutenant André Mornet, gave the 'spy' short shrift, designating her '*un redoubtable adversaire de la France*', a Messalina with the deaths of thousands of French soldiers on her conscience. Sentence was pronounced after ten minutes of deliberation. Margaretha Geertruida Zelle was found guilty on eight counts and sentenced to death for conspiracy and espionage. All legal costs were moreover to be borne by the defendant.

The allied press expressed nothing but delight at the verdict. *Le Journal* dubbed her '*a sinister Salomé who toyed with our soldiers' heads before the German Herod*'. The *Daily Sketch* featured her photograph alongside that of an angelic Canadian nurse, serving as a clear message to womanhood as to where they should look for a role model in these troubled times. In The Hague the Netherlands Ministry of Foreign Affairs attempted to intervene,

but President Poincaré rejected all requests for clemency.

On 13 October 1917 Mata Hari was brought from the condemned cell in Saint-Lazare to Vincennes for execution. She was dressed in her best and assured one of the nuns who had attended her in prison that '*vous allez voir une belle mort*'. It was her final performance and she carried herself like a trouper, refusing to be blindfolded and handcuffed. While the firing squad made ready she blew her lawyer a jaunty kiss. Then twelve shots tore through the air. Henry G. Wales, a British witness reporting for *International News Service*, described the scene as follows: '*She did not die as stage actors or film stars do when shot down. She did not throw her hands in the air (...). Instead she appeared to collapse. Slowly, inertly, she sank to on her knees, her head still upright and without the slightest change of expression in her face (...). A subaltern drew his revolver (...) Bending forward he placed the barrel of the revolver almost – but not quite – against the spy's left temple. He pulled the trigger and the bullet went straight into the brain. Mata Hari was truly dead.*'

Re-enactment of Mata Hari's execution in 1917, probably from a French silent film of 1922. Collection Roger-Viollet, Paris.

'What's the matta, Mata?'

Henry G. Wales was in error. Margaretha Zelle may have been truly dead, but not so Mata Hari. As Julie Wheelwright so perceptively observes in her book *The Fatal Lover. Mata Hari and the Myth of Women in Espionage*, that volley of gunfire at the rear of the Château de Vincennes simultaneously signified the comeback of Mata Hari, the celebrated dancer of yesteryear. The moment she was no more the wildest rumours at once began to do the rounds. She was supposed to have parted her furs at the crucial moment and so knocked the soldiery for six with her dazzling nudity. Or, alternatively, she had been rescued at the eleventh hour by a mounted lover – upon a snow-white steed, needless to say – who spirited her away before the very eyes of her execution squad.

Mata Hari became the subject of a virtual industry in cheap spy thrillers, half-baked 'serious' studies, stage plays, and musicals. She also inspired a number of films. The best-known of these is undoubtedly George Fitzmaurice's *Mata Hari* (1932) starring Greta Garbo and Ramon Navarro, whose dreadful English we have to thank for the immortal line '*What's the matta, Mata?*' For the rest the film is above all a vehicle for Garbo. The costumes are magnificent, the screenplay somewhat less so, and Mata Hari's guilt is established beyond a shadow of a doubt. Margaretha's brothers felt that the film went too far in violating fact – in particular the scene in which Garbo murders a Russian general – and demanded compensation, as well as making an unsuccessful bid to block the film's European distribution. In 1965 another *Mata Hari* movie was to appear with Jeanne Moreau in the title role, but this too played fast and loose with history.

Until the 1960s few people had any doubts as to Mata Hari's guilt. So strongly was this view entrenched that when during the Second World War Josephine Baker offered her services to the French resistance the head of France's counter-espionage was initially hesitant because he remembered the Mata Hari story and was not inclined to commit a similar boo-boo with yet another 'coloured' siren. Then came the Cold War, during which fear of reds under the beds and Big Brother and his ubiquitous ears and eyes was too potent for any reappraisal of the received view.

Only since the seventies has it become accepted more and more widely that the facts were never so serious as they were painted by the French judiciary at the time. As early as 1949 public prosecutor Mornet admitted in a radio interview that there was hardly enough substance to the Mata Hari case to bring a cat to book. And as recently as 1996 the French jurist Léon Schirmann petitioned the government for a reopening of the case against Margaretha Zelle, but his application was pronounced inadmissible. Since then he has joined forces with the Fries Museum-based Mata Hari Foundation to file a renewed application to this end. Finally, the end of 2000 saw the publication of *Mata Hari, la sacrifiée* by Jean-Marc Loubier, who has also been responsible for founding the Association pour la réhabilitation de Mata Hari.

The definitive story will in any event remain unwritten until the due date of release of the French archives in 2017. Hopefully these are being better cared for than Mata Hari's earthly remains. For only in July 2000 the Paris Museum of Anatomy announced that a recent inventory had revealed that the mummified head of Mata Hari which had been in its keeping had inexplicably vanished. Spirited away by a passionate admirer, a collector of the macabre, or simply mislaid? Just one more unanswered question for the file on Mata Hari.

FILIP MATTHIJS
Translated by Sonja Prescod.

BIBLIOGRAPHY

HUISMAN, MARIJKE, *Mata Hari (1876-1917): de levende legende.* Hilversum, 1998.
WAGENAAR, SAM, *Mata Hari: niet zo onschuldig....* Amsterdam, 1981.
WHEELWRIGHT, JULIE, *The Fatal Lover. Mata Hari and the Myth of Women in Espionage.* London, 1992.

A frica

Is Very Far Away

Belgium and its Colonial Past in Congo

In contrast to many other European countries, Belgium never seemed to have many colonial ambitions. During the first wave of colonisation, from the fifteenth and sixteenth centuries, circumstances were distinctly unfavourable. The Southern Netherlands, the precursor of modern Belgium which only became independent in 1830, were, largely for political reasons, unable to develop a seafaring tradition in spite of attempts by Ostend shipowners to establish colonies – in the Canary Islands for instance. During Europe's second wave of expansion in the late nineteenth century, the young Belgian state pursued economic expansion at home. It was the first continental country to develop into an industrial nation. The only Belgian who still dreamed of turning the country into a colonial power was King Leopold II, who reigned from 1865 until his death in 1909.

Leopold cherished high ambitions for Belgium, which naturally would also enhance his own standing. He regarded the acquisition of a colony as the crowning accolade for little Belgium's industrial success. The King explored nearly every continent for an opportunity to lay his hands on extra territory. But he could generate little enthusiasm for this within the ultra-cautious economic elite, while the political elite – consisting largely of the same people – was afraid that overseas adventures would be too costly for

The steamboat *Princess Clementine*, laden with rubber, on the River Congo. Photo Royal Archives, Brussels.

The missionaries of Kimuenza and their pupils. Photo Royal Archives, Brussels.

the treasury and hence the taxpayers. The socialist movement, which was relatively powerless but gaining in support, felt that colonial expansion would swallow up resources that should be devoted to social emancipation within Belgium. Furthermore, they were afraid that the military input required would put the lives of 'working lads' at risk for a cause that would be of no benefit to the working class.

Leopold's own country

The fact that Belgium nevertheless did embark on an ambitious colonial adventure in the last quarter of the nineteenth century can therefore be attributed to the initiative of one man, Leopold II. He seized his chance to rake in, as he put it, his slice of the African 'cake': the immense Congo. Still almost impenetrable, Central Africa had not been explored and no colonial claims had been laid upon it. It was the Anglo-American journalist and explorer Henry Morton Stanley who mapped out the region and found in Leopold a financial backer and patron. The European powers already active in Africa had little difficulty in agreeing with Leopold's plans. Belgium might be an industrial power and one of the world's leading exporters, but militarily and diplomatically it was insignificant. And whatever was allocated to Leopold would at least be kept out of the hands of other major colonial competitors. Furthermore, the King appeared, at least outwardly, to be committed to praiseworthy humanitarian concerns – spreading Christian civilisation and combating the slave-trade. And what was even more important for the other European colonisers was Leopold's promise to respect free trade in 'his' colony so that everyone could benefit commercially. An intensive lobbying campaign that even extended to the United States ensured that Leopold got what he wanted.

Congo became literally *his* colony. The Belgian government, for financial reasons, would have nothing to do with Leopold's plans but it was prepared to accept that the King, in his personal capacity, should become the sovereign of the new Congo Free State and even the personal owner of a large part of it, the so-called Crown Domain.

How Congo would be exploited economically only became clear as the huge territory – about 80 times as large as Belgium – was opened up. At first Congo mainly produced ivory, but this was soon overtaken by rubber for which there was a large and growing market, fuelled by its use, amongst other things, for bicycle and car tyres as well as for numerous industrial applications.

For the production of rubber, Leopold imposed a harsh regime of forced labour on the Congolese. The systematic military pressure and intimidation that accompanied it led to violence, brutality and atrocities which wreaked havoc among the Congolese population. Exploitation, hunger, sickness, terror and outright massacres caused a demographic 'shortfall' that has been estimated at over ten million persons. The images of hacked-off hands – the punishment for Congolese who failed to achieve their production quotas – date from this period, though it is not clear how widespread this barbaric practice was. These excesses provoked international protest in a campaign which included among its supporters the American writer Mark Twain. Although the campaign, like Joseph Conrad's *Heart of Darkness* (1902), expressed a genuine humanitarian indignation, colonial rivalry also played its part since very little had come of Leopold's promises of free trade in the Free State.

Congo in Leopold's rubber coils. Cartoon in *Punch*, 1906.

Although a great deal of money was being made in Congo, virtually none of it benefited the colony itself. King Leopold, who never set foot there, used the proceeds to build up his personal fortune and to finance prestigious public works in Belgium, particularly in Brussels and Ostend. By building parks, avenues, buildings and monuments, the King wanted to give his country a grandeur which the political classes, in his eyes, were too petty, too tight-fisted and too narrow-minded to do. The cost of all this, however, together with the international discredit into which his Congolese adventure had brought him, obliged Leopold in 1908 to transfer control of Congo to the Belgian state, which accepted the territory more out of necessity than imperial ambition.

The Société Générale and the Church

During the half century that Congo remained a colony, Belgian politics showed practically no interest in it. Successive governments, whatever their political make-up, went no further than a cost-benefit analysis: all that was required was that Congo should bring in more money than it cost. So when the colonial budget started to show a structural deficit in the 1950s there were few who opposed decolonisation. This lack of interest meant that the actual rulers of the Belgian Congo enjoyed a high degree of political and financial autonomy. This went so far that when Belgium was occupied by Nazi Germany during the Second World War, voices were raised in Congo in favour of giving the colony a neutral status. The desire to continue trading with both the Germans and the Allies outweighed any sense of (financial) solidarity with the motherland in its war effort. When at that time the United States obtained the monopoly on Congolese uranium – which was used for the atom bomb that destroyed Hiroshima – it occurred without the Belgian authorities having any say in the matter.

The actual running of the colony was in the hands of a few powerful groups, the colonial companies and the Church, who worked closely with the colonial administration. It was not until the early decades of the twentieth century that it became apparent that Congo had immense mineral reserves, including copper, gold, diamonds, uranium and cobalt. Only then did the colony attract the attention of the economic interest groups that were concentrated in a few conservative capitalist holdings with a strong aversion to risk. The most important of these was the Société Générale, which set up numerous subsidiaries in the Congolese mining industry. The Union Minière du Haut-Katanga, which was engaged in extracting copper in the southeastern province of Katanga, even grew into what was effectively a state within a state.

The Catholic Church undertook wide-ranging missionary work in Congo. Large numbers of Belgian, mainly Flemish, priests and nuns travelled to the colony to face an often hard and thankless existence. The missionaries took a grand view of their task: not only did they have to convert the Congolese (in which task they engaged in a grim struggle with their Protestant competitors), but they also tried to instil western, Catholic norms and values into an 'uncivilised' local population. At the same time they constructed a wide educational and medical infrastructure for, just as in Belgium, the Church

considered the expansion of schools, hospitals and cultural institutions as the backbone of a social network in which Christian faith could flourish.

The Société Générale is investing: a provisional bridge on the River Kenge in 1894. Photo KADOC, Leuven.

A Belgian family in Ango in the 1950s. Photo Royal Archives, Brussels (© H. Goldstein).

A model colony with apartheid

Belgium's colonisation was not one of settlement. Only a small elite was allowed to settle in Congo. Colonisation was rooted in a marked paternalism that regarded the Congolese as immature children who needed to be educated. They therefore had to be permanently surrounded by a white, Belgian class of teachers, engineers, doctors, managers, officers and officials. Underlying this was a barely disguised racism: blacks were not considered capable of taking responsibility or carrying out any task which was regarded as in any way 'sophisticated'. Racial segregation turned Congo into an apartheid regime. Whites and blacks each had their own residential districts and social facilities; the death penalty was only imposed on blacks, not on whites; higher education was virtually closed to Congolese and so on. And the greatest racial barrier was created by the huge difference in income between blacks and whites. The regime did allow for a middle category, the so-called évolués, the Congolese who 'civilised' themselves by studying and adopting a western (i.e. Belgian and petty bourgeois) life style. But those who aspired to this had to take special exams and submit to inspections of their homes, during which they had to show that they used a toilet or ate with a knife and fork.

Nevertheless, at first sight the Belgian Congo seemed to be a model colony. It had an excellent administrative, medical, educational and transport infrastructure and it achieved a general level of development that was comparable to, for instance, the Portugal of that time. But when in the late 1950s the decolonisation of Africa became inevitable, it was clear that Congo was not going to be an exception. Bloody riots in the capital, Leopoldville, in 1959 made that perfectly apparent, much to the astonishment of the Belgian colonists who, blinded by racial prejudice, had expected more gratitude from their black pupils. Nevertheless, no Belgian government would have been prepared to wage a colonial war to prevent in-

The Congolese painter Célestin Nzita and his wife in their Léopoldville home. The interior is a testimony of their efforts to be 'evolués'. Photo Royal Archives, Brussels (© J. Makula Inforcongo).

Colonial propaganda; the text on the sign reads: 'three grateful children'. Koninklijk Museum voor Midden-Afrika, Tervuren.

dependence, despite speculation along such lines in right-wing circles and in the conservative milieu of the young King Baudouin.

By then there was little that could be done to block the colony's independence and in any case, although the term had not yet been coined, Brussels already had a 'neo-colonial' future in store for Congo. Political sovereignty might be handed over to the Congolese but the instruments of state power would remain in Belgian hands. The officer corps in the army as well as the executive ranks of the administration were staffed exclusively by Belgians. The economic balance of power also remained completely unchanged, though most of the colonial companies did move their headquarters from Congo to Belgium. The colony was therefore totally unprepared for its independence planned for 30 June 1960. No indigenous elite had emerged and political life, still in its infancy, had only been able to develop along lines of traditional tribal loyalties. Only one important political party opted for Congolese nationalism and a genuine independence struggle: the Mouvement National Congolais (MNC) whose leader, Patrice Lumumba, became Congo's first Prime Minister.

Only a few days after 30 June 1960, Belgium's post-colonial construction collapsed. The blunt refusal to Africanise the army led to a violent mutiny by the rank and file. Many Belgians fled the country, leaving the Congolese state structure fatally weakened. Old tribal rivalries degenerated into violence and the country descended into chaos. The rich copper province of Katanga under the leadership of Moise Tshombe declared itself independent, after which the United Nations (UN) despatched a large body of troops to restore national unity in Congo. This operation brought the UN to the brink of bankruptcy and occasioned the death in murky circumstances of the UN Secretary-General, Dag Hammarskjöld. And yet the Katangan pariah state enjoyed the barely-disguised support of Brussels. With the active co-operation of King Baudouin, who feared that the legacy of his predecessor Leopold II would be lost in the Congolese debacle, right-wing circles in the

Congo, 30 June 1960:
Patrice Lumumba (l.) takes
the floor. King Baudouin
(r.) is shocked by his words.

Mobutu in Kinshasa, April
1977. Photo Henri Bureau /
SYGMA.

Belgian political, economic and aristocratic establishment viewed the Katangan secession as an opportunity to protect their interests and 'arrange matters' in Congo. This megalomaniac scheme gave rise to huge political tensions in Brussels itself.

An estranged motherland

The Congolese crisis soon became 'internationalised' and was thereby caught up in the Cold War. Washington feared – wrongly – that Prime Minister Lumumba would lead Congo and all its strategic mineral wealth into the Soviet sphere of influence. Instructing the CIA to work out a plan to have Lumumba murdered, it organised a coup d'état against him. Brussels too wanted to get rid of Lumumba because he constituted a serious obstacle to Belgian neo-colonialism. In early 1961, the Prime Minister was murdered in Katanga. The UN crushed the Katangan secession and Joseph-Désiré Mobutu, the army's Chief of Staff, assumed power in Congo with the backing of the US and Belgium. By 1965 nothing was left of the young Congolese democracy.

For nearly a quarter of a century Mobutu ruled Congo with an iron fist. He built up a predatory dictatorship based on the violent repression of opposition and the use of bribery and favouritism to buy support. The large-scale and systematic corruption that ensued drove Congo – or Zaire as he renamed it – ever deeper into economic, social and administrative decline. Nevertheless, Mobutu could always rely on Western support in spite of many ups and downs, especially in Belgian-Zaire relations. Things only changed when Zaire's economic importance for Belgium evaporated and the United States lost interest in Africa after the Soviet Union brought the Cold War to an end. Mobutu hoped to shore up his position by playing a role in the growing tensions elsewhere in Central Africa, which culminated in the tragic genocide in Rwanda in 1994, but it did him no good. A revolt in East Zaire, instigated by Rwanda, drove him from power in 1997 and the rebel leader, Laurent-Désiré Kabila, took over power and renamed Zaire the Democratic Republic of Congo. Although much was expected of him, Kabila too turned out to be a dictatorial and short-sighted ruler. He sank even deeper into the Central African imbroglio and became involved in a hopeless conflict in which he lost control over a large part of Congolese territory. In January 2001 Kabila was killed by one of his own bodyguards and succeeded by his son Joseph.

At the dawn of the twenty-first century, it is apparent that Belgium has become completely estranged from Congo. The younger generation has not the slightest affinity with it and lacks the nostalgic attachment which some of the older generation might still feel for the ex-colony. Since 1999 the Belgian government has tried to use this shift in sentiment to pursue the role of honest broker in Central Africa, arguing that Belgium's long familiarity with the region can now be applied 'objectively' without emotion or any hidden economic agenda. On the other hand, the deep indifference of Belgian public opinion has not made these diplomatic efforts particularly rewarding. It remains to be seen whether the Belgian Prime Minister's visit to Congo in June 2001 will bring some fresh hope for the future.

It is also increasingly clear that Belgian-Congolese ties had never rested on an honest pursuit of solidarity or development. The popular mythology of spreading civilisation and Christianity, of exoticism and jungle heroics, was coloured by racial prejudice and ignorance. Behind it the reality remained hidden. Even academic historiography, which until recently had praised the 'civilising work' of Leopold II, has fallen strikingly silent on the subject. Only recently has there been a growing realisation that there are huge gaps in Belgium's collective awareness of its colonial past. That is why in 2000 the Belgian parliament decided to set up a commission to investigate the role played by Belgian politics in the murder of Patrice Lumumba and the circumstances in which it occurred. Because nobody has any idea.

MARC REYNEBEAU
Translated by Chris Emery.

Joseph Kabila, President of Congo. The poster behind him shows the late Laurent-Désiré Kabila.

Robin Hood in the Polders?

Poverty in the Netherlands and the Western World

Our culture is strongly geared towards material values. People who have a high income or some capital are reckoned to be better off than those who do not. People on low incomes, or with no paid work, are quickly considered as inadequate. Personally I have little sympathy with this point of view, but that is irrelevant. Very few can resist the temptations of higher consumption, which means that 'poor' is readily associated with 'unsuccessful' and 'rich' with the opposite. Happiness is often associated with riches. Innumerable research studies have indeed shown a connection between the two, although there are limitations. Up to a certain level increase in income goes with increase in happiness. However, beyond a certain (minimum) income this connection ceases to exist. At that point increase in income produces no further increase in happiness, which leads some people to speak of the 'economy of sufficiency'.

For one reason or another the – in world terms – high income enjoyed by all Dutch people does not lead to the feeling that we are all rich. That is due to the fact that when people become dissatisfied with their material position, they are not looking at the situation world-wide, but only at a limited group in their own immediate environment.

Poverty affects the lives of many. Poor people are often less healthy, poor children come into contact more frequently with the police, and poor people participate less in cultural activities. Poor people have less understanding of society, less trust in the authorities, and consequently are less able to find out where they can get help. The provisions which do exist seem often not to be taken advantage of by those they are intended for.

What is poverty?
In a certain way income and capital are unequally distributed. Table 1 illustrates this in the case of income. For instance, it appears that in 1996 the lowest 25% of those drawing income received 4.9% of total income. The 25% at the top of the income ladder were getting 52.4%, a good ten times as much. If one compares the lowest and the highest 10% or 5%, then the differences are far more than ten times as great.

All kinds of government measures tend to reduce the unequal distribution of purchasing power. It would seem we are taking from the rich to give to the poor – Robin Hood in the polders.

Table 1: Distribution of personal incomes in the Netherlands

David Vinckboons,
Distribution of Bread at the Monastery Gates. c.1610.
Panel, 35 x 53 cm.
Nationalmuseum,
Stockholm.

	1996	1985	1990	1993	1994	1995	1996
	x 1000	as % of income					

Distribution of personal incomes

Lowest 25%	2756	3.4	5.1	4.9	5.1	5.1	4.9
Second 25%	2756	15.8	15.3	15.5	15.4	15.1	15.2
Third 25%	2756	27.7	27.4	27.7	27.5	27.4	27.5
Highest 25%	2756	53.1	52.3	51.9	52.0	52.3	52.4
Total	11023	100	100	100	100	100	100

Distribution of purchasing power

Lowest 25% group	3835	13.2	12.6	12.3	11.9	12.2	11.7
Second 25% group	3835	20.0	19.7	20.0	20.0	19.9	20.1
Third 25% group	3835	26.1	26.3	26.7	26.8	26.6	26.8
Highest 25% group	3835	40.7	41.4	41.0	41.3	41.2	41.3
Total	15341	100	100	100	100	100	100

Source: *Jaarboek Welvaartsverdeling*,1998, p.8

If the differences in income are considerable, the distribution of capital is even more skewed, as table 2 shows. About half of those with capital have less than 50,000 guilders. Between 1950 and 1996 the gap widened still further.

Table 2: Distribution of capital assets for households in the Netherlands

	1990 f1000	1993	1994	1995	1996
Average capital	110 x100	122	134	136	158
Capital bracket (1000 guilders)					
Less than 50	3540	3657	3580	3597	3437
50 to 100	710	773	766	693	718
100 to 200	870	863	912	933	1003
200 to 500	510	727	806	873	982
500 to 1000	150	194	225	241	269
1000 and above	80	95	111	116	139
Total	5860	6309	6401	6454	6549

Source: *Jaarboek Welvaartsverdeling*, 1998, p. 9.

In 1996 more than 970,000 households had a low income. Their income was at most some 250 guilders or so per month above income support level (1 guilder = approx. £ 0.3 or $ 0.5). Almost 424 thousand households had already been trying to manage on a similarly low income for at least four years in succession. Comparatively few households on such a prolonged low income have a younger person at their head. This is because for most people, in the course of their lifetime, their income first of all increases and then falls, and after pensionable age it remains the same. Younger people initially experience a sharp rise in income because they find (better) paid work, or because their earnings increase by reason of their age or experience. Thus, for them, a low income is in most cases not prolonged. This increase in income continues until they reach middle age. Relatively few (prolonged) low incomes are to be found then in households whose head is between 25 and 55 years of age. After that time, an increasing number of people cease work or change to part-time working, which causes their income to go down. Those who continue working until they reach pensionable age still experience a drop in income because the old-age pension (basic Old-Age Pension and supplementary pension) is normally at most 70 percent of final earnings. Anyone then on a low income is unlikely to see it ever again increase. Thus, in 1996 one in five households of over-65s were on a low income. For 190,000 of these households that low income was long-term. As regards purchasing-power, the low-income threshold more or less equates with the 1979 income support level. This threshold is adjusted annually in line with inflation, but that has not always happened with the minimum income guarantee. As a result, over the years the guaranteed minimum income has come to lie ever further below the low-income threshold. In 1996 for a (married) couple without children the low-income threshold stood at 2,140 guilders a month, that is around 200 guilders above the guaranteed minimum income applying at that time. The low-income threshold was also above the guaranteed minimum income for the other frequently occurring household types. In exceptional cases the guaranteed minimum income can be higher than the low-income threshold for a particular household. This can occur, for example, where direct blood relations (parent and child) live together and are both entitled to the old-age pension. Such instances are thus relatively few and far between.

Table 2 is concerned with the capital of all households in the Netherlands. Next, some data on the capital of people with a low income (table 3). This is to be understood as the balance of possessions and debts. In this context 'possessions' means specifically bank accounts, effects, real estate (including the personal dwelling), and investment capital. House contents, household effects, ready cash and car are not included. Debts include the mortgage and other debts (consumer credit). In around a quarter of cases the low-income households have negative equity, that is, their debts exceed their assets. In the majority of cases we are looking at negative equity of a few thousand guilders. Of course, negative equity also occurs in households above the low-income threshold, but to a lesser extent. Of householders above the low-income threshold in 1996 11% had negative equity, and of the households below it 26%.

The great majority of low-income households have means which lie between a couple of thousand guilders of negative equity and at the highest 5,000 to 10,000 guilders worth of assets, thus next to nothing (see table 3). Yet there are households below the low-income threshold who have considerable capital. This occurs particularly among people who are self-employed. Of these, half have capital of at least 65,000 guilders, and a quarter even have capital of more than 270,000 guilders. This small group clearly occupies a special position and cannot be considered as poor.

Marinus van Reymerswaele, *The Tax Collector* (detail). Panel, 82 x 71 cm. Galerie Leegenhoek, Paris.

Table 3: Capital of low-income households[a], 1996[b]

	Households (x 1,000)	1st quartile (x f1,000)	2nd quartile (x f1,000)	3rd quartile (x f1,000)
Working	195	0	5	61
inc. self-employed	67	4	65	270
Non-working[c]	752	(0)	2	9
On income support	130	(1)	1	4
On unemployment benefit	218	(2)	0	3
Unfit for work	81	(1)	2	9
Pensioner	311	2	6	14
Total[d]	953	(0)	3	12

a. The table shows the position as of 1 January 1996. The data are for households in the previous year.

b. The benefits shown in the table are significant as follows: respectively 25%, 50% and 75% of households have capital below the value given in the table.

c. Includes all those not in work.

d. Includes other non-workers and those of unknown social-economic category.

Source: *Armoedemonitor*, 1998, p.15.

The best definition of poverty, it seems to us, is that a person is poor where s/he is in receipt of less than half of the average income in his/her country. When this definition is used, increasing inequality in income-distribution almost automatically means greater poverty. This concurs with the research of Van Praag and Kapteijn previously referred to.

During the 1980s inequality in disposable income increased in many countries. In the Netherlands the increase was between 5 and 10%. In the USA the increase in inequality was even greater: between 16 and 29%. The UK was among the countries where the increase in inequality was 30% or more.

A criterion for poverty which is loosely akin to that just mentioned is that a person is considered to be poor if s/he earns less than half of the median income. Median income is determined by ordering all incomes from low to high and taking the one which lies precisely in the middle. By this definition 6.7% of the population of the Netherlands lives below the poverty line. Of the Western countries, the Anglo-Saxon countries fare the worst when this definition of poverty is applied. The percentage of the population deemed to be poor is 11.1% in Ireland, 11.7% in Canada, 12.9% in Australia, 13.5% in the UK and at least 19.1% in the USA. It is a matter of many tens of millions of people. Thus the most powerful country in the world also has the highest percentage of poor people. That is a dubious reputation that provides food for thought as far as the value of its economic and social system is concerned.

You get what you deserve?

Behind the justification of policy to combat poverty is the moral question: to what extent is poverty a culpable state? That is to say: brought about by one's own fault? The more convinced people are that an individual can do little about it, the readier society will be to make financial sacrifices to combat poverty. The opposite is also true. If it can be readily demonstrated that someone has fallen into impoverished circumstances through their own fault or by free choice, willingness to help will fall off. 'You get what you deserve' aptly reflects what is meant here.

The answer to the question whether the poor themselves can prevent their poverty has considerable influence upon the kind of policy advocated for combating poverty. If poverty is completely outside the control of the individual poor person, then there is little to do but give money without imposing conditions. The economist W. Drees Jr. once reproached the socialist PvdA party, who, in his opinion, clearly supported this policy, for breeding poverty by so doing. If poor people really can influence their situation, then in extreme cases help should be absolutely refused, because people will sort themselves out. Such a position is, quite rightly, seldom taken.

However, it is mostly assumed that individuals can exert some influence on their position, and not without reason. People have free will, which allows room for choices. Any policy for combating poverty must then be aimed at building in stimuli that will encourage people to improve their own situation.

Nonetheless there are groups for whom such stimuli, by definition, can play no part. The elderly with no supplementary pension can scarcely be asked to re-enter the employment market. Much more can, even must, be asked of other groups, such as the young unemployed. Precisely where to draw the line, nobody knows. More research into this matter is urgently needed here.

Whether or not one considers it important to have a policy to combat poverty and the increase of wealth is a subjective choice. The most effective kind of policy is one which takes from the rich to give to the poor. But this is a very generalised presentation of affairs. Space will not allow me to go further into it here. Otherwise I would certainly discuss at length an institution such as the right of inheritance, as something which perpetuates inequalities.

In general, one can say that in the West there is a majority in favour of containing both poverty and wealth within certain bounds. And to some extent this has been successful, albeit least so in the Anglo-Saxon countries.

If one wishes to pursue a policy, then redistribution of income is an obvious one. Put in very general terms, this can be done by making certain goods and services available to the poor at less than cost, or for free, through social services and insurance and through progressive taxation. Another very obvious measure for combating poverty is to take minimal incomes out of the tax system. I will give you an actual example. The net old age pension for a widow is something over 1,400 guilders a month. If she receives a gross supplementary pension of rather less than 40 guilders a month, she still has to pay more than 1,200 guilders per year in income tax. Such people are on the minimum guaranteed income and yet have to pay tax on this most slender of incomes. That is indefensible.

From cradle to grave

Let us pause for a moment and consider the kind of policy that can be implemented to combat differences in income, and therefore poverty. Government policy especially is of critical importance here. This is apparent, for example, in the readiness to impose progressive taxation, or to increase the number of highly educated people via an expansive education policy, thus causing top incomes to fall because of competition. More important in general for the combating of poverty is the extent to which government interferes in economic life. As was demonstrated earlier, differences in income are smaller in mainland Western Europe than in the Anglo- Saxon countries. As regards the extent and method of government influence, in this context there is a clear distinction between the Rhineland (Western European) model and the Anglo-Saxon (UK, USA).

The Rhineland model is characterised by a firm government control of economic affairs and a relatively high number of regulations to remove all sorts of causes and effects of a low income. This can give the citizens concerned the feeling of being looked after from cradle to grave, thus making them less inclined to take responsibility themselves for managing their financial affairs.

The Anglo-Saxon model is characterised by a government which finds it has less work if there is a more equal distribution of incomes and more is left to market forces. The aforesaid market forces employ scarcity and power as criteria for remuneration for labour. That leads to huge differences in income and to considerable poverty, which, in the Rhineland model especially, is in turn reduced by numerous government measures. This is what was typically called for by the social-democratic parties until some years ago; a role that has now been taken over by the green-left.

On the basis of the above, the ideal would seem to be to find a way of combining a lot of individual responsibility with a generous government to care for those who fall into poverty through no fault or failing of their own. Given the role of incentives, which many people still need, this is no simple matter. The area of disagreement referred to leads to the old problem: someone has to decide who is poor by reason of their own fault or failure, and who not. That is in many cases very difficult, and often impossible.

The 'Third Way', propagated by many social-democrats is in fact an attempt to combine a high level of personal responsibility with government interference in many areas, to correct the market outcomes.

Levelling... but how?

Research constantly shows that the majority of the population consider differences in income to be too great. Thus the existing level of poverty is found to be unacceptable. In other words, there must be some levelling of incomes. Some people are uneasy about this. I will dwell for a moment on the removal of incentives to effort and on tax evasion.

The most frequently heard argument against drastic levelling is that it removes the incentive to (greater) achievement. So far, it has been hard to find evidence for this. However, the same goes for the opposite. That still gives us very little to go on. I accept that drastic levelling certainly reduces in part the stimulus towards making an extra effort. But the question is, precisely where does this begin, and how great is the effect?

However, less effort also has its positive sides. Complaints about stress are widespread, especially among personnel in higher positions, but also elsewhere. The number of people falling out of the 'production line' is enormous. In the Netherlands there are almost 900, 000 people classified as unfit for work, out of a working population only eight or so times that number. Previously a constant increase in production meant an ever-increasing attack on the use of finite natural resources. Moreover it is possible that for many people a fairly consistent lower income is so important that they opt for this in preference to a situation with a higher average income, but a great many variations above and below.

One possibility open to those who wish to reduce differences in income, is to levy progressive taxes. A frequent objection to this is that it leads, or can lead, to tax evasion. However, this is something that could be lived with. Capital is fairly to very mobile, but employment is not. And income from employment accounts for three quarters of the differences in income. Yet the possibility of tax evasion cannot be excluded. I can see two possible ways of tackling this. The first has been suggested some time ago by the former German Minister of Finance, Lafontaine. It consists of harmonising tax rates within the European Union. The rumpus this provoked was mainly concerned with his proposal that these tariffs should be decided by majority vote within the EU. Although for a common problem that is not such an illogical system.

If this idea were translated into reality people could also flee to countries outside the EU. But here too – the second possibility – tax evasion could be limited if countries agreed that immigrants would still be taxed for a number of years according to the rates for the country from which they had emigrated.

JAN BERKOUWER
Translated by Sheila M. Dale.

BIBLIOGRAPHY

Armoedemonitor 1998. Sociaal en Cultureel Planbureau. The Hague, 1998.

BERKOUWER, J. and A. HOOGERWERF (ed.), *Markt, ongelijkheid, solidariteit: op zoek naar een herkenbare PvdA.* Tilburg, 1996.

ENGBERSEN, G., J.C. VROOMAN and E. SNEL (ed.), *Effecten van armoede. Derde jaarrapport armoede en sociale uitsluiting.* Amsterdam, 1998.

GOUDZWAARD, B. and H.M. DE LANGE, *Genoeg van teveel – Genoeg van te weinig: Wissels omzetten in de economie.* Baarn, 1986.

Human Development Report 1999. New York / Oxford, 1999.

Jaarboek Welvaartsverdeling 1998. Feiten en cijfers over inkomen en consumptie in Nederland. Voorburg / Heerlen, 1998.

PRAAG, B.S.M. VAN and A. KAPTEIJN, 'Further evidence on the individual welfare function of income. An empirical investigation in the Netherlands'. In: *European Economic Review* 4, 1973.

TINBERGEN, J. and J. BERKOUWER, *De toekomst van het democratisch socialisme.* Rotterdam, 1994.

WOLFSON, D., 'In Memoriam Willem Drees'. In: *Socialisme & Democratie,* 55, no. 12, 1998.

Faced Love

The Work of Toon Tellegen

After reading Toon Tellegen's poems for a while, I always ask myself – oh, I ask myself a lot of things at that point, but also: '*What is a poem again, exactly?*' Something consisting of words, that much is certain, a construct created out of language, with lines the length of which has been determined by the poet and not by the printer. Good. That gives one something to hold on to. A person who is reading or has just read Tellegen is in great need of something to hold on to. Those poems by Tellegen, they consist of language, they have lines, so that part is all right, but they still create confusion. From the moment you so much as glance at them. At the lines and the blank spaces. It makes no sense. There's no consistency there. Sometimes a line is very long, while in the very same poem another line is broken off after only five words, in order to make the next line consist of only one word: '*I must never agree with / it.*'

There's a line like this in a poem entitled 'Conditions which a poem must fulfil' ('Voorwaarden waaraan een gedicht moet voldoen'). Nothing is said about form in that poem. But perhaps the statement '*I must never agree with / it*' does apply to the form as well. For nobody would agree with such an odd line-break. One might even call it painful. '*It must be painful*'.

However, this poem *is* instructive and could perhaps serve as a kind of key to the other poems. It says, for example, that one must search for the logic which a poem keeps letting drop. This, as a statement, presents no problem, but then it also says that this searching must be done '*on my knees and then flat on my belly*' and that a lantern and a magnifying glass should be used as well. Nobody has any trouble with the expression 'you have to search for it with a lantern' (meaning: 'it is very rare'), but we never take it literally. And if somebody, or even a poem, drops logic, we don't generally assume that this logic will be lying around somewhere else. Things become even crazier in this poem, for it is then said that the poem must '*lift*' itself (more or less understandable, you just take it metaphorically), it must always lift itself '*out of its humble chair*'. Reading metaphorically becomes a lot more difficult now, and yes indeed, if we hadn't thought so already, now the fat is in the fire: the poem must '*open the windows / and sing – loudly, hoarsely, absurdly –*'. Of course, '*opening the windows*' could stand for 'broadening one's outlook', 'letting in a fresh breeze', but while I am writing this, the Tellegen-infection has already progressed too far. I now immediately think: how does one broaden one's outlook? By pushing? By stretching? And once inside, what havoc such a fresh breeze could wreak! There it is: 'Hello, I am the fresh breeze'. There's probably also a poem by Tellegen in which people, shivering, start shouting that they don't need it, or, conversely, grab the fresh breeze by its coat and plead with it to stay. And what does that all mean then?

So a poem must sing: '*of love and of me, / the scent of roses and immortality, almost convincing, about it', / and more painful still it must be, far more painful still.*'

Love, roses, immortality and '*about me*'. That suddenly sounds quite old-fashioned – poets and roses, it used to be such a standard combination that there's hardly a poet who still dares to use the word 'rose'. And here we have another typical Tellegen-word: '*almost*'. It must be '*almost*' convincing.

There's another poem, in which, a propos of nothing and between quotation marks, a question is asked: '*What is your favourite word?*' Answer: '*Almost*'. Question: '*Why?*' Answer: '*It is never entirely.*'

So what a handy key this poem is! And what's really so terribly painful about roses and immortality? What could be '*far more painful*'?

In any case, a few things can be deduced from this poem: that all expressions can be taken literally, that this leads to an odd view of the world, that despite that something wants to be expressed, nevertheless, that a poem must be painful, above all, and that it must sing, be it hoarsely and absurdly. This last condition seems to be the least problematic of all.

'Do not wake with a kiss!'

Some of Tellegen's poems I find tremendously painful. This one, for example:

The one said, very softly:
'Should I just leave?'
'Yes,' said the other, even softer.

'Will I be coming back?'
the one asked, almost inaudibly.
Yes, thought the other
and shook her head.

What makes it painful are the words '*softly*', '*even softer*', '*almost inaudibly*' – they suggest that these things cannot be said easily. The last '*yes*' is even completely inaudible, it is only being thought. It is therefore the most painful, for the '*no*' is expressed silently, with a shake of the head, against the will of both, you think, and at the same time it can't be completely against the will of '*the other*', for otherwise she could perhaps still, very, very softly, have said '*yes*'. But people sometimes don't do or say what they most want to do or say. This is illogical – illogicality is a must for Tellegen.

Has this poem raised itself to open the windows, has it sung hoarsely and absurdly? Not really. It has been painful, and rather than loudly it has sung very softly. Softly suits Tellegen better anyhow, although there's shrieking in his poems as well. But remarkably often his people whisper or talk softly. Or remain silent – when they shouldn't. Sleeping Beauty, for example, who hears the prince leave, his mission unfulfilled, because he has found a letter beside her pillow: *'Do not wake with a kiss. / Not under any circumstances. / Not even after a hundred years.'* She remains silent when she hears his tired footsteps go down the stairs again and *'her heart was torn apart'*. So why didn't she say anything, why didn't she look up, if she was able to peer through her eyelashes, if she can hear the prince, why is that letter there in the first place? What does this Sleeping Beauty really want? She probably doesn't know herself. Perhaps she is filled with longing. As people often seem to be permeated with silent longing in Tellegen's poems, perhaps for a world in which ideas and feelings, one person and another, one person and himself, *could* coincide. But such a world doesn't exist, not here, with us, and certainly not in this poetry. Characters are burdened by themselves and by their thoughts, literally again, of course (*'A man, pounding on his thoughts:/ "You're always, always making me sad!"'*). As Tellegen shuffles the literal and figurative use of language around and substantiates and personifies abstract ideas – so Peace can walk by wearing a blue coat, and Longing has strange clumsy hands – such words and ideas stop being self-evident, and that seems to be his intention. People tear themselves apart and they can continue doing so endlessly, they say that they are *'close to despair'* and then other voices are heard, *'rapt voices, splashing voices': "Me too! Me too!"'*

The question remains: what does it all mean? Words are liberated this way, ideas are liberated – but we, who make use of those ideas, who would like to be able to count on some things, become desperate. That is to say, we are *'close to despair'*. Me too!

In the world of the animals, about which Toon Tellegen writes in his brilliant animal stories, things often happen in the same way, but here it seems less oppressive, more light-hearted. There's the cricket, for example, very curious about what it really was he felt, who therefore turns himself inside out, to find out. Literally, of course. So we now have a cricket, who's turned inside out. The thrush and the ant see him. *'Can you see my feeling?'* the cricket asks. *'You do know what feeling is? It must be there somewhere.'* But the other two can't see anything. No thoughts either. The cricket turns himself outside in again, they eat some honey and the cricket adds: *'I always think my feeling must be red, pale red. (...) A pity you couldn't find it.'*
Also rather absurd, but not something that makes one despair.

Outlook on language

Sometimes Tellegen's poems resemble paintings by Salvador Dali. They always make me despair as well. Or scare me. In those paintings and in these poems one sees a surrealistic world, a world in which one cannot be sure of anything, although there is much that resembles the familiar world, which at the same time seems to say: this is the *real* truth. There time doesn't progress

Toon Tellegen (1941-).
Photo by Willy Dee.

the way you think – it always, on its own initiative, progresses more quickly or more slowly. In that other world death isn't the way you think either, death will be standing in a doorway, or people will be dying beneath your window, while they call out that it's a very easy thing to do – in the familiar world too death shows a different face each time. Sometimes everyone is afraid of it, at other times someone suddenly finds it rather easy, dying. Still, here, '*with us*', it never seems to be the way it is with Tellegen. Who can simply write: '*And yet life is not a fatal journey / and it never ends badly. For no one. / On the contrary!*'

Ah, indeed, on the contrary. Perhaps death can be regarded as a good end, that is also possible. Perhaps the word '*fatal*' doesn't apply to it at all. The word '*fatal*' doesn't seem to apply to these poems in any case, only, at most, as a word of which nobody knows what it means anymore.

Nothing fatal ever happens to the animals in his stories either, although one would sometimes say that it did. The elephant, for example, falls again and again from the tree, from a great height. It does hurt, but he's never crushed by it, the elephant. The consequences of the fall don't really matter, it's the fall itself that's important. Especially, maybe, the word 'to fall'. And the fear this word engenders. The elephant seems to have landed in a fear-of-falling-dreamworld, in which one is forever going up to great heights, utterly convinced that one will fall. Fall hard. And it happens, but that's all that happens.

Also, there comes a day when everybody is gone, except the squirrel. Who at first thinks, '*They must be somewhere*', but after a while he isn't so sure of that anymore. '*Perhaps they were nowhere.*' It sounds like a child talking about death, which it doesn't understand. It could be a fatal story, but in the afternoon everybody is there again, suddenly. The squirrel excitedly rushes up to his friend, the ant, and asks: '*Where were you?*' '*I don't know,*' the ant said and shook his head. And the butterfly, fluttering laboriously behind him, said: '*We don't know.*'

We don't know either. It is scary, but it ends well. They weren't dead, they had perhaps only been thought away. Again something has been taken literally: '*I see no one*' or '*Where is everybody?*' Gone.

In his stories and poems Tellegen never wants to start with the things that we take for granted – that we mean 'deadly' when we say 'fatal', that death is the worst thing that could happen to us, that despair is unusual and that we know what love is. The stories and poems of Tellegen do not present a view of the world, they present a view of language, and that is something quite different.

Everybody is or seems to be in despair in Tellegen's world. Not just because all those voices keep shouting that, but because, as a matter of course, desperation strikes again and again (oh no – there comes another one). Quite often we are presented with 'people', it might be 'a man' or 'someone' or 'we', who don't know what to do with those words that, outside of Tellegen's language world, always seem to fit seamlessly into a sentence. Happiness. Anger. Death. Love. Truth. Not the most trivial of concepts.

Perhaps Tellegen's work shows us that we too don't really know what we are talking about, when we say that we know what love is, when we say that we are torn apart by doubt or that we are facing the truth. Tellegen's method tends to be to take something like that literally: '*You must, they said, face the truth. / Now! Immediately! / I faced the truth.*'

This is absurd. Nobody will ever stamp his foot and demand that you face the truth '*now!*' and nobody will ever react to it by doing that. For all of a sudden it has become unclear what it really means, 'facing the truth'. And because everything becomes possible once we are able to '*face the truth*', 'love' is then also faced in that same poem, and '*thoughtlessness with its gigantic wings*' and '*the simplicity of the moonlight on my wall*'. This last phenomenon you can face literally but not metaphorically. And as you read along, you begin to face the fact that you don't have the grip on things you thought you had and that you never had it. That mostly you just throw words around and pretend that it is perfectly clear what they all mean. That it isn't Tellegen who is pulling the rug out from under them, but we ourselves, who had thought we had tamed the words by ceasing to wonder what they actually mean. Love. That's one example. Perhaps it is that, that and sorrow, that Tellegen talks about the most. '*Does anybody know what love is?*' Well, everybody seems to know. But it is also often shouted or whispered that love doesn't exist. And then all of a sudden it does exist. Or perhaps people just can't stop embracing each other, however brilliantly it has been proved that love doesn't exist.

Love is extraordinarily elusive.

Just say that it isn't so.

MARJOLEINE DE VOS
Translated by Pleuke Boyce.

A Story and Four Poems
By Toon Tellegen

The sun was shining and the squirrel and the ant were sitting in the grass on the river-bank. Above them the willow rustled, in front of them the water burbled, and in the distance the thrush was singing.

'In my opinion,' said the squirrel, 'I am happy now.'

The ant said nothing and chewed at a blade of grass.

'I think,' said the squirrel, 'that I could never be happier than I am now.'

'Well…' said the ant. 'And if a honey-cake came flying by with a note on it saying: for the squirrel and the ant…?'

'Yes,' said the squirrel. 'Then I should be even happier. But happier than that is impossible.'

'Well…' said the ant. 'And if I'd been planning to go on a journey and I said: squirrel, I'm not going, I'm staying with you, all right?…'

'Yes,' said the squirrel. 'You're right. Then I should be even happier…'

'And if the cricket was throwing a really big party tonight, and if you suddenly got a letter from the whale with an invitation, and if today the sun didn't set any more, and if everything smelt of fresh beech-nuts…?'

The squirrel didn't answer. He looked at the sparkling water and thought: so actually I'm not really that happy after all…

He looked sideways at the ant. But the ant had his eyes shut, chewed at his blade of grass and let the sun shine on his face.

What am I then? the squirrel wondered. If I'm not very happy…

It was as if a cloud had come between him and the sun. He couldn't answer that question.

In the distance the thrush fell silent and the nightingale started to sing, just like that, in the middle of the day.

Hey, thought the squirrel, what's going on? He felt a stirring in his eyes. Tears? He wondered. Are those tears? He heaved a deep sigh, folded his tail behind his head and stared at the sky. I just won't think any more, he thought. But he knew that that was very difficult.

So they lay side by side on the river-bank, the ant and the squirrel.

'How lovely it is just lying here relaxing, squirrel,' said the ant a long time later. The squirrel said nothing.

'I've never been so lovely and relaxed before,' said the ant.

I wish, thought the squirrel, that just once I could be sitting on a branch with my legs crossed with the ant down below shouting up: you're right, squirrel, I admit it, you're absolutely right…

The sun slipped slowly down the sky, the river burbled and in the distance the blackbird sang. The squirrel just looked and just listened and didn't think about anything any more.

From *Maybe They Were Nowhere* (Misschien waren zij nergens). Amsterdam: Querido, 1991.

A long life stands at the door.	Een lang leven staat voor de deur.
What shall we have it do?	Wat zullen we het laten doen?
We'll have it knock.	We laten het kloppen.
It is tired and mistrustful.	Het is moe en achterdochtig.
It has lost its keys.	Het is zijn sleutels kwijt.
Trains go by,	Treinen rijden voorbij,
travellers nodding and dozing.	reizigers die dommelen.
We'll have long life reach up on tiptoe	We laten het lange leven op zijn tenen staan
and look inside,	en naar binnen kijken,
we'll have it see love, nagging worries and irrational fear,	we laten het liefde zien, en muizenissen en redeloze angst,
have it hear conversations about the blue of tomorrow,	laten het gesprekken horen over het blauw van morgen,
the grey of yesterday	het grijs van gisteren
and the eternal red of now,	en het eeuwige rood van nu,
yearning are the guests	reikhalzend zijn de gasten
and sparkling their sorrows,	en schitterend hun smarten,
long life heaves a sigh and presses its nose to a window –	het lange leven zucht en drukt zijn neus tegen een raam –
on the table a cherry pie.	op de tafel een kersentaart.

At the end of the day,
when someone comes dashing up bearing love,
when you're tired and clumsy and you've just got snarled
in a tangle of fears
-
what are you to do,
what are you to do with the love, downy, edgy,
that someone still brings you?

I remember a boy
who went back over his steps
and thought:
almost someone has loved me passionately,
almost I have been dizzy with happiness!

And almost he'd sung it out loud,
almost he'd started running, that boy,
one fine morning
in the country.

Conditions which a poem must fulfil

It must be painful –
always, come what may.

I must never agree with
it.

With a lantern and a magnifying glass I must –
on my knees and then flat on my belly –
hunt for the logic
that it keeps letting drop.

It must lift itself – let there be no doubt about that –
it must always lift itself out of its humble chair
and open the windows
and sing – loudly, hoarsely, absurdly –
of love and of me,
the scent of roses and immortality, almost convincing,
about it,

and more painful still it must be, far more painful still.

Aan het einde van de dag,
als iemand aan komt hollen met de liefde,
als je moe bent en onhandig en toevallig net verward
in een warnet van angsten
–
wat moet je doen,
wat moet je met de liefde doen, donzig, schrikachtig,
die iemand je nog brengt?

Ik herinner me een jongen
die op zijn schreden terugkeerde
en dacht:
bijna heeft iemand hartstochtelijk van mij gehouden,
bijna ben ik duizelig van geluk geweest!

En bijna had hij dat gezongen,
bijna was hij gaan hollen, die jongen,
op een ochtend
in het land.

Voorwaarden waaraan een gedicht moet voldoen

Het moet pijnlijk zijn:
altijd, hoe dan ook.

Ik moet het er nooit mee eens
zijn.

Met een lantaarn en een vergrootglas moet ik –
op mijn knieën en vervolgens op mijn buik –
de logica zoeken,
die het telkens laat vallen.

Het moet zich verheffen – daar mag geen twijfel over zijn –
het moet zich altijd verheffen uit zijn nederige stoel,
de ramen opendoen
en zingen – luidkeels, schor en onzinnig –
over de liefde en over mij,
de geur van rozen en onsterfelijkheid, bijna geloofwaardig,
om zich heen,

en nog pijnlijker moet het zijn, nog véél pijnlijker.

From *Poems 1977-1999* (Gedichten 1977-1999). Amsterdam: Querido, 2000.
All translations by Tanis Guest.

Portrait

of the Child as Sitter

Children of a Golden Age

Strange as it may seem today, until fairly recently it was thought that in early modern Europe children were not very highly valued and were appreciated not as children but simply as a kind of proto-adults. Research by various historians has shown convincingly that this is a misconception. The way in which children are regarded may vary through time and space; but parents love their children and care about them, and they have always done so.

That this loving care is only rarely reflected in the visual arts appears to have a very prosaic reason. Portraiture as a genre in painting has only come into being since the fifteenth century, and its status since then has always been very low. Even today in auctions and art sales portraits are rarely considered precious as such. It is a famous sitter that makes a portrait attractive; otherwise it has at least to be by Titian or Van Dyck to make a really high price.

Paintings were valued and painters were admired because of their skill, and the way to show excellence in painting portraits was in the handling of faces and hands. The painting of clothing, jewellery and background was considered craft rather than art and did not offer the average painter an opportunity to stand out from his many colleagues. And it is precisely this low status of portrait painting that explains why children's portraits are so rare in European art. To fit in with existing portrait galleries and with tradition a painter was almost obliged to portray children at full length, which implied lots of clothing and background and very little real artwork. Child portraiture was the lowest form of this poorly rated genre, and that remained the case for many centuries.

When we look at the numbers of such works, there appears to be one exception: the Low Countries. Especially in the seventeenth century – the so-called Golden Age of the Dutch Republic – comparatively many children's portraits were painted. In the rest of Europe only the highest nobility saw fit to have their children painted, often together with their parents. Individual portraits of children and youngsters were in many instances made with the purpose of making the heir known to his future subjects or as a tool in the very serious game of finding a profitable match. In the Dutch Republic there was no royal court and the old nobility had little direct political influence,

Jan Mijtens, *Willem van den Kerckhoven and his Family*. 1652 / 1655. Canvas, 134 x 182 cm. Haags Historisch Museum, The Hague.

but in the cities there was a large group of wealthy citizens who aspired to aristocratic status.

These people were proud of their newly-gained riches and displayed a marked self-confidence. A favourite way of showing off in public was the group portrait of men in public service of the kind for which painters like Rembrandt and Frans Hals have become famous. For private consumption, the really rich had themselves painted in family portraits or in portraits of individual family members. In this group children's portraits are still a rare exception, but compared with the rest of Europe their number does stand out. For the first time ever, a large number of these children's portraits have been brought together in an exhibition devoted solely to this subject. This exhibition was on show in the Frans Hals Museum in Haarlem (7 October - 31 December 2000) and in the Antwerp Royal Museum of Fine Arts (21 January - 22 April 2001) and came with an impressive catalogue published both in Dutch and in English.

Real or metaphorical

One of the problems facing the organisers of this exhibition was to distinguish between actual portraits on the one hand and genre paintings on the other. In the latter category the persons symbolise specific emotions or tell a story which is in most cases intended as a lesson in good behaviour. This involved a great deal of research into the provenance of the paintings themselves as well as into the genealogy of the supposed sitters. Of course this

did not lead to a positive result in every case, but where it did the genealogical information is given in detail in separate entries in the exhibition catalogue. No specific distinction was made between portraits of individual children (or sometimes small groups of children) and family portraits in which one or both parents are shown together with their offspring.

Such family groups were particularly popular in the Northern Netherlands in the seventeenth century. Quite often the painting depicts not only the living offspring, but also those who died before the painting was made. Deceased children are most often portrayed as little angels or *putti*. A fine example of this is Jan Mijtens' *Willem van den Kerckhoven and his Family*. The painting was originally completed in 1652, but when a new son was born to the family, he was added to the painting in 1655, showing the importance attached to having the family portrayed in its entirety. Also included in the background is a black servant boy leading a horse. Since the Van den Kerckhoven family seems to have had no direct connection with the Dutch West Indies Company or the slave trade, the inclusion of this servant boy must be seen as an indication of the family's wealth.

As a type source for the composition of family portraits like this one, the authors of the exhibition catalogue refer to the wings of altarpieces and memorial tables which were fashionable until the time of the Reformation. In the Dutch Republic painters used this model rather freely and experimented with the composition and the grouping of the figures in the painting. More traditional – but also twenty years older – is a comparable work by the Antwerp master Cornelis de Vos: *Anton Reyniers, Maria Le Witer and their Five Children*. Here the merchant Anton Reyniers and his two sons occupy

Cornelis de Vos, *Anton Reyniers, Maria Le Witer and their Five Children*. 1631. Canvas, 170.3 x 244.1 cm. Museum of Art, Philadelphia (W.P. Wilstach Collection).

Govert Flinck, *A Girl as Flora*. c.1640. Canvas, 117 x 90 cm. Musée des Beaux-Arts, Nantes.

the left side of the painting, while his wife and their three daughters fill the right hand side. Between the two parents, who are seated, is a table covered with an oriental carpet. Against the back wall and above the table we see a painted double portrait, most probably depicting Anton Reyniers' parents. An illegitimate daughter of whom we have documentary evidence is not included in the painting.

Where the children portrayed could not be identified, the problem arises whether or not we have a portrait in the strict sense of the word. A case in point is *A Girl as Flora* by Govert Flinck. The girl wears a fantasy costume and carries a large bunch of flowers and obviously represents Flora, goddess of flowers and springtime. Without the girl's identity and with no clue to the context in which the painting was made, this work cannot strictly speaking be seen as a portrait. That it has been included in the exhibition nevertheless is probably due to its high quality. In the catalogue it is compared with Rem-

brandt's *Saskia as Flora* (1634), which is not a portrait even though in this case the identity of the model is known.

In yet another painting we see a *Boy Training his Dog*. Again the sitter has not been identified; the painting is by Ludolf de Jongh. The scene is a common one in Dutch paintings of this period and is a metaphor for effective child-rearing. Only the fact that in this case the young boy and the dog are so prominently the main subject of the painting tends to suggest that in this case we actually do have a portrait (with an unknown sitter). A similar instance is the portrait of an anonymous *Four-Year-Old Girl with Cat and Fish* by Jacob Gerritsz. Cuyp.

Ludolf de Jongh, *Boy Training his Dog*. 1661. Canvas, 97.8 x 71.4 cm. Virginia Museum of Fine Arts, Richmond (The Arthur and Margaret Glasgow Fund).

Jacob Gerritsz. Cuyp, *Four-Year-Old Girl with Cat and Fish*. 1647. Canvas, 108 x 80 cm. Private collection.

Children at their finest

In the exhibition the paintings are grouped thematically. The first group shows 'The New Family', the rise of the nuclear family of parents with their children that became the norm in the sixteenth century. Also included here are examples of late fifteenth-century portraits of individual youngsters as young rulers or rulers-to-be. Sixteenth-century portraits of children of rich citizens are grouped under the second theme: 'The First Steps'. 'Learning and Playing' is a self-explanatory title. Here children are shown in their daily occupations, sometimes with one educating the other as in the rather baroque *The Education of Anna Maria Trip by her Sister Margarita as Pallas Athena* by Ferdinand Bol. Related to this is the group of paintings in which the children are dressed up as – in most instances – mythological figures. Of course, the above-mentioned double-portrait by Bol fits into both themes. In others, boys appear in full hunting dress complete with dog and bird of prey.

Very intimate and moving are the post-mortem portraits. Here we see a rather documentary and anonymous painting of the Dordrecht quadruplets. Inscriptions give the names of the children and the number of days and hours each of them lived as well as a line from Psalm 127 on a banderole: '*Lo, children are an heritage of the Lord: and the fruit of the womb is his reward.*' Individual portraits of infants and toddlers on their deathbeds occur as well and have lost nothing of the power to move over the ages. More clearly than anything else they show the grief the parents must have felt at the loss of their dearest possession.

The final theme is the apotheosis of the exhibition. Here we see 'Children at their Finest', beautifully executed portraits of seventeenth-century children in beautiful clothes, often surrounded by toys and caught by the painter in the same natural and spontaneous way we now expect from a professional photographer. In this group we also find again the highest nobility of the Dutch Republic, for instance in the portrait painted by Adriaen Hanneman

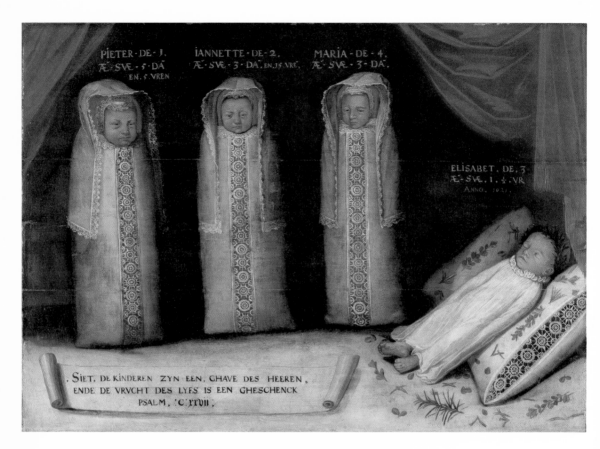

PIETER·DE·I·
Æ·SVÆ·5·DA
EN·5·VREN

IANNETTE·DE·2·
Æ·SVÆ·3·DA EN·15·VRE·

MARIA·DE·4·
Æ·SVÆ·3·DA·

ELISABET·DE·3·
Æ·SVÆ·1·½·VR
ANNO·1621·

·SIET· DE·KINDEREN· ZYN·EEN· GHAVE· DES·HEEREN·
ENDE· DE·VRVCHT· DES·LYFS· IS· EEN· GHESCHENCK·
PSALM· ·CXXVII·

of the young *William III, Prince of Orange* and showing the influence of Anthony van Dyck, and that of the two sons of the Utrecht nobleman Philibert van Tuyll van Serooskerken who are portrayed by Gerard van Honthorst as hunters in a classical mythological scene.

Snapshots

However, the exhibition does not lure the (re)viewer with beautiful paintings only. It is definitely the children themselves who fascinate and amuse – and sometimes deeply move – even the modern public. *Helena van der Schalcke* was painted at the age of two by Gerard ter Borch. She looks quite lost in the dark and undefined space in which the painter placed her, but still she gazes at us confidently. With her white dress, heavy gold chain and wicker basket she already holds the promise of the lady she would become, as we know, for a tragically brief time. Helena died at the age of twenty-four, having recently been married to a merchant from Haarlem. An anonymous *Girl at a Virginal* by Cornelis de Vos is dressed in precious clothes

Anonymous, *The Children of Jacobus Pietersz. Costerus and Cornelia Jans Coenraadsdochter (The Dordrecht Quadruplets).* 1621. Panel, 75 x 104 cm. Dordrechts Museum.

Gerard van Honthorst,
*Hieronymus and Frederik
Adolf van Tuyll van
Serooskerken.* 1641.
Canvas, 123 x 138 cm.
M.A.O.C. Gravin van
Bylandt Stichting, The
Hague.

Gerard ter Borch, *Helena van der Schalcke*. c.1648. Panel, 34 x 28.5 cm. Rijksmuseum, Amsterdam.

with a great deal of lace and looks at us as if about to ask whether this is the right pose. The painting is like a snapshot, and the same can be said of the *Boy (possibly Jacob van Oost jr)* by the Bruges painter Jacob van Oost sr.

It is perhaps not surprising that quite a lot of the children's portraits are painted by the father of the sitter. The combination of paternal love and artistic craftsmanship results in an intimacy which even today we can sense and recognise. The most fascinating and at the same time most puzzling portrait in the exhibition, however, was the anonymous *Girl with a Dead Bird*, which was exhibited in Antwerp only. It is a painting about which virtually nothing can be said with certainty, except that it is deeply moving.

LAURAN TOORIANS

To bring the world of these children alive, the exhibition also showed some actual toys from the period. Toys from around 1600 are rare and only the most costly examples survived as heir-looms. Others have been discovered recently in archaeological excavations. In an essay in the catalogue Annemarieke Willemsen describes these toys (real and painted) and '*the culture of play in the Netherlands around 1600*'. Of special interest is also that for each of the paintings there are separate descriptions of the dress of the children. These have been done by Saskia Kuus, who has also written an introductory essay on 'Children's Costume in the Sixteenth and Seventeenth Centuries'. Other essays deal with the position of children in the Protestant North and in the Catholic South and with the scope for education in the Netherlands during this Golden Age. The book (Jan Baptist Bedaux & Rudi Ekkart (eds.), *Pride and Joy. Children's Portraits in the Netherlands 1500-1700*. Ghent / Amsterdam, 2000) appeared both in a Dutch and in an English edition.

Anonymous, *Girl with a Dead Bird*. c.1520. Panel, 36.5 x 29.5 cm. Koninklijke Musea voor Schone Kunsten, Brussels.

he

Wry Aesthetics of Co Westerik

The painter Co Westerik (1924-) is a universally esteemed artist. He is a loner in the post-war art of the Netherlands. He is not part of any trend, school or movement and is not linked to any prevailing fashions or tendencies. He is not an innovator. On the contrary, his craftsmanlike approach to painting, using well-prepared canvases, underdrawing and a meticulous build-up of coats of tempera and oils, is based on age-old painting practices. He also adheres to tradition, that of Dutch realism, in his depiction of everyday scenes. In his approach to his subjects, however, and in his style, Westerik is utterly unique.

Co Westerik is a highly disciplined man. He works a full day in his studio every day. Yet he has produced very few works. He paints no more than five canvases a year, and often just two or three. He does, though, produce countless sketches, drawings and prints. Westerik is without doubt a good graphic artist and an absolute master of drawing, but he considers his paintings to be the most important: '*In a painting everything has to be weighed up: it is a more serious matter, a matter of greater consequence...*'

He sees drawing as a way of developing subjects, and the same applies to his graphic work. Each and every one of his paintings is an outstanding work. Westerik paints apparently simple, everyday scenes, such as a boy with a bicycle, a schoolmaster with a child, a swimmer or a man with a gramophone. But the way he renders these images is extraordinarily insistent. These innocent scenes exude a sense of unease. The scenes conceal pain, sorrow, fear, loneliness, death and desolation.

This was already apparent in *Skippers* from the early fifties. Two boys and a girl are skipping in the street. An ostensibly cheerful and light-hearted image. Westerik placed the scene in a shallow space. Immediately behind the playing children is a brick wall, in front of which all that can be seen is a narrow strip of paving stones with gas company manhole covers. The perspective is distorted: the paving stones slope downwards to the front. This pushes the children even closer to the edge of the picture. It as if, in this shallow space, the skipping rope cannot even turn completely, and its movement does not correspond to the children's leaps. The children do not have any contact with each other. The undefined and constrained space, the gas com-

pany manhole covers and the children's solitude produce a feeling of op-pression, rather than the cheerfulness and unconcern associated with this subject.

Schoolmaster and Child, painted in 1961, causes a similar feeling of dis-comfort. It shows a teacher, but only half his body, with a crying child in front of him. The teacher has his hand on the child's head to comfort him. But is he actually comforting him, or are we here being drawn into a horri-ble drama? The teacher is not paying attention to the child, but is looking at us. His comforting hand can also be seen as a threat. He is pressing the child's head, which barely extends above the edge of the painting, and with his other hand clasps the child's shoulder or neck. The child's eyes are open wide. The scene takes place against the background of a wall, so that here too no escape is possible.

Westerik often squeezes figures into a frame or setting that is much too restricted, so that all one's attention is focused on what is depicted.

Co Westerik, *Skippers.*
1953-1954. Canvas,
107.5 x 107 cm. Becht
Collection / © SABAM
Belgium 2001.

A very striking example of this is *Woman in a Small Space*, from 1978. We see a woman on her back in a space into which she hardly fits. Both her shoulders touch the sides and her head the ceiling. The limits of the setting make the woman's vulnerable posture, with bare shoulders and a slightly bent neck, even more palpable.

Co Westerik, *Schoolmaster and Child*. 1961. Canvas, 88.5 x 110 cm. Becht Collection / © SABAM Belgium 2001.

Like all Westerik's work, *Schoolmaster and Child* is based on a real-life event. Westerik tells us: *'That was our teacher. He played the violin and could grab hold of your ear at the same time: he was a creep, a real bastard, and so deceitful: for the parents' evening he would be all charm. One never forgets a thing like that, and later it becomes a painting.'* The basis of his paintings is in the end always a personal observation or occurrence. They provoke an emotional and physical reaction and are then transformed by the painter. He does countless sketches and drawings, and if the subject continues to hold its own he ventures into painting. He tries to express the essence of the occurrence. *'In my case it is never a matter of aesthetics in the decorative sense. ... Oh no, it's about something completely different. There are things that are necessary as part of the image, but the essential thing is the idea, the mental things that are made visible and tangible.'*

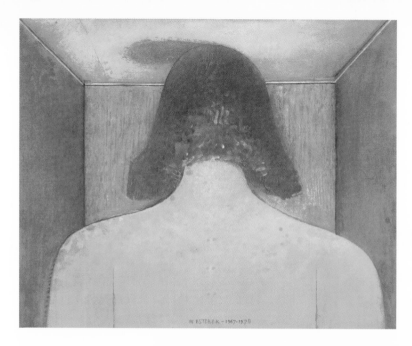

Co Westerik, *Woman in a Small Space.* 1967-1978. Canvas, 40.5 x 50.5 cm. Museum Boijmans van Beuningen, Rotterdam / © SABAM Belgium 2001.

Co Westerik, *Dying.* 1992. Panel, 48 x 54 cm. Private collection / © SABAM Belgium 2001.

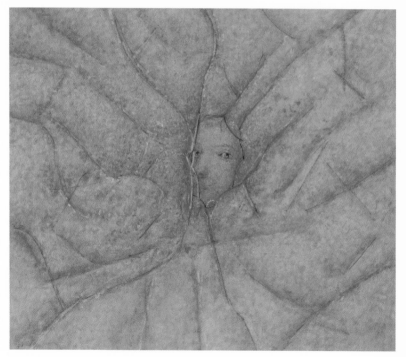

Playing with scale

Yet Westerik's observations are very specific and individual. A very clear example of this is *Dying* from 1992, based on the death of his daughter. He painted her face vanishing into an enormous fold of flesh, like an inverted birth. But there are other, less emotional examples. The *Cut by Grass* series

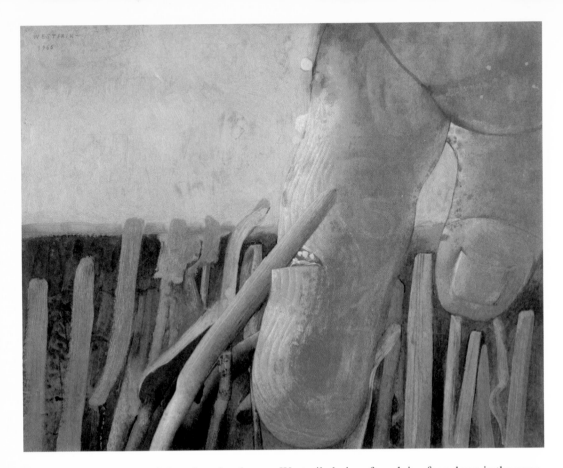

Co Westerik, *Cut by Grass no. 1*. 1966.
Panel, 60 x 75 cm. Stedelijk Museum Amsterdam /
© SABAM Belgium 2001.

is based on the pleasure Westerik derives from lying face-down in the grass, smelling the damp earth, looking at the grasses from close up, and the physical experience of cutting oneself on grass. This subject fascinated him so much that he painted it several times. The first time was in 1966, the last in 1975. The image is extremely simple, being no more than a blade of grass cutting a finger. The way Westerik elaborated on the subject was always different, and yet all the paintings elicit the same reaction, the desire to turn away and at the same time to look again.

One version depicts an index finger and a thumb venturing into the world of grass (no. 1). They disturb the order of the upright blades of grass. One of them penetrates the flesh of the index finger. The wound looks like a little mouth, eagerly biting into the grass. In *Cut by Grass no. 5*, the penetration of the finger into the world of grass has been developed even further. The blades of grass are like swords in combat with the finger. This confrontation results in the appearance of bright red drops of blood. In no. 3 the scene has been reduced to its essence: a blade of grass cuts into a fingertip. No blood this time, but distinct light and shadow effects that make the confrontation highly dramatic. In *Cut by Grass no. 4* the blades of grass sway around the finger. One of them seems to have fused with the finger.

In all these paintings something happens to the scale and the perspective. Westerik shows the image from very close up, filling the picture and very close to its surface, with an empty space behind it. This enhances the effect

Co Westerik, *Cut by Grass no. 4*. 1974.
Panel, 60 x 75 cm.
Groninger Museum /
© SABAM Belgium 2001.

Co Westerik, *Cut by Grass no. 5*. 1975.
Panel, 60 x 75 cm.
Gemeentemuseum,
The Hague / © SABAM
Belgium 2001.

of observing blades of grass from very close up. It is as if he has zoomed in on them, so that the grass and the finger become monuments in a landscape.

Playing with scale is a thread that runs throughout Westerik's work. He does it in a variety of ways, by his framing, as in *Woman in a Small Space*, but also by zooming in on individual parts.

Under the skin

Another constant theme in his work is his interest in skin. This can be seen in *Cut by Grass*, but is sometimes even more explicit, as in *Woman in a Small Space*, where the freckles and marks on her shoulders and neck are clearly visible. The depiction of skin is of crucial importance to Westerik. It is in the skin that his feelings are revealed: '*The minor element that always plays a part in my work consists of experiences that you unconsciously feel tingling in your skin, not the grand, theatrical frightened reaction to a threat; my fear is more refined, more sensitive, more a pulsing under the skin. It is what one does not see that interests me most, and which I want to reveal: for example by opening a leg, or creating a situation which you might not otherwise so easily come across, but which everyone has nevertheless unconsciously perceived - this imprints itself in the skin.*'

In this quote Westerik reveals what makes him so special. With very oddly chosen images, in a distorted perspective and a different scale, he is repeatedly able, while focusing on physicality and flesh, to make tangible such major themes as pain, fear, desolation and death.

SASKIA BAK
Translated by Gregory Ball.

All quotations taken from Johanneke van Slooten, 'De ontdekking van de huid. De geschilderde werkelijkheid van Co Westerik'. In: *Co Westerik, Zelfportretten 1946-1999*. Exh. cat. Teylers Museum, Haarlem, 1999.

n

the Belly of the Boa

The Work of Peter Verhelst

Until recently Peter Verhelst (1962-) was one of Flemish literature's best-kept secrets. True, his disturbing poetry and novels had been much praised by critics and a select band of readers; but he seemed too difficult for the public at large. But although the level of difficulty is no whit reduced, since the beginning of 1999 Verhelst has been among the most widely read and acclaimed of young Flemish writers. Two factors have played a part in this.

Firstly, his decision to write for the theatre. Verhelst's first work for the stage, *Maria Salomé*, appeared in 1997; performed by the Kaaitheater under the direction of Jan Ritsema, it was a great success. Since then the most celebrated producers and companies have been falling over each other for the chance of putting on works by Verhelst. The extreme violence and emotion to be found in the scripts is often reinforced by extreme production techniques, in which shocking video images are combined with deafeningly reverberating dance music and hysterically screeching actors. The storm also has its calm interludes, moments of almost serene reflection in which melancholy and a longing for surcease become apparent. Audiences were enthusiastic about this combination of vicious aggression and disarming tender-

Peter Verhelst (1962-).
Photo by David Samyn.

ness. And the critics had to concede that this contemporary, almost modish literature displayed a large measure of intelligence, self-awareness and critical insight.

The second step to fame came in 1999, when the novel *Tonguecat* (Tongkat) was awarded two prestigious prizes. In the spring of that year it received a Flemish prize, the Golden Owl, followed in the autumn by the Dutch Bordewijk Prize. In the interim the book had also been shortlisted for the much publicised Libris Prize. October 2000 saw the seventh impression of the novel, a phenomenal and chaotic explosion of half-mythical, half fairy-tale stories about terrorism and viruses. Evidently Verhelst can allow himself to go his own, totally unorthodox way with no fear of losing his audience.

'Can language commit suicide?'

One possible reason for this probably lies in the directness of Verhelst's style. His language is full of metaphors from the human body. Scars, blood, body cavities, organs and other body parts make up the core of Verhelst's imagery. According to himself, his aim is to develop a language which can be administered to the reader as directly as an injection or a blood transfusion. But the directness of his works is an illusion. Closer inspection reveals that everything is perfectly thought out and structured. It may all seem very corporeal and concrete, but it is also highly cerebral and abstract. Hence the recurring image of decapitation: the author would really like to be able to write without his head, but of course he can't. Literature will never have the immediacy of a musical composition, a dance, an orgasm. To achieve that kind of ecstasy it would have to deny itself. And that brings us to the most characteristic aim of Verhelst's writing: he wants to create works which annihilate themselves and transmit directly what cannot be put over in words.

Self-annihilation is the key word in Verhelst's view of literature. To express that abstract process in concrete terms he often uses the image of the snake that consumes its own tail and so ultimately destroys itself. '*How can a page once written on become virgin white again?*' – so runs the first line of Verhelst's second novel, *The Muscle Alphabet* (Het spierenalfabet, 1995). The narrator defends a '*self-destroying art*' which consists of '*works which are so perfect that they anihilate themselves. (…) Works which interact so powerfully with themselves that as a result they start to contract. Works which turn in on themselves so much that they explode*'. What he means, in fact, is not explosion, which is directed outwards, but implosion. Language has to be dislocated from the inside out. '*Can language commit suicide?*' the poet wonders in *Palate* (Verhemelte, 1996), a collection in which the open sky ('*hemel*' in Dutch) of Icarus is replaced by the enclosed space of the palate ('*verhemelte*'). It is in that body cavity that language acquires its spoken form. To undermine language the writer will have to undermine physicality.

No wonder Verhelst's work swarms with physical dislocations: viruses and terminal illnesses alternate with anorexia, suicide, self-mutilation. Literature becomes a scar, the mark of a wound. '*My scars are my fleshly flowers,*' Maria Salomé says in the play of that name, '*my orchids. Each scar is the signature of a lover and is shaped like some part of his body.*' All Verhelst's works display an extreme cultivation of trauma. His Icarus only wants to fly so that he can fall. '*I'm so good at suicide,*' he says, '*that my body can't get enough of it.*' And indeed, it is possible to regard Verhelst's work as one endless suicide.

'Leave your body to art'

That suicide begins with Verhelst's first published work, the collection of poems entitled *Obsidian* (Obsidiaan, 1987). Four paintings by Francis Bacon provide the starting-point for the volume's four parts. In a claustrophobic world of cages and enclosed spaces the characters both love and destroy each other. They liquefy in sexual ecstasy, then congeal and become sharp as glass. From the cutting glass it is but a small step to the snipping scissors and the axe – instruments indicative of decapitation and castration, which feature more and more prominently in the poems, establishing unsuspected links with the equally prominent flower imagery. At first sight the language of flowers is a gentle one, but in Verhelst it refers literally and figuratively to cut flowers, flowers so sharp and dangerous that they leave scars on the skin. This symbolism is at the heart of Verhelst's fourth collection, *White Flowers* (Witte bloemen, 1991), in which he uses Baudelaire's '*fleurs du mal*' as a symbol for an art that distils beauty and gentleness from destruction and aggression. This process of distillation has ritual and religious dimensions; but what we have here is a most unorthodox religion, one which looks for the sublime in the terrible.

In art of this kind, everything is constantly changing into its opposite: love turns to aggression, softness congeals, a kiss becomes a scar, a caress a beheading. It is a kind of mirroring, a theme that crops up in all Verhelst's books. In *Master* (1992), the next volume after *White Flowers*, the protagonist stands in the middle of a hall of mirrors. Everything he sees is endlessly reflected, so that he himself disintegrates into a myriad mirror-shards. His world is a chaotic jumble of slides in a viewer. Even more is this the case with the central figure of *Palate*: imprisoned in a virtual reality, he is subjected to a barrage of images crammed with eroticism and destruction. At first he is encased in the supple armour of a rubber suit, but this gradually hardens and stiffens until it turns into a warhead, a bomb that explodes into a million pieces. In this way he becomes a work of art, a splash of paint like those on a Jackson Pollock painting. '*Leave your body to art,*' is the ironic comment; the body has exploded and thus left a work of art to posterity. Verhelst regards this collection as completing his poetic work. Officially he does not write poetry any more; but his poetic nature still expresses itself with undiminished force in his novels and especially in his plays, which can be thought of as poems for many voices.

A body of myths

What was perfected in *Palate* had already been foreshadowed in Verhelst's first novel, which – not coincidentally – bears the title *Fluid Armour* (Vloeibaar harnas, 1993). The book is about an architect who tries to design a house which would reproduce in stone the body of St Sebastian. This martyr appears in many of Verhelst's works; he symbolises the body that destroys itself and by that very act becomes artistic. The protagonist does not achieve his objective, however; he falls (just like Icarus), damages his back and spends the rest of his life in rigid armour. Through a helmet he is confronted with virtual reality images, in which his beloved comes more and more to resemble Salome, who as a reward for her dancing asked for, and received, the head of John the Baptist. It is no coincidence that *Salomé* is the title of an intriguing photo-novel on which Verhelst collaborated with the photographer Patrick de Spiegelaere.

Since 1996 Verhelst has linked his almost archetypal world of eroticism and death directly to the equally archetypal world of folk-tale and myth. *The Colour-Catcher* (De kleurenvanger, 1996) is a gruesome fairy-tale about a Lorelei who follows the young man she loves everywhere until in Venice she drags him into the deadly water. The total union of girl and boy in one sexless being ensures both divine ecstasy and hellish destruction. In *Tonguecat* the mythical Prometheus is the central figure of a series of stories about revolution and terrorism, set in a fairy-tale land where the hellish heat of the underworld is gradually engulfing the heavenly cold of the world above. *Swelling Fruit* (Zwellend fruit, 2000) is a collection of horrific tales centring on the family of Agamemnon. Beneath their loving family life smoulders a world of incest, adultery, parricide and infanticide. The ethical and critical dimensions become ever more apparent: without moralising, Verhelst is discussing the ways in which our society channels ecstasy and the explosion of passions.

Endless self-annihilation

Perhaps nowhere is Verhelst's world expressed in such sober and concentrated form as in his work for the theatre. Simple sentences and highly effective images present the complex world of creation and destruction with such clarity that all the tender horrors come to seem almost natural. And that very naturalness is disturbing and impressive. Characters and events are reduced to an almost archetypal simplicity, but still everything remains eerily ambiguous. That is evident in *Romeo and Juliet* (Romeo en Julia, 1998) and in its sequel *Red Rubber Balls* (1999). The lovers destroy each other, but find no rest. Even in death they continue to grow and spread as tumours inside each other. Love lives on in the form of a virus or a cancer. That is also the form it assumes in Verhelst's latest play, *Arse!* (Aars!, 2000), in which he reduces the Oresteia to its essence: a family drama. The members of the family love each other too much, the one wants to possess the other completely and that is possible only in death. Yet again the snake consumes itself: '*Layer upon layer lover piles himself on lover / like grave upon grave, / (…) Then there begins the digestion, the liquefying, / the slow dissolution in the belly of the boa.*'

Anyone who looks at Verhelst's work as a whole will see how much that process of digestion refers to his oeuvre as well. One book is chewed over again in another, everything begins slowly to deliquesce and to dissolve. In 1994 Verhelst used a pentagram to illustrate the cohesiveness of his work. Within it he placed his volumes of poetry and his main themes such as decapitation, mirrors and castration. Grateful as we should be for this explanation, it is already to some extent obsolete. The simple figure has been drastically revised, relativised, perhaps even annihilated by Verhelst's later work. And it is this endless self-annihilation, above all, that makes Verhelst an important writer. In the space of thirteen years he has constructed a totally individual oeuvre, with a style and themes which are immediately recognisable even as they continue to provide unexpected fireworks.

BART VERVAECK
Translated by Tanis Guest.

Matador

That death like a man dressed in red trickles
Down the curve of the hill, until it comes
to a stop round your feet as naturally as a
mirror
relaxing around your feet before shattering.

(Inside-out man who draws me to him
and buttons me up like a golden jacket; from the heavens
roses will fall; I see a woman's mouth
telling dream backwards and a pale handkerchief.

The man opens the wrong side of the mirror;
kneeling or like a statue with my back
to him or making a Veronica first, I shall
magnetise that black peril with my fleshy cloth
as though that head were fixed to my hips with laths.)

The sun is the halogen lamp of death.

A bloodshot eyeball staring at the sky.

Kneeling on the red hooded cape
I raise my sword to the heavens;
the bright blue altar smiles
and she shows her breast
and her child,
Madonna-of-the-Red-Flower,
lead me
to the Lamb.

From Master. Amsterdam: Prometheus, 1992.

Matador

Dat dood als een roodgeklede man druppelt
over de kromming van de heuvel om rond je voeten
tot stilstand te komen met de vanzelfsprekendheid van een
spiegel
die rond je voeten uitrust alvorens uiteen te spatten.

(Binnenstebuiten gekeerde man die me aantrekt
en dichtgeknoopt als een gouden jasje; uit de hemel
zullen rozen vallen; ik zie de mond van een vrouw
droom achterstevoren uitspreken en een bleke zakdoek.

De man opent de verkeerde kant van de spiegel;
of geknield of als een standbeeld met mijn rug
naar hem toe of eerst Veronica doen, zo zal ik
dat zwarte gevaarte magnetiseren met mijn vlezige doek
als zat die kop met latjes aan mijn heupen vast.)

De zon is de hallogeenlamp van de dood.

Een ontstoken oog dat in de lucht tuurt.

Geknield op de rode kapmantel
hef ik mijn zwaard op naar de hemel;
het hoogblauwe altaar glimlacht
en zij toont haar borst
en haar kind,
Madonna-van-de-Rode-Bloem,
leid me
naar het Lam.

Self-Portrait as an Earthworm

All I did was cut it free,
it was the woman who fixed my skin to the frame.
Leaning forward. Patience settled in her lap, rubbed
congealed candle-grease like white paint (her love) into
the stretched skin and she had only to nod. And to smile.

Over it now move the insects, my thoughts, in pursuit
of aimlessness. (On the skin one can hear a scratching
of tiny claws.) Do they hope for a night that will let them
stiffen up – gleaming, senseless rings upon senseless fingers?
Not to think any more. At last not to have to
hope.

That helpless dream of being caught
that coils its way out of them:
it subsides. (It's only asleep.)

My wife puts an arm round each child.
They watch.

Every word that we think turns
in wet, purple circles,
curls up in a fleshy noose
till I lie trussed up like an earthworm.

Somewhere someone whispers
(or is it the ground sweltering in the heat):
don't believe me.

Believe
but never believe
in me.

It's better that way.

From *The Tree N.* (De boom N.). Amsterdam: Prometheus, 1994.

Zelfportret als regenworm

Ik heb haar alleen maar losgesneden,
het was de vrouw die mijn huid in het raamwerk aanbracht.
Voorovergebogen. Geduld kwam in haar schoot zitten, wreef
als witte verf gestremd kaarsvet (haar liefde) het opgespannen vel
in en ze had maar te knikken. En te glimlachen.

Daarover bewegen zich nu de insekten, mijn gedachten, ze jagen
richtingloosheid na. (Op het vel is gekras hoorbaar van klauwtjes.)
Hopen ze op een nacht die hun toelaat
op te stijven – glimmende, zinloze ringen over zinloze vingers?
Niet meer te denken. Eindelijk niet meer te moeten
hopen.

Die weerloze droom gepikt te worden
die zich daaruit te voorschijn kronkelt:
ze gaat liggen. (Ze slaapt maar.)

Mijn vrouw legt een arm rond elk kind.
Ze kijken.

Elk woord dat we denken draait
natte, paarse cirkels,
krult in een vlezige lus op
tot ik ingebonden lig als een regenworm.

Ergens wordt gefluisterd
(of is het de grond die zindert van de hitte):
geloof mij niet.

Geloof
maar
nooit in mij.

Zo is het beter.

Utopia (Icarus/study 11)

Casts were made of our bodies, deceptive
replicas that breathed, sweated, covered in streamers
swarmed in wind-tunnels. They were catapulted into the air
and when they were just about to fan out, they smashed
to bits on an invisible wall. We were ecstatic
at the air-paintings that they created.
Fresh casts were smeared all over with metal.
As we took our place in those Iron Maidens
we dreamed aloud of the art-work that we would become.
We were hoisted up. Singing. Offering a cheek.
We breathed, sweated, were catapulted into the air
and felt ourselves escape from Jackson Pollock's hand.
Melting we dripped down the walls in threads. Pulsating
stains on the ground. Beads of quicksilver. Bubbles. Harnesses
swung from the ceiling. I had to keep on repeating
to myself I CONSIST OF A BODY I CONSIST OF A BODY
to convince myself that my body existed. That
thing. They held mirrors in front of us so they could see
exactly when we stopped breathing. We stopped on time.
We were brought back to consciousness with the aid
of electricity. I did not wonder why. Certainly not
when I saw my own face: through the closed left eyelid
a strip of white gleamed like a line of cocaine.
I did not hate myself. By now my only self-image
was composed of dizziness, disorientation,
nausea, a lack or an excess of pain. I pulled myself
up by my hair, dancing over a blue crackling
floor, whipped on by a force that was so great
that it threatened to crush us, but instead of that
we felt fresh pain go through us like a scalpel.

From *Palate* (Verhemelte). Amsterdam: Prometheus, 1996.

Utopia (Icarus/studie 11)

Van onze lichamen werden afgietsels gemaakt, bedrieglijke
maquettes die ademden, zweetten, met vlaggetjes bedekt
wemelden in luchttunnels. In de lucht werden ze gekatapulteerd
en net als ze op het punt stonden uit te waaieren, sloegen ze
tegen een onzichtbare muur te pletter. We waren verrukt
over de luchtschilderijen die ze veroorzaakten.
Nieuwe afgietsels werden ingesmeerd met metaal.
Terwijl we plaatsnamen in die IJzeren Maagden,
droomden we luidop van het kunstwerk dat we zouden worden.
We werden opgetakeld. Zingend. Een wang aanbiedend.
We ademden, zweetten, werden de lucht in gekatapulteerd
en voelden ons ontsnappen aan de hand van Jackson Pollock.
Smeltend dropen we van de muren af in draden. Pulserende
vlekken op de grond. Kwikdruppels. Opwellingen. Harnassen
bungelden aan het plafond. Ik moest in mijn hoofd blijven
herhalen IK BESTA UIT EEN LICHAAM IK BESTA UIT EEN LICHAAM
om mij te overtuigen van het bestaan van mijn lichaam. Het
ding. Ze hielden ons spiegels voor om te weten wanneer
precies we ophielden met ademen. We hielden op tijd op.
We werden terug bij bewustzijn gebracht met behulp
van elektriciteit. Ik vroeg me niet af waarom. Zeker niet
toen ik mijn eigen gezicht zag: door het gesloten linkerooglid
heen lichtte een streep wit op als een lijn cocaïne.
Ik haatte mezelf niet. Ik had alleen nog een beeld van mij
dat samengesteld was uit duizelingen, desoriëntatie,
misselijkheid, gebrek of overvloed aan pijn. Ik trok mezelf
aan mijn haren overeind, dansend over een blauw knetterende
vloer, opgezweept door een kracht die zo groot was
dat die ons dreigde te vermalen, maar in plaats daarvan
voelden we verse pijn als een scalpel door ons heen gaan.

Electra will make a speech
A message to the corpses

ELECTRA No more food.
No fluids.

For reasons of hygiene I have decided
To kill time now only with myself.
It will improve the quality of my conversation.
I have nothing to say to you.
You don't speak to me any more.
Certainly not about companionship.
Or about love.

Or do you after all want to hear something about happiness?
Better if we had been a stomach
with two exits, so that we could have digested
and voided ourselves twice as quickly,
so that without shame we could have been ourselves:
a turd.
As warm as the nights when I visited him.

When I die, it dies with me.
Death himself will snip it carefully out of my stomach
and lay it on a bed of white flowers.

Take me too by my ankles like a baby.
Hang me upside down.
A smack is enough
To start me singing.

No father now.
No mother now.
I have stuffed up my bum
With my brother's flesh.

Nothing left.
No father now.
No mother now.
No children now.
No word now.

ELECTRA WITH
EARS STOPPED UP
EYES CLOSED
MOUTH SEWN SHUT
SEX BLOCKED UP

SMILING

**SOMEWHERE AN ARSE HANGS LIKE A MOON
IN THE PITCH-BLACK SKY
JUBILANT
HOPEFUL
REJOICING
RESOUNDS**
ALLE MENSCHEN WERDEN BRÜDER...

From Peter Verhelst & Luk Perceval, Arse. Anatomical Study of the Oresteia (Aars. Anatomische studie van de Oresteia). Amsterdam, Prometheus, 2000.

Arse (Aars, 1999-2000), written by Peter Verhelst and Luk Perceval. Photo by Phile Deprez / courtesy of Het Toneelhuis, Antwerp.

Extract from *Tonguecat*

Seen from a distance, the town dances like a swarm of midges in the evening air. The closer you come, the higher the buildings pull themselves up out of the ground. Flesh-coloured bricks. Flesh-coloured sky. Flesh-coloured sun bleeding to death behind a church. The town heaves like a snakepit, stinks like a dungheap, sticks to your skin like leeches that you have to remove from your face every evening. You look at your face and it looks like something that's been too close to some fire. Blotchy. Hairless. Covered in scabs. Cracked. Like baked dough.

You lie down on a bench and you've just got off to sleep when a policeman shakes your elbow. 'This is a station square, not a bedroom.' When he sees your face his hand automatically goes to his pistol. As you get out of there you feel his eyes burning into your back like two bullets.

You wouldn't believe how much edible stuff can be found in a dustbin.

Perhaps a country gets the capital it deserves. It's strange. The disease raging here is called demolition. If you ask me, there's more being knocked down than built here. The result is that areas of devastation are created in the town itself. I avoid them, not because of the danger – the night-beasts here are after money, drugs or bodies – but because there is no food to be found and nothing to stop the wind. The first few nights I spent in the parks, well out of sight of the police. But it was impossible to sleep there. Men tapped me on the shoulder, but soon made themselves scarce when I turned my face to the moonlight. It wasn't the sight of my ravaged skin that chased them away, but my age. I have seen men buying boys whose voices were barely beginning to break. I've seen girls without breasts who disguised themselves as women. I realised before they did that they'd have had more success without the disguise. My initial reaction was, where are their mothers for God's sake, but the question recoiled on myself. Where is my son?

I had gone back after the fire, but with the houses reduced to smouldering heaps it was hard to know where I was. Eventually I identified the market square by the blackened grave-mound rising above it. No trace of my children. No charred bodies. Only a little black doll which I thought must be the soldier, a doll that crumbled to nothing when I prodded it with the toe of my shoe.

Perhaps my mother's heart was playing tricks with my eyes, but I found footprints in the ash. They were the footprints of Prometheus. Why? Because. They were so deep I could tell he was carrying her on his back. I put my feet in those impressions and started walking. I was right. Near the river I saw that she had got down from his back. Four footprints. They were walking close together.

Sometimes her feet were between his, with the toes towards him. I stood in her footprints and felt his mouth on mine.

From Tonguecat. A Brothel of Stories (Tongkat: Een verhalenbordeel). Amsterdam: Prometheus, 1999.

Poems and extracts translated by Tanis Guest.

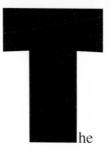he

Turd as Be-All and End-All

of the Cosmos

The Work of Patrick van Caeckenbergh

In the last forty years Belgian contemporary art has made quite a contribution, albeit unassumingly, to the desecration of Art as a Higher Aesthetic Value. While in the sixties Pop Art did its half-hearted ironising work in major art countries such as Great Britain and the United States (imitated with a fair degree of intellectualism in France by Nouveau Réalisme and politicised in Italy through Arte Povera), Belgium had its Marcel Broodthaers, who really kicked the whole art scene in the groin. A frustrated poet, Broodthaers switched to visual art *'because it was easier to achieve success in that field'*. He was to take the shine off the existing art scene with his anarchistic way of thinking and working and at the same time build a whole new and highly personal universe. The term 'individual mythology' did not surface in international art criticism until the early seventies, but it was already applicable to Broodthaers. Along with Joseph Beuys, Broodthaers is now regarded as one of the pioneers of contemporary art: it was not the aesthetic finished project that was important, but the thought process, the unmasking, the marginalisation, the calling into question of every achievement.

The global art scene was to pay for that in the seventies and a part of the eighties with the soporific epigonism known as 'conceptual art', which inflicted its stupefyingly boring non-art upon the world.

Fortunately there was little Belgium, which continued to improvise and tinker, though its contribution went largely unnoticed: Belgium was to build its own, mildly anarchistic version of the 'individual mythology', first and foremost with Panamarenko, of course, but over time also with Jef Geys, Guillaume Bijl, Thierry de Cordier, Jan Fabre and others. In the last ten years they have been joined by younger artists like Luc Tuymans, Peter Rogiers, Wim Delvoye and Patrick van Caeckenbergh.

Van Caeckenbergh (1960-), even more than the others, has constructed a fantastic mental world in a bid to protect himself against the lacklustre outside world. As the artist himself once said: *'I have created an inner island for myself and fritter away my time exploring and fortifying it. (...) What drives me is the luxury of solitary discovery.'*

Patrick van Caeckenbergh is an amateur genealogist, who looks for links

Patrick van Caeckenbergh, *Astronomie Pittoresque. Part II.* 1996. Mixed media (collage), Ø 170 cm. Photo by Felix Tirry, courtesy Zeno x Gallery.

of every description between every possible living being and cosmic phenomenon. This he does in drawings, collages and through writing, as well as in his three-dimensional work. He is also an explorer, a cartographer, philosopher and machinist, intent on investigating *ad infinitum* the cosmic structures and trees of life. But he has no illusions about the futility of the task: that infinity is about as big as an amoeba's intellect.

Digestive system

Patrick van Caeckenbergh's oeuvre to date can be divided into three stages. Broadly speaking: between 1978 and 1984 he experienced an almost delirious craving for structure, the need for answers to vital workaday questions like why we are made of flesh. Van Caeckenbergh calls that period '*Un Pied d'Oeuvre*'. A key work from that time was his *Memory-Motel*, a temporary home for memories which he arranged in a 'living box', an 'archive platform' and a 'sceptical tank': all places or rooms in which Van Caeckenbergh inventorised his whole living and working pattern.

The artist summed up the second period, which lasted into the early nineties, with the word '*Abracadabra*' (That was also the name of an exhibition at the London Tate in the summer of 1999, where his work attracted more than its fair share of attention.) '*Abracadabra*' was a quest for an ideal, magical way of understanding the world. Everyday phenomena such as

Patrick van Caeckenbergh, *'The Very Life'*, Part I: *'I spoke with quadrupeds, birds and fishes until...'*. 1993. Installation in the Kunsthalle Lophem (Bruges). Photo courtesy Zeno x Gallery.

decay, disintegration and lies crept in, the sacred beetles were created, the trees of life – so typical of his work –, a stained glass window made from pornographic cuttings, a horse constructed of kitchen utensils, and vegetables bottled in preserving jars.

Perhaps the most important work in this period was the *Chapeau*, a folding table containing all the information in the world, which the artist wore as a leaden (sixty- kilogram) hat on his head. Ironic absurdity was – and still is for that matter – never far away with Van Caeckenbergh: one of his finest works was called *The Grave*, in which six jolly garden gnomes hump a box of Caran d'Ache crayons on their shoulders. It is a monument for the grave of six great artists: Joseph Beuys, Constantin Brancusi, Marcel Duchamp, Marcel Broodthaers, René Magritte and Andy Warhol.

The third and current period in the oeuvre of Van Caeckenbergh is the large-scale project *'The Very Life'*, which he started in 1990. In this project the artist assumes the role of a pet animal whose digestive system, body gases and domestic paraphernalia have a small but inescapable effect on the universe.

'The Very Life' consists of different phases, all of which answer to storybook titles. In Part I, called *I spoke with quadrupeds, birds and fishes until...*, the artist investigated the instinctive behavioural patterns of animals. He established (among other things) that some of man's basic needs have an instinctive animal origin and can be neutralised by channelling their energy into useful, socially harmless patterns of behaviour.

In Part II, *Allow the whole, stirring continuously, to simmer gently until...*, the artist turns his attention to anatomy and appears as a pet in his own little sitting-room.

Part III is called *I sat under the ground and huddled away I slept a whole winter long until...*: here the artist turns to look at the world of plants and stars. It should be understood as an attempt to break free from the physical obstacles of the earth, which is seen as a place of destruction and overproduction.

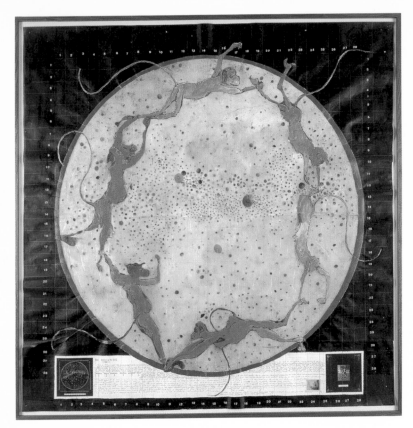

'*The Very Life*' comprises the most diverse works and installations. A fine example is the *Ventriloquist*: the self-portrait of a man with no head or feet, but with an impressive digestive system, which can assimilate and filter all the incoming substances until only the turd remains as the ultimate tangible result. In a recent work *Le Confiturier* (1999), an anthropomorphic assemblage of gas cylinders, water tanks, gas pipe nozzles, kettles and cooking pots, all the seasonal fruits can ferment and be turned into jam. Here again we have the world system of germination, maturation and decay, contained in the fantastic but also melancholy image of the jam man.

Patrick van Caeckenbergh,
Le Confiturier. 1999.
Sculpture, mixed media.
Photo courtesy Zeno x
Gallery.

The hole behind the skirting-board

The artist himself appears in almost every work, reproduced in tiny photographs and wearing a dressing-gown and slippers. He puts himself on a par with the beetles and the caterpillars, tiny creatures all engaged in their Sisyphean tasks of pushing along a ball of dung, of consuming the world. In *The Beetles*, one of the first works in '*The Very Life*' project, Van Caeckenbergh is seen sitting on such a ball of manure in the pose of Rodin's *Thinker*, while two beetles rotate the ball like a planet.

From 'fatal craving for structure' to 'the exploration of the unconsciously instinctive and of material systems': the universe of visual artist Patrick van Caeckenbergh lies somewhere between the Milky Way and a dark

Patrick van Caeckenbergh, *The Milky Way*. 1994. Mixed media (collage), 185.5 x 186 cm. Photo by Felix Tirry, courtesy Zeno x Gallery.

Patrick van Caeckenbergh, *Volière*. 1999. Installation in the Tate Gallery (London), various works. Photo by Pjerpol Rubens, courtesy Zeno x Gallery.

mouse-hole, half concealed behind a skirting-board. That mouse-hole really exists in his oeuvre: the little hole in the skirting-board (which had already appeared in several installations) has a little door with a nameplate 'Van Caeckenbergh'. The artist Patrick van Caeckenbergh has turned himself into a household pet, a biological cog in countless ordered systems, from the circulation of the blood through the star-spangled sky to the digestive system.

In essence, all the large and small installations he has ever made are based on one crucial notion: ever since the Enlightenment man has been feverishly searching for unravelment, order, orientation and regulation. In a word: Reason is King. In this new world there is less and less room for imagination, semblance, poetry and half-truths. But Van Caeckenbergh does precisely that: concerns himself with the seemingly insignificant and petty.

So the description 'melancholy' seems to be a fitting one for the work of Van Caeckenbergh: the *Sehnsucht* or melancholy hankering for the world of creative chaos is expressed in the etymological meaning of the word 'melancholy', Greek for 'black' ('*melan*') plus '*kholia*' ('khole', 'bile'). In Van Caeckenbergh's mouse-hole it is pitch-dark. And black bile or choler adust was formerly supposed to be secreted by the suprarenal glands and to cause melancholy.

MARC RUYTERS
Translated by Alison Mouthaan-Gwillim.

o

their Downfall, Eyes Wide Shut

About the Novels of Thomas Rosenboom

The report by the panel of judges for one of the Netherlands' literary prizes referred to Thomas Rosenboom as a 'young writer'. An extraordinary description. It is certainly the case that the media have long had an appetite for 'cool' young writers. But Rosenboom was born in 1956. Leaving aside his actual age, the phrase 'young writer' cannot even be applied to Rosenboom in the sense of 'new writer'. After all, his debut with the volume of stories *The Folk at Home* (De mensen thuis) was in 1983. Since then he has devoted his energies to a distinctly unfashionable variant of the historical novel. And his stylistic hallmark is a crazy kind of old gents' language, as the following phrases from his latest novel *Public Works* (Publieke werken, 1999) demonstrate: '*Anijs, now a corpulent man, had donned a dignity which had matured from an acquired status to an inner quality. His round face gleamed like a newel post that had grown greasy from the touch of many a hand.*'

So there must have been another reason for describing Rosenboom as a young writer. With the appearance of his very first book, the Dutch weekly paper *Vrij Nederland* called him a virtuoso: '*What next for a young writer who displays such clear virtuosic tendencies; satisfied with his own talent, without a trace of doubt? The three long stories which make up "The Folk at Home" are written with a disturbing facility, showing a Vestdijkian lust for storytelling, reflection and fabulation.*' The comparison with the Dutch writer Simon Vestdijk is a telling one because Rosenboom has been a *wunderkind* of Dutch literature from the outset. The eternal *wunderkind*. Nor was recognition slow in coming. *The Folk at Home* was awarded the Lucy B. and C.W. van der Hoogt Prize, a prestigious distinction for a debutant. In 1995 he was awarded the Libris Prize for Literature for *Washed Flesh* (Gewassen vlees, 1995), and *Public Works* received the Libris Prize in 2000. No mean feat, given the modest size of his oeuvre – his only other book is the novel *Deserving Friend* (Vriend van verdienste, 1985).

Yet one might well ask what the immense popularity of Rosenboom's historical novels says about the state of Dutch literature. Taken together with the rise of autobiographical prose and the egodocument, does it suggest a regressive tendency? The answer is both yes and no. The question of whether Rosenboom does actually write historical novels is hotly debated, for instance. According to the Libris judges' report, *Public Works* is too grotesque, not realistic enough for a historical novel. It sits between a historical evocation of town and country at the end of the nineteenth century, and a psychological analysis which frequently cuts to the quick of individuals whose self-created problems are their downfall.

The theme of evil

Rosenboom's approach to the historical novel is quite unlike that of his Dutch colleagues. After all, the average historical novelist is a plodder who is so absorbed by his subject matter when preparing to write his creative prose – no publication is left unread – that he comes unstuck the moment he must make a selection from the pot-pourri of the past. He could always hurl the whole load of studies and reference books out of the window, but instead of doing so, he conscientiously sets about working all the facts and figures into his prose. With the result that not only does the background come between writer and reader, any larger picture of the subject also disappears under the copious documentation. After the death of the prolific S. Vestdijk in 1971 it seemed as though the genre of the historical novel in the Netherlands – with the odd exception such as Hella Haasse whose work has been much translated into English – had died with him. That is, until Thomas Rosenboom's *Washed Flesh* appeared on the scene. It is not the historical information on the eighteenth century which stays in the mind after reading this book, but a powerful image of the troubled inner man who is the anti-hero. Over and above an interest in authentic detail, which Rosenboom does not shy away from, the historical novel demands a high level of sophistication in a writer who is to avoid falling into the trap of studiousness. After all, the readers of historical novels are not primarily looking for information, or they would have chosen history books. Or put another way, the scenery should not dominate the stage. Rosenboom's work embodies the difference between a real historical novel and the old-fashioned biographical romance which is of little literary interest.

In Rosenboom's books the past evokes the present, as in all successful historical novels. In S. Vestdijk's *The Latter Days of Pilate* (De nadagen van Pilatus, 1938), for example, the historical character of Pontius Pilate reminds one of a weary British colonial official who, eager to return to his home country, is consequently completely uninterested in a trouble-maker like Jesus. Rosenboom's aim is not to describe the century in which his story is set; he is focused on his characters. As he said in an interview: '*My heroes must be absorbed to the fullest extent in their dramatic struggle.*' Which makes his books psychological novels. And what makes those novels so refreshingly contemporary in comparison with historical novels of the past, is their removal of the traditional division of the narrative universe into good and evil.

Rosenboom's characters all have in common that, through their idiosyncratic reasoning, they achieve the opposite of what they are aiming at. They try to control events, but ultimately they are digging their own graves. They are, in the writer's own words, absolutist, totalitarian figures. Characters who, from the best of motives, set their sights on rising above themselves, only to become the victims of the evils they have created.

The main theme running through Rosenboom's oeuvre is evil. His first stories are exercises involving brooding, gloomy adolescents. The theme really comes into its own in the psychological thriller *Deserving Friend*. In this novel, based on a famous Dutch murder case from the nineteen-sixties, mutual blackmail ensures the characters keep a stranglehold on one another. The overall picture painted by the novel is of the final convulsions of class society in the Netherlands.

The opening of the masterly novel *Washed Flesh* is truly emblematic of Rosenboom's themes. The lame boy Petrus sacrifices his cat to make an impression on other boys. The animal's paws are dipped in tar so that walnut shells will stick to them, thus rendering its claws useless. Petrus then places the animal on the slippery ice where a fierce wind is blowing. *'Thus was the animal entrusted to the wind and the eternal ice, it began to slide on its shells and was still looking at Petrus when the wind turned it around. Only now did the tail thicken, the cat stiffened it like a flagpole which only increased its speed. (…) After a while he saw the animal walking again, but he knew: towards the slippery ice – as long as it had the strength, it would keep itself upright with the wind behind it. With one hand shading his eyes Petrus watched his cat. Nothing else was alive, only the dancing little red flame in the distance. For a moment it seemed to stand still, then it went out and all that was left was the mineral glassiness of the ice, gleaming brightly with an antimony sheen.'* I know few images which capture the human condition – what people do to themselves and others – so concentratedly as this scene which has its origins in a historical rural tradition of animal abuse.

Thomas Rosenboom (1956-). Photo by Klaas Koppe.

A far-off past

In an interview Rosenboom revealed that he does not regard the historical novel as a contemporary story in historical clothing. What he finds so attractive about the genre is the distance from his own time. Losing yourself in a far-off past. That is why he set *Washed Flesh* in the eighteenth century and *Public Works* in the Amsterdam and rural Hoogeveen of the late nineteenth century. No-one will deny that every fibre of these books breathes the particular period of the past in which they are set. I suspect that what Rosenboom is referring to in this statement is the writer's experience of creating such books, not the reading experience. Rosenboom researches a period until he knows everything there is to know about it. But that does not interfere with his creativity: for *Washed Flesh* he created an archaic-sounding 'historicising' language which comes across to the reader as perfectly fitting and natural. *Public Works* may be full of bucolic expressions and obscure phrases, but Rosenboom reveals himself to be a less pastoral and less constrained writer than previously.

However pleasant it may be for the writer to immerse himself in another time, the reader experiences Rosenboom's historical novels as very much of his own time. One example: The young bailiff Willem Augustijn's craving for sugar in *Washed Flesh* is very reminiscent of a more modern addiction to cocaine. Besides its plot and the stream of anecdotal events, *Public Works* is a psychological piece about the personal and social consequences of childlessness. The writer has spoken about this: '*In my environment I distinguish between two sorts of people. People who have children and people who do not. The people who have children are in my eyes the true adults. They bear responsibility day in and day out. They do not pursue exclusively their own pleasure, do not only put themselves first (...) This is a reflection of how I feel. I myself have no children, and no job which binds me to society. This is why in recent years I have started to feel increasing repugnance towards my occupation.*'

Pride and fall

If *Public Works* is about childlessness on the psychological level, at a thematic level it is a tale of manifold pride which comes before a fall. In this respect it is comparable to *Washed Flesh* which tells the story of the young eighteenth-century bailiff Willem Augustijn van Donck, who attempts to set up a sugar factory and a colony for the poor in the small town of Hulst. As the story unfolds, however, this patrician young man slides ever deeper into his delusions until a pistol shot puts an end to his life. In *Public Works* this eighteenth-century character has made way for two nineteenth-century gentlemen: Christof Anijs, a somewhat older apothecary who concerns himself with the peat cutters of Hoogeveen, and his cousin Walter Vedder, an Amsterdam violin-maker who, under the pseudonym of Veritas tracks the progress of the public works of Amsterdam, suddenly finding himself personally involved when a grand hotel is planned for the site where he lives. Rosenboom describes the 'history' of an architectural anomaly in Amsterdam. The front elevation of the nineteenth-century Victoria Hotel close to the Central Station contains two seventeenth-century facades. Fascinatingly, for some inexplicable reason the hotel was built around these little houses. *Public Works* portrays the circumstances which led to this, as imagined by Rosenboom, at a time when public works were shaping Amsterdam. Within a short space of time the Concertgebouw, the Rijksmuseum, the Amstel Hotel, American Hotel and the Central Station all came into being. It is against this backdrop that Rosenboom brings his characters' tragic lives into existence.

Anijs, in his sixties, feels inferior to his new, young, university-educated colleague Halink. But he is determined to hold his own. With a devout belief in science and progress, he hands out medicines without a doctor's prescription, clothes himself in a white doctor's coat which he has stolen from the local doctor, and cures the poor peat-cutters in the area. Not only does he cut free the tongues of those suffering from speech impediments, he also gives a child and a dog highly unsuitable, strong tablets. He even performs a puncture with a circumcision knife on a woman in labour who is in difficulty. The baby is born dead. His intentions are good, but his megalomania huge. He even likens himself to Moses, when he succeeds in shipping the peat-cutters and their families as emigrants to the promised land of America. As a character, he is almost the twin brother of Monsieur Homais, the Voltaire-reading pharmacist in Flaubert's *Madame Bovary*.

Anijs' Amsterdam cousin Walter Vedder is just as arrogant. Like Anijs he is self-made and unqualified, having worked his way up from joiner to vio-lin-maker. He, too, thinks he is a man of the world, but at the same time feels unrecognised by his fellows. Which is why he doggedly sabotages the ne-gotiations when the firm which wants to build the Victoria Hotel on the site where his seventeenth-century house stands alongside others, tries to dis-cuss things with him. The representative of the enterprise makes a generous offer: twenty thousand guilders, whereas the actual value of the property is five thousand. Vedder, however, insists on fifty thousand, an impossible price, views his own lack of flexibility as 'negotiation' and the other party's refusal as a 'bluff'. The most tragic aspect is that he is also negotiating on behalf of his next-door neighbours, two simple old people who trust him implicitly, and who, like him, end up with nothing.

Rosenboom depicts the behaviour of the two cousins as 'boyish'. They constantly misinterpret the signals from the world around them, and they suffer as a result of their childlessness due to infertility. '*Ah, no children...! How often does it not happen that it is precisely those people with the largest hearts who are denied the blessing of children?*' Vedder even dreams of a family. When he finds himself in conversation with a widow and her small son, his thoughts take flight: '*Everything had changed, so suddenly and so completely; he had changed too. The late sun on his face: so peaceful! The time: much later...The widow's hand on his forearm: he felt so light, it was as though he was dancing, and as he did so along the path between the teth-ered horses which to him seemed like an avenue, he could feel not just the young mother on his arm, but also the child she was leading on her other arm. His progress was immense, manly, full of dignity, the people moved aside as a matter of course: he had become a family.*'

The cousins, on the threshold of progress, meddle with affairs that are be-yond them, great public concerns like big business and the struggle to over-come poverty and disease. They are shown to be unfit for such work, and yet they achieve great things through their boyishness. The poor emigrants ar-riving at their destination are eternally grateful to Anijs and Vedder. Vedder comes to a wretched end: the Victoria hotel is simply built around his hou-se and that of his neighbours, he receives no money but has already given a guarantee to pay fifty thousand guilders for the peat-cutters' crossing to America. He dies just in time. Anijs ends up in hospital, his wife deserts him, the medical disciplinary committee has forbidden him to practise as an apothecary, but at the end of the novel there is a prospect of happiness in love.

Rosenboom is the cruellest writer in the Dutch-speaking world. What he does to the cousins in his uncaring superior prose, the way he leaves them to go round in circles within their own limitations, the way he leads them eyes wide shut to their downfall, displaying their more than human humanity, is not so much malicious, it is frankly devilish.

JEROEN VULLINGS
Translated by Jane Fenoulhet.

'No, I am sorry, I cannot give you a fertility medicine.'

The clicking of the knitting needles in the side room had stopped, and for a second all Anijs could hear was the murmuring of his blood. There was nobody else in the chemist's shop, only Johanna Bennemin.

Her head bowed low, she remained standing in front of the counter. She seemed not to grasp that he had refused her request and repeated her question once more. At his renewed refusal she began to nod, then at last she turned around, went outside and darted away past the window.

Fertility medicine for an unmarried girl: the request had been too strange even for amazement, and it must have pained Martha, on top of the disappointment that Little Pet had not come along with his sister. A fly buzzed above the sweet counter, a horse stamped the ground in the stable of Hotel Thomas. Anijs closed his eyes in resignation.

'Fertility medicine… how old is that child, actually?'

Martha's sharp voice still took him by surprise. Bracing himself, he pushed the dividing door wider open. As always, she sat by the window, her feet up on the little footstool, in winter on a warmer. He face was even more drawn than usual, but inspired pity nevertheless, on account of the childlessness.

'But I didn't give it to her, did I?' he said in an apologetic, yet aggrieved tone.

Only now did she look right at him, scornfully. 'You didn't give it to her, you say? You didn't give it to her?' She seemed on the point of bursting into laughter. 'Chris, there's no such thing! Or if there is, give some to me…'

He endured her mockery while it lasted, it was all he could do, and even when, bitterly, she resumed her study of life insurance he did not immediately leave: she so dearly wanted a policy, but he thought the premium too high.

Back in the chemist's shop, with the dividing door closed, Anijs fleetingly saw the pale face of Johanna in front of him, its grey eyes like two steel marbles in a weighing scale, then his thoughts returned to their usual course; surely nothing had changed, nothing had happened? Slowly the old disquiet crept up on him. What was preventing his new colleague from paying him a visit? He remembered Halink as a quiet, almost timid young man, but how to explain this stand-offishness? Or was he too busy telling his customers about photography? Even the most diffident characters turned to such things when it was a matter of winning the favour of the ignorant public – perhaps he was actively engaged in fitting out a photographic studio, and that was why no-one had dared to mention the new Unicorn…

Anijs wiped the sweat from his brow. It was five o' clock, the maid was taking the prescriptions round, nothing more would happen today. Suddenly decisive, he took his comb out of his breast pocket, and bent towards the reflective glass protecting the diploma on the wall. Would it not be a friendly gesture if he were himself to call by to show his interest? He combed his moustache, thought that he looked distinguished, took up his hat – the young fellow had obviously heard a thing or two about him, and probably did not dare to disturb him in his manifold activities; he was clearly the sort who preferred to bide his time!

The door slammed shut behind him, its bell tinkling. As he went past he nodded to Martha in the window, then he looked fixedly ahead. The late summer heat hung like a vapour over the canal, there were hardly any people about, the bridges at the Cross were hazy in the distance. Johanna was no longer in sight, had clearly taken the back path to the rise.

Purposefully he hastened along the canalside as he generally did on his way to a meeting or a bedside. In the way fat people do, he leaned backwards slightly to counterbalance his stomach, which stood even prouder as a result, but which was less bosomy than otherwise: what was Halink up to? Those who saw him greeted him confidently, here a woman in a doorway, there a peat-carrier on the deck of his barge; in his usual manner he waved back, without breaking his stride, after all he was always in a hurry, if never so nervous as now: what did Halink have in mind?

There were brief, repeated glimpses of the hinterland between two houses, he had already passed the town hall, and suddenly the white outline of the bridges at the crossing stood out sharply against the glaring light. When a moment later he also caught sight of the sign with the golden unicorn he stood still, panting. With his large white handkerchief he again wiped the sweat from his brow, like an opera singer, then continued on his way, but slower now, cautiously.

It was busier this close to the Cross. On the bridge over the main canal stood three old women. Here, too, his appearance, as familiar as it was striking, attracted attention, but he no longer noticed, nothing penetrated, he needed all his strength to proceed through the thick air which stuck in his throat as he sucked it in. The Unicorn was virtually on the corner. He took the last few steps, turned to face the shop window – and breathed out.

No photographic camera, not even a microscope was to be seen, nothing at all had changed, the same packets and phials were still in the window just as good old Van der Wal had once arranged them. With a sigh of relief, he again allowed his gaze to glide slowly upwards over the faded velvet and on along the milky glass half-partition between the shop-window and the dark room behind it, and found himself looking straight into Halink's face just above it. He was startled, breathed in again, more deeply: poor thing, like a shopkeeper with no customers the new colleague was standing staring out of the window! All the same, he managed a smile and motioned him to come in.

His reined-in senses now also relaxed and like fresh air, the surroundings he had been avoiding rushed in to fill the vacuum at the heart of him. The pump in front of the town hall squeaked in the background, the tepid canal water smelt of fish, on the bridge nearby the three women leaned in concentration towards the spectacle of the old apothecary calling on the young one. Laughing, Anijs waved up to them, then he opened the door. Even the sign saying 'Have you forgotten something?' was still hanging on the inside!

There were indeed no other customers inside. Instead of coming to greet him, Halink had walked back to position himself behind the till, beside which stood Van der Wal's old scales. Straight away Anijs again felt the aloofness of their first encounter at the time of the handover, but above all, he also recognised the old gloom and the cool scent of tea and honeycomb. While they were still shaking hands across the counter he could already see that here inside The Unicorn remained unchanged as well: blast it! Had the young chap no ambition at all? Did he not know how fast science was advancing in the times that were now unfolding?

From *Public Works* (Publieke werken). Amsterdam: Querido, 1999, pp. 31-35.
Translated by Jane Fenoulhet.

Many

Waters to Bridge

Bridges in the Netherlands

1999 saw the completion of the Netherlands Bridge Society's three-part publication *Bridges in the Netherlands 1800-1940* (Bruggen in Nederland 1800-1940. Utrecht, 1997-1999), under the scholarly general editorship of J. Oosterhoff.

The importance of bridges to the life of a country such as the Netherlands is almost impossible to overestimate. Simply, in the words of the General Introduction to *Bridges in the Netherlands*, this is '*above all a land of water. It is therefore hardly to be wondered at that there are a large number of bridges, that bridge-building has a long and rich tradition, and that many remarkable bridges have been built. Prominent among these are the movable bridges in the construction of which Dutch engineers have always been supreme.*' Indeed, the Netherlands arguably has the highest bridge density in the world, and its bridges, quite aside from their historical, technical and functional significance, often also determine the look and character of the topography. What follows is an abbreviated account of the history of Dutch bridge-building, topped off with descriptions of a number of bridges which are in one way or another of particular interest.

The most immediately striking aspect of the Netherlands, and the one with which the country is most commonly associated, is indisputably the physical structure of the northern and western parts: flat and low-lying, often barely above sea level, and criss-crossed by innumerable watercourses of natural origin that were later standardised or canalised and eventually complemented by man-made canals. Although these deltaic features are by no means unique, the Dutch context – especially to the west – is in a category of its own in having for centuries past coincided with a high population density, intense economic activity founded on commerce, and comparatively great wealth. In combination, these geophysical and socio-economic factors favoured the early development of a dense transport network. At first, because of the practical obstacles to building and maintaining roads in marshy soil in the north and west of the Netherlands, this was chiefly a matter of waterways. In the nineteenth century the infrastructure was expanded by the addition of rail and tramways and, from 1900, the road system made rapid strides.

In total contrast to this, the middle, east, and south of the country are gently rolling and in South Limburg even hilly here and there – terrain where rivers tend to become depleted at times of lower rainfall, and fast-moving in wetter seasons, so that there was no question of developing water-borne traffic, except on the great rivers. Moreover, this higher, drier, better-drained land was better suited to road construction, and roads have existed in these regions throughout recorded history. All the same, in order to expand the inland waterways network still further, canals also began to be constructed here from 1800 onwards.

Geographical conditions have had two important consequences for the evolution of Dutch bridge-building technology. First, except in South Limburg, there was no requirement for the long, high, multi-span viaducts and aqueducts that are such a feature of, for instance, the German and French valleys – and which in Britain even carried canals over roads. Second, the geography of the north and west promoted the development of movable bridges, a class that before 1800 was very rare elsewhere. The reason for this is that in conditions where the land barely rises above the water, the erection of fixed bridges is a daunting technical, and financial, proposition even today. For a start, to ensure sufficient clearance for shipping, it requires the construction of steeply inclined bridge approaches. The solution at which Dutch engineers arrived was to develop different types of movable draw and swing bridges, always constructed of wood. Then as now, the movable bridge is recognised as a specifically Dutch area of engineering expertise.

Turning to fixed bridges, it might be supposed that crossings over the lower reaches of great rivers such as the Rhine and Maas (Meuse) would of necessity involve bridgeworks with enormous spans, but in fact the river bridges are of average width in comparison with similar bridges in similar geographical settings elsewhere. The reason for this is that shortly after entering the country the Rhine splits into two arms, the Waal and IJssel, which are both of moderate width. Because of this no river bridge in the Netherlands has a span in excess of 300 m, whereas the suspension bridge built in about 1960 over the Rhine at Emmerich in Germany, for instance, required a span of 500 m.

Bridges through the ages

A difficulty which in the past presented an apparently insurmountable obstacle to bridging these big rivers at their widest was the perennial problem of floating winter ice. Indeed, for centuries it was doubted whether it was possible at all to build bridges capable of withstanding the enormous blocks of ice shunting downstream into the delta.

The earliest river bridges in the Netherlands were Roman constructions, and these were not equalled for many centuries. Remains of Roman bridges have been found along the Waal to the west of Zaltbommel at Zuilichem, and by the Maas at Cuyk. At Maastricht there was another Roman bridge which was continually renewed until the thirteenth century. Later bridges of note were the great fourteenth-century Maria Theresia bridge over the Roer (in Germany: the River Ruhr) at Roermond, and the fifteenth-century wooden bridges over the IJssel at Kampen, Deventer and Zutphen.

Smaller in scale but important to the history of bridge-building were the bridges across castle moats which not only gave access to the castle gate, but also formed part of the castle's defences. In time these bridges evolved from a simple plank or two thrown across the moat into drawbridges, which first appeared in the thirteenth century. More typically Dutch was the influence of the urban environment on the development of bridge engineering. Especially in the west and north of the country, towns were defined by the characteristic canals which began life as moats curved around the inner city walls and ramparts. As towns expanded, so the number of canals was increased, giving rise to the concentric canal belts of which Amsterdam's is the largest and most striking example. Bridge-building across the canals most probably began in the course of the thirteenth century.

At first the bridges were built entirely of wood, supported by portals where wider waterways needed to be spanned. The disadvantage of wood was its perishability. Not only was maintenance costly, but most bridges had to be entirely renewed every twenty years or so. From the sixteenth century onwards, therefore, wood gave way to masonry, the durability of which more than offset the greater building expertise and investment needed for the initial construction.

Dramatic changes in bridge-building came with the industrial revolution, which in the Netherlands by and large took place in the nineteenth century, when iron began to be used. The first Dutch iron bridge is generally acknowledged to have been the Stokkenbrug over the Zalmhaven (salmon port) in Rotterdam, a double bascule bridge which was completed in 1837 – almost six decades after the Iron Bridge over the Severn at Coalbrookdale.

As elsewhere, the development of the railways was from the start an important stimulus to building in iron. Thus the Amsterdam-Haarlem-The Hague-Rotterdam railway (Hollandsche IJzeren Spoorweg), built between 1837 and 1847, incorporated no less than 98 bridges, of which 12 were movable. One of the most formidable challenges to bridge-building in the Netherlands had always been bridging the great rivers. Now, with the advent of the railway age, iron superstructures made this possible. The first great iron rail bridge was the bridge across the IJssel at Westervoort of 1856, soon followed by the bridge across the Maas at Maastricht. From 1864, after the completion of the IJssel bridge at Zwolle, the pace accelerated, resulting in the construction of 21 more large river bridges before the century ended. The most spectacular of these was undoubtedly the bridge over the Lek at Culemborg, whose span of 155 m was for ten years the longest in the world.

Because of the destructive force of winter ice, engineers long shied away from placing piers in the rivers, resorting instead to the construction of extended spans. (In this context it is interesting to note that whereas the building of the railways took place within the framework of an overall national policy, the construction of road bridges was dictated purely by local and regional interests. This, of course, is indicative of the scant importance attached to the road network in the nineteenth century, when national routes were still barely an issue.) Impressive bridges were similarly built across the major canals.

The twentieth century

With the introduction, in about 1900, of reinforced concrete – which had first been used in France and Germany in the latter half of the nineteenth century – Dutch civil engineers immediately stopped using brick for the substructure and superstructure of bridges, though for facings brickwork and natural stone continued to be the norm. The first full-scale Dutch reinforced concrete bridge was in all probability the Schollenbrug across the Watergraafsmeer Ring Canal in Amsterdam, which was built in 1900, measured 14 m between its piers, and was designed by L.A. Sanders of the Amsterdam Wittenburg Cement and Iron Works. At this stage the government was concerned to promote the use of iron and steel for bridges, leaving the development of reinforced concrete to private contractors.

The twentieth century marked the start of a focus on road bridge construction, as from about 1900 onwards the automobile necessitated the expansion of the road network. At first this was a desultory and piecemeal process, but after the First World War a more coordinated approach set in, culminating in a national policy for infrastructural development of the road system. The first national road-building plan (Rijkswegenplan), which was adopted in 1927, duly incorporated an intensive bridge-building programme. To implement this programme a separate bureau was created, in 1928, within the Department of Public Works (Rijkwaterstaat), the government agency established in 1798 for the national administration of waterways and traffic. Among the bridges scheduled under the 1927 plan was the bridge across the Waal at Nijmegen which was completed in 1936 with a span of 244 m, thus becoming the biggest arch bridge ever built on the continent. The programme also provided for large-scale bridge-building across the inland waterways. In the meantime, until about 1930 road traffic across the great rivers continued to rely, as it always had done, on ferries and on ship bridges (as at Deventer, Doesburg, Westervoort, Arnhem, Vianen and Hedel).

After the wholesale destruction of the infrastructure during the Second World War, the first priority was to restore the rail bridges across the great rivers. Financial constraints and shortage of materials meant that some of these replacements were somewhat ramshackle, but most were later replaced by modern welded lattice work constructions. Road bridge construction remained piecemeal in the initial post-war years, until the advent of standardised prestressed concrete and prefabricated units in the 1950s on the one hand, and steep increases in car ownership from the 1960s on the other, provided the incentives for the rapid construction of many new bridges. To sum up this period generally, with a few rare exceptions there was little to mark out Dutch bridges from mass-produced constructions being put up all over the world. The rare exceptions concerned prefabricated prestressed bridges which – thanks to the highly-developed inland water transport system – were easier to put in place in the Netherlands than elsewhere. The highpoint of this type of bridge-building was undoubtedly the Zeeland Bridge, built in 1962-1964 across a closed-off arm of the sea in the south-west of the Netherlands. On the whole, though, bridge construction was targeted at keeping abreast with demand on the road and rail infrastructure, always using the latest steel and concrete technology.

Landmarks

From the 1980s onwards a more aesthetically-orientated outlook set in. There was more money around, and public interest in how things *look* was increasing. Besides, landmark architecture was now an established matter of international prestige. The Department of Public Works and Waterways regularly began to consult authoritative planners and architects, and international competitions were launched for the design of major bridge projects.

The tide began to turn with smaller works, such as footbridges in parks and over motorways, but the real turning point came in 1994-1996 with the Erasmus Bridge in Rotterdam. This bridge, designed and revered by architects, heavily criticised at first by structural engineers, and much discussed by administrators, above all cleared the air for a fresh outlook on bridge-building.

The closing years of the twentieth century have witnessed especially interesting developments in movable bridges. In particular, an approach combining the skills of civil engineers and architects, and incorporating the latest in hydraulic mechanisms and electronic steering, has given rise to bridges some of which are truly revolutionary in conception, while retaining a quintessentially Dutch character. Examples of this are the Kloosterbrug across the Drentsche Hoofdvaart, the rail bridge at Dordrecht, and the Slauerhoff bridge across the Harlinger Trekvaart at Leeuwarden in Friesland. That the trend towards thought-provoking bridge-building in the Netherlands continues apace is demonstrated, among other things, by the number of leading international architects competing for new Dutch bridge projects.

MICHEL BAKKER
Translated by Sonja Prescod.

1

1. St Servatius Bridge (Sint-Servaasbrug) over the Maas at Maastricht.
The name of the town derives from the Latin *mosae trajectum*, referring to the bridge built by the Romans on this site, which for centuries remained the only one over the lower Maas (Meuse). The timber bridge essentially retained its original form until 1275, when it simply fell apart. Tradition has it that the actual moment of collapse occurred during a procession, killing dozens of people. Plans for a re-placement, masonry, bridge slightly north of the old one were at once drawn up, resulting in the construction of the still extant St Servatius Bridge between 1280 and 1298. The medieval bridge had nine semicircular arches of Namur stone and a span of about 12 m, with on the Wyck side one span of about 20 m, with wooden supporting beams and roof. The bridge was designed to be rapidly dismantled, or even fired, in times of war. In the course of comprehensive restoration between 1932 and 1934 the Wyck side was widened to 50 m, spanned by a fixed iron bridge which, in 1962, was converted into a movable (lift) bridge. Note the great stone span to the right which was replaced by the modern, movable part.

2

Zwolle

3

2. Bridge over the IJssel at Westervoort, 1853-1856, first design.
Following the completion, in 1845, of the Amsterdam-Utrecht railway, demand soon arose for a continuation of the line into Germany. This required a bridge over the IJssel at Westervoort, which had to allow for strongly fluctuating water levels and large volumes of floating ice coming downstream in winter. The railway was in the first instance built as a Dutch state enterprise, but the construction of the extension was tendered out to the private Netherlands Rhine Railway Company (Nederlandsche Rhijnspoorweg-Maatschappij) which was largely financed by British capital. The first design for the bridge, by W.C.P. Baron van Reede van Oudtshoorn of the Department of Public Works and Waterways, was for a twin-track four-span bridge with at the centre a swing bridge for two navigable channels of 15.2 m. This design was later modified by widening the spans on either side of the movable bridge to allow for still greater throughflow of water and ice. The contractor was the London firm of Thomas Brassey.

3. High Bridge (Hoge Brug) at Zwolle, 1883.
Built in 1882/1883 for the passage of 'pedestrians, handcarts, and cattle', this bridge, which is known locally as the 'high bridge' or 'high railway bridge', has three iron spans of about 36 m supported by iron beams, with masonry abutments. The wooden deck is between iron profiles of the 'lensligger'' or 'visbuikligger' type developed by the German engineer F.A. von Pauli around 1855. The engineer responsible for the design was M.J. Schuurbecke Boeije of the Netherlands State Railways, whose

4

known interest in mathematics must have accounted for his choice of the Pauli design. The bridge was comprehensively restored in 1993.

4. Bontebrug at Dokkum, 1869.
The Bontebrug over the Kleindiep in the inner city is a pedestrian crossing of 2 m width. Originally constructed of cast iron, its 20.2 m span made it the longest bridge of this material ever built in the Netherlands. The deck was of wood resting on three cast iron arched structures which were 1.7 m high at the abutments. In the body of the arches were circular openings. The bridge was renovated in 1986 and the cast iron replaced by welded sheet iron.

5. Viaduct over the Veeweg (Cattle Path) at Klimmen / Voerendaal.
The viaduct has a total length of 68 m with a central span of 14 m between the piers, and on either side identical sections spanning

5

11.95 m. This construction of 1914 is of a type sometimes known as a 'concrete, high-deck arched bridge', but with three spans, a departure which according to the available evidence had not previously been attempted in the Netherlands, and was thereafter repeated but once, at Bergen op Zoom. As the only one of its kind, the viaduct became a listed monument in 1997.

6

Pons Campensis

7

8

6. The Corn Bridge (Koornbrug) in Leiden. The Koornbrug is of great antiquity, and was originally known as the St Cornelius Bridge. It acquired its present name in 1443 when it became the location of the corn exchange. In 1642 it was enlarged in stone; the contractor was Jan Claesz. van Warmont, and the stone was supplied by Cornelis Gijsbersz. van Duynen, the official municipal master mason.
In 1825 J. de Sauvage constructed the wooden roofs at either long side according to a design of the municipal architect, Van der Paauw.

7. Third Bridge over the IJssel at Kampen, 1598: 'Pons Campensis'. Because earlier bridges on the site had always been susceptible to severe damage from storm floods and ice, the builders of this bridge decided to reduce the number of spans. Originally the two wide central spans were supported by portals. Above were high triangular 'gallow' trusses acting as main beams. These main beams supported rafter-like structures which were horizontally braced. In 1785 this bridge, like its predecessors, was in due course replaced. This is a detail from the map of Kampen, Johannes Blaue, c.1650.

8. Wooden Float-Bridge over the North Holland Canal (Noordhollandsch Kanaal) at Koedijk. This bridge consists of a raft and a pair of cattle-bridges with flaps, connected to the abutments on

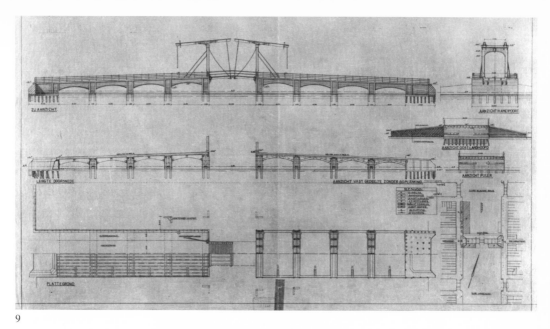

9

10

either side. When the bridge is opened the raft is pulled between the portals beneath the decks of the cattle bridges. Of the eighteen such bridges that were built over the canal this is the sole example which technically still conforms to type. The bridges were standardised to a span of 15.5 m and a total length of 42.5 m. The Koedijk bridge is constructed of pine and oak and was built in 1821; the contractor was Tijmon Kater of Monnickendam. The canal itself was constructed to a design by the hydraulic engineer Jan Blanken Jansz. This illustration shows a model of a float-bridge of oak and mahogany, c.1820. The model shows two alternative mechanisms for raising the cattle-bridges: to the right by means of four winches and chains, to the left by means of levers. (Rijksmuseum, Amsterdam, Marine Models Room).

9. Skinny Bridge (Magere Brug) over the Amstel in Amsterdam.
Built in 1670 as a pedestrian crossing, this bridge had thirteen navigable spans, and one central draw-bridge. On account of its

narrowness it soon became colloquially known as the 'skinny' bridge. In 1840, by which time it was also being used by horse-drawn traffic, the bridge was overhauled. A double draw-bridge was introduced and the number of navigable spans reduced to nine, which by and large resulted in its present form. The present bridge is the result of the 1969 restoration. This

illustration shows the plan of bridge No. 242, Department of Public Works, Amsterdam, 1933 (Gemeentearchief, Amsterdam).

10. Timber 'Earhole' Bridge (oorgatbrug) in Friesland.
Prior to 1800 there were two kinds of movable bridges: draw-bridges, which were by far the

majority, and swing bridges. There was also a third variety, known as an earhole, or mast hole, bridge. This consisted of a fixed bridge in the middle of which were two hinged, leaning flaps which when opened gave clearance to tall ships' masts.

11

12

11. Ship Bridge
(Kraneschipbrug) over the
Merwede Canal at
Meerkerk, 1886.
Built in 1886 as part of the
reconstruction of the former
Zederik Canal into the
Merwede Canal, the desig-
nation of ship bridge, rather
than pontoon bridge, is due
to the fact that, like the ship
bridges on the great rivers,
the movable part opened by
a swivel action around
posts. The floating element
was about 28 m long. The
four vessels were originally
of wood, but were replaced
by steel pontoons in 1910.
Each pontoon was 8 m

long, 3 m wide, and had
a total height of about 1 m,
of which half was submerged. When the canal was
improved in the early 1990s
the bridge was retired from
use. In 1997 it was moved
in its entirety to the outer
harbour of the Prins
Hendrik Maritime Museum,
where it remains on permanent display with its mecha-
nism in working order. The
Netherlands Bridge Society
played a major part in this
conservation project, in ac-
knowledgement of which it
was awarded the Nether-
lands Heritage Prize in
1999.

12. Zeeland Bridge over the
Oosterschelde, 1962-1965.
The bridge spans an arm of
the North Sea in the
province of Zeeland and
connects Noord-Beveland
with Schouwen-Duiveland.
5,131 m long, it is con-
structed of large prefabricated concrete elements and
is the longest bridge in the
country; until 1972 it was
also the longest bridge in
Europe. The bridge was
also a new venture in that it
was the first (partly private-
ly financed) toll bridge in
the post-war Netherlands.
The bridge forms a continuous tube of prestressed con-

crete consisting of 52 T-
sections on 52 piers, each
spanning 95 m. The sec-
tions are connected with
transverse pins and shock
absorbers. There are two
road traffic lanes and a cycle path. The movable part
(40 m) consists of a double
bascule bridge. In total the
bridge has 54 piers.

13. Rail bridge across the Old Maas at Dordrecht, 1993-1994.
Even though tunnels have in recent times been the preferred option for potential pressure points where land and water routes converge, remarkable feats of bridge engineering nonetheless continue to be achieved. A case in point is the Dordrecht rail bridge with its monumental lifting portal of four 65 m piers that are mounted on hinges and connected over the track by square tubular movable beams of 48 m clearance; to open and close the bridge takes just one minute each way. About 5,500 tons of steel went into the construction of the combined fixed and movable bridges.

14. Erasmus Bridge in Rotterdam, 1994-1996
This bridge in Rotterdam across the New Maas consists of an assymetrical steel cable-stayed bridge with a total length of 802 m and a bascule bridge with a single steel flap. The most striking feature of the bridge is a bent pylon which is 79 m high and, for the record, weighs 1600 tons. The total span of the suspension bridge is 260 m, with a navigable channel of 50 m through the bascule bridge. The cables have a total length of 6,180 m. Opened in 1996, the bridge is known as The Swan because of the profile presented by the cables and pylon.

Photos 1-14 courtesy of Nederlandse Bruggen Stichting, Zoetermeer.

13

14

15

15. Klooster Bridge across the Drenthe Ship Canal (design by Haskoning) at Assen / Kloosterveen, 1998-1999. This steel bridge is of a very unusual type. Commissioned by the municipality of Assen, it was constructed in 1998-1999. It has an overal width of 14 m; the section spanning the canal is 7.5 m long. Due to the elevated position of the hinge the deck is completely clear of the ground when the bridge is opened, thus providing a framed view to the far bank and the fields beyond. Photo courtesy of Haskoning Architecten, Amsterdam.

Vigour

and Flexibility

Recent Developments in the Dutch Language

Dutch is a strong and vital language. Never before have Belgium and the Netherlands (I will ignore the former colonies and South Africa here) contained so many speakers of the standard Dutch language, which has developed since the sixteenth century above and alongside a multitude of dialects.[1] Never before have there been within the Dutch language area so many members of ethnic minorities who use Dutch as a second language, albeit with widely varying levels of competence. Never before have so many French-speaking Belgians learned to speak Dutch to the best of their ability. Never before have there been so many foreign students following courses in Dutch language, literature and culture at around 250 universities world-wide. Never before has Dutch been so widely taught in secondary schools abroad as it is today, especially in those federal states of Germany which adjoin the Netherlands and Belgium.

The demographic factors to ensure the vitality of the Dutch language are thus firmly in place. The language is being acquired as a mother tongue on a large scale. It is now the standard language of almost twenty-two million speakers of high socio-economic status (almost sixteen million in the Netherlands and over six million in Belgium) within one cohesive language area. While there are other standard languages within that area, such as French in the bilingual city of Brussels and Frisian in the Dutch province of Friesland, they do not pose a threat to Dutch. The institutional factors are also favourable. Dutch is the official language of the Netherlands and the Dutch-language community in Flanders and Brussels, and is used by public bodies: Dutch is the language of the media, education, the judical system, the Church – in short, it is the language of public life. 'Correct' Dutch has acquired status within the language area: it can be used anywhere, in all kinds of situations, and the culture of the past is passed on to future generations in a rich Dutch-language literature. It is a fully-fledged standard language, which can be used to discuss and write about every imaginable topic.

Every living language is subject to change, and Dutch is no exception. Before going into the changes that have taken place in recent decades, I will look at the most important works published on the Dutch language in this period, works which bear testimony to the vitality of Dutch.

New instruments

After a century and a half of diligent labour, the *Woordenboek der Neder-landsche Taal*, a historical dictionary of the Dutch language and the largest dictionary in the world, was finally completed in 1998. This massive work, inspired by Grimm and Murray, is made up of forty solid volumes, together taking up three metres of shelf space and containing more than 88,000 columns spread over more than 44,000 pages. When the initiator of the project and one of its two original editors, Mathias de Vries, died in 1892 the dictionary had reached only the second letter of the alphabet, and De Vries' co-editor, Allard te Winkel, had not seen a single volume published at the time of his death in 1868. Compiling a dictionary is no sinecure, especially where subsidies are meagre and the scale of the enterprise is greatly under-estimated in the preparation phase. And that is precisely what De Vries did midway through the nineteenth century. It was not until 1969, when the dictionary was taken under the wing of the Belgo-Dutch Institute for Dutch Lexicology (Instituut voor Nederlandse Lexicologie; INL) in Leiden, that it was possible to guarantee – with the aid of generous government support – that the task would be completed before the year 2000. After the founding in 1980 of the Dutch Language Union (Nederlandse Taalunie), a supra-national body in which the Belgian federal state of Flanders and the Nether-lands joined forces to promote the language and culture of the Low Coun-tries, the funding of the *Woordenboek* was taken over by this body. The dictionary describes the vocabulary of the language in the period from 1500 to 1921. It is therefore a historical document, which says nothing about the most modern lexical developments in the language. Copiously illustrated with quotations, the history of each word is outlined: its origin in time and space, the morphological and semantic changes it has undergone and its oc-curence in proverbs and sayings.

The history of words is to some extent also a cultural history: for exam-ple, no less than 27 pages are needed to describe the word '*water*', and com-pound words beginning with '*water*' take up a further 215 pages. The com-pilation of such a large, academic dictionary is unlikely to be repeated, even in a revised version or a version which includes the most modern vocabu-lary; information and communication technology such as the Internet and CD-ROM) offer other possibilities, and a large electronic word archive com-prising the entire vocabulary of the Dutch language from the earliest times to the present – the Language Database run by the INL referred to earlier – provides the basic for modern lexicography.

1984 saw the publication of the first edition of a comprehensive academ-ic work on the Dutch language and its grammar: the *Algemene Nederland-se Spraakkunst*, or ANS for short, written by the Flemings G. Geerts and W. Haeseryn and the Dutchmen J. de Rooij and M.C. van den Toorn. The production of this work, which was made possible by the support of the Dutch Language Union, was originally an initiative of the International Association for Dutch Studies (Internationale Vereniging voor Neerlandis-tiek; IVN) in reponse to the serious need from abroad for a complete, mod-ern description of contemporary Dutch. A second, completely revised edi-tion was published in 1997 in Deurne (Belgium) and Groningen (The Netherlands). This new edition comprises two stout volumes and a total of more than 1,900 pages. A fifth author, K. Romijn from the Netherlands, joined the four-strong team who had worked on the first edition. The ANS is aimed at a wide foreign readership who already have some knowledge of Dutch, as well as at native Dutch-speakers who wish to test their use of the language against the standards of grammaticality and acceptability. Although the work seeks to be primarily descriptive, it is also normative: items which do not form part of the Dutch standard language (e.g. dialects) are ignored, or are marked with labels such as 'outmoded', 'jargon', 'informal' and 'regional'.

Finally, under the editorship of M.C. van den Toorn, W.J.J. Pijnenburg, J.A. van Leuvensteijn and J.M. van der Horst, and with the collaboration of fourteen other authors, a modern history of the Dutch language was published in Amsterdam in 1997: *Geschiedenis van de Nederlandse Taal*. This extensive work of 700 pages includes the results of recent research and contains a wealth of bibliographical references. An introductory chapter is followed by seven further chapters dealing with the 'external history' (the fortunes of the language in the political, social, economic and cultural context) and the 'internal history' (developments in the sounds, declension and conjugation, in the derivation and compounding of words, in vocabulary and in the combinatory possibilities of words to form larger wholes such as word groups and sentences). The work covers the full historical span of the language, from Old Dutch (dating from before 1200) to Modern Dutch. The book concludes with chapters on the Dutch language in Belgium and on Afrikaans, the Dutch-based language of South Africa. Although the chapter on modern Dutch, written by M.C. van den Toorn, begins around 1920, considerable attention is devoted to developments in recent decades. I have made grateful use of this chapter.

The times they are a-changing

At the end of the 1960s society and culture were undergoing sweeping changes, changes which also had an impact on the language. The generation born after 1945 was reaching adulthood. Young people rebelled against their elders, against established authority: there were protests against the war in Vietnam, against nuclear weapons and against the undemocratic structure of university education and industry. Society was secularising at a rapid rate. Women were demanding equal rights. Growing prosperity increased people's ability to travel the world in their free time, while the same time attracting large numbers of foreign workers, especially from the countries around the Mediterranean Sea and the former Dutch and Belgian colonies in Africa and Central America. These immigrants brought their mother tongues with them, and the Netherlands and Flanders rapidly evolved into multilingual communities, including 270,000 Turkish-speaking and 45,000 Kurdish-speaking Turks, 85,000 Arabic-speaking and 195,000 Berber-speaking Moroccans. More than 250,000 Surinamese settled in the Netherlands, along with 70,000 Antilleans and Arubans. The total number of speakers of a mother tongue other than Dutch was estimated at more than one and a half million. In the 1970s the number of students at universities and colleges of higher education increased rapidly. At the end of the 1960s higher education had primarily been the preserve of the elite, the privileged. This is now no longer the case: higher education has become accessible to young people from all ranks of society. International co-operation, especially within the context of the ever-expanding European Union, is blurring national borders. I have already referred to the creation of the Dutch Language Union, that unique supranational collaborative venture between Belgian Flanders and the Netherlands, in 1980.

The anti-authoritarian attitude of young people has led to greater tolerance in the use of language than in the past, to a blurring of norms according to the claims of those who defended the 'civilised', 'correct' use of language which has been the province of concerned individuals and language politicians for more than a century. This tolerance extended to informal language use in terms of vocabulary, but above all in terms of pronunciation. Traditionally, the professed ideal was that it should be impossible to hear from someone's pronunciation from which region or social class they came. Everyone had to strive to achieve this as yet unattained ideal. The general consensus was that those who came closest to it were the educated inhabitants of the urban conglomeration in the western part of the Netherlands known as the '*Randstad*'. They came close to the ideal, but did not achieve it, although the educated Dutchman is often firmly convinced that he has done so: the fact that he is instantly recognisable as a 'Hollander' is something he is often not aware of.

It now seems likely that this ideal will never be achieved. Dialectal and social variants of the standard language (for many still a contradiction in terms) are increasingly tolerated. Dialectal or social pronunciation features which serve to reinforce the solidarity of a certain group are deliberately employed by some people in the standard language. Others use such variants because of indifference towards any norms. The fact that increasingly large sections of the population, through education, radio and television, are coming into contact with what was in the past generally regarded as 'correct' Dutch, has not been able to stem this process of divergence. While dialects may be slowly disappearing, being levelled out and absorbed into larger regiolects, the standard language can be broken down into regionally and socially coloured standard variants.

The shift in norms is also reflected in a changed attitude on the part of many Flemings. Now that the linguistic battle waged by the Flemish against the 'frenchification' of their language has been fought and won, many of them no longer strive to achieve the Northern Dutch standard. From the nineteenth century the Flemish movement, in its bid to shake off the dominance of French, had sought alignment with the standard language that had developed in the Netherlands, on the premise that unity is strength. The modern Fleming is self-aware and no longer needs the northern norm. This changed attitude in Flanders is reinforced by the rapid changes in language use by their northern neighbours as regards vocabulary and, above all, pronunciation. The changes in the northern part of the language area are not held in high esteem in the south: Flemings believe that the Dutch speak the language poorly. A Flemish norm is developing for generally accepted use of the language in the southern part of the language area.

Increasing internationalisation is also changing the function of Dutch. The use of English as a scientific language, at conferences and in publica-

aa p | n oo t | m ie s | w i m | z u s | j e t
t eu n | v uu r | g ij s | l a m | k ee s | b o k
w ei - de | d oe s | h o k | d ui f | s chā-pe n

tions, has resulted in some functional loss of Dutch, but is necessary in order to guarantee the ability of the Netherlands and Flanders to keep up with international scientific developments. The same applies to the use of English in the business community: if industry and commerce wish to maintain their important position in the world, then a knowledge and command of the major world languages, and especially English, is essential. Consequently, a great deal of attention is rightly devoted in Belgian and Dutch schools to developing a command of foreign languages. The growth in the number of bilingual (Dutch-English) secondary schools, and especially the increasing use of English as the medium of instruction in universities, does however pose a threat to the position of Dutch. Students have a right to be educated in their mother tongue. Moreover, education in the mother tongue ensures that Dutch will continue to be an ackowledged language of science and scholarship.

The European Union recognises eleven official languages, including Dutch, and every expansion of the Union will add another language. All these languages have equivalent status and equal rights, which means that a great deal of translation and interpreting is called for. This multiplicity of languages is not only very expensive, it also causes practical problems. In contrast to what happens in official meetings and documents, therefore, in their mutual dealings officials and members of the European Parliament use one of the 'working languages': English and, to a lesser extent, French. The more member states accede to the Union, the greater the chance that English will become the working language. The Treaty of the European Union does not permit the sanctioning of the use of working languages. Moreover, there is little chance that the Treaty will be amended in favour of a single working language, i.e. English; France, in particular, would resist such a move. The increasing, unofficial use of English is unavoidable, however, and this too has led to some functional loss for the Dutch language.

Internal changes

Changes in vocabulary and pronunciation are related most clearly to the external changes outlined earlier. The Dutch have always been happy to borrow words from other languages. Since the Second World War the most important source of these loan words has been English, and English loan words such as 'hotpants' and 'floppy' made their way easily into everyday Dutch usage. The Dutch also have no qualms about using quasi-English words of Dutch invention: the word '*showmaster*', a television presenter, does not occur in English. The many minority languages also contribute to this enrichment of the Dutch vocabulary: '*falafel*' denotes an Arab, '*pilav*' a Turkish dish. Loan words are important from the point of view of cultural history, but they do not bring about an essential change in the 'host' language. Social and cultural changes create a need to adapt the vocabulary. To meet this need, words are borrowed from other languages or existing words are used to create new ones, such as '*betaalpas*', a combination of '*betaal*' (pay) and '*pas*' (card or pass) which is used to designate cards that can be used to make electronic payments and withdraw cash from ATMS.

The generally accepted pronunciation is also changing, though much more clearly in the Netherlands than in Flanders. The letters *v* and *z* are increasingly pronounced without vibration of the vocal cords, with the result that they sound more like *f* en *s*: the word '*vanzelf*' thus becomes '*fanself*'. The letter *r* is pronounced less and less distinctly, sounding more and more like an English *r*, whether this sound is formed at the front of the mouth as in Scotland or at the back of the mouth as in French. The vibration of the tongue is disappearing, with the result that words such as '*rood*' (red), '*goot*' (gutter) and even '*groot*' (great) are becoming almost indistinguishable from each other. The diphthong *ei*, which has the written forms *ei* and *ij*, is being pronounced by more and more Dutch-speakers almost like the *i* in the English word '*five*'. In a related development, the vowel sound *ee* is increasingly coming to sound like the diphtong *ei*, similar to the sound in the English word '*late*', as the gradual disappearance of the old *ei* sound creates room for a new, similar sound. In a comparable development, the vowel sound *oo* is changing almost into an *ou* as in Enlish 'go', so that the Dutch for 'big toe' is increasingly pronounced '*groute tein*' instead of '*grote teen*'. All these sounds were already found in a number of Dutch dialects: all that is happening is that the norm for 'correct' pronunciation of the standard language is changing.

One change which is not based on borrowings from a dialect is the recent shift in the pronunciation of the letter *s*. This sharp sibilant is increasingly acquiring a 'softer' pronunciation, almost like *sh* sound in English 'shower'. All these changes in pronunciation have been set in motion by highly educated young women, working for radio and television. It is frequently the case that women are the vectors of language change.

The grammatical and structural language changes are much less striking; a period of a few decades is too short for this. All Germanic languages have developed over the centuries from synthetic to analytic languages, with characteristic developments including the loss of cases and other declensions, the emergence of large numbers of prepositions and conjunctions, the disappearance of verb conjugations and an increasingly fixed word order. German has changed least in an analytical direction, English the most; Dutch occupies an intermediate position. New prepositions are still emerging: the Dutch noun '*richting*' (direction) is increasingly being used as a preposition in competition with '*naar*' (to): '*Ga richting het wonder, ga richting Jezus*' (Go to the miracle, go to Jesus), as a recent advertising text had it. There is a growing tendency to use the preposition '*om*' to introduce an infinitive without there being any expression of purpose: '*deze beslissing is moeilijk om te begrijpen*' is then the equivalent of '*deze beslissing is moeilijk te begrijpen*' (this decision is difficult to understand). In the past, the use of '*om*' to introduce an infinitive was permitted only in sentences where the word group introduced by *om* expressed a specific purpose, with the sense of 'in order to': '*ik ga naar de dokter om beter te worden*' (I'm going to the doctor to get better). The distinction between cases, including in pronouns, is disappearing: the direct object form '*hen*' (them) is giving way to the indirect object form '*hun*' (to them), which is even replacing the subject form '*zij*' (they), despite the best efforts of the education system: '*hun hebben gelijk*' instead of '*zij hebben gelijk*' (they're right). And '*meer*' (more) and '*meest*' (most) are increasingly being used instead of the comparative and superlative adjectival forms: '*de meest makkelijke verf*' (the most easy paint) instead of '*de makkelijkste verf*' (de easiest paint). English influence has played a role here.

The disappearance of cases and the more rigid word order are undermining the use of the indirect object, which centuries ago had a dative form without a preposition. There is no dative form in the sentence '*hij geeft het zijn vader*' (he gives it his father), and increasingly a preposition is therefore being used: '*hij geeft het aan zijn vader*' (he gives it to his father). The first position in the sentence is generally occupied by the subject of the sentence. If an indirect object is placed in this position, it is now often reinterpreted as a subject: '*passagiers worden verzocht niet te roken*' (passengers are requested not to smoke; plural form of '*worden*' to match the plural form '*passagiers*') instead of '*passagiers wordt verzocht*' (singular form of '*worden*' conveying the sense of 'it is requested that passengers do not smoke'). There are also instances of a new synthesis: '*Jan z'n boek*' alongside the old synthetic '*Jans boek*' and the newer analytic '*het boek van Jan*' (all with the meaning 'Jan's book'), and '*een computer gestuurd programma*' alongside '*een programma dat door de computer gestuurd wordt*' ('a computer-driven program' versus 'a program (that is) driven by the computer'), with a participle being used rather than a declined verb form.

Other recent changes cannot be explained on the basis of such a general trend. A couple of examples: in a sentence such as '*meer auto voor uw geld*', which was first used by Dutch Ford dealers as a translation of the English 'more car for your money', or '*een beetje politicus*' (a bit of a politician), '*auto*' (car) and '*politicus*' (politician) are treated like adjectives and nouns such as '*suiker*' (sugar) ('*een beetje suiker*' – a little sugar) which, unlike 'auto', never occur in the plural form. The preposition '*met*' (with) is moving from the middle of a word group to the front: '*met naar mijn overtuiging grote gevolgen*', alongside '*naar mijn overtuiging met grote gevolgen*' ('with in my view major consequences' versus 'with major consequences in my view'). The verbs '*denken*' (think), '*zeggen*' (say) and '*hebben*' (have) are increasingly being used, especially in conjunction with the word '*zoiets*' (something like), and especially by young people, in combination with the preposition '*van*' in sentences such as: '*ik heb dan zoiets van niet alweer steengrillen*' (and then I sort of think, not stone-grilling again), '*hij dacht van nee*' (he thought not) and '*ik heb zoiets van het kan me niet schelen*' (I sort of think, well, I couldn't care less). The scope of the verb '*doen*' (do) is also widening: '*doe mij maar een pils*' (I'll have a beer, make mine a beer). Words such as '*waarop*' (on which) are virtually never split any more: '*de stoel waarop ik zit*' as opposed to the more traditional '*de stoel waar ik op zit*' (the chair on which I'm sitting, the chair I'm sitting on). The word '*dat*' (that, which) in sentences such as '*het boek dat ik lees*' (the book that I'm reading) is increasingly being replaced by the word '*wat*' (what): '*het boek wat ik lees*'. According to the grammatical rules, the word '*dan*' cannot be left out in sentences such as '*houd je van vlees, dan braad je in boter*' (if you like meat, (then) you fry in butter), because the sentence begins with a conditional form. One manufacturer disregarded this rule totally with its advertising slogan '*hou je van vlees, braad je in Croma*'. This trend is increasing: '*wil je iets drinken, pak je het zelf*' (if you want a drink, you get it yourself). Finally, word order changes in sentences such as: '*dat soort dingen moet ik vaak aan denken*', in which the word '*aan*' is left near the end of the sentence and does not move to the front of the sentence with the rest of the group to which it belongs, are also becoming more common alongside '*aan dat soort dingen moet ik vaak denken*' (I'm often reminded of things like that).

A changing perception of norms also undoubtedly plays a role in syntactic changes, though less clearly than with pronunciation. These changes are also less noticeable, and in many cases we do not know whether particular syntactic phenomena were already present in the spoken language. What can be said in general, however, is that things which formerly occured only in the spoken language may now also be used in the written language; what in the past was regarded as careless language usage is now acceptable. In short, what was not permitted in the past is now allowed. Attributing this to language change can perhaps be defended from an educational standpoint, but is not scientifically accurate. A linguist describes the use of language in all its variation, and if possible provides an explanation for that use. Judgments are a matter for the language politician, not the linguist.

JAN W. DE VRIES
Translated by Julian Ross.

NOTE

1. see *The Low Countries* 1997-98: 163-172.

'Printed

matter bursting with question marks'

Fifteen Contemporary Poems

Selected by Jozef Deleu

K. Michel (1958-)
Rules of Thumb

If the house is infected, they said
in my grandparents' village,
shut a pig up in it overnight
the evil will go into the beast
and by morning the place will be perfectly clean

In the structure that every life is
comes the moment that's known as being
up shit creek with no paddle, a leak
has put Rorschach ink-blots all over the walls
and it smells of something that once
got hidden away in a long-ago game

Look round the table and try
to work out who'll be the mark,
so runs a golden rule for poker-players
if you can't spot the victim
then there's only one possibility

So this brand-new day I say
To the face in the shaving-mirror
when you're in a hole stop digging
be prepared to take things as they come
look around you, search every room
and if you can't find the pig
then you're it

Vuistregels

Is het woonhuis besmet, zeiden ze
in het dorp van mijn grootouders
sluit dan een varken een nachtlang op
het kwaad kruipt in het beest
en alles is de volgende morgen schoon

In het bouwsel dat elk leven is
breekt er een moment aan dat heet
goede raad was duur, een lekkage
heeft de muren bedekt met rorschachfiguren
en het ruikt naar iets dat ooit
tijdens een oud spelletje werd verstopt

Kijk de tafel rond en probeer
uit te vinden wie de sigaar zal zijn,
zo luidt een gouden tip voor pokeraars
zie je het slachtoffer niet
dan rest er maar een mogelijkheid

Dus zeg ik deze nieuwe dag
tegen het gezicht in de scheerspiegel
stop met graven als je in de put zit
wees bereid au & ja te zeggen
kijk om je heen, doorzoek alle kamers
en vind je het varken niet
dan ben jij het

From *Water Studies* (Waterstudies). Amsterdam: Meulenhoff, 1999.
Translated by Tanis Guest.

Hugo Claus (1929-)
What to Talk About

What to talk about this evening? Talk, too,
in a land that we recognise, bear with,
rarely forget.
That land with its farcical genesis,
its damp climate, its dubious stories
about its past,
its people, grasping till their last collapse
among the cauliflowers.
They continue to multiply
in a paradise of their inventing,
greedy for happiness, quivering, mouths full of porridge.
Just as in nature
which strips our undersized hills of their pelts,
shrivels our meadows, pollutes our air,
the unsuspecting cows go on grazing.

Talk about the writings of this land,
printed matter bursting with question marks
on the patient paper
which time and again shies from its history
and escapes it in a fog of shorthand.
Talk about the heavy curtains
that people close over themselves.
But we can still hear them, the stinking
primates that assault each other in rooms.
Just as in nature
the hibiscus gives off no scent,
the innocent cows do that, sinking
into the sodden ground.

Talk in that land of glistening grass
In which man,
intemperate worm, dreaming carcase,
lingers among the corpses that dead as they are
are still obedient to our memory.
Just as our nature expects a single, a simple
miracle that some time will finally
explain to us what we were,
not just this decrepit spectacle
thrown together by time.

Talk about that time which, they said,
would leave its imprint as trademark and palimpsest?
We lived in a time of consumption
And being useful.
What defence against that?
What festive plumes in the arse?

Waarover spreken

Waarover vanavond spreken? En spreken
in een land dat wij herkennen, dulden,
zelden vergeten.
Dat land met zijn koddige genesis,
zijn klam klimaat, zijn voze verhalen
over vroeger,
zijn bewoners, hebberig tot hun laatste val
tussen de bloemkolen.
Zij blijven zich vermenigvuldigen
in een paradijs dat zij verzinnen,
tuk op geluk, sidderend, pap in de mond.
Zoals in de natuur
die onze ondermaatse heuvels onthaart,
onze weiden verschroeit, onze lucht vergast,
de argeloze koeien blijven grazen.

Spreken over de geschriften van dit land,
drukwerk vol vraagtekens
op het geduldig papier
dat steeds opnieuw schrikt van zijn historie
en daarvoor vlucht in verhullend snelschrift.
Spreken over de overgordijnen
die men dichttrekt over zichzelf.
Maar wij blijven ze horen, de stinkende
primaten die elkaar in kamers belagen.
Zoals in de natuur
de hibiscus geen geur verspreidt,
dat doen de schuldeloze koeien die zakken
in de doorzeken aarde.

Spreken in dat land van glinsterend gras
waarin de mens,
onmatige worm, dromend karkas,
verwijlt tussen de lijken die dood als zij zijn
blijven gehoorzamen aan onze herinnering.
Zoals onze natuur een enkel, enkelvoudig
mirakel verwacht dat ooit uiteindelijk
zal verhelderen wat men was,
niet alleen dit aftands spektakel
ineengeflanst door de tijd.

Spreken over de tijd die, zei men,
zou beklijven als brandmerk en palimpsest?
Wij leefden in een tijd van verbruiken
en bruikbaar zijn.
Welk verweer daartegenover?
Welke feestelijke veren in de kont?

What singing in the cellar? Maybe.
Say it. Maybe.
A couple of scratches on slate
and there's the outline of your beloved.
Then fingerprints in clay are her hips.
Phonemes of joy sometimes resounded
as she, when she, called to you like a cat.
Talking about her presence
calls up the blue hour of twilight.
Just as in nature
 the pitiless, glassy, azure blue
of our planet seen from Apollo.
And although simply from talking
your party hat starts to weigh heavy
and the life-line on the palm of your hand
starts to fester
still, notwithstanding, despite all of this
to honour the vigour
of the shadows that populate us,
the shadows that beg for comfort.
And still stroke her shoulder-blade.
Like the spine of a hunchback.
Still greedy for a savage happiness.

Welk liedje in de kelder? Misschien.
Zeg het. Misschien.
Een paar krassen in leisteen
en dat is dan de omtrek van je geliefde.
Vingerafdrukken in klei zijn dan haar heupen.
Fonemen van vreugde weerklonken soms
als zij, toen zij, naar jou riep als een kat.
Spreken over haar aanwezigheid
wekt het blauw uur van de schemer.
Zoals in de natuur
het ongenadig, glazig, blauw azuur
van onze planeet gezien vanuit Apollo.
En al begint van louter spreken
je feestmuts zwaar te wegen
en begint de levenslijn in je handpalm
te verzweren
toch, niettegenstaande, desalniettemin
de bloei vereren
van de schaduwen die ons bevolken,
de schaduwen die bedelen om troost.
En toch haar schouderblad strelen.
Als de rug van een bultenaar.
Toch tuk op een wreedaardig geluk.

From *Cruel Happiness* (Wreed geluk). Amsterdam: de Bezige Bij, 1999.
Translated by Tanis Guest.

Frank Koenegracht (1945-)
Epigram

Epigram

My soul is invisible and flows on and on
but I stay as calm as a Sunday window
and in my fantasy I sit
twice as still as all of you think
while everything that is dark comes creeping up
like a slow and ugly fly.

And all our thinking's like a little dog
at the bend in the road.

Mij ziel is onzichtbaar en stroomt aldoor
maar ik blijf zo kalm als een raam op zondag
en in mijn verbeelding zit ik
tweemaal zo stil als jullie denken
terwijl alles wat donker is komt aansluipen
als een langzame lelijke vlieg.

En al ons denken is als een hondje
in de bocht van de weg.

From *Everything Falls* (Alles valt). Amsterdam: de Bezige Bij, 1999.
Translated by Paul Vincent.

Lut de Block (1952-)
Daughter and I

Dochter en ik

We walked both bleeding along Keyserlei.
Daughter and I. No word passed between us,
no misunderstanding. Nor any link
between her silence and my conscious lack of speech.
Only a hand put out to stop me falling.
A stupid stone, she said. Take care.
The child is mother to the woman.

I'm blooming[1], she said when I tried to tell her
that life is bleeding and cannot be stayed.
She burst out laughing, couldn't help herself.
But isn't bleeding somehow blooming too?
And that she hankered after something wanting,
gaiety, nonsense, jabber of boys in the street.

Ewe-lamb upon my lap, how she had grown.
Spring was still barely here and she so blithe.
Weightless we walked like that,
side by side, and hand in hand,
we walked both blooming along Keyserlei.

We liepen beiden bloedend langs de Keyserlei.
Dochter en ik. Geen woord was tussen ons,
geen misverstand. Ook geen verband
tussen haar zwijgen en mijn gewild niet spreken.
Alleen een hand die me het vallen zou beletten.
Een stomme steen, zei ze. Opletten.
Het kind is moeder van de vrouw.

Ik bloei, zei ze toen ik haar zeggen wou
dat leven bloeden is en niet te stelpen.
Ze klaterlachte, kon het ook niet helpen.
Of bloeden niet een beetje bloeien is?
En dat ze snakte naar gemis,
geluk, gelul, gelal van jongens in de straat.

Ooilam op mijn schoot, wat werd ze groot.
De lente was nog iel en zij zo blij.
Gewichtsloos liepen wij,
zo zij aan zij, en hand in hand,
zo beiden bloeiend langs de Keyserlei.

From Entre deux mers. *Amsterdam: de Arbeiderspers, 1997.*
Translated by Tanis Guest.

1. This poem contains an untranslatable play on words. In colloquial
'Flemish' Dutch *'bloeden'* (bleed) and *'bloeien'* (bloom) sound the same
and are practically indistinguishable.

Leonard Nolens (1947-)

Albatross

That travel, those trips of yours the last few years,
All of them alibis of a seasoned albatross
To fly yourself to sleep henceforth, all of them
Flights of fancy in seventh heaven, all of them
Pretexts for not landing ever, anywhere any more
On your feet, never again waddling from your desk

To your bed.

You calmed down from that turbulent atlas in your head.
Serene from places that had not yet seen your tears.
Your thirst for adventure? Curious sadness,
Forced up from the chair of a bookish boy.
What did you read? 'Look, I land in a street,
And slowly, noiselessly my wings close

In a woman.'

From *Passer-By* (Voorbijganger). Amsterdam: Querido, 1999.
Translated by Paul Vincent.

Albatros

Dat reizen, die reizen van jou de laatste jaren,
Allemaal alibi's van een doorwinterde albatros
Om je voortaan in slaap te vliegen, allemaal
Uitvluchten hoog in de zevende hemel, allemaal
Smoezen om nooit, om nergens meer neer te komen
Op je poten, nooit meer waggelend van je tafel

Naar je bed.

Rustig werd je van die woelige atlas in je kop,
Sereen van plekken die je tranen nog niet zagen.
Je zucht naar avontuur? Nieuwsgierig verdriet,
Opgestuwd uit de stoel van een lezende jongen.
Wat las je? 'Kijk, ik strijk neer in een straat,
En langzaam en geruisloos gaan mijn vleugels dicht

In een vrouw.'

Eva Gerlach (1948-)

Tumult

They're odd creatures, the dead,
pushing into you, sitting with their
cavities in your knees, their phalanges
in your fingers writing a letter,
just as sluggish as you are, as poorly informed
about weather forecasts and mercy, about doubt and prices

and when it's dinner time, bedtime,
time to take the dogs for a walk,
time to make a baby, to bury a husband,
they're always there, compliant,
docile, with their crests and spikes their pubes
over your sex their craniums holding your
senses their bones round your marrow

inside you, clickclickclick. Only
your skin damps their tumult a little.

From *Nothing More Constant* (Niets bestendiger). Amsterdam: de Arbeiderspers, 1998.
Translated by Tanis Guest.

Drukte

Het is raar gesteld met de doden,
schuiven in je aan, zitten met hun
holtes in je knieën, hun kootjes
in je vingers een brief te schrijven,
even sloom als jezelf, even beperkt op de hoogte
van weerbericht en genade, twijfel en kostprijs

en als het etenstijd, bedtijd,
tijd is om de honden uit te laten,
tijd om een kind te krijgen, een man te begraven,
altijd lopen zij, meegaand,
volgzaam, met hun kammen en doornen hun schaambeen
boven je geslacht hun schedelpan rond je
zinnen hun graat om je merg

in je door, tiktiktik. Alleen
je vel dempt hun drukte een beetje.

Peter Holvoet-Hanssen (1960-)

Song for the Dead

Upsy-daisy, there we go, from hobby-horse to hearse across the cobbles.
It drizzled when grandmother was buried.

In September her daughter scrubs the grave though no one
drops by. My knees are wrecked, she reflects. So many
wasted years. Give me a jab if I get Alzheimer's. Or:
poor *bonne-maman* was scared the rabbits in the cemetery
would gnaw at her toes. When my time comes, I'll have myself
cremated. Mr Death's a gourmet in the ground.

In the fog over the graves: a room at her place. Grey
dove stares at the box, doesn't recognise her. 'It's only twenty
degrees and the TV guide has no decent programmes. You're
surely not sleeping with that man from downstairs? How can you? He's
a thief, I'll hide my money!'

The smell of burning potato tops. Mother says goodbye
to the swans. Oppressive air, mud sucking. Arthritis
in the shoulder. Quickly home.

A play on the radio in the living room. No one listens.
The hit parade. Anti-wrinkle cream. And a rosary in the drawer.

From *Houdini's Straitjacket*
(Dwangbuis van Houdini).
Amsterdam: Prometheus, 1998.
Translated by Paul Vincent.

Dodenlied

Hopsa, faldera. Van hobbelpaard tot lijkauto over de kasseien.
Het druilde toen grootmoeder werd begraven.

In september schrobt haar dochter het graf al komt er nooit
iemand langs. Mijn knieën zijn kapot, mijmert ze. Zo veel
verloren jaren. Geef mij een spuitje als ik Alzheimer krijg. Of:
arme bonne-maman had schrik dat de konijnen op het kerkhof
aan haar tenen zouden knagen. Als het zover is, laat ik mij
cremeren. In de grond is magere Hein een lekkerbek.

In de mist over de graven: een kamertje bij haar thuis. Grijze
duif staart naar de buis, herkent haar niet. 'Ik heb maar twintig
graden en de televisiegids geeft geen goede programma's. Gij
slaapt toch niet met die man van beneden? Hoe kunt ge! Hij is
een dief, ik verstop mijn geld.'

De geur van brandend aardappelkruid. Moeder neemt afscheid
van de zwanen. De lucht drukt zwaar, de modder zuigt. Artritis
in de schouder. Vlug naar huis.

Een hoorspel op de radio in de woonkamer. Niemand luistert.
De hitparade. Anti-rimpelcrème. En een rozenkrans in de lade.

Esther Jansma (1958-)
Archeology

If we really have to dress ourselves,
against the cold for instance, or in the name of this or that,
in the remnants of some past or other,
stories and aids to memory that tell

nothing except that we were there
in the time that was here before this today
if we can sustain ourselves in the here and now
only by here and now ceaselessly inventing ourselves

then preferably in a simple way, with clothes.
You sit at the table. Suddenly you see
someone crossing ice, the cold taking hold of him

or some other ending and you say: look,
here you have his shoes, his leather coat, his gloves.
'Where is time? Time is here.'

From *Time is Here* (Hier is de tijd). Amsterdam: de Arbeiderspers, 1998.
Translated by Esther Jansma.

Archeologie

Als we ons dan toch moeten kleden,
tegen kou bijvoorbeeld, of in naam van iets,
in resten van dit of dat verleden,
verhalen en geheugensteuntjes die niets

vertellen dan dat we er al waren
in de tijd die bestond voor dit heden –
als wij onszelf alleen in het nu kunnen bewaren
door onszelf voortdurend uit te vinden in het nu

dan liefst eenvoudig, aan de hand van kleding.
Je zit aan tafel. Opeens zie je hoe iemand
ijs overstak, hoe hem de kou beving

of een ander einde en je zegt: kijk,
hier heb je zijn schoenen, leren mantel, wanten.
'Waar is de tijd? Hier is de tijd.'

Miriam Van hee (1952-)
Drawing

in the end we want to see the same
thing every time: a house between the trees
like the one children never tire of
drawing: a door, a window, a slate roof
and in the window a family and of course
we mustn't forget the chimney
with smoke curling up from it
in the empty bits mountains appear
a bird here and there
and snow perhaps so that
it's warmer there inside

we're not easily satisfied
take a new sheet, in the middle
again that house between trees, a door,
a window, a slate roof and
the telephone wires, shall we put those in
or better not?

From *The Connection between the Days* (Het verband tussen de dagen).
Amsterdam: de Bezige Bij, 1998.
Translated by Tanis Guest.

Tekening

tenslotte willen we steeds opnieuw
hetzelfde zien: een huis tussen de bomen
zoals kinderen het onvermoeibaar
tekenen: een raam, een deur, een leien dak
en achter het raam een familie en laten we
vooral de schoorsteen niet vergeten
waar rook komt uitgekringeld
op de lege plekken komen bergen
hier en daar een vogel
en sneeuw misschien waardoor
het binnen warmer wordt

we zijn niet gauw tevreden
op een nieuw blad, in het midden
weer dat huis tussen de bomen, een raam
een deur, een leien dak en
de draden van de telefoon, doen we die
of toch maar niet?

C.O. Jellema (1936-)

Hunt

Flat on its back its long and spoon-shaped ears,
huddled along the furrow lay the hare,
and I, as I came closer to it, pretended,
thus failing in my task as beater,
it had not been seen, not its eyes bulging
with fear, blank as if it saw not me,
not the wide freedom behind me, but
a nothing in itself, a hole it lay in front of,
too deep, too wide to dare to jump across.
Then in a second, once a step of mine
had passed it, it was gone – turning
(cursing from the ditch bank, but no shot),
I saw it running to the horizon,
already just a dot on white and frozen clay.

What will its end have been? Braised
in wine, under a car or simply
of old age among the cold furrows –
when in spring in the field at home
the hares tumble, I think of it:
how fear can be a sudden source of strength
that frees you right down to your beating heart.
Perhaps, if the hole that grows in me
becomes too deep, too wide to jump across,
by God, a hare will speak for me (for even
a beast that knows fear has a soul that is
saved), if only because I remember
that morning, that one step, and that instinct
with which existence survives by its own strength.

From *Dream Time* (Droomtijd). Amsterdam: Querido, 1999.
Translated by Paul Vincent.

Drijfjacht

Plat op de rug zijn lange lepeloren,
gedoken in de vore lag de haas,
en ik, terwijl ik naderbij kwam, deed,
mijn taak van drijver dus verzakend, of
hij niet gezien werd, niet zijn ogen puilend
van angst, blikloos alsof niet mij hij waarnam,
niet achter mij de wijde vrijheid, maar
een niets in zich, een gat waar hij voor lag,
te diep, te breed om nog te durven springen.
Toen, met een stap van mij aan hem voorbij,
in een seconde was hij weg – me wendend
(verwensing uit de slootwal, doch geen schot)
zag ik hem rennend naar de horizon,
al haast een stip op wit bevroren klei.

Hoe zal zijn einde zijn geweest? In wijn
gestoofd, onder een auto of gewoon
van ouderdom tussen de koude voren –
wanneer in 't voorjaar op het veld voor huis
de hazen buitelen, denk ik aan hem:
hoe angst een plotselinge kracht kan zijn
die je bevrijdt tot in je kloppend hart.
Misschien zal, als het gat dat groeit in mij
te diep, te breed wordt om te kunnen springen,
bij god, een haas mijn voorspraak zijn (want ook
een dier dat angst kent heeft een ziel die wordt
verlost), al was het maar doordat die morgen
mij heugt, die ene stap, en dat instinct
waarmee bestaan zich redt op eigen kracht.

Gwy Mandelinck (1937-)

Rack

You're ironing. With your foot turned,
planted inward, you seem contemplative.
The instant that you threaten me, nose, lip go up.
They bare a set of teeth. Your head turns red

and you besprinkle royally the suit
that I was in. Your hottest innerside
steams down on me. It is a rack
that board, you bend me to your will.

From *Raid* (Overval). Amsterdam: de Arbeiderspers, 1997.
Translated by Pleuke Boyce.

Pijnbank

Je strijkt. Terwijl je voet naar binnen staat
gedraaid, lijk je ingekeerd te zijn.
Zodra je mij bedreigt gaan neus en lip omhoog.
Die geven tanden bloot. Je hoofd wordt rood

en je besprenkelt breed het pak
waarin ik zat. Je heetste binnenkant
komt stomend op mij neer. Een pijnbank
is die plank, je zet mij naar je hand.

Hagar Peeters (1972-)

'Shall I walk part of the way with you?'

Indeed. You may walk along as far as the traffic-lights,
or as far as the next tunnel.
As far as the third street on the right,
as far as the entrance to the park.
As far as the hospital, till we're past
the hospital, as far as my front door.

You may walk along till we're in my room,
till that glass of this or that,
till I've brushed my teeth
or till the first light of morning
falls over the clothes on the chair.

Till the construction workers start work,
till school has begun again,
the civil servants take a break
the shops have closed
or till the last train leaves.

Till after waking up but before breakfast,
till after breakfast but before lunch,
till after lunch but before supper
you may walk along.

From *Enough Poetry about Love for Today* (Genoeg gedicht over de liefde
vandaag). Amsterdam: Podium, 1999.
Translated by Pleuke Boyce.

'Zal ik nog een eindje met je meelopen?'

Ja hoor. Je mag meelopen tot het stoplicht,
of tot de eerstvolgende tunnel.
Tot de derde straat rechts,
tot de ingang van het park.
Tot bij het ziekenhuis, tot voorbij
het ziekenhuis, tot aan mijn huisdeur.

Je mag meelopen tot in mijn kamer,
tot het glaasje van het een of ander,
tot ik mijn tanden heb gepoetst
of tot het eerste ochtendlicht
over de stoel met kleren valt.

Tot de bouwvakkers aan het werk gaan.
tot de school weer is begonnen,
de ambtenaren pauze houden
de winkels zijn gesloten
of tot de laatste stoptrein gaat.

Tot na het ontwaken maar voor het ontbijt,
tot na het ontbijt maar voor de lunch,
tot na de lunch maar voor het avondeten
mag je meelopen.

Piet Gerbrandy (1958-)

In spaces spiders creep between the pipes.
I want to crush the beast that mars me so.

Tongue flays itself on quirk of ivory reefs.
Brain wrack themselves for source of sustenance.

I want to rip the plasters from the drains.
The thing that stills me smoulders in the corner.

Cheerfully I want to pour despair more wine.
What can is bound to be and worse than thought.

I want away and nowhere to move on.
I seek a sheltering spot to lay me down.

I shall effect a feast that pleases me.

In ruimten kruipen spinnen tussen buizen.
Ik wil het beest verslaan dat mij vergalt.

Tong slaat zich rauw op gril van elpen klippen.
Hoofd breekt zich over bron van lijfsbehoud.

Ik wil de pleisters van de goten rukken.
Het voorwerp dat mij stilt smeult in de hoek.

Blijmoedig wil ik wanhoop wijn inschenken.
Wat kan zal ooit en erger dan verwacht.

Ik wil ver heen mij nergens voort bewegen.
Ik zoek een bergzame plek om neer te zijgen.

Ik zal een feest begaan dat mij bevalt.

From Surly and without Hate (Nors en zonder haten). Amsterdam: Meulenhoff, 1999.
Translated by Tanis Guest and Piet Gerbrandy.

Stefan Hertmans (1951-)
First Steps

He ran into the street without a glance
and I, becoming like him more and more,
thought he could make it to the door.

But he turns round and away, cars racing
along the prom. Now he's almost there
I'll never get to him in time.

Just as my father, all his life,
could dream of my hand, as small
and quick, able to slip between two bars
into the depths of rock and water.

Life passes in a wink.

Then I grab him – he unafraid,
His eyes wide open and so calm –

I with that fatal smash
That will not leave
My life and body.

Eerste stappen

Hij liep de straat op zonder kijken
en ik, die soms op hem begon te lijken,
dacht dat hij zo op huis aan kon.

Hij draait zich om, de auto's razen
op de dijk. Nu hij er bijna is
kan ik hem nooit bereiken.

Zo is het dat mijn vader levenslang
kon dromen van een hand, al even klein
en snel, die tussen spijlen van een reling
kon ontglippen, in de diepte rots en water,

een leven in een wenk.

Zo grijp ik hem, hij zonder schrik
en ogen rustig open.

ik met een doodsmak in mijn lijf,
die ik een leven lang niet kan
ontlopen.

From Goya as a Dog (Goya als hond). Amsterdam: Meulenhoff, 1999.
Translated by Gregory Ball.

Leo Vroman (1915-)
The Last World Peace

What is a great conflict about?
Look tonight long and dead
dead silent out among the stars
back to this little earth
and nothing will stay great.
What really stays from afar
of our great self-esteem?
Nothing in eternity
to fight for so it seems
and what else is the use of war?

I myself, once caught in one
saw eternity yawn in the dead
-ly boring endless time
of our hopeless wilting hope
for freedom – or else a cup of cocoa
with only endless sleep to follow.

People! How sweet you are created!
How gorgeously you fit! How neat!
I love you deeply, but I'll keep
one eye open while I sleep:
somewhere your most horrid weapon
must almost be complete.

From *Details*. Amsterdam: Querido, 1999.
Translated by Leo Vroman.

De laatste wereldvrede

Waarom draait een groot geschil?
Kijk vannacht eens lang en dood
doodstil vanuit de sterren
naar deze kleine aarde
en niets blijft groot.
Wat blijft eigenlijk van verre
over van onze eigenwaarde?
Niets in de eeuwigheid
om voor te vechten zo gezien en
waar kan een oorlog anders nog toe dienen?

Ikzelf was eens in een daarvan gevangen
en zag de eeuwigheid al gapen in de dood
saaie eindeloze tijd
van ons hopeloos verslappende verlangen
naar vrijheid of desnoods een kopje chocola
met niets dan eindeloze slaap daarna.

Mensen! Hoe zoet is men geschapen!
Hoe prachtig past men bij elkaar!
Ik ben verliefd op jullie, maar
ik ga met één oog open slapen:
ergens is jullie vreselijkste wapen
vast bijna klaar.

René Magritte, *The Agitated Reader*. Canvas, 92 x 73 cm. Private collection / © SABAM Belgium 2001.

he

Long and the Short of It

Short Film in Flanders

Flemish film-maker Nicole van Goethem died on 3 March 2000. Along with a handful of other names (including Raoul Servais and Lieven Debrauwer), she was one of the main international figures of Flemish film. In 1987 her *Greek Tragedy* (Griekse Tragedie) was awarded an Oscar for best short animated film. Raoul Servais (see p. 268) did even better: in 1966 he won first prize at the Venice Festival for *Chromophobia*, followed in 1971 by the Jury Prize in Cannes for *Operation X-70* (Operatie X-70), and a Palm d'Or in 1979 for *Harpya*. Flemings are also proud of Lieven Debrauwer, who is not an animator. He received a Palm d'Or in Cannes in 1997 for his short film *Leonie*. Flemish feature-length films have rarely won awards at this prestigious level. Short films are more successful. Why?

The answer is simple: because more short films are made in Belgium than feature-length films. To be precise, roughly a hundred every year. Producing a short film is a relatively simple matter in Flanders, partly thanks to subsidies from the Ministry of the Flemish Community. Government participation in feature-length films is much more limited.

This sizeable support for short films does not mean that these works are shown in mainstream cinemas. Short films can only be seen at film festivals and occasionally in small cinemas or cultural centres, as the supporting programme for a feature-length film. Sometimes a short film is included in a compilation programme which does the rounds of cinemas with little or no commercial focus.

Very exceptionally, they are shown in series on television. There are also a number of specialist initiatives in Flanders where short film-makers meet each other. *Het grote ongeduld* (The Great Impatience), an event organised by the Vrije Universiteit Brussel, has for years shown work from film schools. In the autumn of 2000 the Canvas Prize was awarded to the film *Maria* by Fien Troch, which a few months later also received an award at the Brussels film festival. The prizes at the Ghent film festival went to two jolly animations: *Papa Trompet* by Evelyn Verschoore and *BZZ* by Benoît Feroumont.

The festival of short film held in Leuven, *Leuven Kort* (Leuven Short) has also become a fairly dynamic affair in recent years, despite a lack of re-

Lieven Debrauwer, *Leonie* (1997). Photo by Chris Walraed / courtesy Lieven Debrauwer.

sources. In 2000 the organisers made a virtue of necessity and moved their festival to the Internet. This proved quite a success: in the first week of the festival more than 33,000 short films were launched via modem and computer. From a technical point of view, this channel is still in its infancy as regards film. The films have to be played in a fairly small window, the image sharpness is rather poor, and the movements are anything but smooth. Moving images demand a very high line capacity. If you don't have a broadband modem, it becomes an almost impossible task. And yet the medium works for short films, however limited the quality may be. There are any number of websites for short films (the best known being the American www.atom-films.com) and it seems likely that the distribution of short film via this channel will only increase. Quite simply, there is no cheaper form of distribution.

The surfers who visited the festival's web-cinema chose the animation *Dickhead* as the best short film; the jury selected *Pygmalion* by Björn Deneve. Neither were really high-flyers.

Many short films are entered in several festivals at the same time, so if you miss one gathering, you can often catch up at the next event. Short films are rarely shown individually; they tend to be mounted in succession on a long reel and shown under the heading 'The Short Film', as a competition or confrontation. Occasionally a producer will set up several short film projects at the same time in order to bring them out as a single whole. *Brussels my Love* (Bruxelles mon amour) is a recent example of this. In collaboration with Brussels 2000 and the Canvas television channel, the young production company Corridor devised a triptych, bringing together the filmmakers Kaat Beels, Peter Vandekerckhove and Marc Didden around a central theme: Brussels. The three short films merge nonchalantly into each other, producing a medium-length film of around fifty minutes which consists of three chapters: *Hannah* (Beels) *Louise* (Vandekerckhove) and *Cheb* (Didden). Each chapter uses a handful of characters to try and present the atmosphere of Brussels' 'Europe Quarter' – not the dominant presence of the Euro-architecture, but the contrast between that and the ordinary life in what remains of this old and today sadly neglected residential district. We see two

Kaat Beels, 'Hannah', from *Brussels my Love* (Bruxelles mon amour, 2000). Photo by Piet Goethals / courtesy of Corridor, Brussels.

old lovers wrestling with the relationship they have just ended; a meeting between a priest and a landlady at the funeral of an Irish immigrant; the despair of Cheb following the death of his mother; his uncertainty about his future in Brussels. The composition of this portrayal and also the cross-fertilisation between the different components is a considerable success. The result is a piece of urban existentialism which is reminiscent of Marc Didden's 1980 debut *Brussels by Night* and of the first feature-length film by Alex Stockman, *Forbidden to Sigh* (Verboden te zuchten, 2000). Stockman was a co-founder of the Corridor production company; he is also a maker of short films who has now turned to making feature-length films. The reverse of this process almost never happens: a feature-film maker who returns to short film. Here we have the exception to the rule, however: Marc Didden made his first short film after four full-length films.

Five years ago Fugitive Cinema, the collective based around director Robbe de Hert, set up a similar project about Antwerp, *Elixir d'Anvers*, but the producer got into insurmountable financial difficulties and was forced to close down at the end of 1997. There is an important lesson here: short films only lose money.

Computer animation

Contrasting with the low level of interest among the public at large is a high degree of unity in the film community regarding the relevance of the genre. Short films feature at every major film festival, usually in the form of a competition. Short-film makers who win prizes receive an admission ticket from the film community to the world of full-length films.

The transition from short to long is rarely made in Flemish animated film. The most recent attempt dates from 1996, with Servais' *Taxandria*. This does not mean that there is nothing but trouble and affliction in the animated film industry. Quite the reverse: the activities of the brothers Bert and Geert van Goethem, the makers of the fine seven-minute animated musical *Just to Be Part of It*, with an ironic caterpillar playing the lead role, are particularly promising. Geert van Goethem (together with Linda Sterckx) was also the producer of the short animated film *BZZ* by Benoît Feroumont. As mentioned earlier, this work won the short film prize at the last Ghent festival. Both *Just to Be Part of It* and *BZZ* were made in a fairly traditional animation style, but the expertise and the originality of the script are unusual.

There is also a great deal going on in Flanders today in the field of computer animation, but this manifests itself mainly in other domains: special effects, 'ride-films' for amusement parks, all kinds of work for corporate and advertising films and of course the multimedia world. Worth mentioning are the *A Viagem* project by the Trix production company at the Lisbon World's Fair in 1998, and *The Raptoms*, a digital feature-length film being developed by the production company IIM (Imagination in Motion) for Twentieth Century Fox. The project appears to be somewhat comparable with the international ambitions of Raymond Leblanc's Belvision studio in the 1960s.

Short-film makers as long-distance runners

There are also a fair number of examples in Flanders of short-film makers who have made the leap to their first feature film. One such example is Renaat Coppens' *Misstakes* (Misstoestanden), a Flemish film through and through, containing a number of nice moments and based on the world of the *Kiekeboe* strip cartoon. We follow the Kiekeboe family as they become entangled in a ridiculous intrigue in which diamonds and a beauty contest are the focal points. And that's how Renaat Coppens portrays it: action without psychology. Around that action he sets up a complicated construction about a couple of people who are making a film – a film about the Kiekeboe family, of course. The film was aimed at a wide audience, but was a box-office flop because of Coppens' somewhat unorthodox treatment of this popular strip cartoon figure.

Misstakes was co-financed by the Kinepolis group, which in recent years has ventured into the field of production in addition to its activities in showing and distributing films – just like the old Hollywood studios. The same group had earlier provided funding for Renaat Coppens' short film *Gabriel*, which in 1999 won the short film competition at the Ghent film festival. *Gabriel* is about an 'innocent child' who dreams that he is an angel. He is destroyed by those around him (nuns), and this drives him to an innocent suicide. Or does he go to heaven? Visually this is a very attractive film but the content is very romantic and *déjà vu*. This is not uncommon with Flemish films. On the other hand, it cannot be denied that the maker of this film knows how to handle the camera and has a feeling for catching images.

Over the last ten years Coppens has himself been involved in various capacities in many of the films referred to in *Misstakes*. He has also directed commercials, television programmes and three short films: *Gabriel* (1998), *Kandit* (1997) and *My Way* (1993). The existence of the short film is often justified as providing an apprenticeship for full-length films. Coppens' training is broader, as is immediately obvious from the homogeneity of the actors' interpretations in his *Misstakes*. Directing actors has always been a weak point in Flemish cinema, and directing soaps may provide better experience for this than a short film.

In *Film 1* by Willem Wallyn the relationship between the feature-length film and the preceding short-film project is more direct. *Dear Jean-Claude*, Wallyn's first short film, won an award at the Brussels festival of 1998.

Renaat Coppens, *Gabriel* (1998). Photo courtesy of Renaat Coppens.

Renaat Coppens, *Misstakes* (Misstoestanden, 1999). Photo courtesy of Renaat Coppens.

A year later *Film 1* was shown. Both projects show a film-maker experimenting with his medium, with audiovisual means of expression, with narrative techniques. *Dear Jean-Claude* mixes together various image formats: 35 mm negative film and videotape. The story is set at the offices of Studio BBB – 'Bons Baisers de Belgique' – a studio specialising in taping video messages. A young Moroccan called Mohammed has a fixation on the actor Jean-Claude Vandamme, in whom he recognises himself. The Belgian Vandamme is a stranger in Hollywood, Mohammed is a stranger in Belgium. *Dear Jean-Claude* is a plea for tolerance, for equality. All in all a complex and ambitious project, but one which is clumsily put together.

The theme of social engagement returns in *Film 1*, this time in the form of a crusade against sensationalism in the media and press. This theme and story-line are also among the interests of Dominique Deruddere in *Everybody Famous!* (Iedereen beroemd), nominated for an Academy Award in 2001. As in *Dear Jean-Claude*, we see Wallyn restlessly experimenting with form. The film is recorded on video, and printed onto film at the final stage only – a cheap method of production which has recently become increasingly popular.

Wallyn never gets much further than a collection of ideas, sometimes simply jokes. The little mistakes in the short film have turned into big mistakes in the full-length film. As with Coppens' *Misstakes*, the main focus is on experimenting with style. This may indicate that this film-maker has not yet found the story that he wants to tell.

The short film *October Night* (Oktobernacht), made by Danny Deprez en Jean-Claude Van Rijckeghem, took part in the same competition as *Dear Jean-Claude* (Brussels, 1998). The two of them went on to make the full-length film *The Ball* (De bal), which I personally found artificial but which was reasonably well received at the Berlin film festival.

Vincent Ball, *The Bloody Olive* (1996). Photo courtesy of Multimedia, Asse.

It takes more than style

We will round off with the box-office flop *Man of Steel* (Man van staal), which a year later won an important youth prize at the same Berlin festival. It was made by Vincent Bal, one of the most renowned Flemish makers of short films. *Man of Steel* may not be a perfect film, but it is undoubtedly the work of a film-maker with potential. He has a well-developed sense of style but, unlike Coppens or Wallyn, he doesn't retreat into it. That is what makes *Man of Steel* a warm and charming film in spite of its shortcomings. The central character is the teenager Victor, who has to deal with two problems: the death of his father and his awakening erotic feelings for girls in general and Fania in particular. The events take place in Ostend on the Belgian coast, but also in Victor's head. In his imagination he is the 'Man of Steel', a science-fiction hero who experiences wild adventures on distant planets. His exotic adventures there form a striking parallel to his experiences on earth.

The best-known of Bal's short films is *The Bloody Olive* (1996), a *film noir* pastiche which demands respect owing to its great stylistic control. The three protagonists, Mylène, Sam and Werner, excel in constructing murder plots. Then at the drop of a hat the alliances change, the dead stand up again and we find ourselves in a new twist. This game with peripeteia bears little resemblance to the feature-length *Man of Steel*, except in the nostalgic way in which it is framed. *The Bloody Olive* is also completely different from Bal's short film *At the Seaside* (Aan zee), about a family – father, mother, son and daughter – on holiday. Father is an amateur film-maker who spends his time taking pictures of his high-spirited family. The son will discover on that same day that his father is an adulterous father. The theme of loss of innocence is a recurrent one in the work of Bal. He prefers to situate his films in an 'innocent' timeframe, such as the years of economic growth after the Second World War when technological progress was still received with general enthusiasm. He also evokes those same 1950s in a short dance film which he made for the cultural broadcaster Arte: *Joli Môme* (1997), named after a song of the same name by Léo Férré. The choreography designed for this film by Daniel Larrieu is performed by Laurence Rondoni and exudes an atmosphere of dubious sensuality à la Audrey Hepburn. In *Tour de France* (1994), this time set four-square in the 1970s, we see two boys hanging around listlessly. They meet two girls from the Catholic youth movement and this marks the start of an erotic exploration, akin to that undergone by Victor in *Man of Steel*.

Many of Bal's films are dominated by an emphatic stylistic concept: the science-fiction world in *Man of Steel*, *film noir* in *The Bloody Olive*, the combination of amateur black and white images with 'normal' images in *At the Seaside*. In *Tour de France* and *Joli Môme* style is kept in the background, though still recognisable from the pleasure the film-maker derives from evoking the atmosphere of the time. Bal exhibits an almost fetishistic interest in objects with a nostalgic 'charge': the dodgems and celebrity posters in *Joli Môme*, the radio, the caravan, the Catholic youth movement uniforms in *Tour de France*, the beach attributes, the *femme fatale* requisites, the amateur camera in *At the Seaside*, and the list continues in *The Bloody Olive* and *Man of Steel*.

It goes without saying that the short films produced by film-makers cannot be isolated from their full-length works. This relationship may be expressed in a striking continuity (in style and theme), but this is not always the case. Short films are after all often made by young film-makers who have yet to find their story and their style. Their projects show ample evidence of enthusiasm, but are also often romantic and somewhat superficial. They are often single-idea films. Strangely enough, many young film-makers absorb the necessary image-making skills fairly quickly. The ability to work with actors is usually less evident and often remains a problem in Flemish film.

The digital solution

It may be that the latest generation of short film-makers, with their digital films, can change this. Digital film has taken off enormously in the last five years. The heavy equipment is left at home and film-makers set out with cheap, easily managed digital video cameras. The films are edited on the PC and only 'printed' on 35 mm film in the final stage. Making films in this way costs a fraction of what it costs to make a fully-fledged old-fashioned celluloid production. Scenes can now be shot and reshot, again and again, and the film-maker can improvise to his heart's content, because videotape is virtually free. As the definition of the image is coarser than on traditional celluloid, the camera is kept close to the actor's skin where possible. The less refined camera style gives actors unprecedented freedom. The new medium automatically generates a more unfettered acting style.

There is an interesting contrast in this respect between *Maria* by Fien Troch, which won the Flemish Community Prize at the 2001 Brussels festival, and *50cc* by Felix van Groeningen, which received a special jury prize. *Maria* is a traditional 35 mm film dealing with a topic familiar in Flemish cinema: the Fleming who has gone off the rails (as, for example, in *Forbidden to Sigh*). Els Dottermans plays a rock singer whose natural relationship with reality, with her husband, children, parents, is broken. The photography appears nonchalant at first sight, but it is a studied nonchalance. The film is attractive, but it remains a true exercise in style.

50cc is a digital video film containing no well-known actors, which deals with teenagers at the height of their puberty. Three girls travelling to Italy meet five boys on their way to a 50cc motorcycle race. They end up in the Seca petrol station run by Sam and his girlfriend. And there they spend the whole length of the film – 45 minutes! – hanging around. Their boredom is not boring, however, because the performance of the actors is rich in detail, nuance and imagination. The dialogue is in Ghent dialect. Comedy and seriousness, the exalted and the vulgar, alternate in a natural way. Felix van Groeningen held extensive improvisation sessions with his actors, and it shows. Even though the script by the young film-maker is not exactly a high point in film literature, in *50cc* he achieves a rare authenticity and naturalness in the acting performances.

For me, the Flemish short film would benefit more in the medium term from forceful acting projects such as *50cc* than from the familiar Flemish *sérieux* of short films such as *Maria*, however successful these may be.

The new digital media will in any event exert a great influence on the production-methods of films both long and short. Films in which the acting is more important than the carefully thought-out photography will be less likely to be shown in the traditional way. It is likely that short film-makers will also begin using these new techniques. The short film, including in Flanders, will thus become an even more accessible genre – at least for the makers.

ERIK MARTENS
Translated by Julian Ross.

http://www.kortfilmfestival.be

Felix van Groeningen, *50cc*
(2000). Photo courtesy of
Felix van Groeningen.

Riposte

to Death

Esther Jansma's Poetry

Esther Jansma (1958-).
Photo by David Samyn.

Mourning. Cherishing the dead. Examining, delaying, outwitting, toying with, and renaming death, in order finally to let go of it again. This is the essence of Esther Jansma' s work.

Esther Jansma, born in 1958 in Amsterdam, made her debut in 1988 with *Voice under my Bed* (Stem onder mijn bed), an impressive collection of poems, whose tight form and grim subject matter immediately made an impact. The poems are constructed in compact stanzas, with short sentences. They have a strong rhythm which never sinks into a metric drone; alliteration and more particularly assonance are what carry it. Even so, Jansma's language always remains close to spoken language: anyone who has heard her give a reading knows how naturally her poems accord with her own voice and intonation.

The tight form naturally also fits the content. Jansma often chooses the perspective of a child, using the short, peremptory or defiant sentences that children often utter when playing together. In *Voice under my Bed* play is a vital element, as the children in these poems, sisters, see themselves confronted by matters they can barely grasp or bear, which nevertheless have a strong influence on their lives: parents divorcing, a father dying and an inaccessible, domineering mother. The violent emotions are made manageable and bearable by both the children's play and the effective form of the poems. In one of his poems the Dutch poet Lucebert wrote that poetry is child's play; Jansma is not likely to quarrel with that.

Despite all the loss *Voice under my Bed* concludes on a hesitantly positive note, with poems about a pregnancy. In one of them the following lines occur, which always spring to mind when pregnant friends tell me how taken by surprise they feel by the new life within them: '*Sometimes I am afraid. I don't / get it at all. How perfect is a god, / who one day must fall?*'

Mourning pervades Jansma's second book even more strongly. Her first child died at birth. *Flower, Stone* (Bloem, steen, 1990) is entirely devoted to despair, rage and the painful acceptance of this loss. In an interview with the Flemish newspaper *De Morgen* Jansma said that she wrote the poems largely because her feelings could find no words and met with no response. This collection too contains extremely compact poems in which the poet flirts

257

time and again with death, entices it towards her and manages to get a certain grasp on it.

In *Blow Hole* (Waaigat, 1993), her third book, Jansma makes a deliberate attempt to distance herself from the dark, introverted subject matter of the first collections. Influenced by American and South American poetry, her poems become more anecdotal. Stories to cheer herself up, Jansma called them in the above-mentioned interview. Yet even in the stories of children playing the invocation of sorrow and death returns again and again.

Four years after *Blow Hole* Jansma's novel *Picnic on the Winding Stairs* (Picknick op de wenteltrap, 1997) appeared. In short passages of poetic prose she tells the story that had also dominated *Voice under my Bed*. Her traumatic childhood experiences are dealt with by three voices: the Head, the one that analyses and investigates everything; Age, fearful and conservative; and the Romantic, passionate and rebellious. The childlike logic behind the sentences uttered by the voices is captivating: '*One more of those things that have never been proved,*' says the Romantic. '*Someone disappears and everyone begins to weep. I can't stand it! When is someone really going to do some research into disappearing? Someone could just as easily have gone to live somewhere else, or after being dead for a while he could suddenly wake up again!*'

In the grown-up world this kind of argument is bound to be shrugged off as silly. But in the face of death everyone is a Simple Simon, and such an attitude may be all we have to hold on to. This is certainly so in Esther Jansma's work. With the return to the first great loss in her life and to the deadly serious game of resistance to it, it seems as if *Picnic on the Winding Stairs* has completed a cycle and the poet has now found herself again.

Holding on and letting go

But life goes on and death continues to wreak havoc. Not only did Jansma lose a fellow poet – the Fleming Herman de Coninck – who was a close friend, she also lost her second child. '*I certainly don't want to be branded as the eulogist of dead children,*' Jansma says adamantly. Nothing is less likely. In the perfection of their form the poems in one of her most recent collections, *Time is Here* (Hier is de tijd, 1998), which received the 1999 VSB poetry prize, the most prestigious prize awarded for poetry written in Dutch, rise far above sheer autobiography.

Jansma's approach has undergone a change. Where pent-up anger and rebellion were the hallmark of her first volumes, serenity and wisdom are more what typify the poems in *Time is Here*. There is, however, no question of resignation; using powerful constructions she continues to search for a foothold, a riposte to death. In the splendid opening poem 'Safe House' ('Behouden Huys'), which is about explorers who are forced to spend the winter in the Arctic, Jansma writes:

I want
words, to hear what I must do, first
order, second order, tasks are
the veins and arteries of this house, rhythm
that fills the void, tell me
what to do, suffuse the white
with words like hunting cooking
chopping chores….

There is less active rebellion, more surrender, stoical forbearance here. The difference can be sensed even in the form: the poems are longer and more compelling and the sentences within them too. The beauty of the language sometimes gives the poems in *Time is Here* an exquisite tenderness and intensity. Take the poem 'Descent' ('De val') written '*to swap the small dingy death (and when is death not dingy and small?) for a grand colourful death, one with fishes, diamonds, ribbons and bows etc.*' 'Descent' is an attempt to delay death for a while, to embellish it, to demarcate it, preserve it, bear it.

One of the poems in *Time is Here* is also the first poem in Jansma's next book *Turrets* (Dakruiters, 2000). 'Absence' ('Afwezigheid') tells us: '*What was said repeats itself, missing / is manifold, keeps opening up in the now / and you don't know how.*'

The constantly recurring sense of loss and the childish revolt against it are once more at the heart of the collection. But now more than ever Jansma seems to be investigating indomitability itself. It is this that makes many of the poems so compelling. These are no empty utterances resigned to the inadequacy of language.

Combining an almost effortless flexibility with intense concentration, Jansma discovers that tightly clutching on to death, studying it and giving it form are all parts of a process of acceptance and letting go:

...... How a rose
against all odds so gracefully, balding so gradually,
in curves like question marks, goes down in history,
beats me. Or did I arrange it so myself here,
because I'm really missing it, the point of it all,
hinted at by
curves like question marks?

And so the cycle concludes with a bold statement addressing life and the living: '*I've done with questions. From now on I will know things.*'

'*Only the first-rate can cope with loss / that is to say: learn to get again,*' one of the poems announces. Jansma is a past master in bringing home to the reader the convergence of death and life, of holding on and letting go, of having and not understanding, and this is what makes her one of the most important poets of our time.

KOEN VERGEER
Translated by Elizabeth Mollison.

Five Poems
by Esther Jansma

Voice under my Bed

Like the dust under your bed
they become, he said. But they don't know
that they're dead, he said; they know
nothing.

Their fall out of time
races out past the bounds
within which we wake in the morning, he said.
Beyond there is nothing, he thought.

You give your helplessness
a voice under the bed and the names
of gods, he said. For he didn't yet know
that he was dead.

From *Voice under my Bed* (Stem onder mijn bed). Amsterdam: de Arbeiderspers, 1988.

Stem onder mijn bed

Als het stof onder je bed
worden ze, zei hij. Maar ze weten niet
dat ze dood zijn, zei hij; ze weten
van niets.

Hun val uit de tijd schiet
de grenzen voorbij, waarbinnen wij
's morgens ontwaken, zei hij. Daarachter
ligt niets, dacht hij.

Jullie geven je onmacht
een stem onder het bed en de namen
van goden, zei hij. Want hij wist nog niet
dat hij dood was.

Prologue

I wrap her in tissues of words,
I want her panting with language
I write to everyone; I want
no sound untouched by her.

I want to hear her everywhere, I want her
to break rules and to be born
over and over again, in ever different ways.
I want a thousand lives for her.

And in a thousand people
she can play at dying.

From *Flower, Stone* (Bloem, steen). Amsterdam: de Arbeiderspers, 1990.

Proloog

Ik hul haar in weefsels van woorden,
ik wil dat ze ademt van taal,
ik schrijf iedereen aan; ik wil
geen klank onaangeraakt door haar.

Ik wil haar overal horen, ik wil
dat ze spelregels breekt en steeds
opnieuw en anders wordt geboren:
ik wil duizend levens voor haar.

En ze mag in duizend mensen
spelen, dat ze doodgaat.

Descent

We crossed the Styx.
The ferryman lay drunk in his ship.
I held the tiller and we sank like stones.

Water like the earth exists
in layers, transparent ribbons, gleaming strata
of ever smaller life, less warmth.

In your hair bubbles blossomed,
the current drew your head backwards
and stroked your neck.

Stones waved with arms of algae and ferns,
sang gently gargling 'peace'.
They cut your clothes away.

Fish licked the blood from your legs.
I held your hand tight. I wanted to comfort you
but we fell too quickly and there are no words

that exist without air, my love
stayed above, blue balloons, short-lived beacons,
marking the site of the accident

before they drifted away. Your mouth opened wide.
Your face went red, your hands sought for
balance, sought for my arms.

You tried to climb up inside me.
You were a glassblower with a cloud of diamonds
at his mouth. I held you like a kitten.

I stroked your fingers.
You didn't let go.
You slept and I stroked your fingers, let go.

From *Time is Here* (Hier is de tijd). Amsterdam: de Arbeiderspers, 1998.

De val

We kruisten de Styx.
De veerman lag dronken in zijn schip.
Ik hield het roer en we zonken als stenen.

Water bestaat als de aarde
in lagen, transparante linten, glanzende strata
van steeds kleiner leven, minder warmte.

In je haren bloeiden luchtbellen,
de stroom trok je hoofd naar achter
en streelde je hals.

Stenen wuifden met armen van algen en varens,
zongen zachtjes gorgelend 'vrede'.
Ze sneden je kleren los.

Vissen likten het bloed van je benen.
Ik hield je hand vast. Ik wilde je troosten
maar we vielen te snel en er zijn geen woorden

die zonder lucht bestaan, mijn liefde
bleef boven, blauwe ballonnen, bakens voor even,
de plaats markerend van het ongeluk

voordat ze verder dreven. Je mond ging open.
Je gezicht werd rood, je handen zochten
evenwicht, zochten mijn armen.

Je probeerde in me omhoog te klimmen.
Je was een glasblazer met een wolk van diamanten
aan zijn mond. Ik hield je vast als een katje.

Ik aaide je vingers.
Je liet niet los.
Je sliep en ik aaide je vingers, liet los.

Absence

Like roses opening, you don't see it,
a rose is a rose is, is suddenly knowing:
what was said repeats itself, missing
is manifold, keeps opening up in the now

and you don't know how. You lie in the heart
and you wait and nothing seeks you, nothing
sleeps you to the light, keeps unfolding itself
while falling into itself.

From *Turrets* (Dakruiters). Amsterdam: de Arbeiderspers, 2000.

Presence

I've done with questions. From now on I will know things.
From now on she's not a rose but Julia

and her sleep is not the sleep of things.
From now on she can be known and I'm going to live

for a long time in a house with her and feed her,
I teach her to talk and she tells me how things are

while she keeps changing. She keeps using different words.
Sometimes I cut her hair. Then her head changes.

Myself I change so slowly that she doesn't notice,
when she's grown up

I have been always old and happy.

From *Turrets* (Dakruiters). Amsterdam: de Arbeiderspers, 2000.

All poems translated by Tanis Guest.

Afwezigheid

Zoals rozen openen, je ziet het niet,
een roos is een roos is, is plotseling weten:
wat werd gezegd zegt zich weer, missen
is veelvoud, blijft opengaan in het nu

en je begrijpt niet hoe. Je ligt in het hart
en je wacht en niets zoekt je, niets
slaapt je naar het licht, blijft zich ontvouwen
terwijl het valt in zichzelf.

Aanwezigheid

Ik ben uitgevraagd. Vanaf nu ga ik dingen weten.
Vanaf nu is zij geen roos maar Julia

en is haar slaap niet de slaap van de dingen.
Vanaf nu kan zij gekend worden, ga ik heel lang

met haar in een huis wonen en haar eten geven,
leer ik haar praten en vertelt zij me hoe het is

terwijl ze steeds verandert. Steeds gebruikt ze andere woorden.
Soms knip ik haar haren. Dan verandert haar hoofd.

Zelf verander ik zo langzaam dat zij niets merkt,
wanneer zij groot is

ben ik altijd al oud en blij geweest.

hronicle

Architecture

Architecture and National Identity

In recent years it has been almost impossible to keep up with the attempts made to describe the distinct character of Belgian – and in particular Flemish – contemporary architecture, and to identify and promote it as such. In countless exhibition catalogues and publications connections have been drawn between the most diverse oeuvres by reference to an underlying design culture or paradigm. References, for instance, to the highly individual approach of architects and their aversion to bureaucratic procedures, or to their search for simplicity. Formal principles of design, design approaches and constructed banality are effortlessly welded together in defence of a supposed national – or Flemish – identity.

Homeward. Contemporary Architecture in Flanders is an attempt to develop a new paradigm for contemporary Flemish architecture: one based on urban planning. At least, this is what Steven Jacobs claims in his introduction to the publication. However, instead of contributing a new paradigm, the book appears to take issue with the existing paradigms and the label 'Flemish' in general. The only feature that links the ten structures presented (nine buildings and one urban planning design) is their location. They are all examples of designs conceived for and in Flanders. But how does this English publication differ from the *Yearbooks of Flemish Architecture* (Jaarboeken Architectuur Vlaanderen)*, which, every two years, catalogue Flanders' latest architectural achievements in word and image? By selecting a limited number of designs, the authors of *Homeward* have at least attempted to avoid the format of the Yearbook with its short, descriptive texts. Moreover, they dispense with the customary dichotomy between a sharp analysis of the morphology of the

Flemish landscape and the glorification of isolated and autonomous architectural objects. The authors of *Homeward* emphasise the context in which a number of prominent designs were created. They also describe how architects approach specific requirements relating to urban planning or the landscape and incorporate these in their designs. Although the selection contains no surprises, this approach is justified and even commendable. The reader is thus able to understand the problems and challenges architects face in Flanders today (peripheral urban development, suburbanisation, ribbon development, etc.) and how they implicitly or explicitly influence a design. The statistics relating to living patterns and land use in Flanders support the general approach, but are not explained in the text.

In his aphoristic contribution to *Homeward,* the philosopher Dieter Lesage rightly describes the cultural identity of Flanders as an artificial construct, a synthetic delimitation. Perhaps the same could be said of the 'Dutchness' of the architecture discussed in two other recent publications: *The Artificial Landscape. Contemporary Architecture, Urban Design and Landscape Architecture in the Netherlands,* edited by Hans Ibelings, and *Superdutch. New Architecture in the Netherlands* by Bart Lootsma. Both authors, who also made the *Architecture in the Netherlands Yearbook 99-00,* emphasise the need among Dutch architects to draw on their own cultural tradition and identity. Ibelings and Lootsma are quick to point to Calvinist and Humanist criticism of the worldly wealth of the Golden Age – which still profoundly influences the Dutch character even today. They also point to tradition in the treatment of the built environment, which is based – as was the case with the major water-management projects – on a sober and pragmatic application of technology and planning. It is well known that in the Netherlands, in contrast to Belgium, everything is regulated and every square kilometre is subject to planning. In the Netherlands even teenagers, junkies and prostitutes have not escaped the urban planning pro-

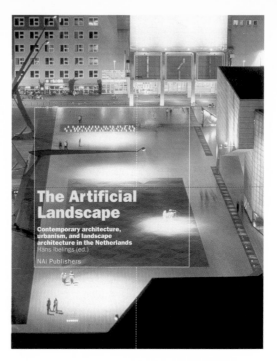

cess, and the places where they meet and work have been designed and institutionalised. Young people can now meet and 'hang around' in specially designated areas known as *'hangplekken'*. The same applies to prostitutes, who can now work in special 'drive-in' spots and tolerance zones. Moreover, the Netherlands has a strong culture of consultation – the so-called 'polder model' – and everyone is allowed his/her say. Unfortunately, the polder model has little room for radical proposals, which are often stifled in the quest for consensus and compromise. Nevertheless, Ibelings and Lootsma have detected in recent Dutch architecture completely new responses to this situation that involve searching for the potential that lies hidden in a commission. Designers have found a way to escape the iron grip of regulation by dealing inventively and creatively with the restrictions imposed, for example by using irony or extreme logic.

According to Ibelings, the Dutch landscape is artificial and therefore transformable. In the 1990s, the concept of the 'transformability' of (urban) landscape gave designers new inspiration. The knowledge that the landscape was transformable brought a new freedom for architects, urban planners and landscape architects, and is the subject of this publication.

The projects presented in *Homeward* are conducive to deep reflection. In *The Artificial Landscape*, however, they degenerate into a form of background music accompanying a superficial argument. Ibelings presents an overview of more than 130 projects from some sixty design studios in the Netherlands. Discussion of the projects is kept to a minimum and is linked to a particular key word, thus forming a sort of 'lexicon' of Dutch architecture. With its collage of text and image, the book is a typical product of the postmodern age in which we live; an age in which architecture is increasingly becoming a consumer good. Nine explanatory texts and a selection of important texts on Dutch architecture published in recent years give this publication the necessary gravitas.

In *Superdutch*, Bart Lootsma presents twelve 'radical' design studios (of which MVRDV, Neutelings Riedijk and OMA are the best known) which combine internationalism with a typically Dutch realism and pragmatism. It is somewhat surprising that Lootsma describes these firms as 'radical' because they have all found a place in the Dutch architectural establishment

– and done so with remarkable ease. Lootsma's argument is based on the concept of 'second modernity', borrowed from the sociologists Ulrich Beck and Anthony Giddens. This concept is characterised by countless new rules and regulations, by consultation and jurisprudence. This means that the architect has to respond to a context that is no longer purely morphological or typologically defined, but instead has several hidden layers of rules, provisions and requirements set by various external parties. Examples are the requirements relating to climate control, noise, security and fire, and those set by individuals for their living environment (e.g. privacy). The design studios Lootsma discusses acknowledge the ascendancy of the modern age and are focussing on how to control it. They identify limiting conditions and rules using diagrams, statistics and datascapes etc. in order to allow themselves a certain freedom of movement and realise their hidden agenda. The book presents a wide selection of interesting and often innovative buildings that represent this architectural approach. The biographical texts accompanying the well-documented projects could, though, have been rather more critical in tone.

DIETER DE CLERCQ
Translated by Yvette Mead.

Kristiaan Borret, *et. al.*, *Homeward. Contemporary Architecture in Flanders*. Antwerp: de Singel, 1998; 210 pp. ISBN 90-75591-09-8.
Hans Ibelings (ed.), *The Artificial Landscape. Contemporary Architecture, Urbanism and Landscape Architecture in the Netherlands*. Rotterdam: NAi Uitgevers, 2000; 304 pp. ISBN 90-5662-156-4.
Bart Lootsma, *Superdutch. New Architecture in the Netherlands*. Princeton, NJ: Princeton Architectural Press, 2000; 256 pp. ISBN 1-5689-823-99.

The theatre of the Brakke Grond. Photo by G.J. van Rooij.

De Brakke Grond, a Flemish House in the Netherlands

In the heart of Amsterdam, by the Nes, within the ring of canals, stands an old building called De Brakke Grond, which means 'Brackish Soil'. The oldest document relating to it dates from 1626. The property has spent most of its long life as an auction house for tobacco, but it has also done duty as a steam-powered print-works, a dance-hall and a theatre. In the mid-1970s it was occupied for two years by squatters, until it was bought by the Flemish Government with a view to turning it into a Flemish cultural centre.

The Amsterdam architect Arthur Staal was commissioned to renovate the structure. On 23 May 1981, now completely restored, the complex opened its doors. The tastefully arranged centre houses a handsome theatre which has become well-known in Amsterdam, a gallery ('t Wit Lavendel), an exhibition hall, a smaller theatre, rehearsal and presentation space, conference rooms, living-quarters for the director and, of course, a café-restaurant which is if possible even more famous.

Initially De Brakke Grond was given a very broad remit, which was more strictly formulated in 1999. The task of the Flemish Cultural Centre is to publicise the cultural life of Flanders in the Netherlands and to develop a permanent forum for the entire country. It provides a platform for outstanding artistic and cultural developments from Flanders and promotes Flemish-Dutch cultural co-operation. In particular, De Brakke Grond tries to establish contacts with those in a position to make Flemish cultural life more widely known in the Netherlands – people like journalists, critics, arts programmers, museum directors, organisers of cultural events, etc. Dutch artists too are an important target group, for De Brakke Grond seeks to encourage dialogue between Flemish and Dutch artists. Finally, it also aims to reach a wide range of policy and opinion-formers.

At first things did not go smoothly for De Brakke Grond in its new role as a Flemish cultural centre under the aegis of the Minister for Culture of the Flemish Government. In its early years new directors followed one another in rapid succession. But under Guido Vereecke, the present director, things calmed down and on 6 April 2000, in the presence of Queen Beatrix of the Netherlands and King Albert II of Belgium, he was able to celebrate De Brakke Grond's twentieth anniversary with a symposium on cultural co-operation between the Netherlands and Flanders.

De Brakke Grond carries out its mission by organising a wide variety of cultural initiatives and events. Most of these take place in its own premises, but on occasion it also supports events elsewhere. In the case of the performing arts De Brakke Grond has from the beginning worked closely with the [Nes]theatres (formerly the Theaterunie). They hire out part of their facilities for Dutch productions and jointly organise some others. Many a major Flemish theatre and dance production has had its Dutch premiere in De Brakke Grond. The problem is, though, that the halls there are on the small side and not always available; so the Flemish cultural centre also helps Flemish artists to plan their 'careers' in the Netherlands and does its best to ensure that where appropriate Flemish companies are able to graduate to larger Dutch theatres. In the programming of theatre, dance and music alike, efforts are made to present as much recent and innovative work as possible.

Major exhibitions are also organised on a regular basis. Altogether De Brakke Grond has over 500 m² of exhibition space at its disposal. In the beginning it was mainly the great and famous artists who were shown; but these days the preference is largely for young artists who have yet to make their name internationally. As far as possible this young talent is exhibited in an international context. A great deal of importance is also attached to continued promotion of the artist. A network of contacts has been built up with galleries, art institutions and museums, to give artists the opportunity to develop their later careers more successfully.

Other art-forms such as film and literature (including journalism and essays) are also catered for, while readings and discussions are regularly organised.

Ultimately, the aim of De Brakke Grond is to become the main point of reference for anyone seeking information on art and culture from Flanders.

In its twenty years of existence the Flemish cultural centre De Brakke Grond has evolved into the first port of call for anyone in the Netherlands who is interested in Flemish culture. And this is no Flemish cultural reservation but an open house, always mindful of its Dutch and international context.

DIRK VAN ASSCHE
Translated by Tanis Guest.

Flemish Cultural Centre De Brakke Grond,
Nes 45 / 1012 KD Amsterdam / The Netherlands
Tel. +31 20 622 90 14 / http://www.brakkegrond.nl

John Appel's *André Hazes – The Film* (André Hazes – Zij gelooft in mij), winner of the Joris Ivens Award at the 1999 IDFA.

Film and Theatre

Facts and Fakes The Amsterdam International Documentary Film Festival

At the time of the first Amsterdam International Documentary Film Festival (IDFA) in 1988, the Dutch documentary industry was defunct. The stream of documentaries that for years had been showing in the news cinemas had dried up, while the movie theatres rarely showed anything but feature films. Television companies too seemed to have lost interest in non-fiction films. It was a far cry from the middle years of the century when the Netherlands enjoyed a flourishing tradition of documentaries, with internationally acclaimed film-makers like Bert Haanstra, Herman van der Horst, John Fernhout and Joris Ivens.

In 2001 much has changed. Dutch documentaries are once again among the international trendsetters, the broadcasting companies are financing and regularly showing (Dutch) documentaries and even in the cinema the non-fiction film is no longer an oddity. Perhaps it is over-generous to credit this turn of events entirely to the IDFA, which organised its 13th event in 2000. Nevertheless, it is a fact that the IDFA has been the catalyst in reviving the documentary climate in the Netherlands while at the same time gaining an international reputation for itself. In 2000, the IDFA was the largest documentary film festival in the world.

The festival's success has inevitably had its critics. In 1999 one of them, the film teacher Stefan Majakovski, organised a single afternoon's 'off-IDFA' documentary event that in 2000 grew into a genuine alternative festival lasting several days. Rumour has it that in 2001 it will become even more professional. The IDFA's reaction to this has been fairly laconic: the organisers' attitude is that every respectable festival has a shadow event. After all, the Berlin Film Festival has its Panorama and Forum sections and, more recently, the independent American Sundance Film Festival has Slamdance. According to press reports, the IDFA's director and founder, Ally Derks, felt honoured that people now take the IDFA seriously enough to make the effort to channel their criticisms in this way. Nevertheless, he also seemed to imply that it was time to get down to business. There's a real festival to be organised.

Yet not so long ago the IDFA was itself a kind of alternative festival, a reaction against the relative lack of interest in documentary production shown by the Film Festival in Utrecht (then known as *Nederlandse Filmdagen* and later the Netherlands Film Festival) and the international Rotterdam Film Festival. The 1960s and 70s were the years of the Festikon, a festival of education and creativity that, entirely in the spirit of a time when it was believed that society could be remoulded, focused attention on the documentary film, especially as an instrument for awakening social conscience. But when this festival quietly bled to death, it was not at all certain that another documentary festival would take its place.

From the ashes of the Festikon, however, came Menno van de Molen and Ally Derks and with the support of a small group of students of Dutch and Theatre Studies and strong backing from the Dutch journalist and documentary maker Jan Vrijman, they supervised the birth of the first IDFA. They took over Festikon's legacy of social criticism and in that same year, before a small audience, organised their first festival. By the following year, the young and enthusiastic team had built up so much credit that the government agreed to give the festival long-term financial support.

In the years that followed the IDFA grew to be the third largest film festival in the Netherlands, with an international allure that was important to film-makers and others in the industry. A number of other initiatives attached themselves to the IDFA, such as the international FORUM for the co-financing of documentaries, the Docs for Sale documentary market, and recently the Jan Vrijman Fund, set up to finance documentary films from developing countries, analogous to the Hubert Bals Fund which is linked to Rotterdam's International Film Festival. The Scenario Workshop, originally organised during the festival itself, now spreads over a period of several months. Under the guidance of a Dutch documentary maker, with guest appearances by various producers, commissioning editors for television and representatives of film financing organisations, the participants each produce a complete scenario for a documentary film. The best scenario then receives a 'completion' prize of 275,000 guilders to enable the winner to turn his or her ideas into a film of about one hour's duration.

All these side-activities would obviously lose their attraction without a strong festival programme and interest from abroad. The first IDFA event coincided with the political thaw taking place in the then Soviet Union. As a result, in 1988, the festival was able to present a survey of old and new documentaries from the Soviet Union that gave westerners an often disconcerting picture of that country during and after the periods of *glasnost* and *perestroika*. Bringing these films to an international public has since been recognised as one of IDFA's most important achievements.

Its association with the former soviet republics greatly influenced the IDFA programme in subsequent years: from the first year, when the Armenian film *Island* (Ktsjsiner) by Reuben Gevorkjanz and Karin Junger's *Birthplace Unknown* were joint winners of the Joris Ivens Award and the next year when the winner was the Latvian *The Crossroad* (Skierskala) by Imantis Seletskis, to the 1993 winner *The Belovs* (Belovy) by the Russian film-maker Victor Kossakovsky.

Until the film industry in the former soviet republics collapsed in the mid-1990s, films from those countries remained important for setting the tone of the IDFA programme. So too were American documentaries in the direct cinema, or *cinéma vérité*, tradition, with the veteran Frederick Wiseman as a fairly regular contributor. In general, the programming focused mainly on the west. And although the IDFA claimed to support the 'creative documentary', films that were too poetic or impressionistic were often rejected in favour of those with greater social orientation. But although journalism often prevailed over artistic quality, it also meant that the IDFA became a place for reflection on the representation of current events, such as the war in the former Yugoslavia.

Despite the fact that its very first award went to the debut documentary of a Dutch film-maker, Karin Junger, the IDFA's relationship with Dutch documentary makers has been less close than one might expect. For a long time, its regulations did not allow a Dutch documentary to be entered in the competition if it had already been shown in a cinema or on television, which in effect amounted to the IDFA demanding to show the premieres of Dutch documentaries. Eventually an exception was made for films that had already appeared at the Dutch Film Festival in Utrecht, although this did not result in many more Dutch winners. In 1994, Jos de Putter won the prize with *Solo, the Law of the Favela* (Solo, de wet van de Favela), an impressionistic film about budding young footballers in Brazil dreaming of a career in football. And there were two consecutive Dutch winners in 1999 and 2000. The first was the opening film by John Appel, *André Hazes – The Film* (André Hazes – Zij gelooft in mij), a campy portrait of an Amsterdam folksinger who, in spite of his considerable success with rather sentimental Dutch popular songs, would far rather be a blues singer. The following year it seemed almost certain that the same formula would also work for Roel van Dalen's *Ajax – Hark the Herald Angels Sing* (Ajax – Daar hoorden zij engelen zingen), a film about the popular Amsterdam football club, Ajax. But against all expectations, the Joris Ivens Award went to an entirely stage-managed documentary *The Sea that Thinks* (De zee die denkt), a debut production on which its director Gert de Graaff had worked for twelve years.

Awarding the prize to a film far removed from the traditional documentary concept put back on to the IDFA's agenda the whole question of the criteria and standards people expected of a documentary. Already in the 1990s, in parallel with other cinematic developments, the phenomenon of the fake, fictitious, sham documentary had turned up at the IDFA when Kevin Hull's *Relics – Einstein's Brain* opened the festival in

1994. The film was not announced as a staged documentary, so audiences were completely confused. A crazy Japanese scholar searching for Albert Einstein's brain? It just wasn't possible. Or was it?

The Sea that Thinks can best be described as a philosophical enquiry into the nature of reality. The film poses the question whether everything might not be mere illusion. It makes use of optical illusions and cinematic tricks, such as making the central character the scenario writer of the film in which he already appears to play the leading role. These are questions that go beyond the process of filmmaking, questions which everyone, child, adolescent or adult, will have asked themselves. In turning the theme into a film, one could say that *The Sea that Thinks* investigates the basic conditions for making films about reality, in other words, for making documentaries. In this film, director De Graaff shows himself to be entangled in his own doubts as to the legitimacy of his cinematic claims to reality. The dilemma of the documentary maker has never been so clearly presented.

DANA LINSSEN
Translated by Chris Emery.

IDFA
Kleine-Gartmanplantsoen 10 / 1017 RR Amsterdam / The Netherlands
Tel.: +31 20 627 3329 / Fax: +31 20 638 5388
http://www.idfa.nl

A Painter Film-Maker Homage to Raoul Servais

The internationally renowned Flemish maker of animated films, Raoul Servais (1928-), can look back on a glittering career. With a relatively small number of animated films, only twelve over forty years, he has won prizes at all the world's major film festivals. In October 2000, to mark its 27th anniversary, the International Film Festival of Flanders organised an exhibition in honour of the man who is known as the father of Flemish and Belgian animated film. Entitled *A Painter Film-Maker's Journey*, the exhibition had already been a success in Annecy and Montreal.

Through the use of films, drawings, paintings, photographs and digital images, the viewer was drawn into the fantasy-rich world of ideas of an artist who time and again has astonished the world with innovative screenplays; not least by the combination of live action with animation, the so-called *'Servaisgraphy'*, which he developed himself. In short, the exhibition portrayed his whole evolution from experimental autodidact to grandmaster of the animated film.

To mark this exhibition a catalogue was published, written in both French and English, which took the form of an extensive and beautifully illustrated biographical essay about the artist. Its author was Philippe Moins, art historian and co-director of the Brussels Animated Film Festival.

Moins' account of the life and work of the Ostend painter and film-maker is both meticulous and absorbing. He relates how, as a five-year-old, Servais was already fascinated by the cartoons of Felix the Cat that his father projected for him; how he then attempted to animate his own childish drawings; how he made his own camera out of a cigar-box; in short, how his driving enthusiasm for the moving picture was rooted in his childhood. Some time later he came into contact with the late Henri Storck, the father of the Belgian Documentary School, who before the war ran his own 'Ciné Club d'Ostende'. Later on, together with the Ostend painter Maurice Boel, Servais breathed new life into the film club. Of particular importance is that Moins places Servais' development in its socio-cultural context, which is fascinating for those with an interest in the Flanders of the time and more especially in 'old' Ostend, 'terminus of the continent', queen of the seaside resorts and the town of James Ensor.

In the end, Servais received a formal artistic education at the Royal Academy of Fine Arts in Ghent, where he studied in the department of decorative arts. He drew, painted and designed posters, made designs for murals, carpets and stained-glass windows … all with great enthusiasm. But his passion for the animated film remained.

In 1953 he helped René Magritte to transpose the latter's *Le Domaine Enchanté* on to the circular 'Salon des Lustres' at the Knokke casino. According to Moins, it was Magritte's work that introduced Servais to surrealism, which, together with the expressionism of such artists as Constant Permeke, remained a permanent influence on his work. It was only in 1957 that Servais had the means to take his first steps in the world of the animated film. He worked for three years on *Harbour Lights* (Havenlichten, 1960) which, although barely completed, promptly won the first prize for animation at the Antwerp Festival. *Harbour Lights* is full of imperfections but, according to Philippe Moins, contains all the hallmarks of the 'Servais touch'. In the first place, there is the international accessibility of the film. Beneath the *'childlike surface'* there lurks a metaphorical layering that is the result of a lengthy thought process: *'To bring his ideas to life he deliberately takes a distance from what is, at the specific point, the canon of animation film, and turns to the plastic arts.'* Indeed, from the beginning Servais distanced himself from the conventional animated film. His background as a painter enabled him to adapt his style to any subject, constantly making references to the artistic trends of the time. This anti-Disney style perfectly suited his basic theme: the struggle for individual freedom and creativity.

Harbour Lights is about a small streetlight which the larger lights are always making fun of. However, it wins everyone's respect after going to the help of a faulty lighthouse. Servais uses animation for functions that lie beyond the scope of live action: *'the heroes of the film being a lantern, a lighthouse and above all … the light, used as a narrative and dramatic element.'* His humanist message is serious, but it is packaged in a humorous and playful style with more than a touch of

Raoul Servais, *Night Butterflies*
(*Nachtvlinders*, 1998). Photo
courtesy of Raoul Servais.

the cartoonesque. His anti-commercial, craftsmanlike approach ensured that on the basis of the characteristics described above he secured a unique place in the international world of animated films. 1960 was not just the year of his first festival award; it was also the year of his appointment as a teacher at his old college, the Royal Academy of Fine Arts in Ghent. Freed from material worries, he was now able to start building up his own oeuvre. A few years later, in 1966, he founded the very first department of animation in Europe. His influence on his students was so great that even today people talk of the Ghent school of animation.

Every three or four years, the film-maker came out with a new production: *The False Note* (De valse noot, 1963), *Chromophobia* (1966), *Sirene* (1968), *Goldframe* (1969), *To Speak or not to Speak* (1970), *Operation X-70* (1971), *Pegasus* (1973), *Sir Halewyn's Song* (Het lied van Heer Halewyn, 1976), *Harpya* (1979), the long animated film *Taxandria* (1994) and *Night Butterflies* (*Nachtvlinders*, 1998). With these eleven films Servais won more than fifty festival awards, including the Palme d'Or at the Cannes Festival for *Harpya*. Philippe Moins has done us a great service by thoroughly analysing these films and using his knowledge of art history to bring out their links with the plastic arts.

In an epilogue to this unique publication, the film critic Jan Temmerman devotes a few pages to the significance of Servais's school for animated film, the talents of whose ex-students have received world-wide acclaim.

Deservedly, Raoul Servais was president of the International Association of Animation (ASIFA) from 1985 to 1994; no small achievement for the painter film-maker who, as autodidact, discovered animated film for himself.

WIM DE POORTER
Translated by Chris Emery.

Philippe Moins and Jan Temmerman, *Raoul Servais. Itinéraire d'un*

peintre cinéaste. A Painter Film-Maker's Journey (French-English publication with separate Dutch translation). Ghent: Raoul Servais Foundation, 1999; 119 pp.

Multicultural Theatre: Diversity Unites

The relationship between Politics and Art has always been a difficult one, as history amply demonstrates. Examples abound of outrageous political attempts either to outlaw or to propagate particular forms of art. In the Netherlands it was the famous liberal statesman Johan Rudolf Thorbecke (1798-1872) who first publicly advocated the autonomy of art. His opinion that governments ought to refrain from passing judgement on artistic matters has been cited remarkably frequently in the course of various debates over the past two years, particularly with reference to the performing arts, and even more specifically where the government has attempted deliberately to stimulate cultural diversity in the theatre.

Rick van der Ploeg, the Social Democrat Secretary of State for Culture, seemed to be taking an advance on his vision of a peaceful and tolerant multicultural society when he set aside a large sum of money to subsidise immigrant talent in the theatre. Much of the ensuing discussion hinged on whether this well-meaning piece of positive discrimination might not be confused with social welfare. A national newspaper commented: '*Van der Ploeg presents himself as the minister for integration and cultural diversity. He should be given the portfolio for dreams and fantasy.*' (*De Volkskrant*, 29 May 1999)

Quite apart from that debate, one can rejoice in the fact that immigrant participation in both Dutch-speaking and foreign-language theatre has been going on for years, long before the government decided to attach importance to it. A company with an impressive record in this field is Onafhankelijk Toneel from Rotterdam which practises the art of theatre in all its forms, from repertoire to opera, from musicals to modern dance. In 1995 its artistic director, Gerrit Timmers, dramatised a novel by the French-Moroccan Driss Chraïbi, *La civilisation, ma mere! ...,* as *Civilisation, my Mother!* (De beschaving, mijn moeder!). The actors, of Moroccan origin, performed the play in Arabic, a translation for Dutch members of the audience being provided by electronic supertitles. Quite apart from the quality of this hilarious and moving production, it was an experience in itself to sit in an audience with both Moroccan – by origin - and Dutch spectators. Especially striking was the contrast in their response: the Dutch, traditionally reserved and hiding themselves in anonymity; the Moroccans, exuberant and loudly expressing their approval or disapproval.

Onafhankelijk Toneel has enjoyed mounting success with similar productions in which different cultures encounter each other. In 2000 they put on an interesting version of Shakespeare's *Othello* in which the leading role, the famous black Moor, was played by a white Dutchman. The actor Bert Luppes depicts a confused Othello who becomes hopelessly entangled in the web of an Arabic-speaking environment. Like *Civilisation, my Mother!*, this production was also performed in Morocco where the Dutch members of the company again experienced, and even more strongly, the contrast in audience response. Added to that was the fact that by Moroccan standards the production was, to put it mildly, controversial, which led to a (non-violent) confrontation between Islamic and Christian attitudes and principles.

Onafhankelijk Toneel is a tightly-knit ensemble that for the last thirty years has been producing theatre which is both widely discussed and of consistent and critically acclaimed quality. But newcomers to the world of theatre, too, have been doing sterling work in the field of cultural integration. Made in da Shade, a group from Amsterdam who aim to produce '*theatre for new times in old cities*' has been enjoying growing popularity among the young by integrating video and hiphop into their productions and more particularly by adopting the richly variegated, multinational jargon of their youthful audiences. In doing this they make no attempt to draw special attention to the diversity of language and culture which characterises their productions. That diversity is as self-evident as the pluriform society that the group is attempting to reflect.

There are also other companies in the Netherlands that work on similar lines, that is to say without regard to cultural politics or the whims of fashion. One example is the DOX theatre group from Utrecht, where young amateurs under the guidance of professional theatre makers have been producing work of high quality. Or RAST in Amsterdam, a company that combines Turkish and European theatrical traditions into a new theatrical form. And then there are also the institutions and production companies, like the Volksbuurtmuseum in The Hague and Cosmic Illusion in Amsterdam, who consciously strive to integrate the ethnic minority groups of which there are so many in the Netherlands.

Compared with the modest but commendable tradition of multicultural theatre built up in the Netherlands over recent years, what has been achieved in Flanders rather pales into insignificance. That said, the rare initiatives that do exist in this field are highly promising and encourage hopes of further development in the near future. And in Flanders too politicians have now recognised the social importance of co-operation between the various population groups; where in the past a few projects, mainly concerned with employment, had indeed been devised to encourage cultural involvement among minority groups, there now also exist two separate multicultural organisations with guaranteed government subsidies. These are Woestijn 93 in Antwerp, a production company for theatre, literature and music whose artistic director is Hazim Kamaledin, originally from Iraq, and the Ghent dance company Hush Hush Hush, headed by the choreographer Abdelaziz Sarrokh who comes from Morocco.

Among the most talked-about productions of 2001

Het Waterhuis, *Thousand and One Nights* (Duizend en één Nacht, 2000; three directors). Photo by Menno Leutscher.

was undoubtedly *Not All Moroccans Are Thieves* (Niet alle Marokkanen zijn dieven), which was intended for anyone of fourteen years old and over and was put on by HetPaleis of Antwerp in collaboration with DAS Theater. Working with a large group of actors, both trained and untrained, more than half of them not of Flemish origin, its director Arne Sierens created '*a parable about possession, justice and the weird tricks fate plays*'. Taking Dostoievsky's novel *Crime and Punishment* and Robert Bresson's film *Pickpocket* as his starting-point, Sierens and his motley company embarked on a rehearsal process that proceeded by fits and starts but eventually resulted in a performance which was decidedly confrontational. Largely because – as the title itself suggests – stubborn clichés about 'foreigners' are punctured and critical questions asked of all those who claim to be involved with issues of social and cultural integration. In May 2001 a French-language version of *Not All Moroccans Are Thieves* was performed at the KunstenFESTIVALdesArts in Brussels.

Returning from Flanders to the Netherlands, we have to stop off briefly at Het Waterhuis in Rotterdam. This is yet another example of a company which tries to connect with a changing society and does so not just in the theatre but also in other locations: in centres for asylum-seekers, for instance, and in unoccupied houses. The group focuses primarily on children and young people; in 2000 and 2001, for example, they have been performing *The Girls of Aboke* (De meisjes van Aboke) for children from the age of ten. In a sober production of a play by the dramatist Chaib Massaouda, a Moroccan by origin, the harrowing story is told of the 139 girls at a boarding school in Aboke, northern Uganda, who fell victim to one of the cruellest rebel armies in the world. Whereas this production is intended to raise social awareness among its young audiences, the same company's *Thousand and One Nights* (Duizend en één Nacht)**,** performed in various towns in 2000**,** appeals to the sense of humour of young and old alike. Three directors are involved, one of whom is the Moroccan Youssef Ait Mansour who also acted in *Civilisation, my Mother!*, referred to earlier.

For a Secretary of State who wants to encourage the participation of minorities in cultural life, *Thousand and One Nights* must have been a dream production. In Rotterdam, this magical fairy tale began in broad daylight next to the theatre in the city centre. From there, the audience was taken to a working-class district in the south of the city, in the kind of bus recognisable only by those who have holidayed in exotic places. Here, in three different locations, all within walking distance of each other, the story of the artful Sheherezade and the cruel king Shahria was played out. In the first, a school attic, children and young people from the neighbourhood joined the audience. There the first story began, providing as it were a framework for the stories which were to follow, starting in a second location, an office building under construction, and finally in an empty grocer's shop with boarded-up windows. There, the actors of Het Waterhuis were joined by oth-ers from Maatwerk, a Rotterdam company of professionals who perform with mentally handicapped people. Making good use of Sheherezade's seductive arts, the cruel king is led up the garden path and finally branded as a slave for the rest of his life. Ultimately, therefore, this is a variation on the same theme of women's emancipation that in a less informal way lay at the heart of Onafhankelijk Toneel's productions.

Like Made in da Shade and other new groups, Het Waterhuis goes about the integration of minorities in an unforced and self-evident fashion, as regards both the company and their audiences. It is 'self-evident' in the sense that it is not merely a slavish response to a cultural policy that places a premium on multi-cultural initiatives. The ideal is, after all, independent of the economy and art of politics.

Nevertheless, sometimes art and politics do meet unexpectedly in a clash as painful as it is unavoidable. This was demonstrated by the commotion surrounding Onafhankelijk Toneel's planned production in 2001 of *Aïsha or the Women of Medina* (Aïsja of de vrouwen van Medina), again with Moroccan actors. In the final stages rehearsals had to be called off, mainly because of religious objections on the part of some of the cast, who found themselves supported by Moslem extremists who could not always be identified. To put Aïsha, the wife of Mohammed, on stage would be regarded as a serious offence against the laws of Islam.

For a number of reasons it was too dangerous for the performance to go ahead. So at the end of November 2000 Gerrit Timmers, the producer, cancelled the production, which led to political involvement by the Christian Democrat party in Parliament. Where ignorance and fear threaten to prevail and ideals and ideologies come into conflict – there, it seems, the liberal spirit of Thorbecke can no longer thrive freely. However much might be achieved in the sphere of multi-cultural theatre, in real life the road ahead is still long and hard. It was summed up in the words of Gerrit Timmers when he wrote in his diary on 26 November 2000: '*With an aching heart I take leave of a production which might have built a bridge of mutual understanding between Muslims and others, between Moroccans and Netherlanders, between men and women.*' (*TheaterMaker*, January 2001).

JOS NIJHOF
Translated by Chris Emery.

Split Screen The Flemish Search for a Cinematographic Identity

Belgian cinema has often been thought of as one of the most undervalued in Europe. Researchers will have great difficulties in finding relevant literature on it. However, in recent years there have after all been some extremely useful publications on the subject.[1] The latest is *Split Screen*, the first full English-language monograph on Belgian film history.

In this book, the American scholar Philip Mosley

Robbe de Hert, *Soft Soap*
(Lijmen, 2001).

asserts that Belgian cinema deserves more attention than the few footnotes it has been allotted in general film histories, and he is not referring only to the several recent successes, which have come mainly from the French-speaking community (such as the Cannes Palme d'Or for the Dardenne brothers in 1999). One thing that Mosley considers important is the way Belgian film-makers deal with the complex question of identity in the context of a changing Belgium and its cultural communities. Mosley's highest praise goes to the films of Charles de Keukeleire, Henri Storck and André Delvaux. However, it is no coincidence that they are all film-makers with obviously Flemish roots who switched to French-language productions early in their careers, but who constantly touch on the subject of identity in their films.

This brings us to one of the problems of Flemish film. The development of a fully-fledged feature-film industry before World War II was hampered by the structural difficulties of the limited market and language regions, and the government made little effort to support the many initiatives in this sector. After their avant-garde period in the twenties, both Storck and De Keukeleire soon had to switch to occasional (mainly documentary) film commissions. These ranged from advertising films for private and government institutions and instructional films, to coverage of current events for newsreels. Nevertheless, in Mosley's view the leading role of Flemish-Belgian cinema should not be underestimated, especially with regard to documentary, animation, colonial and experimental films.

This did not prevent initiatives to make feature films for the local market too. Mosley sees Flemish film as having four significant moments in its history. First and foremost is the period in the thirties that started with the film *The Abysses* (De Diepten). Jos Buyse and the cameraman Germain Baert are thought to have made both Dutch and French versions of this film (now probably lost). The most important film from this peri-od is the successful *De Witte* (1934) by the Antwerp director and producer Jan Vanderheyden, who went to Berlin to film it. In Mosley's opinion this film reveals '*the undeveloped state of early Flemish cinema ... since no studios yet existed in Flanders*'. However, the dominant figure in Belgian feature film production at that time was Gaston Schoukens from Brussels, who became the talk of the town with his popular *Familie Klepkens* films.

After the Second World War Flemish feature films evolved only very gradually. According to Mosley it was not until the second half of the fifties that any real innovation in Flemish film took place. An important milestone was the film *Seagulls Die in the Harbour* (Meeuwen sterven in de haven, 1955) by the trio Roland Verhavert, Rik Kuypers and Ivo Michiels. As the first Belgian film at the Cannes Film Festival, it was praised by critics but proved to be less successful in local theatres. And yet new talent did develop in its wake. In addition to the highly promising Paul Meyer (*De Klinkaart*, 1956) and Emile Degelin, the Antwerp Filmgroep 58 was formed, its members including, as well as Kuypers, various young film-makers such as Harry Kümel, Robbe de Hert and Patrick Le Bon. In Mosley's view, these film-makers, '*raised on the best of Hollywood and international art cinema*' proved that by 1960 Flemish-Belgian cinema '*had entered an era of greater artistic accomplishment, one that culminated in systematic state intervention*'. In the meantime Storck, De Keukeleire and also Paul Hasaerts had attracted international attention with exceptionally creative art films.

A third significant moment, in Mosley's opinion, was the establishment of a culturally inspired film policy in 1964. It is interesting to see how Mosley judges the influence of these state measures for direct support on actual film production. His controversial thesis is that the Flemings, in contrast to their French-speaking countrymen, were more aware of '*the potential of cin-*

ema as a vehicle for the construction of a clearly defined regional identity'. It is therefore 'unsurprising that mainstream Flemish cinema turned in the early 1970s and again in the 1980s to the canon of Flemish literature as a means of self-validation'. Even a 'left-wing maverick like Robbe de Hert began to direct Flemish "heritage" films and popular comic revivals'.

Mosley does not see this as being entirely negative, but he does point out that it also became the Achilles heel of Flemish film. This would lead to a new response in the eighties, when 'a new wave of directors, more interested in original subject matter and cultural pluralism' attempted to shake Flemish cinema out of 'a complacency born out of years of well-funded but increasingly ossified auteurist production'. Here Mosley refers to films by Marc Didden or Dominique Deruddere. There is nothing new about daring statements like this and there is good reason to doubt them (was Flemish cinema ever 'well-funded'?). But they are in line with certain critics who claim that the mechanisms of governmental support (selection committee, cultural evaluation criteria, and so on), controlled the content and form of film production for many years.

This brings us to our criticism of *Split Screen*, which is that its approach is rather more broad than deep. The reader is overwhelmed with a huge number of filmmakers, film technicians and film titles, but there is very little depth to the book. *Split Screen* is merely a good reference book based on existing Belgian sources, with Mosley himself carrying out little, if any, original research. Nevertheless, even now it is clear that this English-language work will soon become *the* international reference book on Belgian film.

DANIËL BILTEREYST
Translated by Gregory Ball.

Philip Mosley, *Split Screen. Belgian Cinema and Cultural Identity.* Albany, NY: SUNY Press, 2001; 251 pp. ISBN 0-7914-4748-0.

NOTE

1. Specifically: J.P. Everaerts, *Film in België: Een permanente revolutie.* Brussels, 2000; F. Sojchet, *La Kermesse héroique du cinéma belge.* Paris, 1999; M. Thijs, *Belgian Cinema – Le Cinéma Belge – Belgische Film.* Ghent / Brussels, 1999.

Sphere of Operations: the World
Tone Brulin's Theatre of Dreams

From 1943 until 1946 the young Antoon van den Eynde (1926-) studied stagecraft at La Cambre, the National School of Architecture and Decorative Arts in Brussels. Years earlier, the English theatre philosopher Edward Gordon Craig had written to La Cambre's founder Henry van de Velde: '*We must teach our students to fly, intoxicated by air*'. In 2000 Van den Eynde, who had by then spent many decades creating theatre under the pseudonym of Tone Brulin, wrote: '*As students of the school of Van de Velde we wanted to dream of a new type of theatre in which the actors could dream as well as fly like Craig wanted his students to dream and fly. A new type of theatre can't be dominated by spoken literature which seems to nail the action to the floor. We felt the need to elevate, to float.*'

The head of La Cambre's drama department when Brulin was studying there was Herman Teirlinck. To Teirlinck, theatre was no mere skilfully presented collection of acquired tricks; it was a dream for the future of mankind. And this utopian vision determined Brulin's ideas on theatre. In his monograph on Brulin, Geert Opsomer comments that whatever new context this man of the theatre found himself in, he always looked for a provisional, contemporary interpretation of that dream of the future.

In the early years of his career the young actor-director-set-builder did very little work in the theatre. During that period his main activity was as a journalist and co-founder of the avant-garde periodicals *Tijd en Mens* (1948) and *Gard Sivik* (1952). In that capacity he introduced the Flemish cultural world to the ideas of Antonin Artaud. Brulin saw Artaud's *théâtre de cruauté* as a possible model for the theatre for the future. He was strongly opposed to the Western dichotomy between life and art: the life that exists in art must be revealed and vice versa, with the aim of helping the individual to discover himself.

Brulin's pet hate was the false aesthetics of the 'neo-classical' drama prevailing at that time in Flanders. As an antidote to this fossilised form he opted for trance, magic and dream. This was eventually to bring about an 'atonal' theatre, in which gestures and instinctive reactions, the impulsive in other words, were more important than recognisable conventions and meanings.

In 1953 Brulin won the Amsterdam Book Week Prize for his play *Two is Too Little, Three is Too Much* (Twee is te weinig, drie is te veel). Since then his plays have been performed by the great Flemish theatres. In the same year he and a friend set up the Nederlands Kamertoneel (Dutch Chamber Theatre), where he introduced works by Becket and Ionescu, among others, and also encouraged original work by young writers. The object of the Chamber Theatre was to bring art and life closer together: there was less distance between actors and audience, the length of performances was limited, and grand gesture and poetic diction made way for subtle underacting.

In 1958 Brulin and the company of the Royal Flemish Theatre in Brussels embarked on a tour of the then Belgian Congo. During this time he also worked as a director in Pretoria at the invitation of the South African National Theatre, and managed to set up another Chamber Theatre there. His time in Africa was for Brulin a shocking first encounter with racism and colonialism. It inspired him to write, among other things, the anti-colonialist *Potopot* and *The Dogs* (De honden) in which he denounced South Africa's policy of apartheid. In 1961, pressure from the South African embassy led to an attempt to ban performance of the latter play in Belgium. Since then Brulin has resolutely maintained his image as a writer who reacts to current events and does not shrink from the resultant

De Nieuw Amsterdam, *Shango* (1997), directed by Tone Brulin (l.). Photo by Jean van Lingen.

protests. This is also apparent from his work with The New Africa Group, a company he established in London together with two South African writer-actors and a black actor from Sierra Leone.

However, this commitment does not mean that Brulin is an out-and-out revolutionary pursuing a political agenda. His involvement is ethical: he is a humanist and existentialist who tries to realise his utopian ideas of theatre to the best of his ability. He is aware that this will always be a work-in-progress, and so he puts his own efforts into perspective: '*It's rather like throwing a box of matches into the North Sea in the hope that one day the North Sea will dry up and then someone will find the matchbox and warm all humanity with it.*'

In the 1960s Brulin had his hands full in his own country: among other things he worked as a television producer and taught at RITCS, the newly-established school for directors in Brussels. But that did not stop him continuing the search for his theatre of dreams. He now became acquainted with Jerzy Grotowski's Living Theatre. Grotowski sees the text of a play as merely the starting-point for the acting itself. Consequently, what is most important is the play as ritual self-expression by the actor and doing away with the 'god-like' status of the dramatist. Brulin was heavily influenced by Grotowski's theories and abjured the literary theatre of text. For him improvisation, music, movement and the training of actors were now the most important aspects; he organised actors' workshops in his own country and also championed Grotowski in the US at workshops and lectures in a number of Drama Departments. At Antioch College, Ohio, he established the Otrabanda Company with a number of his students. In an attempt to reach an audience of non-theatre-goers the company would later sail down the Mississippi on a home-made raft. Wherever they tied up they set up a circus tent and treated the local population to *The River Raft Revue*,

a colourful spectacle of music, dance, clowning, boxing and performance.

In the 1970s Brulin continued his world travels. In the course of his intercultural quest, which took him among other places to the Dutch Antilles and Malaysia, he fell under the spell of popular theatre. The Grotowskian emphasis on experiment and technique, which proved too elitist for the broad audience that Brulin wanted to reach, retreated into the background, making way for an anthropological and intercultural dimension. He now mixed traditional elements with naïve means of expression and topical illusions. Openmindedly he seeks out the universal humanity in other cultures and so constructs a transnational naïve popular theatre. The result was TIE3, the Theatre of the Third World, which he established in 1975: at once popular theatre and world theatre. He himself calls it '*a theatre of contingency*': a performance is put together using all manner of *objets trouvés*, people as well as things. Mythical tales are used to forge a link with current events such as poverty in Indonesia or the position of immigrants in Belgium. When Brulin toured Malaysia with the play *Tak Kotak-Kotak* in 1978 TIE3 performed not only in the established temples of culture but also in the slums. More than ever before, theatre had become for him a continuous process of learning, its ultimate aim the exploration and self-improvement of the individual.

Since 1986 Brulin has worked mainly as a free-lance director, in Sweden, Portugal and Malaysia among other places. He has also set up a new company: Nieuwe Realisaties (New Realisations), with whom in late 2000 he put on the most recent performances of *People of the Void*. This is an adaptation of Wilson Harris' novel *Jonestown*, in which the author uses the mass suicide in 1978 of the sect led by Jim Jones as a model for all cultures that come out of nothing and disappear into nothing again. In Brulin's adaptation the stage is occupied by seven actor-musicians from a range of cultures. Using video images, music, sound-effects, dance and words they evoke a mythical world diametrically opposed to Western rationalism. Both as writer and director, in *People of the Void* Brulin shows himself to be a man who has made the world his sphere of operations. Or, as he put it himself in an interview, *'I believe in the naked simplicity of word and gesture, of ordinary things and simple rituals. For me, theatre is on a par with music and dance. The story is not important.'*

FILIP MATTHIJS
Translated by Tanis Guest.

History

Centre of Rotterdam Taken Out

When the German Luftwaffe bombed Rotterdam on 14 May 1940 some nine thousand people lost their lives, 25,000 dwellings were destroyed, 11,000 buildings, 2,350 shops, thirteen hospitals, two thousand factories and workshops, two theatres, twelve cinemas and the premises of four daily newspapers. This puts the city on the Maas (the 2001 European City of Culture) in the same tragic line-up with Guernica, Coventry and Dresden. On 14 May 1940 an anonymous reporter on the Rotterdam newspaper 'De Maasbode' wrote this eye-witness account of the wiping out of a city:

It must have been around one o'clock when, in the company of the then editor-in-chief of the *Maasbode*, Dr J. Witlox, we left St Anthony's Institute in Nieuwe Binnenweg for the *Maasbode* building, situated on Grote Markt. We had learned that the office was on fire again and we wanted to have a go at saving at least part of the editor's valuable library.

An officer – standing sentry on the corner of Oude Binnenweg and Mauritsweg – explained in answer to our question: 'We aren't allowed to shoot at planes any more, we've surrendered.'

It was just as we were crossing Coolsingel, about to turn into the Passage, that we were surprised by an air-raid warning. And it may be imagination after the event, but we knew at once: we're for it now, something terrible is about to happen.

Meanwhile the alert went on sounding for an abnormally long time, for minutes on end the howl of the sirens (that went right through you) continued to wail above the roofs of a city doomed to die. And so, in the glass cage that was the Passage, we stood and waited for what was to come.

We were with ten, maybe twenty, or so other people. And to this very day I can still picture them clearly: those two giggling bobby-soxers, who could only keep their nerves under control by letting out those strange, high-pitched laughs, the long-faced man saying: 'The whole town's going to go up' (and how quickly he was to be proved right), the man brought in by a soldier, bicycle and all: 'You've got to keep off the street when there's a warning on', and a few other people who had been caught out by the danger signal.

Then suddenly we saw a formation of bombers circling in the sky over the city, still very high up at first. 'There they are!' someone shouted, and we stared in horror at the monsters circling above the roofs of a dying city, taking up position. Still more formations could be heard on their way: indeed, it felt as if something fatal was about to happen.

Coolsingel was deserted and desolate; a soldier with rifle at the ready was walking back and forth in the middle of the wide road. The formation circled lower. What were they going to do? The air-raid warning continued its piercing scream, for an incredibly long time. Surely by now everybody knew that there was an alert on?

But there, in the central warning station, they very probably knew rather more than did we, as ordinary people, in a condemned city centre; there they probably already knew the frightful certainty, that it wouldn't be a bomb here or there, but that this would be a deed to make the world recoil from such a form of warfare.

There are times in life when people risk everything, lose everything or win everything. Who inspired me I do not know, presumably a solicitous guardian angel, but all at once I knew without any question: 'I'm not going to stay in this Passage a moment longer. I'm in a cage, and I'm not going to stay here so much as another second.'

And straightaway I leaped down the Passage steps and ran into Coolsingel. In agitation the people in the Passage yelled after me: 'Come back. You'll get yourself killed' The soldier shouted something, pointed with his rifle in my direction, but I had stopped thinking; I was running, rushing full tilt, alone, absolutely alone, along a deserted Coolsingel, to meet my death or my salvation.

At the very same moment the alert had abruptly stopped sounding. Suddenly the drone of the aeroplane engines came through clearly, and the whole scenario became even more alarming. In fear of my life I ran into Oude Binnenweg and just as I reached it the deafening and fatal din began. Looking round I saw pieces of timber, splinters, stones, clouds of dust flying into the air, suddenly couldn't see the Passage any more, still don't know whether this was the moment it was reduced to rubble and dust or whether that happened later, but one thing I knew then for certain: if ever I had chosen a good moment to flee from a horror out of hell, then that was it.

In Oude Binnenweg panes were shattering, very soon I was wading through a sea of broken glass, but nothing could stop me: I ran, raced towards my temporary lodging, St Anthony's Institute in Nieuwe Binnenweg, that looked to me like a safe haven at that mo-

ment, and truly remained so throughout those days.

I shall never forget that crazy record run, in unbridled terror, with the bombing at my heels, not knowing any more whether bombs were landing in front of me or behind me (and probably much further away from me than I thought), but in mortal fear, which was really nothing to be proud of, but possibly not so difficult to understand, after some experience of bombing raids in the preceding days of the war.

At the gatehouse of St Anthony's, I managed to persuade the sister on duty to let me in (fortunately she recognised me), and at the same time a man slipped in with me, someone I knew and had always considered capable of anything, but never of being able to pray in such a heart-rending manner. Because that was perhaps the most remarkable thing of all: in the corridors of the St Anthony's Institute people were calm; anxious, certainly, (just think of all the hundreds of terminally ill, who couldn't move an inch without help), but full of trust, praying, reciting one rosary after another, right through an entire, devastating bombing raid that shocked the world.

In those hours (it is my impression that it lasted for hours, but it cannot have been for more than an hour and a half before the all-clear sounded) a city was destroyed.

And then the new horror set in. Without house or home, without my family, not knowing whether they were alive or buried under the rubble, I began to roam the battered inner city like a tramp.

It quickly became apparent how frightfully heavy the attack had been; it was heart-rending to see wagons with grievously wounded people, with corpses, with people who were out of their minds; to witness scum who even at a time like this had no scruples over going into deserted houses and stealing whatever took their fancy. We saw them coming away with radio sets, boxes full of shoes; they did not even have time to help the dying. We saw it with our own eyes in the shelter trenches in Hoboken, where bottles of drink looted from off-licences were being passed from hand to hand, where people were drinking themselves insensible, where acts of such barbarity were going on that one would refuse to acknowledge their perpetrators as human.

So it was all that frightful, horrendous afternoon as it slowly turned to evening: incidents of amazing courage, self-sacrifice and humanitarianism occurred side by side with the most bestial forms of selfishness and brutish behaviour.

Dazed streams of people who had been made homeless, who had lost everything, were pouring out of the streets of the city centre. I saw a number of people jump into the water of the Westersingel in sheer terror when a German plane flew low overhead, long after it was known that the city had been surrendered.

It was in the evening that Fate began to exact its toll with the greatest intensity and ferocity. The weather was fine for the time of year, but one thing in particular made the devastation what it was: the wind, a strong, cutting, stiff east wind (it changed later on, but then blew with equal force from the west) fanned the fateful fires that were everywhere to be seen.

And during the hours of darkness we witnessed

a spectacle the like of which will never again unfold itself before our eyes. In dismay, we stood on the top storey of one of the St Anthony's buildings, on the edge of the bombed area, watching a conflagration, a devastation that spread further and further, that quite simply seemed impossible to contain. Bellowing and roaring the flames – without exaggeration as high as houses – were eating their way through the streets of Coolsingel out towards the west. The fire was continually finding fresh food in new hearths. It was horrifying to see how a conflagration of amazing ferocity was developing in the Coolsingel area: whenever petrol storage tanks exploded, whenever warehouses full of oil burst into flames, the flames shot up to a towering height. The whole inner city was slowly becoming one great ocean of fire. Every half hour one saw the blaze eat further in the direction of Schiekade, further towards the east, until finally all the houses of the inner city, and then of Kralingen too, seemed to be one compact mass of fire.

From *Eyewitnesses* (Ooggetuigen, ed. Geert Mak). Ooievaar: Amsterdam, 2000.
Translated by Sheila M. Dale.

Leuven and Louvain-la-Neuve: Aller / Retour

Visitors approaching Leuven by car are greeted by a sign with icons depicting the city's attractions. The town hall represents the Gothic Leuven of Dirk Bouts, the Flemish Primitive painter who left his native Holland to settle in Brabant. Icons representing a brewer's copper and a scholar refer to the local industries: brewing and learning. The fact that the copper and scholar are equally rotund alludes to the success of the economic formula that brings producer and consumer as close together as possible. The consumption of beer and the imparting of knowledge would appear to go hand-in-hand. In Leuven, drinking has always been an essential part of academic sub-culture. English travellers used to write about it and Erasmus used to complain about it. Moreover, both sectors are keen to take on England and Leuven's brewery, with a sizeable stake in the English market, has done so very effectively. The university confronts England in a more rhetorical way, basking in comparisons with Oxford. Both brewery and university assert the value of their wares with a date. In both cases this is clearly a mark of quality rather than a sell-by date. The brewery takes pride in its six-hundred year history, and its bottles proudly inform us that it has existed '*Since 1366*'. In the academic year 2000-2001, the university celebrated the 575th anniversary of its foundation in 1425 – the date on the university's Gothic seal that dates from 1909. Traditions are continually being invented, certainly by the universities (Hobsbawm), so competitors readily accuse each other of falsifying history. With regard to the university of Leuven, it is claimed that the Catholic university founded in 1834 has nothing to do

with the old university (1425-1797), and certainly not with the state university (1817-1835). It is easy to forget that, on the continent of Europe, no university survived the French Revolution unscathed and that only Oxford, Cambridge and the Scottish universities have an uninterrupted history.

The icons of the twentieth-century heritage industry that markets the city allude to the late Middle Ages, when Leuven began to develop an identity and the production of beer and knowledge brought about an economic renaissance. The city had lost its political prominence for good, and a university was thought to be the way ahead. While it is true that the university was founded as a municipal initiative, it happened to fit in perfectly with the plans of the Dukes of Burgundy and the Habsburgs for the Low Countries as a whole. Leuven was to be the educational centre for the professional classes of this embryonic state, as well as its intellectual capital. Although some would disagree, Leuven is the oldest university in the Low Countries. It is older than Leiden and Utrecht in the North and continued to draw Catholic students from there, even after the Belgian Revolt.

The university was famous from the beginning. In less than twenty-five years, it became a microcosm of Europe. Scotland sent a strong contingent, including a certain George Lichthon, whose lecture notes have provided us with the oldest portraits of students and professors (Aberdeen University Library). In the sixteenth century the university reached the pinnacle of its success. After Paris, Leuven was the second largest university north of the Alps. The fact that a Leuven theologian, Adriaan van Utrecht, was elected pope was an enormous source of pride. Posterity has adorned Leuven's 'finest hour' with the aura of a Golden Age. For a decade Leuven was the focal point of Humanism in Europe. In 1516 Thomas More's 'Utopia' was printed there and his friend Erasmus turned the so-called Collegium Trilingue (College of the Three Languages: Latin, Greek, Hebrew) into a much talked-about seat of learning. In no time at all, the university produced a trio of scholars with international reputations who are still a source of national pride today: Mercator, who devised a method of cartographic projection, the botanist Dodoens and Andreas Vesalius, who put Leuven at the forefront of anatomical study. Learned scholars such as John Dee came to Leuven to study. The first denunciation of Luther was printed at about the same time (1520) and slightly later, in 1532, a number of half-hearted advisors left to advise King Henry VIII on his divorce. Leuven was the birthplace of such well-known concepts as '*utopia*' and '*atlas*', and also of the Index, meaning a list of prohibited books (1546). The list became one of the main weapons of the Counter-Reformation.

In the seventeenth and eighteenth centuries, Leuven became the real *pépinière* of the Counter-Reformation. Catholic seminarists from Protestant countries attended separate lectures, the effect being one of many seminaries. The recusants from Elizabethan England were succeeded in the seventeenth century by Irish in habits of every kind and colour. Today, the former monastery of an Irish Order of Friars Minor houses the Irish Institute for European Affairs – and a very commendable pub. In the nineteenth century it was the turn of the Americans and Latin Americans, and in the twentieth century the Asians and Africans arrived, bringing a touch of exoticism to the city. The Catholic label seems to attract people from abroad, another reason for retaining the 'K' ('Katholiek' – Catholic) in the university's name: K.U.Leuven (Catholic University of Leuven), although at home it is often something of a ball and chain.

In the First World War, the burning city of Leuven – *'the Oxford of Belgium'* (*The Times*) – acquired an aura of martyrdom. In 1914 English ships – and English girls too – were christened 'Louvain'. The universities of Oxford and Cambridge offered hospitality to the university of Leuven. The destruction of the university library gave rise to a movement of international solidarity, centred on the John Rylands Library in Manchester. The Americans stole the show with a brand new library building that was, ironically, itself destroyed in May 1940. Goebbels' claim that this was a war crime on the part of the English might be considered a sinister joke by the Nazis. The two world wars led to a response of greater openness towards the Anglo-Saxon world on the part of the university, which in the past had been completely permeated by French culture and heavily influenced by the academic achievements of its powerful neighbour to the east.

There is no doubt that the 1960s, characterised by linguistic conflict and secularisation, caused a shock wave and gave rise to a hitherto unknown academic openness that was averse to cavilling and paternalism. In 1985, in the presence of the Pope, the Rector of the university claimed the right to freedom of research and the right to differ and err. Modernisation inevitably meant a more technocratic approach. In the anglophile climate of the post-World War Two period, Cardinal Newman's *The Idea of a University* was occasionally taken down from the bookshelves and dusted-off again. However, in the course of the 1970s it became clear that Leuven – which, like Oxford, excelled in the humanities – was starting to become more pragmatic and making more room for useful science and technology. Even the Leuven of Letters (scholastics and humanism, orientalism and ecclesiastical history), the mythical Leuven which causes Umberto Eco to rub his hands with glee, had to become 'plugged in' to the future.

In the meantime the university is facing new challenges, all of which are related to its identity: the tensions between establishing regional foundations on the one hand and internationalisation on the other; the legitimisation of its catholicity in a secular society and, finally, the diminishing attraction of the traditional university city. The formula that had boosted Leuven's success, that of a great university in a small city, now seems to be working against it; students today seem to prefer real big cities with more swinging night life and ditto music scene. To many people, 'Catholic val-

This is how Scotsman George Lichthon pictured his professor and fellow students at the Leuven Artes Faculty in 1467. The professor is on his rostrum, while the students are sitting on the floor. All of them are wearing the prescribed academic attire. Leuvens collegedictaat, Aberdeen University Library, ms. 109.

ues' means no more than the standards of propriety of a middle-aged middle class.

The 'Dutchification' of public life in Flanders and the democratisation of education (with a larger influx of students from the lower middle classes) have resulted in the gradual acceptance of the Dutch language at the university. After the language frontier was established in 1962, the continued existence of a bilingual university at Leuven was seen as an anomaly. Eventually the French-language university moved to a brand new university town on the French-speaking side of the language frontier: Louvain-la-Neuve. In tune with the dictates of political correctness, the demands for *'Flemish Leuven'* have recently been likened to the ethnic cleansing in former Yugoslavia, yet the comparison is nothing if not anachronistic. Considering all that has gone before, we must remind ourselves that, figuratively speaking, not a single drop of blood was spilled when the university was divided and the axe was applied to the supposedly centuries-old library (which had been destroyed twice in the past hundred years). The most that can be said is that the split – in particular the legendary division of the library – caused some hilarity abroad. But this was surely a poorly understood Belgian joke. The agitators of the time appeared to draw most of their inspiration from the American civil rights movement and even the war cry *'Walloons out'*, which sounds so hostile today, was little more than an echo of *'Yankee go home'* from the Vietnam demonstrations in which Flemish students also took part.

The division of the university removed the last remaining source of linguistic conflict, and was a response to the new reality of a Belgian nation with a Dutch-language community in the north and a French-speaking community in the south. After thirty years, everyone has at last found their niche. The two universities opened their doors to each other during the anniversary celebrations, which were marked with a series of exhibitions held in both cities with the revealing title *Leuven – Louvain-la-Neuve / Aller-Retour*. A special bus service was even scheduled across the language frontier. As one would expect, the common heritage of the two universities was lavishly displayed. Certain young historians would claim that we should not dwell too much on the past and that a bus, here we are talking about a local bus – a metaphor for the present mass university –, should not be 'tarted up' as an old-timer. In fact they are raising yet again the issue of continuity – of 575 years of Leuven University.

However, both universities took the view that historians should not be killjoys, and the bus was brought out to take its place in a historical parade. We Belgians simply love to celebrate.

MARK DEREZ
Translated by Yvette Mead.

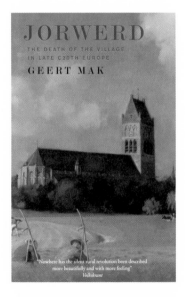

JORWERD
THE DEATH OF THE VILLAGE
IN LATE C20TH EUROPE
GEERT MAK

"Nowhere has the silent rural revolution been described
more beautifully and with more feeling"
Volkskrant

The Death of the Village Geert Mak's Jorwerd

Literary non-fiction is thriving in the Netherlands today, with a lively output of essays, historical studies and biographies, of popular works in biology, psychology, science and philosophy, of books on ethics, euthanasia, art, film, animals, the environment, sport and travel. And, increasingly, these works find their way abroad through translation. A good example is the work of the Dutch journalist Geert Mak. A few years ago, the Harvill Press published his charming historical portrait of his home town, *Amsterdam: A Brief Life of the City* (1997) (see *The Low Countries* 1996-97: 277-278). Now it has brought out his counterpoint to this, *Jorwerd. The Death of the Village in Late Twentieth-Century Europe*, an account of the slow death of the small village in the northern province of Friesland where he spent his youth. I would hope that in the near future Harvill will also publish his latest book, *The Century of my Father* (De eeuw van mijn vader), a family chronicle of the twentieth century.

Jorwerd opens with the poem 'What the Poet Should Know' by the Frisian author Obe Postma, and closes with another of his poems, 'All the Joys of my Life'. In between, the language and literature of the Frisian-speaking minority in the Netherlands are mentioned only in passing, though Mak is quite good on the oral culture of the village, the anecdotes and story telling, the gossip and conversations going on in the shops and in the pub. Himself a city dweller, Mak has a very good ear for the differences that exist, even today, between townspeople and country folk in the Netherlands.

Mak begins with a portrait of the village as it was around 1950, teeming with variety and life everywhere, in the shops and pubs, in the church, the post office and the school, in the bank, the library and the solicitor's office, on the farms, around the harbour, the market and the bus stop. He then goes on to paint the slow but steady disappearance, accelerated from 1970 onwards, of almost all of this: the departure of the horses and the farm hands, the blacksmith, the petroleum man, the huntsman, then the fire brigade, the district nurse and finally the shopkeepers; the closing of the harbour; and the preservation of the church as a monument of cultural and historical rather than religious significance.

In the process, Mak charts the enormous changes that have taken place in the Dutch countryside since the joint forces of mechanisation, European Agricultural Policy and the banks brought about a relentless rationalisation and modernisation. The central theme of his book is the change from a traditional farming community and its daily struggle with nature, into today's struggle of lonely farmers with regulations, paperwork, mortgages and subsidies. Mak is especially good on the human consequences of this *'silent revolution that swept through Europe between 1945 and 1995'*, and he describes the downward spiral many farmers are faced with today – of ever increasing debt, guilt, shame, isolation, depression and suicide. In this respect, the village of Jorwerd has a lot more in common with villages in Britain and Germany – high suicide rates, for example – than with a town like Amsterdam.

Mak's book is an essay in the cultural anthropology of village life that is comparable to the writings on European villages by the cultural critic John Berger. At the same time, Mak offers the reader an oral history of Jorwerd, its rituals and traditions, its customs and conventions. The anecdotes and stories Mak recounts – e.g. of Old Peet, who has never left the village, and his friend Folkert – mark the loss of collective memories and the fading knowledge of the past. There is the stoic resilience of country folk, and the tenacious survival of local clubs and associations, e.g. the summer performances of the open air theatre group. There is also the loss of the silence and emptiness of the Frisian landscape, and the decline of Christianity, in the chapter 'How God disappeared from Jorwerd' which ends with the funeral of old Tsjitse Tijssen. In his last chapter, Mak gives a fascinating account of the disappearance of the traditional Frisian storyteller from village life.

There is, to be sure, a degree of idealisation in Mak's portrait. For instance, he does not really acknowledge that a village could also be a place of small-minded enforcement of social norms and unforgiving long memories; a place where 'newcomers' from the towns were often not particularly welcome; and where the natives sometimes had good reason to leave, to emigrate and try their luck elsewhere. Another idealisation is Mak's view of change, and the pervasive sense of loss in his book. This grand Romantic theme is undoubtedly one of the key attractions of his *Jorwerd* – as could be seen in the Summer of 2000 when this English translation was published, just in time for the great home-coming reunion of Frisian emigrants from all over the world.

All the same, Mak is right to say '*This is not a nostalgic history*'. In his *Epilogue* he gives a hard-hitting account of the ongoing crisis in the countryside, of the devastating consequences of the industrialisation of agriculture, of what happened to the countryside and village life when these were modernised away in the late twentieth century. This is the story of the terminal decline of the village, not just in Friesland, but all over Europe.

REINIER SALVERDA

Geert Mak, *Jorwerd. The Death of the Village in Late Twentieth-Century Europe* (Tr. Ann Kelland). London: The Harvill Press, 2000; X-274 pp. ISBN 1-86046-803-9.

'Going into the world' Dutch Immigrants in Canada

'I believe that Canada offers a man a chance, a chance to show what he can do, a chance to roll up his sleeves, a chance to succeed. Oh, that success must be wonder-

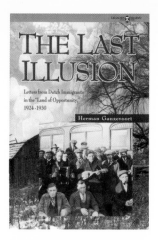

ful! Here I notice the sympathetic and, more often than not, contemptuous glances of my acquaintances. I hear their scornful gossip and scheming, niggling whispering about "that Frans, who can't get into his stride". That's the terrible torment which I'm now going to escape. I'm going into the world'.

This is an excerpt from a letter written by Frans van Waeterstadt, which appeared in the *Leeuwarder Nieuwsblad* on 4 April 1927. Herman Ganzevoort included it in translation in his anthology, *The Last Illusion. Letters from Dutch Immigrants in the 'Land of Opportunity', 1924-1930*. Like so many of those who made their way across the ocean to Canada in the 1920s, Van Waeterstadt was confident that things would work out. Those who read through Ganzevoort's collection of letters from beginning to end will be amazed at the staggering naivety with which many a Canada-bound Dutch traveller embarked upon the great adventure.

Ganzevoort collected excerpts from letters and accounts in thirteen Dutch newspapers. They provide a good picture of the ambivalent emotions experienced by many migrants on leaving their native country and on arrival in Canada, during their first years in the land of the maple leaf and, for some, on their return. By dint of sheer hard work and the ability to adapt, many of the immigrants were able to build a new life for themselves in Canada, but there were also those for whom the '*Land of Opportunity*' proved to be a '*Land of Misery*'. They pined away in that vast country with its severe winters and, consumed by homesickness, returned to the Netherlands.

Ganzevoort, a historian attached to the University of Calgary, is no newcomer to the world of publishing. In fact, he has several books and anthologies about the history of migration to his name, including a pioneering study about the 'Dutch Experience' in Canada: *A Bittersweet Land. The Dutch Experience in Canada, 1890-1980* (1988). In *The Last Illusion*, he confines himself to a part of the 1920s; but it is a fascinating part. Once the wave of migration to Canada in the postwar years had subsided, a new movement out of Europe got under way in the mid-1920s. Growing industrialisation had resulted in a veritable exodus from the Canadian countryside. In particular the young people and the war veterans, who had initially been allocated their own farms, made for the rapidly-growing cities. As a result, agriculture was in urgent need of new immigrants. Dutch farmers, often praised for their energy and great capacity for work, flocked in their thousands to the Canadian prairie provinces. The fact that the United States had tightened its conditions of entry for immigrants only added to Canada's appeal. Semi-official bodies such as the Netherlandic Emigration League and the Central Emigration Foundation of Holland endeavoured to inform and direct the flood of migrants so as to reduce the chances of the venture misfiring. These bodies, however, were not always successful in their efforts, as is sometimes harrowingly apparent from Ganzevoort's collection of letters.

While *The Last Illusion* lays bares the emotional life of the migrants, Frans J. Schryer's *The Netherlandic Presence in Ontario. Pillars, Class and Dutch Ethnicity* is more a theoretical work. Schryer, professor in the Department of Sociology and Anthropology at the University of Guelph, is mainly concerned with the large numbers of Dutch people (not only from Europe, but also from the former Dutch East Indies) who arrived in Ontario between 1947 and 1960. Schryer endorses in part the general picture of the Dutchman who integrates quickly and easily into his new environment. Partly because of the speed with which they mastered English, the Dutch are described as the group with '*the lowest ethnic identity retention*'. Consequently, it is difficult to present them as a homogeneous entity, and yet it would be wrong to play down typically Dutch customs and practices. While the Netherlands underwent what might be described as a social revolution in the 1960s and 1970s, the Canadian Dutch kept up their traditions, many of them closely linked with their Calvinistic (or Catholic) faith. We are reminded here of the much greater resolve, described by (among others) Joan Magee (in *The Belgians in Ontario. A History*, 1987), with which Flemish immigrants in Ontario continued to organise processions and each year commemorated a medieval victory in battle.

Apart from the tell-tale physical indications of Dutch origin, Schryer believes there is also a 'silent' Dutch ethnicity that should not be underestimated, an inconspicuous but deep-rooted form of Dutch individuality. He is referring here to the maintained beliefs or values of the Dutch-Canadian population, which are not immediately apparent to outsiders. Interestingly, too, many immigrant children continue to read Dutch, though English is now their only language of communication. This explains why Canada still has three Dutch-language newspapers. And as consumers the Canadians of Dutch origin have their own behaviour patterns and preferences (such as typical wall tiles, posters and copper trinkets).

All in all, we are given a complex picture of the Dutch in Canada (or more specifically, in Schryer's case, Ontario), in which diversity and uniformity seem to go hand in hand. These two studies are important

pieces of the jigsaw puzzle that represents Dutch migration to Canada. A large part of the puzzle, however, still awaits completion. For instance, much research remains to be done into the various migration movements to the West of Canada. Moreover, the most recent influx of highly-qualified people to growth cities like Calgary and Vancouver provides further material for socio-historical analyses.

HANS VANACKER
Translated by Alison Mouthaan-Gwillim.

Herman Ganzevoort, *The Last Illusion. Letters from Dutch Immigrants in the 'Land of Opportunity', 1924-1930.* Calgary: University of Calgary Press, 1999; 238 pp. ISBN 1-55238-013-0.
Frans J. Schryer, *The Netherlandic Presence in Ontario. Pillars, Class and Dutch Ethnicity.* Waterloo (Ontario): Wilfrid Laurier University Press, 1998; 458 pp. ISBN 0-88920-312-1.

Women in the Dutch colonies

A fascinating but little known aspect of Dutch colonial history concerns the role and position of women in the Dutch East Indies (present-day Indonesia). During the seventeenth and eighteenth centuries – as was shown by Jean Gelman Taylor in *The Social World of Batavia* (1983) and by Leonard Blussé in *Strange Company* (1986) – Indonesian concubines, Chinese go-betweens and rich mestizo wives were often indispensable to the Dutch colonisers in running their empire. It is a theme one also finds in literature, in the nineteenth-century Indonesian folktale of Nyai Dasima and again in the strong female characters portrayed by Indonesia's most important writer of today, Pramoedya Ananta Toer.

Dutch women, on the other hand, made their appearance on the colonial stage mostly after the opening of the Suez canal in 1869, and were then usually dependent on the status, income and career of their husbands. A remarkable number took to writing, and beginning with Mina Kruseman's feminist novel *An Indies Marriage* (Een Indisch Huwelijk, 1872), there is a significant line of Dutch women writers advocating emancipatory ideas for the colonies – from Augusta de Wit, Carry van Bruggen and Marie van Zeggelen in the early decades of the twentieth century, via Annie Salomons and Madelon Lulofs in the 1930s through to Hella Haasse and Beb Vuyk after the war.

Meanwhile, though, Indonesian women had already begun to develop emancipatory ideas of their own. The most important figure was Kartini (1879-1904), who fought for the education of women and their liberation from the shackles of Javanese feudal traditions as much as from Dutch colonial paternalism. Her posthumous *Letters of a Javanese Princess* (1921, originally published in Dutch in 1910 as *Door Duisternis tot Licht*) have continued to inspire Indonesian women in their struggle for emancipation.

The central theme of Elsbeth Locher-Scholten's new book on *Women and the Colonial State* is how, especially and increasingly during the first half of the twentieth century, Dutch and Indonesian women, despite their shared aspirations, were kept apart by their diverging interests and by the colonial conditions of Dutch East Indies society. Her book offers a wealth of new data and archival materials, and many interesting illustrations and maps. There is a helpful glossary of Dutch and Indonesian terms, and a good five-part index (of names, geography, population groups, institutions and subjects) which, however, only covers the main text of the book and not the very extensive notes and the 20-page bibliography at the end.

In the six essays collected here Locher-Scholten discusses a number of key aspects of the struggle for racial and sexual emancipation and equality under colonial conditions. Her perspective is informed both by feminist theory and by the post-colonial views of Edward Said. As she puts it: *'Writing about gender in a colonial context reveals the iniquities and inequalities of the colonial system at its most uncompromising.'*

After a general introduction on 'Gender, Modernity and the Colonial State', Chapter 2 discusses the colonial debate about female labour in the 1920s, in which European notions clashed with Indonesian practices. The analysis is supported with important statistical data on Indonesian women, their professions, wages and work, both in indigenous agriculture and on the large colonial plantations in Java. Chapter 3, on the representation of Javanese domestic servants, sets out how instruction manuals and colonial children's literature defined the role of the Dutch woman as that of a wise but firm teacher of her servants. Chapter 4, on the western lifestyle of European women, documents how *'an illusionary Netherlands in the tropics'* was constructed and promoted through western models for women's clothing, food and manners.

The last two chapters are, to my mind, the most innovative. Chapter 5, on the struggle for women's suffrage in the colonies, reveals how European women carried their 'white woman's burden' and considered themselves part and parcel of the Dutch colonial project; how they fought for their own voting rights, and kept a safe distance from the Indonesian women's movement. The final chapter makes an important contribution to the history of the women's struggle in Indonesia in the colonial era by describing the fierce verbal battles and political demonstrations of 1937, when the colonial government attempted to regulate family life through a new ordinance on marriage. The debate focused – and foundered – on the conflicting views of marriage and monogamy of the colonial government, of the Indonesian women's movement, and of the Islamic religious leaders who scored a memorable victory here.

What emerges from these essays is a detailed picture of the cultural battles that went on in the colonies – over marriage, manners and morality, over relations, intimacy and sexual affairs just as much as over work, education, democracy and the law. Again and again we see Western ideals and conceptions of womanhood in

Djemini, a Javan woman married to the Dutch NCO Piet Scholte, and her daughter Helena ('Lin'), who later became a writer. Early 20th century.

conflict with Indonesian views and colonial realities. And with hindsight, we can see striking and unsettling parallels between the suppression in the thirties of Indonesian nationalists, and the tightening of regulations for women, European as well as native. It is a parallel hinted at in Hella Haasse's novella *Forever a Stranger* (Oeroeg, 1948), where she describes how the Dutchwoman Lida sides with the young Indonesian nationalist Oeroeg against the Dutch colonial establishment.

Back in the thirties, however, *'female solidarity across the colonial divide did not exist'*. For this reason alone, it would be extremely interesting to try and continue Locher-Scholten's history of women's struggle in the Indonesian archipelago up to the present. This would cast an interesting light on the ongoing exploitation of Indonesian women in the sweatshops that produce cheap commodities for global companies. It would also, finally, bring out the common ground between the Dutch historian Locher-Scholten and the Indonesian feminist, poet and philosopher Toety Herati Nurhadi, who – together with her fellow feminist activists – was arrested under the Suharto regime simply for daring to hand out milk to the poor in Jakarta.

REINIER SALVERDA

Elsbeth Locher-Scholten, *Women and the Colonial State. Essays on Gender and Modernity in the Netherlands Indies 1900-1942*. Amsterdam: Amsterdam University Press, 2000; 251 pp. ISBN 90-5356-403-9.

Language

A Gigantic Dutch-Flemish Language Project The Corpus of Spoken Dutch

2001, the first year of the third millennium, is the European Year of Languages. This has been decreed by the European Union and the Council of Europe. In the course of 2001, via the Internet, the media and numerous organised events, the attention of millions of Europeans will be focused on the wealth of language that has made Europe's cultural heritage unique in the world. Everyone, young and old, will be encouraged to learn at least one other language. Language opens doors to people, cultures and employment. Every language spoken in the European Union, whether by many people or by few, will play an important role in the project, and obviously a dynamic language like Dutch is also involved.

Dutch is a medium-sized language. Numerically it ranks sixth in the European Union, in which there are currently eleven official languages: Danish, German, English, Finnish, French, Greek, Italian, Portuguese, Spanish, Swedish and Dutch. The latter is the mother tongue of nearly 22 million people: 16 million Netherlanders and 6 million Flemings. Through this language they experience the 'world', they express themselves, they think, dream and communicate. Dutch is a language with a rich history that has produced great literature and an impressive number of scientific publications. A growing number of foreigners want to learn the language for business, literary, cultural and personal reasons. Dutch is taught in about 250 universities around the world.

The concept of 'Dutch' is a complex one, just as is that of English, German, French etc. As well as Standard Dutch, the general language used within the Dutch-speaking area, there is a wide range of variation: dialects, regional patterns, social varieties (vulgar and posh, for example), specialist languages, group languages and the numerous types of jargon that one finds, for instance, among the young or among computer freaks. Added to that, some leading philologists distinguish two variants of Standard Dutch: those spoken in Belgium and in the Netherlands. The norms applied to Standard Dutch in these two areas are slightly different, particularly in respect of pronunciation and choice of words.

A medium-sized language like Dutch cannot stand still in the rapidly expanding world of speech and language technology. This is the domain of machine analysis, the synthesis of voice and speech patterns and artificial language production. To fall behind at this technological level would ultimately have a damaging impact on the culture and economy of the Low Countries. It would also have a negative effect on the democratic quality of the European Union. Every citizen in the EU should be in a position to participate fully and equally in European society – certainly in respect of his or her language. In the long term, automatic speech recognition and other techniques will facilitate fluent communication between man and machine. However, for the time being technical stunts like that of the science-fiction character Captain Kirk in *Star Trek*, who regularly converses with his spaceship's super-intelligent computer, lie in the (distant?) future. As indeed does machine translation of the subtleties of one natural language into another, such as from Dutch to Spanish and vice-versa.

In multi-lingual Europe, Dutch has to compete with other languages, and particularly with English, which is far and away the dominant language of the digital era. English plays a major role in the development and application of information and communication technology. To some extent this is because for some years English has had the necessary resources for research, such as large databanks of the spoken and written language. As early as 1991-1994, the British National Corpus (BNC) was set up: a huge collection of one hundred million British-English words, spoken and written in context. Taken together they provide a good idea of English as used by speakers of Standard English at the end of the twentieth century. The BNC, however, has not been considered appropriate for American English. There are so many differences in language usage between the two variants that a separate corpus for American English is now being compiled, the so-called ANC, American National Corpus. The design and the goals are similar to those of the BNC.

The BNC is also the inspiration for the Corpus Gesproken Nederlands (CGN; Corpus of Spoken Dutch), a large-scale Dutch-Flemish project that began in 1998. It runs for five years and it is expected that the complete corpus will be available by mid-2003. It will then be possible to apply to the Dutch language the technology developed for English.

The initiative came from Professor Willem Levelt, director of the Max Planck Institute for Psycholinguistics in Nijmegen. The project is financed by the Dutch and Flemish governments and the Netherlands Organisation for Scientific Research. There are two co-ordinating centres: Ghent for Flanders and Nijmegen for the Netherlands. A management committee, chaired by Professor Levelt, bears the final responsibility for this gigantic project. Dozens of experts from North and South are involved, as well as government officials and interested parties from trade and industry. All rights remain in the hands of the Dutch Language Union, an intergovernmental organisation set up by the Belgian and Dutch governments in 1980. Its purpose is to promote close co-operation between Flanders and the Netherlands in the fields of language and literature. Dutch-speakers must continue to play their full part in the concert of the European Union. It is in their own interest as well as that of Europe.

The project is directed at constructing a databank of contemporary 'democratic' Standard Dutch as spoken by 80% of adult Netherlanders and 50% of adult Flemings. One should therefore be able to hear, more or less, if a speaker comes from Groningen, Utrecht, Leuven or Kortrijk. Unlike the British or American corpus, written Dutch is not included in the research: there is already enough available information on that. Because it only involves the spoken language, the size of the database is also smaller: ten million words, about a thousand hours of speech, are more than enough for the CGN. Two thirds of the words (with their context) are from the Netherlands, one third from Flanders. The numerous subjects differ in sex, age, occupation and education. Furthermore, they come from every region of the Dutch-speaking area. A characteristic of their natural use of language is its wide diversity, including the categories of speech: there are conversations in shops and trams, interviews, board meetings, school lessons, a lecture, discussions and debates, a sermon, etc. The subjects are equipped with a microphone that records everything they say throughout the day to everyone they meet. Furthermore, sophisticated interference-free studio recordings are also being made. The millions of recorded words are embedded in spontaneous and natural-sounding sentences. That means that such things as hesitations, slips of the tongue, linguistic mistakes, broken sentences, different talking speeds, coughing, throat-clearing etc. are all recorded. The words are then skilfully and painstakingly analysed and supplied with a phonic (phonetic and phonologic), semantic, lexicological and other linguistic commentary. The idea is to discover what present-day standard Dutch sounds like in all its various forms, and how it all fits together. There have to be recordings of so many different Dutch language utterances that an electronic apparatus such as a speech recogniser will instantly 'understand' everything.

As well as language and speech technology, language digitisation, the CGN is also extremely important for linguistics in its broadest sense: lexicography, phonetics, phonology, syntax, semantics, socio- and psycholinguistics and conversation analysis will all benefit hugely from the results of this project. Moreover, such an in-depth portrait of 'volatile' spoken Dutch is relevant to education. Insight into the actual, daily use of language is indispensable not only for courses in Dutch as a second or foreign language but also for teachers in primary and secondary schools.

If, in 2003, the Corpus Gesproken Nederlands is found to be applicable to scientific, commercial and didactic goals, copyright and distribution will be managed by the Dutch Language Union. On payment of a fee, businesses and scientific institutions will be able to use the CD-ROMs on which the corpus is stored. As with the British model, computer linguists will regularly update this enormous databank and adapt it to the latest technology.

Now especially, in this European Year of Languages, many are coming to appreciate the great importance of the project. There is now a widespread desire on the part of government, science and industry to ensure that Dutch plays an adequate role in the modern multilingual information society. A substantial presence in the field of speech and language technology is important for the Flemish and Dutch economies, for radiating Dutch culture throughout Europe and for European democracy. Digital presence and availability is essential for the status and prestige of Dutch in the Europe of today and of the future. Flanders and the Netherlands have understood that perfectly.

ANTON CLAESSENS
Translated by Chris Emery.

Corpus of Spoken Dutch: http://www.lands.let.kun.nl/cgn/ehome.htm
Dutch Language Union: http://www.taalunie.org

Literature

A Lost World The Novels of Erwin Mortier

The Flemish writer Erwin Mortier (1965-) now has two novels to his name – together hardly more than three hundred pages, but more than enough to warrant the assessment that Dutch literature has been enriched with a new sound. Actually, that was apparent as soon as the first book came out. Mortier's debut novel *Marcel* (1999) met with unanimous praise, in particular for its stylistic qualities. His second book, *My Other Skin* (Mijn tweede huid, 2000), was rightly regarded as a confirmation of that extraordinary debut.

Of course it's not unusual for real talent to need no laborious introductory period and for its value to be immediately recognised, at least by professional readers. That instant brilliance is misleading, however, since it's quite apparent that the author has gone about his task like a craftsman of old, shaping and polishing his sentences before confidently committing them to paper. That is what is so remarkable about Mortier's books: there's nothing at all modern about them. They don't deal with contemporary existence, with the hectic pace of life in the metropolis or outside it. They don't ponder the loss of identity or the extreme pseudo-individualism that marks today's mass culture. There's not a trace of this to be seen, not even on the stylistic level. Mortier writes a pleasantly languid, almost stagnant prose. His language is rich in images, but these are no rank surrealist growths. They are not concerned with an ecstatic crossing of borders, with extreme contrasts or bizarre combinations. Rather, they are an attempt to sensitise the mind to the miracle of an almost forgotten commonplace. Mortier's images lead one into another, branching off in subtle refinement across an entire paragraph or more, using the arbitrary skin of the language to reveal a skin that's more fitting and durable. It's a style by no means stirring or spectacular, but Mortier does force the reader to slow down and use all his powers of concentration. The re-

Erwin Mortier (1965-). Photo by David Samyn.

sults of that effort must be expressed in a different terminology.

That's what the writer seems to be after. Mortier's quest is to capture in images a vanishing world, a world that in the Netherlands is as good as gone. This is the world of the Flemish countryside, of family life that has not yet succumbed to petit bourgeois stiffness, that breathes an almost pre-bourgeois openness and liberality, with plenty of room for uncles and aunts, nephews and nieces. The adults never speak of the dead, and that is understandable. It gradually emerges that the past of the dead is one of Flemish nationalism, marked by that tragic mixture of social frustration, idealism, collaboration and Eastern Front heroism which even today it is difficult to talk about in socially and politically acceptable language, but which does not rule out compassion and solidarity. Even if we resist equating the first-person narrator with the author, there is enough evidence available to place the story in or around 1970 (the existence of TV; someone's disparaging remark about '*de Bietels*' – the Beatles – '*a bunch of apes if you ask me*'). But all the rest *seems* to date from a much earlier time. The authority and status of the teacher and the village priest have something pre-war about them, as do the self-evident class distinctions, the differences between city and countryside and the authority implicit in family relationships. Because the perspective on that world is doubly restricted – by the youthfulness of the first-person narrator (who embodies the narrative consciousness in only a few fragments) and by Mortier's decision not to place this country life in a broader context – I believe the book could have been *written* in 1970 as well, if not earlier.

It is clear that Mortier has no intention of being a modern writer, at least not in the sense of risking everything for smoothness of style and recognition. His concern, rather, is with an ability that seems to be degenerating at top speed: the magical ability to create metamorphosis and transformation, such as we see in the work of great authors like Bruno Schulz and Walter Benjamin, who also took it upon themselves to save a vanishing world.

The grandmother in *Marcel* is a dressmaker, and her work is described as follows: '*There was no one to hear her secret formulas, her mutterings and hummed tunes while she breathed life into one garment after another. The sewing-room was transformed into a magical laboratory, and she into an alchemist. She drew lines with a stick of greasy chalk on feather-light sheets of tissue paper laid out on the table. She guided the predatory jaws of her scissors around the contours of a skirt or the lily-like outline of a bridal gown.*' And this from one of the first-person narrator's secret observation posts: '*In no time my garden acquired the shape of a horseshoe, a bastion of wild leafy growth. In that wilderness I would crouch unseen, on hot days, when my mother called my name and I wanted to be impossible to find.*'

These sentences could just as easily have come from Bruno Schulz's *The Cinnamon Shops* or Walter Benjamin's *A Berlin Childhood around 1900,* both written in the early thirties. As I said earlier, *Marcel* – and *My Other Skin* to a lesser degree – have something unmistakably anachronistic about them, though in the case of books so rich in brilliant sentences I would hesitate to call it an obstacle.

My Other Skin relates to *Marcel* both thematically and stylistically. '*It was in the time before I could really talk. Almost nothing had a name; everything was body*.' What follows, of course, is highly expressive: a world still almost entirely without distances and abstractions, an interior world built of impressions, intuitions and fumbling movements. It is the world of *Marcel*, which here is given a name and a place. The name of the family is Callewijn, people who '*for generations*' have lived in an old house '*below the dike on the Bruges canal*'. The book has all the features of a Bildungsroman. We follow Anton, the main character, as a schoolboy and a young student. It is the seventies, the early eighties – a time of great social and personal change. The tranquillity and security of Callewijn's paradise (or is 'Hof' the name of the village?) is threatened by an encroaching industrial park and a motorway being built near the dike. And the secondary school, with its suffocating tedium, does its sobering work as well. This part of the book is played out against the backdrop of burgeoning (homo)sexuality which Mortier, as always, describes with fine restraint, all the mysteries intact.

The book ends in a minor key. Anton has found a friend in Willem, a fellow student from an urban, intellectual milieu without whom Anton's adolescent existence would have been unbearable. But just as they're about to set off for Ghent to continue their studies all their dreams of the future are brought to a cruel end. Willem is killed in an accident. Anton, more vulnerable than ever, will have to go it alone, finding security in the skin of the language. Undoubtedly he will become a writer.

CYRILLE OFFERMANS
Translated by Nancy Forest-Flier.

Marcel has been translated by Ina Rilke and will be published by Harvill in October 2001. There are also plans for an English translation of *My Other Skin*.

The Babel Guide to Dutch and Flemish Fiction in English Translation

Babel literary guides are known for being handy-sized, upbeat reference books that review works of literature in succinct commentary followed by brief excerpts. Previous Babel guides have been published on French, German, Italian, Portuguese, and Scandinavian fiction. This guide to Dutch and Flemish fiction begins with a compact introduction to some of the latest anthologies in English and continues on through a very quick-paced, alphabetically arranged authors' sampler containing over 100 works of fiction originally written in Dutch – with only one linguistic exception of origin, that of Rink van de Velde's *The Trap* (De fuke, 1966), which is set in wartime Friesland and written in Frisian.

Reviews of anthologies appearing in the opening pages of the *Babel Guide* provide perspective and read collectively as if they were written as an extended introduction. The anthology reviews also give authors not reviewed individually in the guide a much-deserved mention. The review of *Women Writing in Dutch* (1994), edited by Kristiaan Aercke, provides mention of Monika van Paemel, one of the towering figures of contemporary women's writing who warrants wider translation, and Maria Stahlie, an intriguing contemporary novelist and fiction writer who has translated into Dutch three equally intriguing American writers: Alison Lurie, Lorrie Moore, and Tobias Wolff. *Modern Stories from Holland and Flanders* (1973), edited by Egbert Krispyn, gives attention to Remco Campert whose short story, 'Trip to Zwolle' is mentioned – and whose two novels translated into English, *Gangster Girl* (Het gangstermeisje, 1965) and *No Holds Barred* (Liefdes schijnbewegingen, 1963) are books I have read and enjoyed for their 'grey humour'. Other titles of anthologies reviewed in the Babel Guide are *Fugitive Dreams* (1988), edited by E.M. Beekman; *Memory and Agony: Dutch Stories from Indonesia* (1979), edited by Rob Nieuwenhuys; and *The Dedalus Book of Dutch Fantasy* (1993), edited by Richard Huijing. The latter anthology makes a wide interpretation of 'fantasy' to include Gerard Reve's classic spine-chiller 'Werther Nieland,' and lesser-known fiction such as Willem Schòrmann's precursive postmodern story, 'The Unbalanced King', Jan Wolker's 'Feathered Friends', and Jan Arends' 'Breakfast'.

The scope of the Guide encompasses not only the Low Countries, but also colonial and post-colonial

Dutch literature. One gets a glimpse into former days in Indonesia, the Caribbean, and the Congo. Madelon Lulofs, the 'female Multatuli' known in the Netherlands as M.H. Székely-Lulofs, recounts life in Sumatra from a colonialist frame of reference in *Rubber* (Rubber, 1931) and *Coolie* (Koelie, 1932); Jef Geeraerts' *Gangrene* (Gangreen I, 1968) takes readers back to the Belgian Congo in the 1960s. Settings of the fiction provide a multicultural array of locales as well – from Portugal and Brazil (in Cees Nooteboom's *The Following Story* – Het volgende verhaal, 1991) and the Gulf coast of the US (in 'After the Hurricane' by Inez van Dullemen, from *The Dedalus Book of Dutch Fantasy*) to Germany (in *From Berlin* – Krijgsgewoel; Machthebbers: verslagen uit Berlijn en Toscane, 1983 – by Armando), Morocco (in *Abdullah's Feet* – Abdullahs voeten, 1996 – by Hafid Bouazza), and Paris in 1910 (in *Villa des Roses* by Willem Elsschot, 1913).

The blend of classic, mainstream, experimental, modern and postmodern fiction is impressive, if daunting as the subject of condensed reviews. Indonesia and the Dutch East Indies inspire Multatuli's controversial *Max Havelaar* (1860), which called into question the Dutch colonial enterprise in the East Indies, and is surveyed along with Louis Couperus' *The Hidden Force* (De stille kracht, 1900), Maria Dermoût's *The Ten Thousand Things* (De tienduizend dingen, 1956), and Beb Vuyk's *The Last House in the World* (Het laatste huis van de wereld, 1939), published just before the end of the colonial era in the East. The experience of occupation during the Second World War is revisited in Harry Mulisch's *The Assault* (De aanslag, 1982), Rudi van Dantzig's *For a Lost Soldier* (Voor een verloren soldaat, 1986), and Gerhard Durlacher's *Stripes in the Sky* (Strepen in de hemel, 1985), as well as in the stories and novels of Marga Minco and many other writers. History and psychology inspire self-reflexive qualities, places and poses in Jan Cremer's *I Jan Cremer* (Ik Jan Cremer, 1964) that makes him something of a Dutch Jack Kerouac and in the elegant and harrowed lives of men and women of the past in Hella Haasse's historical fiction.

The reviewers make these works come alive, even for readers unfamiliar with Dutch and Flemish literature. Theo Hermans' review of three of Elsschot's novels: *Soft Soap; The Leg; Will-o'-the-Wisp* (Lijmen, 1924; Het been, 1938; Het dwaallicht, 1947) is a wonderful miniature essay. The novels are '*hard-headed unsentimental stories full of black humour but with a soft spot*'; and the last novel of the series, *Will-o'-the-Wisp*, is '*a real postcolonial gem*' that retells the life of an everyman character whose moral education comes at the end of his life, during *a 'taut, mysterious'* encounter with three Muslim sailors in Antwerp's harbour district (see p.46).

The vivid commentaries by the eight contributors to the Babel Guide – Katheryn Ronnau Bradbeer, Jane Fenoulhet, Yann Lovelock, Barry Price, Reinier Salverda, Dennis Strik, Paul Vincent and Theo Hermans – are authoritative and yet accessible for readers new to the works and authors reviewed. Hermans, Professor of Dutch and Comparative Literature at the Department of Dutch, University College London, who selected the texts for review and the contributors, has said that the idea behind the choice of texts was to gather a reasonably representative selection of primarily literary fiction, along with a few books of appeal to younger readers and some titles that could be classified as popular literature.

The guide also contains a second section, beyond the reviews, that provides information on post-war English translations of modern Dutch and Flemish fiction, with bibliographical and publishing details (translator, publisher, number of pages, original title, original date of publication, etc.). Although the number of authors and books reviewed is extensive, I regretted not seeing mention of Maarten 't Hart and Annie M.G. Schmidt. However, the coverage is remarkable as it stands and my longing to see more entries is the best recommendation that I can make for this little gift-guide for all those who enjoy reading Dutch and Flemish literature as I do, primarily in English translation.

RITA INGRAM GIVENS

Theo Hermans, *et al.*, *Babel Guide to Dutch and Flemish Fiction in English Translation.* Oxford: Boulevard Books, 2001; 208 pp. ISBN 1-899460-80-2.

A Strange Host Called Poetry
The Watou Summers

The Watou poetry-summers, which take place every year in the West Flemish village of that name close to the French border, knock the usual tedium of a summer in the country clear out of sight. Each year the organiser and poet Gwy Mandelinck combines poetry, visual art and the existing architecture in a new and original approach. Twenty-one years ago Mandelinck's urge for visualisation became so great that he felt that verses alone could no longer express his thoughts and emotions. From 1983 on he settled on a confrontation of poetry and contemporary art and let the folklore aspect, hitherto a marked feature of Watou summers, go by the board. In 1985 a few artists began for the first time to take full advantage of the local environment, and this became a *leitmotiv* that has run through every summer since. Camiel van Breedam, an assemblage artist, made a mustard gas burial mound with gas masks; from a distance it looked like a heap of dead leaves. And on the Marktplein the painter Godfried Vervisch put up a shed and had graves dug in it. Then he put his paintings in them.

Since 1991 the poetry-summers have taken on the character that has made them well-known both at home and abroad. As their name indicates, it is always the word that is central, however important the influence of the visual arts may be in the two disciplines' confrontation. Not by chance did the 1991 poetry-summer have as its title the line by J. Slauerhoff *'Only in my poems can I live'*. It could be the motto of Gwy Mande-

linck, who in the winter months withdraws from the artistic world and spends his time reading, writing and selecting poetry. With the approach of summer he then brings that indoor world out of doors, putting up the chosen poems in the strangest places. Over the past decade he has increasingly moved away from canonised Flemish poets in favour of a selection with a more international flavour, including new poets. On top of this, lately work has been commissioned from some poets. In 1991 poetry set its stamp on the proceedings immediately and literally, for a number of streets and squares were given poets' names which they still bear today. The visitor too is left with memories which seem burnt into the retina. In 1991, for instance, there was the death-house of Paul Snoek, one of the most important post-experimental poets of the Dutch language-area. 1991 was the tenth anniversary of Snoek's death and his sons Jan and Paul arranged a little room in Watou. You had to work your way in through black hangings and then you saw a chair and a table. A lamp hung low over the table, with under it a fly-swat lying next to a poem by Snoek with the lines *'There's a tear welling up in the soul of my pen / and the flies have shat on my paper'*. On the wall, among other things, the poet's motorcycling kit, smelling of mothballs.

In 1992 Mandelinck for the first time focused on a single visual artist: the recently deceased sculptor José Vermeersch. His hallmark was stocky people and dogs who looked rather like each other. Alongside those seventy figures, all displayed in Watou's Douviehuis, Mandelinck installed a great many poems. But it wasn't just that you could read them; here and there you could also hear poets' voices. For instance, these lines by Hugo Claus kept ringing in your head: *'The time is come Goodbye all those I know / As gas rolls near and climbs the breath / Of him who in my body sits unspeaking // The time is come: 'Goodbye dog-tamer.' // He says: 'Goodbye body like a house.'* Among a group of figures (women, children and dogs), a motionless audience, you saw Claus on a video screen speaking these lines over and over again. His voice pursued you as you went down the barn's creaking steps. From 1992 on the poets' voices became faithful guides through the poetry-summers. Guides to death, almost, for over the past ten years mortality has been a powerful presence in summery Watou. Perhaps this thought strikes you even more quickly when you are confronted with poetry and visual art in tumble-down buildings, in stables or simply in the open air. Not immersed in the comfortable atmosphere of a museum or gallery. In this respect Watou's poetry-summers are always unconventional and contrary. They ambush your imagination: poetry as a strange host radiating mortality.

In 1994 Mandelinck reversed the roles again: the poet Hugo Claus, who of course harbours in his oeuvre a whole range of poets of all complexions, was the central figure. And kindred souls were selected to complement his work. Traces of that memorable summer when a world-class poet consented to be shut up in a village for a whole two months can still be seen here

The Blauwhuys in Watou: the lines on the roof of a shed are from Rutger Kopland's 'Still-Life with Golden Plover' ('Stilleven met gouden plevier'): *'they are asleep in a frozen world, in / an orchid, a kitchen garden, a ditch, / they dream they have been found, taken home, / laid down on that table – but why,'* (Tr. James Brockway)

and there: on the wall of the Wethuis, for instance, the first time that site on the Marktplein had been used.

In 1995 it was the turn of another magician: Jan Fabre. Until then he had always been associated with urban culture, with dark theatres and museums, though his fascination with insects might lead one to suspect that he was capable of other things. And he confirmed that suspicion brilliantly. Fabre took the poems Mandelinck handed him and located them in the space with a fine equilibrium. Unforgettable was the teabags installation in the cellar of the Douviehuis: as you came down the stairs you saw hundreds of teabags swinging in the wind and smelt the wonderful aroma of the tea in the water. And while the teabags mirrored themselves in that water you heard actors' voices simultaneously whispering and stuttering Guido Gezelle's poem 'The Water Scribbler' ('Het schrijverke') about a dancing dragonfly.

In 1998 Gwy Mandelinck joined up with SMAK, the Stedelijk Museum voor Actuele Kunst (Municipal Museum of Current Art) in Ghent. In that year the museum's curator Jan Hoet brought some choice items from its collection to Watou. Gwy Mandelinck came up with verbal fireworks to match them. This time the title was *'Before it disappears and after'*, a line from the Dutch poet Rutger Kopland who turns up every year in Watou; the result was a real feast for the senses. Among other delights, wintry lines by Kopland were set against a summery *tableau vivant* by Mario Merz: tables of glass and granite spread with colourful vegetables.

In 2000, under the flag *Storm Centres,* the poetry-summer voyaged through Europe with a markedly more international choice of poetry. This was mainly because with this theme Jan Hoet wanted to draw attention to smaller countries and language-areas within Europe as centres of turbulence. He selected mainly young, still relatively unknown artists. And again that resulted in a lively confrontation between the genres, with a regular and fascinating fusion. Yet perhaps it was Jan Fabre, again, who provided a high-point, in

a little house on the Douvieweg. Here Death – as we already said, a regular visitor who always lies in wait for you in Watou – almost takes your breath away in the oppressive combination of Peter Verhelst's poems, the claustrophobic little rooms and the voice of actor Dirk Roofthooft, who was responsible for the aural presentation of all the poems. Fabre's *Salvator mundi*, a small globe of beetles with a human backbone rising out of it, offered the visitors' souls little hope of salvation. But then, Watou is not a place for consumers of art to stroll languidly around, for the poetry of its summers is like the dust of the village's roads: it all looks very peaceful, but the words get into your clothes and stick there, longer than you want.

PAUL DEMETS
Translated by Tanis Guest.

FURTHER INFORMATION

Gwy Mandelinck / Kapelaanstraat 2 / 8978 Watou / Belgium
Fax +32 57 38 80 93 / e-mail: poeziezomers@yucom.be

Music

The Essential Guide to Dutch Music

The Netherlands has acquired a reputation for producing well-edited publications in the field of music and maintaining good working relationships with the country's composers. This detailed guide to a hundred Dutch composers is yet another example of these admirable qualities. The editor-in-chief, Jolande van der Klis, supported by a wide group of contributors, has selected a hundred Dutch composers for inclusion in this book, the earliest being Jan Pieterszoon Sweelinck and Cornelis Schuyt while the most recent are not yet fifty years old. The introduction immediately concedes that a second volume with another hundred names could easily be compiled but, be that as it may, the hundred representatives in this first volume are a sensible, 'first-class' selection, the cream of Dutch composers from the baroque to the present day. The editors underline the fact that they wanted to draw particular attention to twentieth-century composers while not losing sight of earlier periods.

The selection is wide, and includes composers who are not Dutch by birth but who, having worked in the Netherlands for a considerable period, have made an essential contribution to Dutch music. The Swedish Klas Torstensson, for instance, is included because he has lived in the Netherlands since 1973. So too are the seventeenth-century German composer Henrico Albicastro and the Flemish Carel Hacquart who in 1678 was the first to compose an opera with a Dutch libretto (*Love Triumphant* – De Triomfeerende Min).

A second factor which has widened the selection is that not only classical composers have been included, but also improvisers, jazz musicians and individuals who work on and with pop music in an innovative way. From the jazz world there are the composer-improvisers Misha Mengelberg and Paul Termos, as well as the composer and bass-player Maarten Altena, who has collaborated with Theo Loevendie, the Netherlands Ballet Orchestra and Louis Andriessen's De Volharding ensemble. Chiel Meijering tries to create a bridge between pop and classical music. Guus Janssen, too,

combines improvisation and elements of jazz and pop with a contemporary 'serious classical' style of composition. Falling between all the genres, Willem Breuker blends 'high' and 'low' art in his music.

The guide makes no distinction between 'major' and 'minor' composers. Each individual receives the same attention, i.e. the same amount of text. The authors' justification for this approach is that while well-known figures obviously cannot be omitted, there is all the more demand for information about those who are less well known. The book is therefore more than just a work of reference; it is also a rich source of information about little-known composers. Who has ever heard of Nicolaes Vallet, a lute-player of French origin, who settled in Amsterdam at the beginning of the seventeenth century? Or, and this is for the connoisseurs, who knows that *Little Kisses* (Kusjes) is a collection of madrigals by the seventeenth-century Haarlem composer, Cornelis Thymanszoon Padbrué? Composers from the Romantic period, too, have been brought back from obscurity, like Daniël de Lange, Johannes Verhulst and Henri Zagwijn. As for women composers, the situation in the Netherlands is no better than elsewhere. Of the hundred composers selected, only five are women: Henriëtte Bosmans, Anna Cramer, Elisabeth Kuyper, Tera de Marez Oyens and Cornélie van Oosterzee.

The best feature of this guide is that it does not confine itself to biographical details but also includes a great deal of clear information about the musical characteristics of its subjects. By limiting the biographical aspect, the guide leads the reader to the actual music. The discussion of each composer is supplemented with a list of selected compositions, a bibliography that, where necessary, includes references to the composer's own writings, and a discography. Distinctive photographs, or portraits in the case of older composers, 'illuminate' the guide.

The book would have been more useful if the lexicon section had been given an introduction that sketched, in broad outline, the evolution of music in the Netherlands, the formation of various groups, the rise of particular centres and their importance etc. As it is, readers have to work out the general trends for themselves from the individual biographies.

The guide originally appeared in Dutch in 1997 under the title *Het Honderd Componisten Boek*. However, for the English edition the articles have been updated to the year 2000. As the title states, this guide is '*essential*'. It is no exaggeration to say that it is indeed an essential source not only as an introduction to Dutch music, but also as a springboard for deeper study.

YVES KNOCKAERT
Translated by Chris Emery.

Gerard van Honthorst, *The Merry Musician*. 1623. Canvas, 108 x 89 cm. Rijksmuseum, Amsterdam.

Jolande van der Klis (ed.), *The Essential Guide to Dutch Music. 100 Composers and Their Work*. Amsterdam: MuziekGroep Nederland / Amsterdam University Press, 2000; 437 pp. ISBN 90-5356-460-8.

The Revival of a Museum in a Revived Building The Brussels Museum of Musical Instruments

In June 2000, the Museum of Musical Instruments (Muziekinstrumentenmuseum, or MIM), moved into the former building of the Old England department store chain near Koningsplein in Brussels. After twenty-two years of plan-hatching, fund-raising and hard work, it was time for the opening – or rather the reopening – of a museum that actually had been in existence for quite some time but was not widely known. What follows here is a brief sketch of the difficult road from creating a collection to finding a fitting way to exhibit it.

Anyone who has spent time strolling around the Kunstberg area in Brussels is certain to have noticed Paul Saintenoy's magnificent, recently restored, Art Nouveau structure. The composition of steel, cast iron and glass – in itself an eye-catcher – is reinforced in its sinuous elegance by its encompassing neo-classical monumentality. There's still something modern about it, and one can imagine how spectacular it must have been around 1900 to see such a structure impart a touch of the up-to-date to an area that conformed so strictly to architectural regulations. Saintenoy's drawings for the building were commissioned by the exclusive Old England department store. The avant-garde design was intended to attract the mainly affluent customers who frequented one of the most fashionable districts of the city.

A stone's throw away, on Regentschapsstraat, was the long-established home of the Music Conservatory, where a museum of musical instruments had been housed since 1877. It was the instrument manufacturer Mahillon who had persuaded the Conservatory's director, Gevaert, to establish a museum in his institute. He put his knowledge and experience at the museum's disposal in exchange for the honorary title of '*conservateur de Musée instrumental du Conservatoire royal de musique de Bruxelles*'. The collection was one of barely twenty in all of Europe, and in the beginning it consisted of the estate of the famous musicologist Fétus and a series of East Indian instruments owned by Leopold II. Mahillon expanded the collection considerably; at the time of his death it numbered at least 3,177 pieces.

The intention, however, was not only to collect the instruments but also to display them, and that's where things always went wrong. In 1924, just after Mahillon's death, his successor, Closson, complained about the pitiful conditions under which the collection was being stored. He did get some action, but the situation was never ideal. The instruments ended up spread over several different buildings around the Conservatory. Even when the museum was incorporated into the net-

Virginals, clavichords and organs in the Brussels Museum of Musical Instruments.

Photo by Jean Boucher / MIM.

work of royal museums in 1992 the event was not marked with a proper exhibition, despite the fact that plans made back in 1978 were slowly approaching completion. It was then that the Belgian state had bought the Saintenoy building to house the museum of musical instruments, but it would take more than twenty years for all the obstacles – most of them financial – to be removed.

Today, the MIM is more than a backstage collection for experts. It can also welcome the public with all the facilities of a modern museum. On display in an area of more than 3,000 square metres are about 1,500 instruments, with the rest of the collection being kept under the best possible conditions. Each of the building's four floors is devoted to one particular subject. On the ground floor one learns all about the folk instruments of Belgium, Europe and beyond, from bagpipes to ukulele to sitar. The basement contains the 'Musicus Mechanicus' department, with information about music and technology. How does a carillon work? What goes into the electronic amplification of music? A sound laboratory has also been installed on this floor, where visitors can try their hand at analysing instrumental sound and learn something about acoustics.

The first floor is devoted to Western art music. We begin with the Greeks and go on from there: how was music made in the Middle Ages, what did Bach's orchestra look like and what about the orchestra from the Romantic period, coming bursting at the seams?

The second floor is all about 'Strings and keyboards'. The popularity of stringed instruments in the world of folk music partly accounts for their enormous diversity. What do guitars and mandolins have in common? How do you make a violin? The significance of stringed instruments is something we almost take for granted, so the museum has them in every shape and size. What exactly are the differences between a virginal, a spinet and a harpsichord? There are plenty of mechanisms to demonstrate the correct answers.

In addition there's the Garden of Orpheus, where children can even touch the instruments; the library, finally open to the public; a real museum shop, where both specialised literature and musically inspired knick-knacks are on sale; and of course the extensive eating and drinking facilities, like those provided by Old England in the building's early years. Finally, the museum concerts, with instruments from the collection played by Belgium's many ancient music specialists, have been reinstated. Reason enough to pay an instructive visit to a revived museum in a revived building.

RUDY TAMBUYSER
Translated by Nancy Forest-Flier.

MIM Hofberg 2 / 1000 Brussels /Belgium
Tel.: +32 2 545 01 30 / http://www.mim.fgov.be

Dirk Jan Struik (1894-2000).
Photo by Klaas Koppe.

D.J. Struik's Marxist Mathematics

In October 2000 the Dutch-American mathematician Dirk Jan Struik peacefully passed away at his home in Belmont, MA, at the age of 106. Struik made his name as the author of *A Concise History of Mathematics*, published in 1948, one of the first books on the history of mathematics in which the influence of social factors is explicitly recognised. This book did more than any other to make mathematics' vast wealth of ideas accessible to a wide audience. It was translated into eighteen languages (including Persian) and is still in print.

Dirk Struik, born in 1894 as the son of a Rotterdam headmaster, studied mathematics and physics in Leiden. As a student of the inspiring theoretical physicist Paul Ehrenfest, a teacher with the ability to make science come alive, he hoped to find a connection between mathematics and socialism. He was a member of the SDP, the Marxist splinter of the Social Democratic Workers' Party (Sociaal Democratische Arbeiders Partij), but mathematics took first place in his life. At about that time he married Saly Ruth Ramler, a Czech mathematician and a gifted ballet dancer. She died in 1993 at the age of 99. In 1922, Struik obtained his doctorate under Professor Schouten of Delft University. His thesis was on an aspect of topology, a branch of pure mathematics, and had to do with tensors. The close relationship between this theory and Einstein's general theory of relativity, formulated in 1915, especially appealed to Struik. He published a great deal on this subject right into his later years, with such works as *Lectures on Classical Differential Geometry*, written in 1950. Even at the age of 101 he wrote a review of a recent history of tensors.

Because of his communist sympathies he had no chance of finding a teaching post in the Netherlands, and in 1924 he left to spend a year in Rome as a Rockefeller fellow. After Schouten's 'intellectual yoke', Struik saw himself in Italy as '*an aristocrat à la Goethe*'. He worked in the Vatican Library, where his interest in the history of mathematics was finally fully aroused. One year later, Struik found himself in the German city of Göttingen, where the work of mathematician Frits Klein gave him '*confidence in the possibilities that Marxism offered for understanding the course of mathematics*', as he put it in an interview sixty years later.

After acknowledging that the Netherlands had little to offer him, and refusing to drop everything and run off to Siberia with his brother Anton (an engineer), Struik turned his gaze westward. In 1926, the great mathematician Norbert Wiener, with whom Struik had become acquainted in Göttingen, brought him to the Massachusetts Institute of Technology (MIT) in Cambridge, Mass. For twenty-five years Struik led a peaceful existence full of mathematical activity and political activism. In 1936 he became the co-founder of the Marxist journal *Science and Society*. In 'On the Sociology of Mathematics', an article written in 1942, Struik laid out his opposition to a Platonic view. Mathematics, he argued, had its origins in a dialectic of interlocking intellectual, social, cultural and economic factors. In 1948, this Marxist approach led to the *Concise History* and to *Yankee Science in the Making*. Struik's study of Dutch mathematics in the time of Simon Stevin (1548-1620) is in the same tradition. According to Struik, Stevin tore down barriers and paved the way for a new phase in the development of capitalism.

The McCarthy period, which Struik called '*half Nazi Germany, half Alice in Wonderland*', led to controversial trials and to the suspension of his MIT appointment in 1951 on account of '*subversive political activities*'. Struik's response was to spend the next four years travelling around the United States giving lectures on the freedom of the press. Finally the charges against him were dropped, and '*the Fifth Amendment Communist*' was reinstated at MIT, which had continued to pay him throughout that difficult period.

In 1960 Struik had to retire from MIT, which grieved him deeply. But driven by an unfailing intellectual curiosity, the publications continued to flow from his pen unabated. He published book reviews until just a few years ago and kept up his correspondence until just before his death. Asked for the secret for his long life, Struik answered, '*3 Ms: marriage, mathematics and Marxism*'.

DIRK VAN DELFT
Translated by Nancy Forest-Flier.

Put the Blame on Baruch

In the past scholars have underrated the significance of Spinoza (1632-1677) as a key figure in the radical thought of the Enlightenment: that is the view of the British historian Jonathan I. Israel, best known for his monumental *The Dutch Republic* of 1995. In his new and equally impressive book *Radical Enlightenment. Philosophy and the Making of Modernity, 1650-1750* he attempts to rectify this situation.

Yet this is more than just a study of the influence of Spinoza. What Israel has in mind is nothing less than a revision of the accepted image of the Enlightenment, in which the Netherlands is consistently allotted the same role as Switzerland: as a haven for persecuted freethinkers from France or England and a place where books banned elsewhere could be published relatively freely. This perspective makes it too easy to forget that the Republic too was a hotbed of radical ideas, which did not fail to have their effect in other countries. To realise this, Israel maintains, one has only to look more closely at the chronology of the Enlightenment.

In thinking of the radicalism of the Enlightenment what comes to mind is always the second half of the eighteenth century, the materialism and atheism of French *philosophes* like Diderot, La Mettrie, Helvétius and Holbach. But this period of the so-called 'High Enlightenment' did not exist in isolation. According to Israel, the daring ideas of Diderot and his fellow-thinkers were in fact merely the culmination of a radical undercurrent in enlightened thinking which goes back to the ideas of Spinoza and the 'free spirits' ranged around him.

It was then, between 1650 and 1680, that we find the real '*crisis of the European mind*', as Paul Hazard called it in a classic study of 1935; though for Hazard the 'crisis' begins only in 1680. For Israel that year marks the start of the early Enlightenment, the time when all the really innovative ideas were developed which then needed only to be consolidated and popularised by the 'High Enlightenment'.

The 'crisis' was the result of the advent of the new science of Copernicus and Galileo and the new rationalism of Descartes, which put an end to the self-evident coherence of faith, tradition and authority rooted since ancient times, both philosophically and theologically, in the scholastic-Aristotelian way of thinking. Descartes' systematic doubt and the new science's mechanistic view of nature shattered all the old certainties and so ushered in the modern age, which then took shape slowly but surely during the Enlightenment and ultimately led to the political and social upheaval of the French Revolution.

So far the story sounds familiar, but Israel argues that it is wrong to regard the Enlightenment as a homogeneous movement. In reality it was extremely heterogeneous, not so much because of the various national differences (indeed, Israel stresses its European nature) but because of the difference between its moderate mainstream and a radical undercurrent. While the moderate *philosophes* gradually found more and more support from government and enlightened elements among the clergy, throughout the entire eighteenth century radical thinkers were subject to bans and persecution – not infrequently with the approval of moderate Enlightenment thinkers, who deliberately distanced themselves from the radical competition in order to preserve their hard-won respectability.

A charge of 'Spinozism' was in practice the most effective stick to beat the opposition with. Israel cites countless examples, drawn from German, French, Dutch, English, Scandinavian and Italian sources, which show how much Spinoza was *the* bogeyman whose name could be used to discredit a seventeenth- or eighteenth-century thinker. To defenders of the traditional order he was a 'monster' whose ideas opened the floodgates to atheism, anarchy and licentiousness.

'Spinozist' as a term of abuse came to be used in a very broad sense, just like 'fascist' after 1945. But in Israel's view it did not thereby become '*vague*' or '*meaningless*'. Rather, he sees this as an indication of the importance of Spinoza's philosophy, which was then far better and more widely known than is generally assumed today.

erywhere, if only through the efforts made by his numerous opponents to refute them.

Why it should have been Spinoza who became the universal scapegoat is no mystery to Israel. He was the first to take all the fatalist, naturalist and atheist notions of the past and make of them a coherent, stable 'system'. On top of that, no other philosopher was so consistently and uncompromisingly modern. In Israel's view, his traditionalist opponents were right: Spinoza *was* the greatest danger threatening the old order.

In his *Tractatus Theologico-Politicus* (1670) he propounded a rigorous critique of the Bible which reduced God's word entirely to the work of man and argued for personal freedom and a democratic republic. In his *Ethica* (published posthumously in 1677) he broke with the Judeo-Christian idea of a personal God by recognising only one substance which as 'God or Nature' determined all things with relentless inevitability. The universe was governed by a determinism as absolute as it was immanent, obedient to geometrical logic, which relativised the distinction between good and evil and gave short shrift to such things as divine revelation, miracles, angels and demons, while mind and body (as 'attributes' of the one substance) proved to be two sides of the same coin.

Precisely because of his radicalism, so Israel suggests, Spinoza's thinking best fitted the mechanistic world-image of the new natural science. Better, certainly, than Cartesianism, which with its dualism of body and spirit still left room for supernatural phenomena; moreover, unlike Spinoza, it did *not* regard movement as a quality of matter and so still kept a place for God as 'first cause'. Whereas the Cartesians were looking to reconcile faith and reason, in Spinoza the 'natural light of reason' was the only route to salvation; in essence a strictly secularised ideal, even though – as witness his equation of nature with God – he continued to use the language of theology.

Such total secularisation was anathema also to moderate Enlightenment thinkers. And so they too went in search of a way of reconciling faith and reason. Israel sees this as explaining the success enjoyed on the continent by Locke and Newton, and by the enlightened 'physico-theology' (which thought that from the order found in nature it could derive the existence of a 'divine architect') and the German metaphysics of Leibniz and Wolff with its God-willed *harmonia praestabilita*. The object in all these cases was to take the wind out of the sails of an advancing radicalism à la Spinoza.

And so, in one of the most provocative chapters in *Radical Enlightenment,* Israel puts into perspective the significance of the 'Anglomania' which reared its head on the continent about 1730 and played off Newton's experimental science and the empiricism of Bacon and Locke against the metaphysical philosophy of Descartes, Leibniz and Spinoza. He does not question the honesty of someone like Voltaire, whose *Lettres philosophiques* (1734) passionately promoted the British ideas. But he is suspicious of the *Encyclopédie* of Diderot and d'Alembert, the most important literary and scholarly monument of the High Enlightenment.

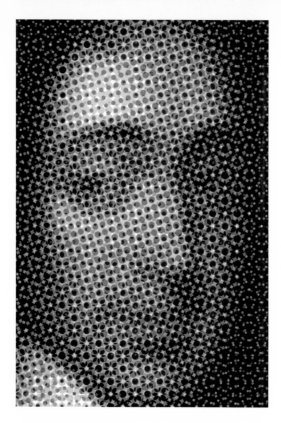

Portrait of Spinoza on the cover of a book published on the occasion of the exhibition *A Stone in Flight – Artistic Explorations inspired by Benedictus de Spinoza* (1997).

To prove his point he uses primary and secondary literature and also his own archival research to investigate various controversies and episodes in the Republic in which Spinoza and his philosophy played a major part: from the legal proceedings against Spinoza's reckless disciple Adriaen Koerbagh in 1668 to the uproar over Pierre Bayle's *Dictionnaire historique et critique* (1697), which devoted considerable – albeit seemingly negative – attention to Spinoza, from the 'Bredenburg squabbles' among the Collegiants of Holland to the protests against *The World Bewitched* (De betoverde weereld, 1691-93), Balthasar Bekker's widely-read attack on belief in witchcraft and black magic. With, of course, all due attention to the tumultuous reception of Spinoza's own writings.

Time and again it is apparent that reactions were by no means confined solely to the Republic. Throughout Western Europe, as far afield as Scandinavia and Italy, these issues were extensively discussed and commented on in the new public domain, which with its salons, coffee-houses, libraries, newspapers and periodicals offered plenty of scope for the keenest of intellectual debate. No matter that Spinoza's works were everywhere banned; his ideas still managed to penetrate ev-

True, d'Alembert's *Discours préliminaire* praises Bacon, Newton and Locke to the skies, but in Israel's view that was because by then they had become 'safe' thinkers. In Diderot's case, especially, his real sympathies lay elsewhere, with Spinoza; it is no coincidence that the *Encyclopédie* devotes five times as much space to him as to Locke.

The question is, to what extent Israel is right. For while Spinoza's ideas may have been better attuned to the secularising implications of the new science, his metaphysics contributed little more to the experimental method of Newton and his followers than a dogmatic belief in the logical structure of reality. On the other hand, it is typical of the late Enlightenment that it increasingly turned away from rigid metaphysical thinking as being too far removed from the scientific empiricism of investigation and experiment.

This is clear, for example, from the *Traité des Systèmes* (1749) by Condillac, a kindred spirit of the Encyclopedists, which dismisses metaphysicians as 'poets' and all systematic philosophy as nothing more than 'words'. But Israel has an answer to this too, for in his *Traité des sensations* (1754) the same Condillac developed a '*sensationalist psychology*' in which all a person's mental activity is reduced to his physical 'impressions' – thus correcting Locke, who still recognised 'reflection' as a separate mental activity. In this way, says Israel, Condillac cleared the way for a purely materialistic conception of mind such as we find later in such '*nouveaux spinosistes*' as Diderot, La Mettrie and Helvétius.

The rift between the High Enlightenment and seventeenth-century radical thought was thus indeed not as great as all that. And Israel argues that the same goes for British deism, which took over the radical torch from Spinozism in the early eighteenth century. This deism is often said to be purely English in origin, but Israel shows that major British deists like Toland, Tindal and Collins lived for long periods in the Netherlands and became acquainted with Spinoza's ideas there; which is not to say, of course, that they can be seen as his uncritical imitators.

The same applies to almost all later radical Enlightenment thinkers. They were still invariably pilloried as 'Spinozists' by their opponents, but theirs was rarely a pure Spinozism. In the case of La Mettrie, for instance, the first full-blooded materialist and atheist thinker, it is doubtful whether he ever made any serious study of Spinoza. Even Israel has to acknowledge that. In La Mettrie, as in Diderot, we find a way of thinking that does indeed display the necessary kinship with Spinoza's philosophy but does not coincide with it.

Far more questionable is the link that Israel draws in his epilogue between Spinoza and Rousseau, a declared deist who in *Émile* (1762) defends human freedom against determinism of any kind on the grounds of the existence of the 'soul'. Despite this, in Israel's opinion, as a political philosopher Rousseau, with his concept of the 'common will', shows a remarkable agreement with Spinoza's political thinking in which the 'common good' is proclaimed as the *ratio* of all politics.

This is taking a very broad view of Spinoza's influence. But Israel is undoubtedly right in seeing Rousseau as a *philosophe* who developed his own ideas 'in dialogue' with a radical tradition which had absorbed Spinoza's thinking over the course of the eighteenth century. More than this he did not seek to demonstrate in his stimulating and pioneering book, every page of which attests to his phenomenal mastery of his material.

When the French Revolution broke out people in the streets sang '*c'est la faute à Voltaire, c'est la faute à Rousseau*'. Israels comes very close to claiming that they should really have been singing '*c'est la faute à Spinoza*', but in the end he contents himself with having placed the crucial importance of Spinozism for radical Enlightenment thought on the historical agenda. With an army of convincing arguments and such a mass of documentation as has never before been mustered in such breadth and richness.

ARNOLD HEUMAKERS
Translated by Tanis Guest.

Jonathan I. Israel, *Radical Enlightenment. Philosophy and the Making of Modernity 1650-1750*. Oxford: Oxford University Press, 2001; 810 pp. ISBN 01-982060-89.

Society

Living inside Belgium

Belgium is remarkable in the unremarkable. If pressed to find a single word to describe life in Belgium, one might well settle for 'easy' .

To many who do not know the country that might sound either like selling it short, or damning it with faint praise. Either way, dull, you might say.

Really? Consider, if you will, the following. A country with a healthy degree of decentralisation, where a top professional career can be followed without always having to repair to the capital to get it. A country which has experienced over 150 years of communal and linguistic conflict with surprisingly little violence: many harsh words, but few blows. A capital city which has rocketed up to being the administrative centre of the European Union and of NATO, without posturing and without ceasing to be green, provincial and habitable.

It is of course not all marvellous. Few would deny that many Belgian towns and villages are visually unlovely; and between them there is too often a reckless ribbon development in which harmony, style and communal responsibility have been sacrificed to individualism. But even here you will find a high quality of life, both material and non-material.

In most European countries citizens enjoy decentralised access to facilities such as education, health,

social services, leisure and sport. In Belgium this extends also to culture, thanks to the dense network of municipal community and cultural centres, many of them with first-class exhibition or performance facilities. A metropolitan cultural hegemony of the West End or Broadway type is unknown here.

The Flemish regional government understands the need to support culture, especially language-based culture, in the light of the tough Flemish struggle for recognition, and in the light of the community-based problems still to be solved. Among Walloons too, there is a new feeling that their culture has to be protected; a preoccupation which differs subtly from that of earlier years, when it was 'simply' a matter of maintaining French-speaking dominance.

Why say all this? The point of it is that the European foreigner living in Belgium gets from living here what he or she puts into it. The 'ease' mentioned above permits you to have only slight and occasional contact with the country, if that is what you want. You don't have to know what is going on, and many foreigners don't. Given the polyglot ability of the Belgians, including those with only a modest education, you don't even have to attempt one of the national languages. The adaptation required of you is absolutely minimal.

In this spirit, many of my own British compatriots living here seem merely to close their eyes and think of Eurostar.

To a superficial observer, the Belgian inter-community debate, in which Flemings are pitched against Walloons, with the small German-speaking community also striving to protect its interests, looks like a squabble over language. It is not; it is deeply political, and from time to time the question is even asked, both north and south of the main language border, whether Belgium can continue to exist as one country. But Belgians get on with things despite difficulties, while the said superficial observer from elsewhere in Europe blithely misses the point.

The Flemish government and community for its part has for some years now been exerting itself to make and maintain contact with foreign residents, to explain to them the issues being debated, and to tell those who want to hear it what is being achieved in Flanders. There are multilingual pamphlets and books, illustrated lectures and guided tours with a choice of language, international cultural evenings and so on, on a scale found in few other countries.

Even more remarkable, if you will forgive the word, is the fact that some Flemish institutions are asking foreigners in private and in public what they think of Flanders. The response can be disappointing. Asked 'What do you think of Flanders?' many might answer (if they tell the truth) 'I don't.'

One image evident even to casual observers is of

course that of the extreme right. Most European countries, including Belgium, have this problem. It is true that candidates from the Flemish far right Vlaams Blok party won an alarming number of seats at recent elections. But it is also true that the democratic parties reacted immediately and jointly by refusing to co-operate with them. No cause for complacency of course, but a reason to be watchful also in drawing one's conclusions. The trap of facile judgement gapes wide, and the foreign observer must be wary of falling into it.

In contrast to immigrants from south-eastern Europe and from the Third World, who have to learn one of the languages, look about them and adapt in order to survive, foreign residents (whether short or long-term) from the European Union are able to take a less strenuous path. The employer completes all the formalities and smoothes the way. The openness and tolerance, the ongoing welcome in one's own language, and the 'ease', can be taken for granted, and they often are. It is significant that extremely few entitled foreigners used their newly acquired vote in the municipal elections of October 2000: from one in twenty in the provinces of Hainaut and Liège right down to one in a hundred and thirty in Brussels, with an average of one in thirty for the whole country. You can attribute this to foreign apathy, or to the unsung Belgian talent for stability, or to both factors working together.

If the Netherlands is, as it claims to be, classless, then by the same yardstick one could categorise Belgium as middle-class. Karl Marx found it the most middle-class country he knew. His remark was meant disparagingly; most Belgians would not take it so. Conservatives in other countries preach the value of the family, which they feel to be threatened. In Belgium the family is alive and well; the feeling of belonging to it is very strong, often to the detriment of one's obligations to a broader group or to the community as a whole. Most Belgian university students go home (i.e. to their parents) at the weekend. At least one political party here complains that it has become difficult for young couples to find a house in the area where they grew up, or near their parents (which is mostly the same thing). All this can sound very strange to a foreigner, especially to an Anglo-Saxon, for whom proximity to the scene of one's youth is in no way a desideratum; often quite the contrary. The complaint about housing is made most often with reference to the Brussels region, ignoring the simple truth that if you push to have the capital of Europe in your country, that can entail disadvantages. One can of course see the preoccupation as a positive sign; it shows that the Belgians still expect their capital to be habitable and affordable, an ideal that most British and French citizens would find utopian with respect to theirs.

The Belgians are indeed no travellers; their home, and their home region, are important to them. Apart from the annual excursion to the Mediterranean or to their own crowded coast, they tend to stay put. But they are used to having foreign bodies in their own country; they have had them as refugees, traders, plunderers, invaders, occupiers, allies, tourists, businessmen and international executives. They are one of the least nationalistic, and most Europhile, nations in Europe. The country itself had an inauspicious start, coming into existence as the combined product of revolt and of nineteenth-century great-power *Realpolitik*. The language boundary cutting across Belgium has in recent history caused more, and more severe, problems than has, for example, the confessional boundary which traverses the Netherlands. For a time one half of Belgium had to accept being dominated by the other half. Now the same two communities have to work out an equitable coexistence. You can see it unfolding before you, voices raised sometimes, but not fists. But you have to take the trouble to watch and listen. No Belgian will reproach you for expressing an informed opinion – he or she will be charmed to learn that you have one.

The appearances, therefore, are deceptive. The calm is that of deep water. And how do the Belgians take it? Their most frequent reaction to the country's dilemmas is to display the one national characteristic known to everyone here, however unobservant: the famous muddling through, for which they have their own national terminology: '*plantrekkerij / tirer son plan*'. Putting it in more eloquent terms, they are pragmatic. And remarkable in the unremarkable.

JOHN MACE

Securing a 'Good Death' under the Law Euthanasia legislation in the Netherlands

On 28 November 2000 history was made in the Netherlands. On that day the Second Chamber, the lower house of parliament, passed the Euthanasia Bill by a majority of 104 to 40. In favour of the Bill, which was introduced jointly by Ministers Borst of Public Health and Korthals of Justice, were the PvdA social democrats, the liberal vvd, d66 left-wing liberals, and the GroenLinks green left. Voting against were the CDA Christian Democrats, the small Christian parties, and the Socialist Party. With this the Dutch put themselves on course to become the world's first nation with a statutory framework for voluntary euthanasia and doctor-assisted suicide. The Bill didn't encounter much opposition when it was presented to the First Chamber on 10 April 2001.

In the interim the Netherlands scooped yet another first on the social front with the solemnisation, on 1 April 2001, of the world's first legal same-sex marriages.

Voluntary euthanasia and doctor-assisted suicide, as before, remain statutory offences (carrying twelve and three years' imprisonment respectively), but under certain circumstances, specified in guidelines enshrined in law, physicians are exempted from prosecution. The decriminalisation process entails a hearing by an independent tribunal – presided over by a jurist, and including an ethicist and a medical expert – which rules, on a case by case basis, whether a practitioner has acted with 'utmost care' as understood by the law. If so, the case is dismissed; otherwise it is referred to the public prosecutor.

The first and foremost criterion for 'utmost care' is that in practising voluntary euthanasia, or doctor-assisted suicide, a physician should have acted strictly in accordance with the patient's wishes. A physician complying with a request for voluntary euthanasia, or doctor-assisted suicide, must be absolutely satisfied that the patient is acting entirely of his own volition. His request for medical assistance should moreover be 'persistent' – that is repeatedly expressed. Furthermore, the physician must be satisfied that from the patient's perspective the issue is one of 'hopeless and intolerable suffering'. This latter formulation replaces what was previously termed an 'intolerable situation'. In addition to this, the patient must be cognisant of his condition, and physician and patient must together have come to the conclusion that this is the only reasonable way to proceed. This conclusion must then be corroborated by at least one further independent medical opinion, which must be based on examination of the patient. The medical procedure requested by the patient must be followed with due care, and a full report submitted to the coroner, who orders a post-mortem, the results of which are reported to the office of the Chief Prosecutor and to the tribunal, which also receives copies of all reports.

Finally the law also enshrines the right of minors (of twelve and over) to voluntary euthanasia and doctor-assisted suicide, though juveniles between twelve and sixteen still require parental consent. For youngsters over sixteen parental consent is not required, but the parent(s) or legal guardian(s) must be involved in the decision-making process. Correspondingly, sixteen is the threshold age for the right to make a 'living will', a principle also embodied in the new legislation. Already 100,000 Netherlanders have such a will, in which they can indicate under what kind of circumstances euthanasia should be performed on them.

Broadly speaking, the new law formalises what was already established practice in the Netherlands, by translating into legislation the policy of toleration that had been observed over the past ten years. In the country as a whole there was a long-felt desire to bring euthanasia out of the twilight zone into the light of day, and to see doctors, who are now bound by strict rules, provided with legal protection. In providing that protection the law makes absolutely clear that the patient does not have the right of self-determination, and that the actual decision is always up to the doctor(s). Ministers Borst and Korthals hope that whereas under the previous system fifty per cent of doctors failed to come forward out of fear of prosecution, all cases of voluntary euthanasia and doctor-assisted suicide will now be reported.

Still, the enactment of the new legislation will not mean the end of the euthanasia debate in the Netherlands. Critics have already pointed to the difficulties inherent in interpreting a phrase such as 'hopeless and intolerable suffering'. In this context, they quote the 'Chabot ruling' of 1994, when the highest court in the land pronounced that purely psychological suffering may constitute due grounds for a physician to practise doctor-assisted suicide. The case concerned a Dr Chabot, a psychiatrist who had decided to assist in the suicide of a severely depressed female patient aged fifty. And what, ask the critics, about the concept of 'weariness of life'? A notorious case in point was that of the 86-year-old former PvdA member of the First Chamber E. Brongersma, who in 1998 said he 'suffered from life itself', and found life to have become 'meaningless'. There was a court investigation going on into his collection of child pornography and he was supposed to be depressive because of the increased public outcry against paedophilia in the wake of the Dutroux affair in Belgium. His GP, who had assisted him in committing suicide, was acquitted by the court just a few weeks before the Euthanasia Bill first came before parliament. Minister Borst too sailed close to the wind when she declared in the course of the euthanasia debate that voluntary euthanasia should surely also be an option for people suffering from the early symptoms of dementia. For, argued Mrs Borst, there were those for whom certain knowledge of inevitable mental deterioration was tantamount to 'hopeless and intolerable suffering'.

Cause enough, then, for sharp reactions from the Roman Catholic bishops, the Dutch Protestant churches collectively, and the Jewish community. Joining in the fray are also individuals such as Willem Jan Otten, the writer, publicist and Catholic convert, who has for years been reproaching his country for its arrogant approach to ultimate questions of human destiny and social good.

The Netherlands was, and continues to be, only too aware that the new law needs to be explained to the world at large and not only to the Vatican – whither Mrs Borst on two occasions travelled to tell the Pope how matters stood – where its provisions are not always fully understood.

In Belgium, meanwhile, developments next door were eagerly followed, particularly since the ruling purple-green coalition government intended to introduce a euthanasia bill very similar to the Dutch one in the Federal Senate in 2001. A joint study by the universities of Brussels and Ghent, which was published in the British medical journal *The Lancet*, found that doctor-assisted death was already occurring on a large scale in Flanders, with a good 39 per cent of all deaths being preceded by medical decisions that could potentially result in shortening life. Indeed, curtailment of the patient's life against his or her wishes was found to be almost three times as common as curtailment by request. To proponents of legalised euthanasia this was as clear a vindication of their case as any.

The painful circumstances surrounding the enactment of the 1990 Abortion Act – which the late King Baudouin refused to ratify – are still fresh in people's memories. His brother Albert II will most likely not go that far, but the actual political and public debate is still going on. Flanders, which is strongly secularised, has more support for the legalisation of euthanasia than does Wallonia, though the contrary used to be the case. Nonetheless, Flanders is divided on this issue across all party lines and social groupings. Finally, while the opposition Christian democratic parties in both parts of the country are solidly against this legislation, the ruling parties are not of one mind. For as the leadership was drafting the bill, its own backbenchers were already submitting amendments.

LUC DEVOLDERE
Translated by Sonja Prescod.

The Netherlands Association for Voluntary Euthanasia (NVVE; Nederlandse Vereniging voor Vrijwillige Euthanasie) provides information and advice on 'legal suicide'. The organisation was entirely committed to the legalisation of voluntary euthanasia (http://www.nvve.nl).

Visual Arts

Brussels: From Cross-Roads to Parking Place

The international exhibition Europalia 2000 Brussels deliberately put the cat among the pigeons and did not shrink from the resultant hubbub. The exhibition *Brussels, Cross-Roads of Cultures* resolutely followed the course taken by the arts, with the emphasis on painting. Starting at the beginning of the nineteenth century, it continued right through to the present day, as if there was no stopping it, as if the roads stretched all the way from the cosmopolitan cross-roads to the visitor's feet. Yet you left the Palace of Fine Arts convinced that the cross-roads was a place busy with artists and intellectuals, especially between 1850 and 1914. And that at the end of the day almost all roads led to Paris. Only the signposts 'Symbolism' and 'Art Nouveau' pointed towards the Belgian capital. Today it is civil servants – European or otherwise – that choke the Brussels ringroad. Brussels is no longer an artistic junction but an administrative one.

The story begins with an early French exile, Jacques-Louis David. The artist spent the years between 1816 and his death in 1825 painting neo-classical scenes in Brussels: drifting on cloud and throne, Mars allows himself to be disarmed by Venus; Achilles furiously draws his sword when Iphigenia prepares to sacrifice herself to ensure a Greek victory. On his Brussels throne, 'monsieur David' submits to the attentions of his disciples. Why return to turbulent France?

More important for the development of modern painting in Brussels is Gustave Courbet's participation in the Brussels salons. As a mediator between North and South, Courbet is very much at home in the Belgian capital where, moreover, he meets fellow freethinkers. His realistic paintings tap a new vein of painters with a social conscience, from Joseph Stevens and Charles de Groux, through Félicien Rops and James Ensor to Constantin Meunier and Eugène Laermans.

Courbet's solid areas of paint have clearly left their mark on Ensor and Vogels, whose northern variant of Impressionism is much more strongly rooted in earth and reality than its sun-drenched French counterpart. Even Hippolyte Boulenger, who painted the landscape around Tervuren out in the open air after the example of the Barbizon school, felt the difference in light sensitivity. His irregular splotches of paint heralded the tachism of the young James Ensor.

The Frenchman who very rapidly gathered the largest following in Brussels was Georges Seurat. Again it was all a question of a French lesson in light. Seurat allowed the light to explode in the colours of the spectrum. People and surroundings break up into a multitude of spots. It is not his painter's hand that mixes the colours, but the eye of the spectator. The world is seen as if under a microscope. After Seurat gained admission to the salon of the leading artists' group Les XX in 1887, many painters fall under the pointillist spell. Willy Finch, Anna Boch, Théo van Rysselberghe, Georges Lemmen, Henry van de Velde, Jan Toorop; none of them is able to resist 'the little dot' entirely.

Jan Toorop is the most modern of the Dutchmen who came to Brussels for a taste of France. The exhibition catalogue presents him successively as tachist, pointillist, symbolist and intermediary between Khnopff and Klimt, Brussels and Vienna. Toorop studied at the Brussels academy in the early 1880s, together with a certain Van Gogh. He joined Les XX in 1885, just two years after its foundation. The Dutch integrated effortlessly into the Brussels art scene. Among the first to settle in Brussels in 1847 was Willem Roelofs and he paved the way for his fellow countrymen. This now rather tame-looking landscape artist, on the cusp between romanticism and realism, was an active member of the Brussels Cercle Artistique. In his wake a veritable artists' colony of Dutchmen (among whom Toorop and Willem de Famars Testas), all looking to break loose from the suffocating Dutch tradition, established itself in Brussels between 1850 and 1890. In prosperous Brussels they saw their way clear to re-assessing themselves artistically and enriching themselves financially. Press and fellow painters embraced them as 'Hollando-Belges', as half-Belgians. Until, sooner or later, they headed northwards again. After their stopover in Brussels, one or two of them caused a furore elsewhere: Laurens Alma Tadema in London, Vincent van Gogh posthumously in Provence. The twin brothers David and Pieter Oyens kept one foot in the Dutch Golden Age while with the other they tested the waters of the contemporary, fashionable art world. As chroniclers they captured on canvas the life of the Brussels painters. David Oyens, for example, depicts an artist scrutinising *L'Art Moderne*, the weekly mouthpiece of Les XX and clever conveyer of French influences.

The first half of the catalogue sparkles with entertaining dialogues and discussions: Stevens chats with Courbet; Boulenger embraces Rousseau; Rops and Klinger gather around Wiertz; Meunier goes to Rodin's for coffee (the two gentlemen exchange pictures); in comradly fashion Laermans and Kollwitz take

Willem de Famars Testas,
Elsene Seen from the
Kroonlaan Fly-Over. 1885.
Water colour, 29.4 x 49.5 cm.
Rijksmuseum, Amsterdam.

pity on the workers; Redon, Khnopff, Burne-Jones and Toorop allow themselves to be seduced by wide-eyed ladies; Van de Velde, Horta and Hoffmann merge art and life in art-nouveau buildings... And then the clamour dies down.

After the First World War Brussels repeatedly missed its connection with the avant-garde. True, gallery owners like Georges Giroux and Paul-Gustave van Hecke did keep their finger on the pulse. Magritte and his Surrealist brothers-in-arms managed to salvage something. Brussels gave the CoBrA movement two letters. Marcel Broodthaers juggled with language, mussels and poetry. But there was a noticeable thinning-out of traffic at the cross-roads. In the end four contemporary artists were surprised at each other's presence. A German, a Spaniard, a Tanzanian and a Belgian kept the image of a cultural cross-roads artificially alive. They stayed on in Brussels. No more, no less. Somewhere along the line, the cross-roads became a non-obligatory parking place for works of art and artists.

KURT DE BOODT
Translated by Alison Mouthaan-Gwillim.

The exhibition catalogue of *Brussels, Cross-Roads of Cultures* was published both in Dutch and French by Mercatorfonds (http://www.mercatorfonds.be).

André Volten, Sculptor in Public Space

André Volten. Sculpture in Private Space. Sculpture in Public Space[1] is a book on the work of André Volten, published in the Netherlands in 2000. The dust jacket round the linen binding is partly gold coloured; this is a reminder of the brass models that define Volten's sculptures in private spaces. The monograph on Volten's sculpture was presented together with a one-man show of his models at the Kröller-Müller Museum in Otterlo. The larger silver-coloured area on the dust jacket refers to the stainless steel that Volten is so fond of using in his sculptures for public spaces. In his article 'Art on Commission', Hein van Haaren deals with this section of his work, while the former director of the Kröller-Müller Museum, Rudi Oxenaar, writes about Volten's sculpture in private spaces. The lucidity of André Volten's sculptures is thus already indicated by the dust jacket of this meticulously designed book.

Both texts are informative. In his article Hein van Haaren says the following, '*It is characteristic of Volten that he himself usually plays the leading part in deciding what his client may or should expect of him. Both experienced and inexperienced customers often welcome this approach to the content of the work.*' And from 1956 to the present, Volten has in fact played this part in at least 112 places in and beyond the Netherlands. Indeed, if one considers all the well-known Dutch sculptors who have built up a considerable body of work, there is none with such a relatively large proportion of sculptures for public spaces.

André Volten, *Sculpture*. 1984-1990. Laquered steel, 2200 x 500 cm. Stationsplein, Lelystad. Photo by Jan Blom / courtesy of the artist.

The two texts are preceded by the strikingly composed 'Autobiographical Notes'. Here Volten describes his independent-minded anarchist father, who led a very hard life as a small fisherman in the Zuider Zee, and his equally principled but milder mother. He explains his ideas on the use of materials and on the placing of sculptures in public spaces. His designs acquire form through his focus on the specific nature of every new spatial situation he is confronted with. And the figures are always associated with the work he is doing at that particular moment. He has a love and respect for the material, a respect for fellow workers and for public space, which he refers to as '*a scarce and vulnerable thing*'.

Volten, who was born in 1925 in Andijk on what is now the IJsselmeer, is still active in 2001 and has built up an oeuvre that shows great inner consistency. The monograph focuses on a selection of his work in both words and photos. Lists of commissions, solo and group exhibitions, catalogues and literature complete the book. This monograph is consequently not an academic catalogue of his oeuvre, but it is the first serious introduction to the consistent work of this industrially-oriented artist. The photos, mainly in black and white, are designed to bring out the individuality of each work.

The square, the cube, the circle, the cylinder and the sphere dominate André Volten's work. They are the natural products of the metal industry, and Volten's lifelong preoccupation with these forms also springs from his wonder: he regards them as archetypes recognisable to all and possessing great beauty. His favourite materials for figures in public spaces are stainless and polished steel, and to a lesser extent, corten steel, bronze and granite. Granite is the hardest stone of all and allows a greater degree of precision of form than any other stone. Stainless steel guarantees the highest degree of precision if the design is executed by a good company. It is this, in addition to its wonderful sheen, that makes it Volten's favourite material. These clear mathematical forms, made in reliable materials, determine the appearance of Volten's work in public spaces.

In addition to this he is fortunate in having a very accurate sense of the appropriate monumental size.

To illustrate the above and as an introduction to the monograph and André Volten's work, I shall look at two figures that I consider to be typical of his work. The first is the twenty-two metre high *Sculpture*, dating from 1990, which stands on the station forecourt in Lelystad.[2] The attention of the passer-by is caught by a whole range of red and blue street furniture: lamp-posts, a phone booth, a billboard, a flagpole, a cycle rack, a post-box, flower boxes, chairs, and litter bins. These colours are repeated in the facade of the station building. Volten probably chose steel for its neutral colour in order to distinguish or separate it from the rest of the 'furnishings'. And the enormous height, which was decided on after a great deal of calculation, was necessary to link together all the stationary accents and the liveliness of the passing traffic in one large gesture. From its large square foot starts a movement which is repeated very precisely as a steel lasso high above its base. This suggestion of a circle is the most

important element in the sculpture. The foremost line of the base appears as the highest point at the rear. With its rigorous sweep, *Sculpture* in Lelystad incorporates the square and circle, round and straight, vertical and horizontal. This sign of welcome and departure may resemble a mathematical principle, but it is dominated by the sureness of the monumental size and vivacity, and the nobility of the gesture.

André Volten has lived in Amsterdam-Noord, the sober, non-historical part of the city, since 1950. When he was almost seventy, a commission contacted the borough of Amsterdam-Noord. Referring to his having remained faithful to the spot for forty-five years – '*an industrially-oriented artist belongs in an industrial area*' is how he puts it – the commission and the borough sought the funding for a monumental sculpture in Amsterdam-Noord. This took the form of *Sculpture for the IJ-Bank*, completed in 1996.[3] The artist, who had always lived on the boundary between land and water, points out the connection between them by means of two stainless steel links, about 5 metres long, permanently clasped together. Even without any knowledge of the sculpture's background, anyone can understand its meaning.

As in Lelystad, the monumental size of *Sculpture for the IJ-Bank* is designed to fit its spatial context. And like the 1990 sculpture, this one too is breathtakingly persuasive. In Lelystad, the expansion returns with deliberation to its point of departure. *Sculpture for the IJ-Bank* is not centrifugal but pressed tightly together, full of latent power. This is achieved by its vivid plasticity. The constantly moving water gives an added lyrical delight to the gleaming stainless steel forms of the sculpture. This is not an external addition to the sculpture. In his talent for the monumental, Volten bases his ideas on the music of the actual space itself.

JOSÉ BOYENS
Translated by Gregory Ball.

NOTES

1. Rotterdam: Nai Uitgevers, 2000; 136 pp. ISBN 90-5662-151-3.

2. Lelystad is one of the two largest cities in Flevoland, which the Netherlands reclaimed from the IJsselmeer, formerly the Zuider Zee, between 1961 and 1986.

3. The IJ forms the port of Amsterdam. It separates Amsterdam-Noord from the old, historical part of the city.

Short takes

Clogs, windmills, tulips, cannabis – these still define the foreigner's perception of the Netherlands. And so, on a rather less superficial level, do the paintings of Rembrandt and Vermeer. We know a great deal about the life of the former. His productivity was impressive. But Vermeer? Hardly any biographical data and a mere 35 paintings attributed to him. But that didn't stop the Delft master becoming a cultural icon.

Mystery lets the imagination run free, and the lack of information on Vermeer means that his life and work provide rewarding subjects for novelists. In *Girl with a Pearl Earring* Tracy Chevalier speculates about the Vermeer household in the 1660s. She observes the domestic tensions between the painter, his constantly pregnant wife, his mother-in-law and a young maidservant who poses for the famous painting of the title, which has also been called 'the Dutch Mona Lisa'.

Girl in Hyacinth Blue by Susan Vreeland is again a voyage through the past, in search of the origins of the 36th Vermeer. Eight linked stories and a succession of owners bring us to the subject of this imaginary canvas: Vermeer's daughter Magdalena. Journeying through time, we also become aware of the shifts in the value and significance of art.

Katherine Weber too imagines a Vermeer. In her psychological thriller *The Music Lesson* a bond develops between the painted woman on the canvas and the main character Patricia Dolan. An Irish-American art-historian, she is drawn into the Northern Irish struggle

for independence by a passionate affair and is forced to choose between the beauty of art and politics.

A choice which Marilyn Chandler McEntyre certainly has no need to make, for in her volume of poetry *In Quiet Light* she takes the mysterious beauty of paintings like *The Milkmaid* and *The Lacemaker* as her starting-point for 'Poems on Vermeer's Women'. A contemplative exercise which in one poem she herself describes as follows: '*Go home. Write about her now. / Give her lines and let her speak.*'

Nor does the stream of studies of Vermeer show any sign of drying up. Anthony Bailey, who has already devoted two books to Rembrandt, sketches a personal portrait of him in *Vermeer: A View of Delft*. He begins his story in 1654 with the great gunpowder explosion in Delft and ends with the echoes of Vermeer's work in Proust and the notorious forgeries of Han van Meegeren. Another fascinating, though more technical, study is *Vermeer's Camera*, in which Philip Steadman attempts to prove that Vermeer employed a camera obscura to paint his near-photographic scenes. And those wishing to learn a lot about Vermeer in a short time will find what they want in *The Little Book of Vermeer*: life, work, technique, themes, style and historical context, all explained in layman's terms in one pocket-sized book.

Twelve paintings by Vermeer and ten by his fellow-townsman Pieter de Hooch formed the nucleus of the exhibition *Vermeer and the Delft School* (Metropolitan Museum of Art, 5 March - 27 May 2001; National Gallery, London, 20 June - 26 September 2001). Around them were assembled works by lesser-known masters and objets d'art of all kinds. Incidentally, the *Woman at a Virginal*, hailed by *The Sunday Times* at the beginning of March as a newly-discovered Vermeer, was not included in the exhibition. There was some confusion here: the work has been known for a long time and according to authoritative experts is not an authentic Vermeer. Wim Pijbes, director of Rotterdam's Kunsthal, put it like this: '*A real Vermeer smiles, but a false one smirks. And this one smirks*'. So we're still waiting for no. 36.

Tracy Chevalier, *Girl with a Pearl Earring*. London: HarperCollins, 1999; 248 pp. ISBN 0-00-225890-0 / Susan Vreeland, *Girl in Hyacinth Blue*. New York: Penguin Books, 1999; 242 pp. ISBN 0-14-029628-X / Katharine Weber, *The Music Lesson*. New York: Picador, 2000; 178 pp. ISBN 0-31-225285-4 / Marilyn Chandler McEntyre, *In Quiet Light: Poems on Vermeer's Women*. Grand Rapids, MI / Cambridge: Wm. B. Eerdmans Publishing Co.; 71 pp. ISBN 0-80-283879-0 / Anthony Bailey, *Vermeer : A View of Delft*. New York: Henry Holt & Company, Inc., 2000; 256 pp. ISBN 0-80-506718-3 / Philip Steadman, *Vermeer's Camera: Uncovering the Truth behind the Masterpieces*. Oxford: Oxford University Press, 2001; 207 pp. ISBN 0-19-215967-4 / Guillaume Cassegrain, et. al., *The Little Book of Vermeer*. Paris: Flammarion, 2001;120 pp. ISBN 2-0801-0549-3 / Walter Liedtke, et. al., *Vermeer and the Delft School*. New Haven, CT, Yale University Press, 2001; 550 pp. ISBN 0-30-008848-5.

If there is one aspect of the Low Countries on which there is no shortage of good information, it is the visu-

Johannes Vermeer, *Lady Writing a Letter with her Maid*. c.1670. Canvas, 72.2 x 59.7 cm. National Gallery of Ireland, Dublin.

al arts. Last year again saw an abundance of splendid books on art old and new from the Netherlands and Flanders. A random selection: *Made in Flanders* on the miniatures of the Master of the 'Ghent Privileges, *Pleasant Places* on landscape engravings and paintings, a fascinating, almost microscopic investigation of Pieter Bruegel's *The Way to Calvary* in *The Mill and the Cross*, and *Raoul de Keyser Paintings 1980-1999* on the Flemish artist who developed his own idiom between figuration and abstraction. And 'mixed media' adventurers like Wim Delvoye also receive due attention.

Many books about art, then, but also some multimedia. The Maerlantcentrum – an initiative by the Catholic University of Leuven and Ghent's Hogeschool voor Wetenschap en Kunst – brings together scientific and scholarly research, new technologies and business with the object of making the historical-cultural heritage of the Low Countries accessible to a broad public. Which all sounds very ambitious, but in practice means that the Centre produces splendid and useful CD-ROMs. Their first offering was on St Bavo's Cathedral in Ghent; next one could click one's way through the

legacy (house and art-collection!) of the seventeenth-century Antwerp burgomaster Nicolaas Rockox. A journey through the past and present of Antwerp's Cathedral of Our Lady is the subject of the Maerlant Centre's third CD-ROM.

G. Clark, *Made in Flanders. The Master of the Ghent Privileges and Manuscript Painting in the Southern Netherlands in the Time of Philip the Good.* Turnhout: Brepols, 2000; 500 pp. ISBN 2-503-50878-2 / Walter S. Gibson, *Pleasant Places. The Rustic Landscape from Bruegel to Ruisdael.* Berkeley, CA / Los Angeles / London: University of California Press, 2000; 320 pp. ISBN 0-520-21698-9 / Michael Francis Gibson, *The Mill and the Cross: Peter Bruegel's 'Way to Calvary'.* Paris: Editions Acatos, 2000. 199 pp. ISBN 2-940-03372-2 / Steven Jacobs (ed.), *Raoul De Keyser: 1980-1999.* Ghent: Ludion, 2001; 272 pp. ISBN 90-554-4286-0 / Wim Delvoye. *Cloaca.* Ghent: Ludion, 2000; 136 pp. ISBN 90-554-4301-8 / Maerlant Centre: http://www.kuleuven.ac.be/upers

In 2001, for the second time in the history of the Academy Awards, a Flemish film was nominated in the category 'Best Foreign-Language Film'. After *Daens* in 1993, this time it was the turn of Dominique Deruddere's *Everybody Famous!* (Iedereen beroemd). However, this satirical tale of a father's desperate quest to gain artistic recognition for his songstress daughter had to cede the prize to *Crouching Tiger, Hidden Dragon*.

The Dutchman Michael Dudok de Wit had better fortune: his short animated film *Father and Daughter* was rewarded with an Oscar. Dutch animators consistently do quite well at the Academy Awards; in 1978 Co Hoedeman carried off a statuette for his *Sand Castle* and in 1995 Dudok de Wit himself received a nomination for *The Monk and the Fish*.

Dudok de Wit graduated from West Surrey College of Art in 1978 and currently lives in London, where he draws and directs television and cinema commercials. He also illustrates books and teaches animation at several English art colleges. *Father and Daughter* had already been hailed as 'Best Short Animation' at the Orange British Film Academy Awards. It is a story without dialogue of a young girl who says goodbye to her father and constantly returns to the place of their parting. In eight and a half minutes her whole life and the twentieth century go by, but her longing for her father remains.

On 15 December 2000 James Brockway died in The Hague at the age of 84. An obituary in *The Guardian* described him as '*a man of disciplined joy*', '*who brought Dutch verse to English audiences and English novels to the Dutch*'. Brockway had come to the Netherlands in 1946 to write, but 'by accident' became a translator. His collection of poetry *No Summer Song* appeared in 1949. Just before his death came *The Brightness In Between*, and between these was only *A Way of Getting Through* (1995). In terms of productivity the poet lagged far behind the translator. Apart from a bulky anthology of work by eight Dutch poets and individual volumes of translated poems by Rutger Kopland and Patty Scholten, he managed to place his translations in British literary journals on some 700 occasions. He even attracted the attention of T.S. Eliot with his translations of Achterberg, and in 1966 he won the Martinus Nijhoff Prize for translation, and was honoured with a decoration in 1997. A further collection of his Kopland translations will be published posthumously. And Brockway's generosity to Dutch letters continues from the afterlife: his legacy to the Dutch Foundation for Literary Production and Translations and the Literary Museum means that deserving translators might in future be rewarded with a James Brockway Prize.

With Brockway's death Dutch literature has lost an important translator and advocate. This is the more regrettable, since in recent years Dutch and Flemish literature in translation has carved itself a greater place in the English-language market. Along with translations of contemporary authors such as Arnon Grunberg, Bart Moeyaert and Marcel Möring, in 2000 there were also a number of reprints of older translations of 'classic' authors like Louis Couperus, Bordewijk and Arthur van Schendel.

It is not just that more and more Dutch-language literature is being translated and published in English; a number of these books have been extremely well received by the press. One such is H.M. van den Brink's *On the Water* (Over het water, 1998). This book on the magical bond and near-perfect sychronisation between two young men training together as rowers in Amsterdam just before the Second World War was described by *Publisher's Weekly* as '*a sensitively written and finely tuned work*'.

Another work that attracted the reviewers' attention was Arthur Japin's debut novel *The Two Hearts of Kwasi Boachi* (De zwarte met het witte hart, 1997). *Booklist* called it '*a powerful study of displacement and disillusionment*'. Japin, who at the end of 2000 became the first Dutch writer-in-residence at NYU, recounts the true story of two West African princes who were sent to study in the Netherlands in the 1830s.

In the academic world, too, interesting translations of Flemish and Dutch literature have appeared. For the most part these are historical texts, as in *Medieval Dutch Drama*. In this volume Johanna C. Prins has translated the plays from the Van Hulthem manuscript (Koninklijke Bibliotheek, Brussels, c.1400-1410). These comprise four so-called *abele spelen* – serious secular plays – each of which is accompanied by a farce. These eight texts are among the earliest secular plays in the Dutch vernacular.

H.M. van den Brink, *On the Water* (Tr. Paul Vincent). London: Faber and Faber, 2001; 134 pp. ISBN 0-571-20152-0 / Arthur Japin, *The Two Hearts of Kwasi Boachi* (Tr. Ina Rilke). London: Chatto and Windus; 342 pp. ISBN 0-701-16870-6 / Johanna C. Prins (ed.), *Medieval Dutch Drama: Four Secular Plays and Four Farces from the Van Hulthem Manuscript*. Asheville, NC: Pegasus Press, 2000; ISBN 1-889-81807-0.

Ever since the Eighties Flanders has had an international reputation for fashion. On 26 May 2001 the fashion year opened in Antwerp, the city which nurtured several of the most renowned Flemish designers. *Landed / Geland* is a project devised by guest curator and designer Walter van Beirendonck. Van Beirendonck did not opt for a string of glamorous parades; instead he put the emphasis on creativity, passion and authenticity. A move away from the catwalks and marketing ploys, then, and back to the essence of fashion – an essence which he sought to capture in a number of exhibitions. *Mutilate / Vermink*, for example, explores in an ethnographic and historical context the ways in which people like to deform or disfigure the human body: from Thai giraffe-women and Chinese girls with bound feet to piercing, scarring and transsexuality. Strikingly, too, the event did not turn into an ego-trip for Antwerp designers. Van Beirendonck made his selection from the cream of international designers.

Following *Landed / Geland, ModeNatie* (Fashion-Nation) will open at the end of 2001. The building will house the ModeMuseum, the Flanders Fashion Institute and the famous fashion department of Antwerp's Koninklijke Academie voor Schone Kunsten.

tel. 0032 70 233 799 / http://www.mode2001.be

With *Dancing Dutch* the Dutch Theatre Institute aims to produce a 'vademecum for foreign professionals'. This is no all-encompassing history of contemporary dance in the Netherlands, but a bird's eye overview of that dance-landscape. Dutch dance owes its present character and international influence to an inspired battle against the lack both of tradition and of facilities and infrastructure. The book casts light on characteristic aspects of the Dutch dance scene, but it also contains brief portraits of a few key figures. For along with government support, the professionalisation of Dutch dance is above all the work of a number of strong individuals. One good example is Hans van Manen, winner of the Erasmus Prize for 2000, a make-up artist and rock & roll dancer who via a crash course ended up in the world of ballet. In 1965 he was the first to put together a male pas-de-deux, and he introduced dancers in gym-shoes and court shoes to the stage.

Coos Versteeg (ed.) *Dancing Dutch. Contemporary Dance in the Netherlands*. Amsterdam: Theater Instituut Nederland, 2000; 172 pp. ISBN 90-70892-61-8.

Early in 2001 more than two hundred original photos by Henri Berssenbrugge were displayed in Rotterdam's Kunsthal.

Dutchman Henri Berssenbrugge (1873-1959) began his career in 1901 as a painter, but his brushes and

The art, strength and vulnerability of Dutch football since the 1960s: that is David Winner's topic in *Brilliant Orange. The Neurotic Genius of Dutch Football*. But he looks beyond the renaissance of Dutch football and combines his account of the game with reflections on Dutch national character. For instance, he links the creative force of Dutch total football with the rise of structuralism in Dutch architecture. Here everything revolves around space: your opponent's space must be restricted by pushing him back, while conversely when you have the ball space must be created. The flexibility of the polderland becomes mastery of the pitch. And so Saenredam, the seventeenth-century painter of imposing church interiors, is ranked alongside Johan Cruyff, the personification of total football: both are neurotic about space. And the author blames the failures of Dutch football on an inherent urge to self-destruction and the innate difficulty with leadership.

Winner tackled the aesthetics of total football with great thoroughness. He spent a year living in Amsterdam and interviewed such diverse figures as the outside-right Johnny Rep, the poet Anna Enquist, the netherlandicist Herman Pleij and the artist Jeroen Henneman. In his enthusiasm to demonstrate the interaction between culture, history and football he sometimes loses his way; but even so, *Brilliant Orange* is a remarkable book on Dutch football as an abstract artform.

David Winner, *Brilliant Orange. The Neurotic Genius of Dutch Football*. London: Bloomsbury, 2000; 246 pp. ISBN 0-7475-4708-4.

Henri Berssenbrugge, photo of Lily Green as *The Witch*, 1925 (collodion printing out paper).

paints were soon relegated to a corner of his studio. In the same year he set himself up in Tilburg as a photographer. Initially he worked dutifully at producing standard retouched portraits in fantasy settings, but the urge to experiment soon manifested itself. Berssenbrugge went in search of new forms of portrait photography. Gradually his backgrounds became more neutral. Taking as his motto 'The more ordinary the better', he started photographing people in their natural surroundings. In his outdoor shots he shows himself the heir of Van Gogh and Millet, recording working people on his plates. He also captured the street life of Rotterdam with a sure hand. Later he was also to experiment with special techniques to make his photographs look more like paintings and thus enhance their dramatic impact.

Ingeborg Th. Leijerzapf and Harm Botman, *Henri Berssenbrugge – Passion, Energy and Photography*. Zutphen: Walburg Pers, 2001; 349 pp. ISBN 90-5730-158-X.

The Netherlands is changing at tremendous speed. And its economic, demographic and social evolution is also reflected in the landscape. In *Atlas of Change. Rearranging the Netherlands* the authors sketch, each in their own way, an image of that changing country. Bureau Must does it with maps, Theo Baart with photos and Tjerk Ruimschotel analyses the developments in their historical and contemporary context. The book's fourth contributor, Tracy Metz, investigates the phenomenon by means of a number of reports and interviews. Among others, she follows a woman commuter who for ten years has been taking the slow train from Amsterdam to the Alexanderpolder and gives the Sudanese refugee Mohammed abd-Alhamid his say. He misses the emptiness of his own country: '*Too green. It's much too green here (…) It shouldn't be so full everywhere*'.

In *Dutch Town Planning Overseas* we learn what the Dutch did with foreign space in the past. To this end its author, Ron van Oers, used not only written texts but also a vast collection of accurate maps.

In the great days of overseas trade by the VOC and WIC (the Dutch East India and West Indies Companies) profit was the supreme good. Consequently, it was important that trading posts and harbour areas were laid out and/or expanded as functionally as possible. And so the strict organisation of the companies was reflected in overseas architecture and town planning.

A fine example of Dutch 'redevelopment' is Colombo. At the start of the seventeenth century it was the last base in Ceylon (Sri Lanka) still held by the Portuguese. In 1656 the VOC captured the town, thus bringing the cinnamon trade entirely into Dutch hands. For 140 years Colombo would be the VOC's Ceylon headquarters. But first the chaotic Portuguese settlement got a proper Dutch face-lift. The central area or Company Town was drastically reduced in size (easier to defend with fewer walls!). Outside that central citadel was built a second district with houses for merchants and workers. This Burgher Town was laid out with straight streets which divided the whole into equal-sized blocks. And in the best Dutch tradition it was all duly provided with a network of sluices, canals and bridges.

Theo Baart, *et al., Atlas of Change. Rearranging the Netherlands*. Rotterdam: NAI / IOP, 2000; 256 pp. ISBN 90-5662-163-7 / Ron van Oers, *Dutch Town Planning Overseas during VOC and WIC Rule (1600-1800)*. Zutphen: Walburg Pers, 2000; 240 pp. ISBN 90-5730-104-0.

In *Contemporary Architects of The Low Countries*, too, town and country planning plays a major role. In this book Hans Ibelings writes about the work of 10 Dutch architects and Francis Strauven looks at 6 Flemings. Each author has also written a general introduction; and these author show just how much Dutch and Flemish architects have constantly to consider how land and space can best be used in a very densely populated part of the world.

Among the Flemish architects discussed in *Contemporary Architects of The Low Countries* is bOb van Reeth. A hefty volume on him and his firm AWG is a recent addition to the 'Architecture monographs' series. It charts his work by means of sketches, plans and photos; and often in his own words, for he has always written extensively about his architectural vision.

'Architects' architecture is not interesting. Building is interesting' says Van Reeth. He himself combines spontaneity and a Sixties-style craving for freedom with technical skill and precision. A striking feature here is the heterogeneity of his designs, which not uncommonly quote from other work. This is his subtle way of resisting the loss of diversity in towns.

The Flemish Government also appointed Van Reeth Architect General for a period of five years from the end of 1998. This makes him the first architect to be given the role of adviser and quality controller for Flemish public architecture. Or, to quote the headline in a Flemish paper, *'Architect Van Reeth to make Flanders more beautiful.'*

Hans Ibelings and Francis Strauven, *Contemporary Architects of the Low Countries* (Tr. Gregory Ball). Rekkem: Stichting Ons Erfdeel VZW; 128 pp. ISBN 90-75862-44-X / Geert Bekaert, *BOb Van Reeth*. Ghent: Ludion, 2000; 192 pp. ISBN 90-55442-99-2.

Urban planning is one of the topics addressed in *Vacant City. Brussels' Mont des Arts Reconsidered*. But the book's main subject is the changing role and significance of museums. On the Kunstberg, in the heart of Brussels, a short stroll from the Central Station, a number of museums and cultural institutions are concentrated. The idea for the whole came from King Leopold II, who dreamed of a grandiose classical museum complex. His plans were not realised in his lifetime, but after a few provisional reorganisations of what was then still the Hofberg the Kunstberg acquired its present appearance with the completion of the Koninklijke Bibliotheek Albert I in 1969.

The Kunstberg is based on the idea that a concentration of cultural institutions can act as an engine of urban development. Now, however, the engine has stalled and the museum quarter has a moribund feel to it. Which is why this book presents the results of a wide-ranging enquiry into a further reorganisation of the Kunstberg. In addition, a number of architectural firms are given the opportunity to put forward their plans and visions for a New Kunstberg.

Vacant city : Brussels' Mont des Arts Reconsidered. Rotterdam : NAI, 2000; 375 pp. ISBN 90-5662-167-X.

In Northern France, some twenty kilometres from the Belgian border, is Lille – a city with a chaotic history which over a period of 1000 years has changed hands twelve times. At one time Lille lay on the southern border of the then Netherlands, but from the seventeenth century on it has been the bridgehead for French expansion to the north.

Despite all its sieges and occupations, the city always survived. Over the centuries its inhabitants became masters of compromise, countering difficult periods and major challenges with a shrewd entrepreneurial spirit. The advance of industrialisation and successive waves of immigration, among other factors, have meant that the urban landscape has been subject to constant modification.

The book *Lille* brings together a number of personal articles and a string of historical 'Episodes' to paint a good picture of this modest but flexible European metropolis. The story begins with the Count of Flanders building a castle on an island in the River Deule in the 11th century and continues to today's Lille of the Eurostar train. In his contribution Robin Thompson, town planner of the county of Kent which in a European context works closely with Nord-Pas-de-Calais, calls the city *'an inspirational example of city regeneration'*. What he finds remarkable is that the city has regenerated itself from the old centre out, while in England the process takes place in the docklands and warehouses on the urban fringe. The Euralille complex designed by the Dutch architect Rem Koolhaas, which together with Eurostar made Lille a gateway to the continent, gives Thompson *'a powerful sense of arrival in the heart of a city which has re-created itself'*. Though he promptly adds that Koolhaas' design is '*rather too geometrical for English tastes*'.

Eric Bussière (ed.), *Lille*. Antwerp: Mercatorfonds, 2000; 271 pp. ISBN 90-6153-455-0.

In 2002 Bruges will be European City of Culture, and the Flemish city is determined that its festival year will not be merely a one-off point on the cultural calendar. It is to be a pivotal year, one which will give the area's cultural life fresh stimuli for the future. In 2000 Bruges was placed on UNESCO's World Heritage list, but Brugge 2002 intends to represent more than the historical city alone. As the organisers put it: '*Brugge 2002 is a city refreshing its memory so that its imagination can take flight.*' Of course there are exhibitions about the city's centuries of history – among them *Jan van Eyck, Early Netherlandish Painting* and *Cloistered World, Open Books* – but there will be contemporary art as well, both within and outside the walls. In addition there are numerous video and photographic projects, concerts (ranging from old music to present-day experiments) and dance performances by, among others, Jan Fabre and Anne Teresa de Keersmaeker. And some new permanent features will enhance the city's image: a pavilion by Toyo Ito, a footbridge on the Coupure and the long-awaited concert hall by the Flemish husband-and-wife team of architects Robbrecht and Daem.

Tel. +32 70 22 33 02 / http://www.brugge2002.be

In 1919 the Dutch historian Pieter Geyl became the first Professor of Dutch Studies at University College London. Running to almost 600 pages, the paperback *History of the Dutch-Speaking Peoples* is a reprint of the two volumes he wrote on the history of the Low Countries in the 16th and 17th centuries, which first appeared in 1932 and was last reprinted in 1966. The book begins with the abdication of Charles V in 1555 and ends with the Peace of Münster in 1648. Geyl gives a masterly account of the Dutch revolt against Spain, the rise and establishment of the Republic and the trade, prosperity, colonial expansion and cultural achievements of the Golden Age.

More history can be found in *The Political History of Belgium*, in which the authors trace developments in the Belgian political landscape since 1830. A good deal of attention is devoted to recent developments such as the electoral success of the Far Right and the increasing influence of the media. And those who have finished the book and still want to know more can turn to *Language and Politics*, in which Els Witte and Harry van Velthoven provide a well-organised guide through the complex labyrinth of Belgian language legislation and the socio-political and cultural complications involved.

Pieter Geyl, *History of the Dutch-Speaking Peoples 1555-1648*. London: Phoenix Press, 2001; 589 pp. ISBN 1-84212-225-8 / Els Witte, *et al.*, *Political History of Belgium*. Antwerp / Brussels: Standaard Uitgeverij / VUB University Press, 2000. 297 pp. ISBN 90-5487-276-4 / Els Witte, *et. al.*, *Language and Politics. The Situation in Belgium in an Historical Perspective.* Leuven / Brussels: Balans / VUB University Press, 1999; 239 pp. ISBN 90-5487-252-7.

FILIP MATTHIJS
Translated by Tanis Guest.

of Dutch-Language Publications translated
into English (traced in 2000)

Aardewerk, A.
A. Aardewerk antiquair
B.V.: 30 years: a choice
from the collection /
A. Aardewerk. Den Haag:
A. Aardewerk antiquair
B.V., cop. 2000. 84 p.
Transl. of: A. Aardewerk
antiquair B.V.: 30 jaar: een
keuze uit de collectie.
2000

Aben, Rob.
The enclosed garden: his-
tory and development of the
hortus conclusus and its
reintroduction into the
present-day urban land-
scape / Rob Aben and
Saskia de Wit; [transl. from
the Dutch: John
Kirkpatrick]. Rotterdam:
010 Publishers, cop. 1999.
256 p.
Transl. of: De omsloten
tuin: geschiedenis en
ontwikkeling van de hortus
conclusus en de herintro-
ductie ervan in het hedendaagse stadslandschap.
1998.

Alberts, A.
The islands / by A. Alberts;
ed., with an introd. by E.M.
Beekman; transl. [from the
Dutch] by Hans Koning.
1st ed. [Singapore]:
Periplus, 1999.
Original English ed.:
Amherst: University of
Massachusetts Press, 1983.
Transl. of: De eilanden.
1972.

Aldo
Aldo van Eyck, works /
comp. by Vincent Ligtelijn;
[transl. from Dutch into
English: Gregory Ball ...
et al.]. Basel [etc.]:
Birkhäuser, [1999]. 311 p.
Transl. of: Aldo van Eyck,
werken. 1999.

Amsterdam
Amsterdam / photogr. and
compilation Herman
Scholten; [text: Frederik
Wiedijk; transl. from the

Dutch: All English
Translations]. Almere:
Bears Publishing, [1999].
127 p.
Transl. of: Amsterdam.
1999.

Anema, Marije
Paris, shopping & restau-
rant guide / [author Marije
Anema; directing ed. Joyce
Enthoven; transl. ed. Becky
Broer; transl. from the
Dutch; photogr. Joris den
Blaauwen].
Breda: Mo'Media, cop.
2000. 219 p.
Transl. of: Parijs, winkel- &
restaurantgids. 2000.

Anne
Anne Frank House:
a museum with a story /
[compilation and ed. Anne
Frank House, Menno
Metselaar ... et al.; final ed.
Hansje Galesloot; ill. Eric
van Rootselaar; transl. from
the Dutch Epicycles,
Lorraine T. Miller].
Amsterdam: Anne Frank
Stichting, cop. 1999. 268 p.
Transl. of: Anne Frank
Huis: een museum met een
verhaal. 1999.

Baarsen, Reinier
17th-century cabinets /
[author: Reinier Baarsen;
transl. from the Dutch: John
Rudge; photogr.: Depart-
ment of Photography,
Rijksmuseum ... et al.].
Zwolle: Waanders;
Amsterdam: Rijksmuseum,
cop. 2000. 64 p.
(Rijksmuseum dossiers)
Transl. of: 17de-eeuwse ka-
binetten. 2000.
(Rijksmuseum-dossiers).

Bakker, Nico T.
History as a theological
issue / Nico T. Bakker;
transl. [from the Dutch] by
Martin Kessler; [ed. by
David E. Orton]. Leider-
dorp: Deo Publishing, cop.
2000. XII, 301 p. (Theological seminar; 2)

Transl. of: Geschiedenis
in opspraak: over de legiti-
matie van het concept ge-
schiedenis: een theologi-
sche verhandeling. 1996.

Bakker, Piet de
The young stork's
Baedeker: travel guide / by
Piet de Bakker; [transl.
from the Dutch: Léonie van
Lieshout; typography/
cartography: Jessica
Zeelenberg]. Zuilichem:
The Catharijne Press, 1998.
40 p. + Lexicon (30 p.)
Special ed. Number of
copies printed: 15; I-XV.
In book case with spine
title: Travel guide.

Bakker, Piet de
The young stork's
Baedeker: travel guide / by
Piet de Bakker; [transl.
from the Dutch: Léonie van
Lieshout; typography/
cartography: Jessica
Zeelenberg]. Zuilichem:
The Catharijne Press, 1998.
40 p. Number of copies
printed: 175; 1 -175.

Bavinck, Herman
The certainty of faith /
H. Bavinck; [transl. from
the Dutch by Harry der
Nederlanden]. Republ.
Potchefstroom: Institute for
Reformational Studies,
1998. 46 p. (Scientific
contributions of the PU for
CHE. Ser. F1, IRS study
pamphlets; nr. 364) First
English ed.: St. Catherines,
Ontario: Paideia, 1980.
Transl. of: De zekerheid des
geloofs. 1901.

Belgian
Belgian fashion design / ed.
by Luc Derycke and Sandra
Van de Veire; [texts by Luc
Derycke ... et al.; transl. by
Gerrie van Noord ... et al.].
Gent: Ludion, cop. 1999.
320 p.
Transl. from the Dutch and
the French.

Benali, Abdelkader
Wedding by the sea /
Abdelkader Benali; transl.
[from the
Dutch] by Susan Massotty.
London: Phoenix, 2000.
186 p.

First English ed.: London:
Phoenix House, 1999.
Transl. of: Bruiloft aan zee.
1996.
Other ed.: New York:
Arcade, 2000.

Berg, Arnoud B. van den
Zeldzame vogels van
Nederland: met vermelding
van alle soorten = Rare
birds of the Netherlands:
with complete list of all
species / [text:] Arnoud
B. van den Berg &[carto-
graphy an diagr.: Cecilia
A.W. Bosman; [red.:
Gunter De Smet ... et al.].
Haarlem: GMB; Utrecht:
Stichting Uitgeverij van de
KNNV; Mountfield: Pica
Press, cop. 1999. 397 p.
(Avifauna van Nederland;
1) Text in English and
Dutch.

Beukman, Manja
The war bride's tale: an
odyssey of cultural shock:
a novel by Manja Beukman
/ transl. from the original
Dutch [and ill.] by Jan
W. Auer; with a pref. by
John Michielsen. 2nd ed.
St. Catharines, Ontario:
Marnie Heus Books, cop.
1999. 185 p.
First English ed. publ. as:
The war bride's tale, or, I
was the bride of a Canadi-
an. 1999.
Transl. of: Ik was de bruid
van een Canadees: roman.
1950.

Beyond
Beyond all bounds: women
about their active role in
conflict situations and as
a refugee / [ed.: Wendela de
Vries; final ed.: Winde
Evenhuis; transl. from the
Dutch: Diane Ricketts; photogr.: Petterik Wiggers].
Utrecht: Humanist Commit-
tee on Human Rights
(HOM); Oegstgeest:
Vrouwenberaad Ontwikke-
lingssamenwerking, cop.
1999. 64 p.
Transl. of: Ongekend ver-
weer. 1997.

Boer, Pim den
History as a profession: the
study of history in France,
1818-1914 / Pim den Boer;

transl. by Arnold J. Pomerans. Princeton, NJ: Princeton University Press, cop. 1998. XV, 470 p.
Transl. of: Geschiedenis als beroep. 1987.

Bolten, Jaap
Dutch banknote design 1814-2002: a compendium / Jaap Bolten; [transl. from the Dutch by Ruth Koenig]. 2nd rev. and updated ed. Amsterdam: De Nederlandsche Bank; Leiden: Primavera Press [distr.], 1999. VI, 398 p.
With a catalogue of all the banknotes issued by the Nederlandsche Bank, originally comp. by P.J. Soetens and for this ed. edited and brought up to date by J.J. Grolle and P. Koeze. First English ed. publ. as: Dutch banknote design: a compendium. 1988. Transl. of: Het Nederlandse bankbiljet 1814-2002: vormgeving en ontwikkeling. Amsterdam: De Nederlandsche Bank, 1999. First Dutch ed. publ. as: Het Nederlandse bankbiljet en zijn vormgeving. 1987.

Bont, Ad de
Mirad, a boy from Bosnia / Ad de Bont; notes: David Burton; [transl. from the Dutch Marian Buijs]. Harlow: Longman, 2000. 161 p. (New century readers) First Dutch ed.: London: Longman, 1995. (Longman literature). Transl. of: Mirad: een jongen uit Bosnië.

Bordewijk, F.
Character: a novel of father and son / F. Bordewijk; transl. [from the Dutch] by E.M. Prince. Chicago: Ivan R. Dee, 1999. 286 p. (Elephant paperbacks) First English ed.: London: Owen, 1966. (Series of translations published under the auspices of the Council of Europe; 25). Transl. of: Karakter: roman van zoon en vader. 1938.

Bouazza, Hafid
Abdullah's feet / Hafid Bouazza; transl. from the

Dutch by Ina Rilke. London: Review, 2000. 123 p.Transl. of: De voeten van Abdullah. 1996.

Breton de Nijs, E.
Faded portraits / E. Breton de Nijs; introd. by E.M. Beekman; transl. [from the Dutch] by Donald and Elsje Sturtevant. [Singapore]: Periplus, 1999.
First English ed.: Amherst: University of Massachusetts Press, 1982. (Library of the Indies).
Transl. of: Vergeelde portretten. 1954.

Bridging
Bridging the divide: 400 years The Netherlands-Japan / ed.: Leonard Blussé, Willem Remmelink, Ivo Smits; [transl. from the Dutch: Martha Chaiklin ... et al.; text ed. English ed.: Jane Milne-Colling ... et al.]. Leiden: Hotei Publishing; Hilversum: Teleac / NOT, cop. 2000. 288 p. Publ. on initiative of the Stichting 400 jaar Nederland-Japan. Transl. of: Bewogen betrekkingen: 400 jaar Nederland-Japan. 2000.

Broekaert, Elisabeth
Let's stick together / [foto's, photogr.:] Elisabeth Broekaert; [liefdesgedichten en tekst, love poems and text: Bart Moeyaert; vert., transl.: David Colmer ... et al.]. Antwerpen: VPMA, [2000]. [103] p.
Text in English and Dutch.

Bruggen, Jakob van
Jesus the son of God: the Gospel narratives and message / Jakob van Bruggen; transl. [from the Dutch] by Nancy Forest-Flier. Grand Rapids, MI: Baker Books, cop. 1999. 307 p.
Transl. of: Het evangelie van Gods Zoon: persoon en leer van Jezus volgens de vier evangeliën. 1996. (Commentaar op het Nieuwe Testament. Derde serie. Afdeling Evangeliën / geredigeerd door J. van Bruggen; dl. 5.)

Bruna, Dick
Boris and Barbara / Dick Bruna; [transl. from the Dutch].
Handforth, Cheshire: World International, 1998. [26] p. (Miffy's library) (World of reading) Transl. of: Boris en Barbara. 1989.

Bruna, Dick
The Christmas book; [transl. from the Dutch]. London: Egmont Children's, 1999. 32 p. (Picture Mammoth) Transl. of: Kerstmis. 1963.

Bruna, Dick
Miffy rides a bike / Dick Bruna; [adapt. from the Dutch by Patricia Crampton]. New York [etc.]: Kodansha International, 1999. [28] p. Transl. of: Nijntje op de fiets. 1982.

Bruna, Dick
Miffy's birthday / Dick Bruna; [adapt. from the Dutch]. London: Methuen Children's Books, 1998. Concertina-type book, [10] p. (Jigsaw story book) Transl. of: Het feest van Nijntje. 1970.

Bruna, Dick
Miffy's first sleepover / Dick Bruna; [adapt. from the Dutch by Patricia Crampton]. New York [etc.]: Kodansha International, 1999. [28] p. Transl. of: Nijntje gaat logeren. 1988

Bruna, Dick
Poppy Pig's birthday / Dick Bruna; [transl. from the Dutch]. Handforth, Cheshire: World International, 1998. [26] p. (Miffy's library) (World of reading) Transl. of: De verjaardag van Betje Big. 1986.

Bruna, Dick
Poppy Pig's garden / Dick Bruna; [transl. from the Dutch]. Handforth, Cheshire: World International, 1998. [26] p. (Miffy's library) (World of reading) First English ed.: London:

Methuen, 1978. (Bruna books).
Transl. of: De tuin van Betje Big. 1977.

Bruna, Dick
Snuffy's puppies / Dick Bruna; [transl. from the Dutch].
Handforth, Cheshire: World International, 1998. [26] p. Miffy's library) (World of reading) Transl. of: De puppies van Snuffie. 1986.

Burggraaf, Gijsbert Pieter Peter
Jonah, the first Israeli missionary, and the great revival among the heathen / Gijsbert Pieter Peter Burggraaf; [transl. from the Dutch by Iz. den Dekker]. Stolwijk: The Smoking Flax; Harskamp: Reformed World Evangelization Foundation [distr.], cop. 1999. 158 p. Transl. of: Jona, de joodse zendeling. Stolwijk: De rokende Vlaswiek, 1997.

Catz, Hans
The eye of the needle: a story from World War II / narrated by Hans Catz; transcribed by his children, Folkert and Petra Catz; transl. [from the Dutch] by Rose-Marjan Hartog. Huizen: H.S. Catz, 1999. 215 p. 23 cm.; Transl. of: Het oog van de naald. 2nd. rev. ed. 1999. First Dutch ed.: 1993.

Claus, Hugo
Desire / Hugo Claus; transl. [from the Dutch] by Stacey Knecht. [New ed.]. New York [etc.]: Penguin Books, 1998. 211 p.
First English ed.: New York: Viking, 1997. Transl. of: Het verlangen. 1978. (BB Literair).

Cock Blomhoff, Jan
The court journey to the shogun of Japan: from a private account by Jan Cock Blomhoff / ed. by F.R. Effert; introduced and annotated by Matthi Forrer; [transl. from the Dutch by Mark Poysden; photogr.

Hayashi Kazuma ...
et al.]. Leiden: Hotei, cop.
2000. 133 p.
Transl. of: De hofreis naar
de Shogun van Japan. 2000.

Conrad, Patrick
Limousine / Patrick
Conrad; transl. [from the
Dutch] by Stephen Smith.
London: Cape, 1999. 298 p.
Transl. of: Limousine: mis-
daadroman. 1994.

Cooper, Dutch
Josie / Sjoerd Kuyper;
[transl. from the Dutch by
Patricia Crampton].
London: Mammoth, 2000.
Transl. of: Josje. 1989.

Costa, Denise de
Anne Frank and Etty
Hillesum: inscribing spiritu-
ality and sexuality / Denise
de Costa; transl. [from the
Dutch] by Mischa F.C.
Hoyinck and Robert E.
Chesal. New Brunswick, NJ
[etc.]: Rutgers University
Press, 1998. XII, 275 p.
Transl. of: Anne Frank en
Etty Hillesum. 1996.

Couperus, Louis
Psyche / Louis Couperus;
transl. from the Dutch by
B.S. Berrington. Cupid and
psyche / Lucius Apuleius;
transl. [from the Latin] by
Robert Graves. London:
Pushkin Press, 1999. 237 p.;
17 cm. First English ed. of
"Psyche": London: Alston
Rivers. 1908.
Transl. of: Psyche. 1898,
and of: Cupido et Psyche,
from: Metamorphoses sive
De asino aureo. 1522.

Crone, Robert A.
A history of color: the evolution of theories of lights
and color / Robert A.
Crone. Dordrecht [etc.]:
Kluwer Academic Publish-
ers, cop. 1999. 282 p.
Transl. and adapt. of: Licht,
kleur, ruimte: de leer van
het zien in historisch perspectief. 1992.
Repr. from: Documenta
Ophthalmologica, vol. 96,
no. 1-3. 1999.

Daum, P.A.
Ups and downs of life in the

Indies / P.A. Daum; [ed.
with an introd. by E.M.
Beekman; transl. from the
Dutch by Elsje Qualm
Sturtevant ... et al.].
Repr. Singapore: Periplus,
1999.
First English ed.: Amherst:
University of Massachusetts
Press, 1987. (Library of the
Indies).
Transl. of: "Ups" en
"downs" in het Indische le-
ven. 1892.
First publ. as story in:
Bataviaasch nieuwsblad,
1890.

De Bode, Ann
Mummy, Mummy, where
are you? / Ann de Bode and
Rien Broere; [ill.: Ann de
Bode; English text by Su
Swallow, transl. from the
Dutch]. London: Evans
Brothers Ltd, cop. 1999.
33 p. (Helping hands)
Transl. of: Waar is mama!
1997. (Hartenboeken).

De Bode, Ann
Pay up or else! / Ann de
Bode and Rien Broere; [ill.:
Ann de Bode; English text
by Su Swallow, transl. from
the Dutch]. London: Evans
Brothers Ltd, cop. 1999.
33 p. (Helping hands)
Transl. of: Bang voor de
bende. 1997.
(Hartenboeken).

De Vos, Dirk
Rogier van der Weyden: the
complete works / Dirk De
Vos; [transl. from the Dutch
by Ted Alkins]. New York:
Harry N. Abrams, 1999.
445 p. Transl. of: Rogier
van der Weyden: het volle-
dige oeuvre. 1999.

Death
Death as a punishment: an
offence against life: reflections on fear, revenge and
reconciliation / [final ed.:
J.M.M. Naber ... et al.;
transl. from the Dutch by
M. Smits ... et al.].
Oegstgeest: Commissie
Justitia et Pax-Nederland,
1999. 83 p. (Commissie
Justitia et Pax-Nederland;
nr. 15) Transl. of: De dood
als straf: een vergrijp tegen
het leven. Oegstgeest:

Commissie Justitia et
Pax-Nederland, 1997.
(Commissie Justitia et
Pax-Nederland; nr. 11).

Dekkers, Dieuwertje
Jozef Israëls, 1824-1911 /
Dieuwertje Dekkers; with
contributions by Martha
Kloosterboer ... [et al.; ed.
Dieuwertje Dekkers ... et al.
text ed.: Mieke van der Wal
; transl. from the Dutch and
ed.: Alison Fisher ... et al.].
Zwolle: Waanders, cop.
1999. 399 p.
Publ. in coordination with
Groninger Museum, Jewish
Historical Museum and
Institute of Art and Archi-
tectural History.
Publ. to accompany the
exhibitions: "Jozef Israëls,
master of sentiments" in
Groninger Museum,
Groningen (December 19,
1999 - March 5, 2000), and:
"Jozef Israëls, son of the
ancient" in the Jewish
Historical Museum,
Amsterdam (December 17,
1999 - April 2, 2000) to
mark the 175th anniversary
of the painter.
Transl. of: Jozef Israëls,
1824-1911. 1999.

Dekkers, Midas
The way of all flesh: the
romance of ruins / Midas
Dekkers; transl. from the
Dutch by Sherry Marx-
Macdonald. New York:
Farrar, Straus and Giroux,
cop. 2000. 280 p.
Transl. of: De verganke1ijk-
heid. 1997.

Dekkers, Midas
The way of all flesh: a cele-
bration of decay / Midas
Dekkers; transl. from the
Dutch by Sherry Marx-
MacDonald. London:
Harvill, cop. 2000. 256 p.
Transl. of: De vergankelijk-
heid. 1997.

Dictionary
A dictionary of medieval
heroes: characters in medieval narrative traditions and
their afterlife in literature,
theatre and the visual arts /
ed. by Willem P. Gerritsen
and Anthony G. van Melle;
transl. from the Dutch by

Tanis Guest; [adapted for
English readers by Richard
Barber]. 1st ed. Woodbrid-
ge: Boydell Press, 1998.
VII, 336 p.
Transl. and adapt. of: Van
Aiol tot de Zwaanridder:
personages uit de middel-
eeuwse verhaalkunst en hun
voortleven in literatuur,
theater en beeldende kunst.
1993.

Dijk, Jan van
The network society: social
aspects of new media / Jan
van Dijk; transl. [from the
Dutch] by Leontine
Spoorenberg. London [etc.]:
Sage Publications, cop.
1999. 267 p.
Transl. of: De netwerkmaat-
schappij. 1991.

Dorrestein, Renate
A heart of stone / Renate
Dorrestein; transl. from the
Dutch by Hester Velmans.
London [etc.]: Doubleday,
2000. 260 p.
Transl. of: Een hart van
steen. 1998.

Dort, Evelien van
The chicken who wanted to
fly / a story by Evelien van
Dort; ill. by Veronica
Nahmias; [transl. from the
Dutch]. Edinburgh: Floris
Books, 1999. [16] p.
Transl. of: Kipje Hip. 1999.

Du Mortier, Bianca M.
Aristocratic attire / [author:
Bianca M. du Mortier;
transl. from the Dutch: Ruth
Koenig; photography:
Department of Photogra-
phy, Rijksmuseum:
Madeleine ter Kuile ... et
al.]. Zwolle: Waanders;
Amsterdam: Rijksmuseum,
cop. 2000. 56 p.
(Rijksmuseum-dossiers)
Transl. of: Regenten
gekleed. 2000.

Du Perron, E.
Country of origin / E. Du
Perron; [transl. from the
Dutch; introd. by Francis
Bulhof]. [Hong Kong]:
Periplus, 1999. XXIII, 438 p.
First English ed.: Amherst:
University of Massachusetts
Press, 1984. (Library of the
Indies).

Transl. of: Het land van herkomst. 1935.

Dutch
Dutch ambulances (1945-1975) / by K.J.J. Waldeck; [transl. from the Dutch: Anton L. Hermans]. Zaltbommel: European Library, cop. 2000. 75 p. (Back in time)
Transl. of: Ambulances in beeld (1945-1975): van ziekenwagen tot ambulance. 1998. (Toen boekje).

Eelman, Marianne C.
Waterfalls and rapids / [written by: Marianne C. Eelman; transl. from the Dutch by K.M.M. Hudson-Brazenall]. 1st ed. London [etc.]: New Holland, 1998. 78 p. (Natural phenomena)
Transl. of: Watervallen en stroomversnellingen. 1997. (Natuur in beweging).

Enquist, Anna
The injury / Anna Enquist; transl. [from the Dutch] by Jeannette K. Ringold. London: Toby, 2000.
Transl. of: De kwetsuur: tien verhalen. 1999.
Partially first publ. in: Hard gras, and other publications.

Enquist, Anna
The secret / Anna Enquist; transl. [from the Dutch] by Jeannette K. Ringold. London: Toby, 2000. 262 p.
Transl. of: Het geheim. 1997.

Euwe, Max
Judgement and planning in chess / Max Euwe; transl. [from the Dutch] by J. du Mont. [New ed.] / ed. by John Nunn ... [et al.]. London: Batsford, cop. 1998. 174 p. (Algebraic classics series) (A Batsford chess book) First English ed.: London: Bell, 1953.
Transl. of: Oordeel en plan. 1952.

Feiter, Wilfred de
What shall I do? That's what I'll do! / [Wilfred de Feiter; ill.: Edwin Hekman; transl. from the Dutch: Barbara Fasting]. Zeewolde: Imagine...IT, cop. 1999. 102 p.

Transl. of: Wat doe ik nu? Dat doe ik nu! 1997.

Fijnekam, Leen
Sails in the wind: windmill area Kinderdijk, picture of a global heritage / Leen Fijnekam [co-ordination]; Nico Knol [photo's]; Rita Vlot [text; transl. from the Dutch: Vertaalbureau De Drechtsteden]. 1st ed. Papendrecht: De Stroombaan, 1999. 95 p., 2 throw-out leafs
Transl. of: Wieken op de wind: molengebied Kinderdijk, beeld van een wereld-erfgoed. 1999.

Forming
Forming merciful brothers / [vignettes: Patrick Kapteijns ... et al.; transl. from the Dutch: Sylvia Dierks-Mallett ... et al.]. Tilburg: General Board Brothers CMM, 1998. 100 p. (Mercy and fraternity; 2)
Transl. of: De vorming tot barmhartige broeder. 1998. (Barmhartigheid en broederschap; 2).

Geus, Marius de
Ecological utopias: envisioning the sustainable society / Marius de Geus; [transl. from the Dutch: Paul Schwartzman]. Utrecht: International Books, cop. 1999. 318 p.
Transl. and adapt. of: Ecologische utopieën: ecotopia's en het milieudebat. 1996.

Gezelle, Guido
The evening and the rose: 30 poems / Guido Gezelle; transl. from the Flemish by Paul Claes & Christine D'haen. 5e, rev. ed. Antwerpen: Guido Gezelle-genootschap, 1999. 116 p. Text in English and Dutch. First English ed. publ. as: Poems. Deurle: Colibrant, 1971.

Gezelle, Guido
That limpid singer: a bilingual anthology of the poems of Guido Gezelle (1830-1899) / ed. by Paul Vincent. Hull: Association for Low Countries Studies

in Great Britain and Ireland (ALCS), 1999. 238 p. (Crossways; vol. 4) Text in English and Dutch. Contains an anthology of his poems.

Ginneken, Lily van
Public art '90-'98: Stroom Den Haag / [text Lily van Ginneken; transl. from the Dutch Pieter Heynen ... et al.; photogr. Rob Kollaard ... et al.]. Den Haag: Stroom, The Hague's Center for Visual Arts; Amsterdam: IDEA Books [distr.], cop. 1998. 112 p.
Transl. of: Kunst in de openbare ruimte '90-'98. 1998.

Goetinck, Marc
Brugge, Sint-Salvators-kathedraal / [Marc Goetinck; transl. from the Dutch: Genoveva Nitz; Photos: Andreas Lechtape]. 1. ed. Regensburg: Schnell und Steiner, 1999. 23 p. (Art guide; no. 2357)
Transl. of: Brugge, Sint-Salvatorskathedraal. 1998.

Goldschmidt, Tijs
Darwin's dreampond: drama in Lake Victoria / Tijs Goldschmidt; transl. [from the Dutch] by Sherry Marx-Macdonald. 1st ed. Cambridge, Mass. [etc.]: MIT Press, 1998. 274 p. First English ed.: 1996.
Transl. of: Darwins hofvijver: een drama in het Victoriameer. 1994.

Good
Good practice: handbook on mentoring of girls and women in or towards technical jobs / [text Ericka Kuyters ... et al.; English transl. from the Dutch: Charlotte Friedman ... et al.; ed. Gertje Joukes]. Amsterdam: VHTO; Delft: UETP-Randstad, 1998. 107 p.
Transl. of: Good practice: handboek over mentoring van meisjes en vrouwen in of op weg naar technische beroepen. 1998.

Goorbergh, Edith A. van den
Light shining through a veil: on Saint Clare's letters to Saint Agnes of Prague / by Edith A. Van den Goorbergh and Theodore H. Zweerman; transl. [from the Dutch] by Aline Looman-Graaskamp and Frances Teresa. Leuven: Peeters, 2000. XI, 339 p. (The fiery arrow collection; 2)
Transl. of: Clara van Assisi: licht vanuit de verborgenheid: over haar brieven aan Agnes van Praag. 1994. (Scripta Franciscana; 2).

Grunberg, Arnon
Silent extras / by Arnon Grunberg; transl. from the Dutch by Sam Garrett. London: Secker & Warburg, 2000. 363 p.
Transl. of: Figuranten. 1997.

Haas, Vincent de
Jesus, the merciful one, our brother / [Vincent de Haas]; transl. from the Dutch]. Tilburg: General Board Brothers CMM, 2000. 104 p. (Mercy and fraternity; 3)
Transl. of: Jezus, de barmhartige, onze broeder. 2000. (Barmhartigheid en broederschap; 3).

Hadewijch
Poetry of Hadewijch / introductory essay, transl. [from the Middle Dutch] and notes Marieke J.E.H.T. van Baest; with a forew. by Edward Schillebeeckx. Leuven: Peeters, 1998. 330 p. (Studies in spirituality. Supplement; 3)
Text in English and Middle Dutch.

Hamaker-Zondag, Karen
The yod book: including a complete discussion of unaspected planets / Karen Hamaker-Zondag; [transl. from the Dutch Wanda Boeke]. 1st. ed. York Beach, Maine: Samuel Weiser, 2000. 323 p.
Transl. of: De jodfiguur ("de vingerwijzing Gods") en ongeaspecteerde planeten. 1998.

Heteren, Marjan van
The poetry of reality: Dutch painters of the nineteenth century / Marjan van Heteren, Guido Jansen, Ronald de Leeuw; with contributions from Wouter Kloek ... [et al.; transl. from the Dutch Annabel Howland ... et al.; photogr. Department of Photography Rijksmuseum, Henk Bekker ... et al.]. Zwolle: Waanders; Amsterdam: Rijksmuseum, cop. 2000. 215 p.
Transl. of: Poëzie der werkelijkheid: Nederlandse schilders van de negentiende eeuw. 2000.

Heyer, C.J. den
Paul: a man of two worlds / C.J. den Heyer; [transl. from Dutch: John Bowden]. London: SCM, 2000. 312 p.
Transl. of: Paulus: man van twee werelden. 1998.

Holland
Holland: land of water, dykes and polders / [compilation: Herman Scholten; text: Frederik Wiedijk; transl. from the Dutch: All English Translations; photogr.: Herman Scholten ... et al.]. Almere: Bears Publishing, [2000]. 47 p.
Transl. of: Holland: land van water, dijken en polders. 2000.

Houtepen, Anton W.J.
God an open question: theological perspectives in an age of agnosticism / Anton Houtepen; [transl. from the Dutch]. London: SCM, 2000. 384 p.
Transl. of: God, een open vraag: theologische perspectieven in een cultuur van agnosme. 1997.

Hoving, Ab
The ships of Abel Tasman / by Ab Hoving and Cor Emke; with an introd. by Peter Sigmond; [transl. from the Dutch]. Hilversum: Verloren, 2000. 144 p. + CD-ROM + modeldrawings
Transl. of: De schepen van Abel Tasman. 2000.

Hullu, Ondine de
Bente learns how to dance in a wheelchair / Ondine de Hullu [text; transl. from the Dutch: Daan Fest; ill.: J.P. Priester]. Son en Breugel: Bock Reha, [1998]. 24 p.
Transl. of: Bente leert rolstoeldansen. 2nd ed. 1998. First Dutch ed.: 1997.

Hulsenbek, Caroline
Amsterdam, shopping & restaurant guide / [author Caroline Hulsenbek; directing ed. Joyce Enthoven; transl. ed. Karin Beurskens; transl. from the Dutch; photogr. Patrick Wissink]. Breda: Mo'Media, cop. 2000. 221 p.
Transl. of: Amsterdam, winkel- & restaurantgids. 2000.

Huygen, Wil
Gnome life / text by Wil Huygen; ill. by Rien Poortvliet; [transl. from the Dutch]. New York [etc.]: Harry N. Abrams, 1999. 32 p.
Transl. of: Leven en werken van de kabouter. 1976.

Huyser, Anneke
Singing bowls exercises for personal harmony / Anneke Huyser; [transl. from the Dutch; photogr.: Benelux Press, Annelies Schoth ... et al.]. Havelte: Binkey Kok, 1999. 113 p.
Transl. by Tony Langham ... [et al.].
Transl. of: Klankschalen en hun therapeutische toepassingen. 1999.

Ibelings, Hans
20th century urban design in the Netherlands / Hans Ibelings; [transl. from the Dutch Robyn de Jong-Dalziel; ed.: Caroline Gautier]. Rotterdam: NAi Publishers, cop. 1999. 175 p.
Transl. of: Nederlandse stedenbouw van de 20ste eeuw. 1999.

Ibelings, Hans
Contemporary architects of the Low Countries / Hans Ibelings and Francis Strauven; red. Jozef Deleu ... [et al.; transl. from the Dutch]. Rekkem: Stichting Ons Erfdeel, cop. 2000. 128 p.
Transl. of: Hedendaagse architecten in Nederland en Vlaanderen. 2000.

Janmaat, R.
The emotional touch: more effective environmental education about the Wadden Area / [Text: Rob Janmaat ... et al.; transl. from the Dutch by Liesbeth Zuidgeest]. Harlingen: Waddenvereniging, 1999. 67 p.
Transl. of: Mensen willen geraakt worden: meer effect met natuureducatie op de Wadden. 1999.

Japin, Arthur
The two hearts of Kwasi Boachi: a novel / Arthur Japin; transl. [from the Dutch] by Ina Rilke. London: Chatto & Windus, 2000. 342 p.
Transl. of: De zwarte met het witte hart. 1997.

Jongh, E. de
Questions of meaning: theme and motif in Dutch seventeenth-century painting / E. de Jongh; transl. [from the Dutch] and ed. by Michael Hoyle. Leiden: Primavera Pers, 2000. 296 p.
Transl. of: Kwesties van betekenis. 1995.

Kemenade, Willem van
China, Hong Kong, Taiwan, inc. / Willem van Kemenade; transl. from the Dutch by Diane Webb. New York: Vintage, 1998. 460 p.
First English ed.: New York: Knopf, 1997.
Transl. and rev. ed. of: China BV: Hongkong Taiwan: superstaat op zoek naar een nieuw systeem. 1996.

Keulartz, Jozef
Struggle for nature: a critique of radical ecology / Jozef Keulartz; transl. [from the Dutch] by Rob Kuitenbrouwer. London [etc.]: Routledge, 1998. VII, 198 p. (Environmental philosophies)
Transl. of: Strijd om de natuur: kritiek van de radicale ecologie. 1995.

Kolk, Hanco
The 7 Provinces / Hanco Kolk, Peter de Wit; [colors: Bea Loomans ... et al.; transl. from the Dutch: Ineke van Osch]. 's-Hertogenbosch: Silvester, cop. 2000. 48 p. (Bryant the Brigand; 1)
Transl. of: De 7 Provincien. 2000. (Gilles de Geus; 8).

Konijn, Elly A.
Acting emotions: shaping emotions on stage / Elly A. Konijn; transl. [from the Dutch] by Barbara Leach with David Chambers. Amsterdam: Amsterdam University Press, cop. 2000. 209 p.
Transl. of: Acteren en emoties: vorm geven aan emoties op het toneel / Elly Konijn, Astrid Westerbeek. 1997.

Kouwenhoven, Arlette
Siebold and Japan: his life and work / Arlette Kouwenhoven, Matthi Forrer; [transl. from the Dutch Mark Poysden; photogr. Ben Grishaaver ... et al.]. Leiden: Hotei, cop. 2000. 111 p. Publ. on the occasion of the opening of the museum: "Sieboldhuis", April 4, 2000 at Leiden.
Transl. of: Siebold en Japan. 2000.

Krabbé, Tim
The cave / Tim Krabbé; transl. from the Dutch by Sam Garrett. 1st ed. New York: Farrar, Straus and Giroux, 2000. 152 p.
Transl. of: De grot. 1997.

Kruijff, A.F.
Future of predictive medicine: a first step towards common policy / A.F. Kruijff, R.F. Schreuder; transl. by Jan Arriens, Julian Ross of an original Dutch adapt. Zoetermeer: Foundation for Future Health Scenario's (STG) / Stichting Toekomstscenario's Gezondheidszorg;

Maarssen: Elsevier gezond-heidszorg [distr.], 2000. 93 p.
Transl. and adapt. of: Toekomstscenario's voor-spellende geneeskunde. 1998, and: Chronisch zie-ken en scenario's genetica. 1999.

Kuitert, H.M.
Jesus: the legacy of Christianity / H.M. Kuitert; [transl. from the Dutch: John Bowden]. London: SCM, 1999. XIV, 285 p.
Transl. of: Jezus: nalaten-schap van het christendom: schets voor een christolo-gie. 1998.

Kusters, John Th.
The internal signposting of receiving, warehousing and shipping departments / aut-hor: John Th. Kusters; final ed.: Dagmar Mulder. 2nd ed. Nijmegen: JEKA, 1999. 39 p.
First English ed.: 1996.
Transl. of: De interne bewegwijzering van goede-renontvangst-, magazijn- en expeditie-afdelingen. 1991.

La Rivière, Leen
The way: bible studies about discipleship for continentals/young conti-nentals and any other youth choir/gospel group involved in music ministry / first edition by Leen La Rivière; additions from Marcel Koning ... [et al.]; ed.: Leen La Rivière; [transl. from the Dutch by Emilie Cuddihy-Versteeg]. Rotterdam: Continental Sound, 1999. 100 p.
Publ. on the occasion of Continental Sound's 30th anniversary, Disciple's 25th anniversary and Euro-Con-tinentals' 15th anniversary.
Transl. of: Op weg: bijbel-studies over discipelschap. 1999.

Lamers, Josee
The added value of Europe-an works councils / Josee Lamers; [transl. from the Dutch Accuwrite]. Haarlem: AWVN, 1998. 207 p.
Study by order of the

AWVN executed by the Hugo Sinzheimer Instituut.
Transl. of: Toegevoegde waarde van Europese ondernemingsraden. 1998.
Leeuwen, Marco H.D. van
The logic of charity: Amsterdam, 1800-1850 / Marco H.D. van Leeuwen; transl. [from the Dutch] by Arnold J. Pomerans. Basingstoke [etc.]: Macmillan; New York: St. Martin's Press, 2000. XV, 242 p., [8] p. pl.
Transl. of: Bijstand in Amsterdam, ca. 1800-1850: armenzorg als beheersings- en overlevingsstrategie. 1990. (ICS-reeks; 2).

Lieshout, Robert H.
The struggle for the organi-zation of Europe: the foundations of the Europe-an Union / Robert H. Lieshout; [transl. from the Dutch]. Cheltenham [etc.]: Elgar, cop. 1999. X, 202 p.
Transl. of: De organisatie van de West-Europese samenwerking. 1997.

Linden, Nico ter
The story goes... / Nico ter Linden. London: SCM Press, 2000. 304 p.
3. The stories of Judges and Kings / transl. from the Dutch by John Bowden.
Transl. of: Het verhaal gaat... . 3: De verhalen van Richters en Koningen. 1999.

Loo, Tessa de
The twins / Tessa de Loo; transl. from the Dutch by Ruth Levitt. London: Arca-dia Books, 2000. 392 p.
Transl. of: De tweeling. 1993.
Other ed.: New York: Soho Press, 2000.

Luijten, Ger
Rembrandt's etchings / [author: Ger Luijten; transl. from the Dutch: Beverley Jackson; photogr.: Department of Photography, Rijksmuseum: Madeleine ter Kuile ... et al.]. Zwolle: Waanders; Amsterdam: Rijksmuseum, cop. 2000. 48 p. (Rijksmuseum-dossiers)

Transl. of: Rembrandts et-sen. 2000. (Rijksmuseum-dossiers).

Mak, Geert
Amsterdam: a brief life of the city / Geert Mak; transl. from the Dutch by Philipp Blom. London: Harvill Press, 1999. XIII, 338 p.
Transl. of: Een kleine ge-schiedenis van Amsterdam. 1994.
Other ed.: Cambridge, MA: Harvard University Press, 2000.

Mak, Geert
Jorwerd: the death of the village in late twentieth-century Europe / Geert Mak; transl. from the Dutch by Ann Kelland. London: Harvill Press, 2000. X, 274 p.
Transl. of: Hoe God ver-dween uit Jorwerd. 1996.

Marie-Anne
The Tommies are coming!: diary of an Oosterbeek girl september 1944 / [Marie-Anne; comp. C. van Roekel]; transl. [from the Dutch] by: A.G. Meeuwsen. Oosterbeek: Society of Friends of the Airborne Museum, cop. 1998. 40 p.
Transl. of: De Tommies komen. 1987.

Marugg, Tip
The roar of morning / Tip Marugg; [transl. from the Dutch]. London: Faber, 2000. 150 p.
Transl. of: De morgen loeit weer aan. 1988. (BBLiterair).

Medieval
Medieval Dutch drama: four secular plays and four farces from the Van Hulthem manuscript / transl. [from the Medieval Dutch] with an introd. by Johanna C. Prins. Asheville, NC: Pegasus Press, cop. 1999.
(Early European drama translation series; 3)

Meer, Jaap J.M. van der
Glaciers and icecaps / [writ-ten by: Jaap J.M. van der Meer; transl. from the

Dutch by: K.M.M. Hudson-Brazenall].
1st ed. London [etc.]: New Holland, 1998. 79 p.
(Natural phenomena)
Transl. of: Gletsjers en ijs-kappen. 1997. (Natuur in beweging).

Meijer, Peter J.
Volcanoes and thermal springs / [written by Peter J. Meijer; transl. from the Dutch by K.M.M. Hudson-Brazenall].
1st ed. London [etc.]: New Holland, 1998. 79 p.
(Natural phenomena)
Transl. of: Vulkanen en thermische bronnen. 1997. (Natuur in beweging).

Meyer, Han
City and port: urban plan-ning as a cultural venture in London, Barcelona, New York, and Rotterdam: chan-ging relations between public urban space and large-scale infrastructure / Han Meyer; [final ed.: Henk Pel; transl. from the Dutch: D'Laine Camp ... et al.].
Utrecht: International Books, cop. 1999. 424 p.
Transl. of: De stad en de haven. 1996.

Miesen, Bère M. L.
Dementia in close-up / Bère M.L.Miesen; [transl. from the Dutch]. London: Routledge, 1998. 208 p.
Transl. of: Dementie dich-terbij: een handreiking aan verzorgenden. 1993. (Cahiers ouderdom en levensloop).

Min, Willemien
Peter's patchwork dream / Willemien Min; [transl. from the Dutch]. Bath: Barefoot Beginners, 1998. [32] p.
Transl. of: De lappendeken. 1991.

Möring, Marcel
In Babylon / Marcel Möring; transl. from the Dutch by Stacey Knecht.
1st ed. New York: Morrow, [2000]. 417 p.
First English ed.: London: Flamingo, 1999.

Transl. of: In Babylon.
1997.

Moeyaert, Bart
Hornet's nest / Bart
Moeyaert; transl. [from the
Dutch] by David Colmer.
Asheville, NC: Front Street,
2000. 127 p.
Transl. of: Wespennest.
Amsterdam: Querido, 1997.
First Dutch ed. publ. as:
Suzanne Dantine. 1989.
(Top)

Moor, Margriet de
The virtuoso / Margriet de
Moor; transl. from the
Dutch by Ina Rilke.
Woodstock, NY: Overlook
Press, 2000.
First English ed.: London,
1996.
Transl. of: De virtuoos.
1993.

Museum
Museum Mesdag: guide /
[ed. Annemiek Overbeek ...
et al.; text Fred Leeman ...
et al.; transl. from the Dutch
Diane Webb; photogr. Thijs
Quispel ... et al.].
Amsterdam: Van Gogh
Museum; Zwolle: Waanders
[distr.], cop. 1999. 95 p.
Transl. of: Museum
Mesdag: gids. 1999.

Netherlandish
Netherlandish art in the
Rijksmuseum / Henk van
Os. Zwolle: Waanders;
Amsterdam: Rijksmuseum,
cop. 2000. 279 p.
Vol. 1: 1400 - 1600.
Transl. of: Nederlandse
kunst in het Rijksmuseum.
Dl. 1: 1400-1600.
2000.

Nieuwenhuys, Rob
Mirror of the Indies: a history of Dutch colonial literature / Rob Nieuwenhuys;
transl. [from the Dutch]
by Frans van Rosevelt; ed.
by E.M. Beekman. Repr.
[Singapore]: Periplus, 1999.
First English ed.: Amherst:
University of Massachusetts
Press, 1982.
Transl. of: Oost-Indische
spiegel. 1972.

Nooteboom, Cees
Rituals / Cees Nooteboom;

transl. [from the Dutch] by
Adrienne Dixon. London:
Harvill, 2000. 153 p.
First English ed.: Baton
Rouge: Louisiana State
University Press, 1983.
Transl. of: Rituelen. 1980.

Offringa, Hans
The house: a moving story /
Hans Offringa; [transl. from
the Dutch: Janet Knol; ed.:
William Ross ... et al.;
photogr.: Etienne van
Leeuwen]. [Groningen]:
Gopher Publishers, 1999.
427 p.
Transl. of: Het huis. 1997.

Palmen, Connie
The friendship / Connie
Palmen; transl. from the
Dutch by Ina Rilke.London:
Harvill, 2000. 261 p.
Transl. of: De vriendschap.
1995.

Peeters, Judith E.M.
Changing coastlines / [writ-
ten by: Judith E.M. Peeters;
transl. from the Dutch by
K.M.M. Hudson-Braze-
nall]. 1st ed London [etc.]:
New Holland, 1998. 79 p.
(Natural phenomena)
Transl. of: Kustvormen:
scheidslijn tussen land en
water.
1997. (Natuur in beweging).

Peeters, T.
Autism: medical and educa-
tional aspects / T. Peeters,
C. Gillberg; [transl. from
the Dutch]. 2nd ed. London:
Whurr Publishers, 1999.
VIII, 126 p.
First English ed.: London:
Jansen, 1995.
Transl. of: Autisme,
medisch en educatief. 1995.

Peeters, T.
Autism: from theoretical
understanding to educa-
tional intervention /
T. Peeters; [transl. from the
Dutch].
Repr. London: Whurr
Publishers, 1999. 188 p.
First English ed.: 1997.
Transl. of: Autisme: van
begrijpen tot begeleiden.
1994.

Peil, Jan
Adam Smith and economic

science: a methodological
reinterpretation / Jan Peil.
Cheltenham [etc.]: Elgar,
1999. XII, 206 p.
Transl. and adapt. of: Adam
Smith en de economische
wetenschap: een methodo-
logische herinterpretatie.
1995.
Thesis Katholieke Universiteit Brabant, Tilburg.

Petri, Catharose de (pseud.
of H. Stok-Huyser)
The liberating path of the
Rosycross: the fourth
Aquarius Renewal Confer-
ence, Basle 1966 / by
Catharose de Petri and
J. van Rijckenborgh; [transl.
from the Dutch]. Haarlem:
Rozekruis Pers, 2000. 103 p.
(The apocalypse of the new
era; 4) Transl. of: Het vrij-
makende pad van het
Rozenkruis. 2nd rev. ed.,
1996. (De apocalyps van de
nieuwe tijd; 4).
First Dutch ed. publ. as: De
apocalyps van de nieuwe
tijd, 1966. 1967. (De apocalyps van de nieuwe tijd; 4).

Petri, Catharose de (pseud.
of H. Stok-Huyser)
The mighty signs of God's
counsel: the third Aquarius
Renewal Conference, Bad
Münster 1965 / by Catharose de Petri and J. van
Rijckenborgh; [transl. from
the Dutch].
Haarlem: Rozekruis Pers,
2000. 43 p. (The apocalypse
of the new era; 3)
Transl. of: De machtige
tekenen van Gods raad. 2nd
rev. ed., 1994. (De apocalyps van de nieuwe tijd; 3).
First Dutch ed. publ. as: De
apocalyps van de nieuwe
tijd, 1965. 1966. (De apocalyps van de nieuwe tijd; 3).

Petri, Catharose de (pseud.
of H. Stok-Huyser)
The new caduceus: the fifth
Aquarius Renewal Confer-
ence, Toulouse 1967 / by
Catharose de Petri and
J. van Rijckenborgh;
[transl. from the Dutch].
Haarlem: Rozekruis Pers,
1999. 55 p. (The apocalypse
of the new era; 5)
Transl. of: De nieuwe mer-
curiusstaf. 2nd. rev. ed.,
1997.

(De apocalyps van de nieuwe tijd; 5).
First Dutch ed. publ. as: De
apocalyps van de nieuwe
tijd, 1967. 1968.
(De apocalyps van de
nieuwe tijd; 5).

Petri, Catharose de (pseud.
of H. Stok-Huyser)
The world brotherhood of
the Rosycross: the second
Aquarius Renewal Confer-
ence, Cawl 1964 / by
Catharose de Petri and
J. van Rijckenborgh;
[transl. from the Dutch].
Haarlem: Rozekruis Pers,
2000. 47 p. (The apocalypse
of thenew era; 2)
Transl. of: De wereldbroe-
derschap van het Rozen-
kruis. 2nd rev. ed. 1992.
(De apocalyps van de
nieuwe tijd; 2).
First English ed. publ. as:
De apocalyps van de
nieuwe tijd,
1964. 1965. (De apocalyps
van de nieuwe tijd; 2).

Pictures
Pictures from the Tropics:
paintings by western artists
during the Dutch colonial
period in Indonesia /
Marie-Odette Scalliet ... [et
al.; English transl. from
the Dutch: Karin Beks].
Wijk en Aalburg: Pictures
Publishers; Amsterdam:
Royal Tropical Institute,
cop. 1999. 160 p.
Transl. of: Indië omlijst:
vier eeuwen schilderkunst
in Nederlands-Indië. 1998.

Pierik, R.L.M.
In vitro culture of higher
plants / by R.L.M. Pierik.
Dordrecht [etc.]: Kluwer
Academic Publishers,
[2000]. V, 348 p.
Repr. of the 4th ed.
Transl. and adapt. of:
Plantenteelt in kweekbui-
zen. 1985.
First Dutch ed.: 1975.

Polak, Marinus
South Gaulish terra sigillata
with potters' stamps from
Vechten / Marinus Polak;
[transl. from the Dutch:
K.H.M. van den Berg].
Nijmegen: Katholieke
Universiteit Nijmegen,

Afdeling Provinciaal-Romeinse Archeologie, 2000. 440 p., 42 p. pl. (Rei Cretariae Romanae fautorum acta. Supplementa; 9) Transl. of: De gestempelde Zuidgallische terra sigillata uit Vechten. 1995. Thesis Katholieke Universiteit Nijmegen.

Port, Mattijs van de
Gypsies, wars and other instances of the wild: civilisation and its discontents in a Serbian town / Mattijs van de Port. Amsterdam: Amsterdam University Press, cop. 1998. IX, 266 p.
Transl. and adapt. of: Het einde van de wereld: beschaving, redeloosheid en zigeunercafés in Servië, 1994. Thesis Utrecht.

Preparation
The preparation and use of compost / by Madeleine Inckel ... [et al.]; English transl. [from the Dutch] by E.W.M. Verheij. 5th rev. ed. Wageningen: Agromisa, 1999. 66 p. (Agrodok; 8) First English ed.: 1981. Transl. of: Maken en gebruik van compost.

Pride
Pride and joy: children's portraits in the Netherlands 1500-1700 / ed. by Jan Baptist Bedaux & Rudi Ekkart; [transl. from the Dutch: Ted Alkins]. Gent; Amsterdam: Ludion, cop. 2000. 319 p.
Publ. on the occasion of the exhibition: "Kinderen op hun mooist" in the Frans Halsmuseum, Haarlem (October 7, 2000 - December 31, 2000), and in the Koninklijk Museum voor Schone Kunsten, Antwerpen (January 21, 2001 - April 22, 2001).
Transl. of: Kinderen op hun mooist. 2000.

Prins, Piet (pseud. van: Pieter Jongeling)
When the morning came / Piet Prins; [transl. from the Dutch by Gertrude de Boer; ill. by Jaap Kramer]. Pella, Iowa: Inheritance

publ, 1998. 158 p.: ill.; 23 cm. (Struggle for freedom series; 1) First English ed.: Neerlandia, Alta: Inheritance Publ. 1989. (Struggle for freedom series; 1).
Transl. of: Toen de morgen kwam. 1980.
First publ. as youth story in: Nederlands Dagblad.

Ree, Hans
The human comedy of chess: a grandmaster's chronicles / Hans Ree; forew. by Jan Timman; [transl. from the Dutch by Willem Tissot ... et al.]. Milford, CT: Russell Enterprises, cop. 1999. VI, 334 p.
Transl. and adapt. of Schitterend schaak. 1967.

Rembrandt
Rembrandt under the scalpel: the anatomy lesson of Dr Nicolaes Tulp dissected / Norbert Middelkoop ... [et al.; transl. from the Dutch Harry Lake ... et al.; ed. Marlies Enklaar ... et al.; photogr. Ed Brandon ... et al.]. The Hague: Mauritshuis; Amsterdam: Six Art Promotion, cop. 1998. 92 p.
Publ. on the occasion of the exhibition: "Rembrandt onder het mes", in the Mauritshuis, The Hague (October 3, 1998 - January 10, 1999).
Transl. of: Rembrandt onder het mes: de anatomische les van dr Nicolaes Tulp ontleed. 1998.

Rembrandt's
Rembrandt's treasures / Bob van den Boogert (ed.) ... [et al.; transl. from the Dutch: Lynne Richard ... et al.]. Zwolle: Waanders, cop. 1999. 159 p.
Publ. in cooperation with Museum het Rembrandthuis on the occasion of the exhibition: "Rembrandt's schatkamer", in the Museum Het Rembrandthuis, Amsterdam (September 25, 1999 - January 9, 2000).
Transl. of: Rembrandt's schatkamer. 1999.

Renne
Animal males and females /

Renne; [transl. from the Dutch]. North American ed. Milwaukee, WI: Gareth Stevens Publ., 2000. (Animals up close) Transl. of: Papa is anders dan mama. 1997. (De natuur op schoot).

Renne
Animal trails and tracks / Renne; [transl. from the Dutch]. North American ed. Milwaukee, WI: Gareth Stevens Publ., 2000. (Animals up close) Transl. of: Ik laat sporen achter. 1999. (De natuur op schoot).

Renne
Animals and their eggs / Renne; [transl. from the Dutch]. North American ed. Milwaukee, WI: Gareth Stevens Publ., 2000. (Animals up close) Transl. of: Ik kom uit een ei. 1996. (De natuur op schoot).

Renne
Animals that live in water / Renne; [transl. from the Dutch]. North American ed. Milwaukee, WI: Gareth Stevens Publ., 2000. (Animals up close) Transl. of: Ik leef in het water. 2000. (De natuur op schoot).

Renne
Why animals have tails / Renne; [transl. from the Dutch]. North American ed. Milwaukee, WI: Gareth Stevens Publ., 2000. (Animals up close) Transl. of: Ik heb een staart. 1997. (De natuur op schoot).

Renne
Young animals and their parents / Renne; [transl. from the Dutch]. North American ed. Milwaukee, WI: Gareth Stevens Publ., 2000. (Animals up close) Transl. of: Ik lijk op mijn mama. 1996. (De natuur op schoot).

Representing
Representing the Japanese occupation of Indonesia:

personal testimonies and public images in Indonesia, Japan, and The Netherlands / ed. by Remco Raben; [authors Michael Baskett ... et al.; transl. from the Dutch: Mischa F.C. Hoyinck ... et al.]. Zwolle: Waanders; Amsterdam: Netherlands Institute for War Documentation, cop. 1999. 239 p.
Publ. on the occasion of the exhibition: "Nederlanders-Japanners-Indonesiërs: de Japanse bezetting van Nederlands-Indië herinnerd", in the Rijksmuseum, Amsterdam (August 7, 1999 - October 24, 1999).
Transl. of: Beelden van de Japanse bezetting van Indonesië. 1999.

Ritsema, Geert
No rose without a thorn: export flowers from India / Geert Ritsema; transl. from the Dutch by Elize Greidanus. Utrecht: The India Committee of the Netherlands, 1998. 38 p.
Transl. of: Geen roos zonder doornen: exportbloemen uit India. 1997.

Röell, D.R.
The world of instinct: Niko Tinbergen and the rise of ethology in the Netherlands (1920-1950) / D.R. Röell; transl. [from the Dutch]: Margaret Kofod (with the exception of chapter two and three). Assen: Van Gorcum, 2000. XIV, 242 p. (Animals in philosophy and science) Transl. of: De wereld van instinct: Niko Tinbergen en het ontstaan van de ethologie in Nederland (1920-1950). 1996.
(Nieuwe Nederlandse bijdragen tot de geschiedenis der geneeskunde en der natuurwetenschappen; nr. 52).

Roeloffs, Pieter
Traces: memoirs of an Indonesian wartime boyhood / by Pieter Roeloffs; (ed. by Donna K. Woodward); [transl. from the Dutch].
Medan: [P. Roeloffs], 1998. 129 p.

315

Transl. of: Memoires van Pieter Roeloffs 1939-1946. 1998.

Ruebsamen, Helga
The song and the truth / by Helga Ruebsamen; transl. from the Dutch by Paul Vincent. 1st ed. New York: Knopf, 2000.
Transl. of: Het lied en de waarheid. 1997.

Runia, Epco
The glory of the Golden Age: Dutch art of the 17th century: drawings and prints / [author: Epco Runia; ed.: Ger Luijten ... et al.; transl. from the Dutch: Barbara Fasting ... et al.; photogr.: Department of the Photography Rijksmuseum ... et al.]. Zwolle: Waanders; Amsterdam: Rijksmuseum, cop. 2000. 156 p.
Publ. on the occasion of the exhibition: "De glorie van de Gouden Eeuw" in the Rijksmuseum, Amsterdam (April 15, 2000 - July 16, 2000).
Transl. of: De glorie van de Gouden Eeuw: Nederlandse kunst uit de 17e eeuw: tekeningen en prenten. 2000.

Schendel, Arthur van
John Company / Arthur van Schendel; transl. and with an introd. by Frans van Rosevelt; ed. with notes by E.M. Beekman.
[Singapore]: Periplus, 1999. First English ed.: Amherst: University of Massachusetts Press, 1983. (Library of the Indies).
Transl. of: Jan Compagnie. 1932.

Schogt, Philibert
The wild numbers / Philibert Schogt; [transl. from the Dutch]. New York: Four Walls Eight Windows, 2000. 159 p.
Transl. of: De wilde getallen. 1998.

Schoots, Hans
Living dangerously: a biography of Joris Ivens / Hans Schoots; [transl. from the Dutch: David Colmer]. Amsterdam: Amsterdam University Press, cop. 2000. 443 p.

Transl. and adapt. of: Gevaarlijk leven: een biografie van Joris Ivens. 1995.

Schreuder, D.A.
Road lighting for safety / D.A. Schreuder; transl. by Adriana Morris; ill. J. Kosterman. London: Thomas Telford, 1998. XIII, 294 p.
Transl. of: Openbare verlichting voor verkeer en veiligheid. 1996.

Schubert, Ingrid
Bear's eggs / Ingrid and Dieter Schubert; [transl. from the Dutch]. Asheville, NC: Front Street, Lemniscaat, cop. 1999. [28] p.
Transl. of: Dat komt er nou van... 1999.

Schubert, Ingrid
There's a hole in my bucket / Ingrid and Dieter Schubert; [transl. from the Dutch]. London: Andersen, 2000. 32 p. (An Andersen paperback)
First English ed.: 1998.
Transl. of: Een gat in mijn emmer. 1998.

Simonis, A.J.
Our father: reflections on the Lord's Prayer / A.J. cardinal Simonis; transl. [from the Dutch] by Barbara Schultz-Verdon. Grand Rapids, Michigan [etc.]: Eerdmans, cop. 1999. 125 p.
Transl. of: Op de adem van het leven: gedachten over het Onze Vader. 1997.

Slotboom, Carl
The train: a play / Carl Slotboom; transl. [from the Dutch] by Louis I. Leviticus. London: Samuel French, cop. 1999. 21 p.
Transl. of: De trein. 1995.

Stadium
The stadium: the architecture of mass sport / ed. by Michelle Provoost; [transl. from the Dutch: Robyn de Jong-Dalziel ... et al.; photogr.: ABC Press ... et al.]. Rotterdam: NAi Publishers, cop. 2000. 183 p.
Publ. on the occasion of the exhibition 'Het stadion, de

architectuur van massasport' in the Nederlands Architectuurinstituut, Rotterdam (June 8, 2000 - September 23, 2000).
Transl. of: Het stadion: de architectuur van massasport. 2000.

Stiekema, Han M.
Flow system therapy: with personal health plan / Han M. Stiekema; [ill.: E. Bonarius]. 4th rev. ed. Amsterdam: PIP Press, 1999. 209 p.
Transl. of: Stroomsysteem en optimale vitaliteit. 1994.

Stoeltie, Barbara
Dutch style: Jan des Bouvrie / [text:] Barbara; and [photogr.:] René Stoeltie; [ed.-in-chief: Irma Goedemondt; ed.: Seegers & Deana; transl. from the Dutch: Susan Hunt]. Hoofddorp: VNU Tijdschriften, 1999. 159 p.
Publ. of: Eigen Huis & Interieur.
Transl. of: Dutch style. 1999.

Swaaij, Louise van
The atlas of experience / Louise van Swaaij and Jean Klare; [transl. from the Dutch]. London: Bloomsbury, 2000. 96 p.
Transl. of: Atlas van de belevingswereld. 1999.

Tepper, Nanne
The happy hunting grounds / Nanne Tepper; transl. from the Dutch by Sam Garrett. London: Flamingo, 2000. 269 p.
Transl. of: De eeuwige jachtvelden. 1995.

The
The Hague City Mondial: the making of a tourist product in a multiethnic city / [text: Amrit Consultancy (Sitla Bonoo ... et al.; ed. English text: Alex Burrough, transl. from the Dutch]. The Hague: City of The Hague, cop. 1999. 96 p.
Transl. of: Reisgids Den Haag City Mondial: een wereld achter de duinen. 1999.

Tjin, Roy
The guide to Suriname / Roy Tjin & Els Schellekens; transl. [from the Dutch] and ed.: Judi & Henk Reichart; [maps: Hebri; photos: Roy Tjin]. [Amsterdam]: Brasa Publishers, 1999. 113, [16] p. photos.
Transl. of: Reizen in Suriname: piranha en mopè. 1995.

Van Riel, Gerd
Pleasure and the good life: Plato, Aristotle, and the Neoplatonists / by Gerd Van Riel. Leiden [etc.]: Brill, 2000. X, 207 p. (Philosophia antiqua,; vol. 85)
Transl. and adapt. of: Het genot en het goede: Plato's Philebus en zijn invloed in de antieke filosofie. 1997. Thesis Leuven.

Vandersteen, Willy
The circle of power / Willy Vandersteen; script and drawings, Paul Geerts; [transl. from the Dutch]. Edinburgh: Intes International, 1998. 56 p. (The greatest adventures of Spike and Suzy)
Transl. of: De gouden cirkel. 1960. (De Avonturen van Suske en Wiske).

Vandersteen, Willy
Highland games / Willy Vandersteen; [transl. from the Dutch]. Edinburgh: Intes International, 2000. 56 p.: Gekleurde ill.; 28 cm. (The greatest adventures of Spike and Suzy)
Transl. of: De knokkersburcht. 1954. (De avonturen van Suske en Wiske; 20)

Vandersteen, Willy
The Loch Ness mystery / by Willy Vandersteen; [transl. from the Dutch]. Edinburgh: Intes International, 1999. 36 p. (The greatest adventures of Spike and Suzy; 5)
Transl. of: Het monster van Loch Ness. 1978. (Suske en Wiske).

Vasalis (pseud. van: Margaretha Leenmans)
Fifteen of her poems /

Vasalis; with transl. [from the Dutch] by James Brockway. Woubrugge: Avalon Press, 1999. [39] p.
Text in English and Dutch.
Transl. of a selection from: Gedichten. 1997.

Velmans, Edith
Edith's story / Edith Velmans. New York: Soho, 1999. 240 p.
First English ed. publ. as: Edith's book. London: Viking, 1998. Based on diaries and letters from the period: February 6, 1946 - December 27, 1946.
Dutch ed.: Het Verhaal van Edith. 1997.

Velthuijs, Max
Frog and duck / Max Velthuijs. London: Andersen Press, cop. 1999. [16] p.
(Frog and friends)
Transl. from the German.
First Dutch ed.: Kikker en eend. 1999. (Kikker en zijn vriendjes).

Velthuijs, Max
Frog and hare / Max Velthuijs. London: Andersen Press, cop. 2000. [16] p.
(Frog and friends)
Transl. from the German.
First Dutch ed.: Kikker en haas. 2000. (Kikker en zijn vriendjes).

Velthuijs, Max
Frog and pig / Max Velthuijs. London: Andersen Press, cop. 1999. [16] p.
(Frog and friends)
Transl. from the German.
First Dutch ed.: Kikker en varkentje. 1999. (Kikker en zijn vriendjes).

Velthuijs, Max
Frog and rat / Max Velthuijs. London: Andersen Press, cop. 2000. [16] p.
(Frog and friends)
Transl. from the German.
First Dutch ed.: Kikker en rat. 2000. (Kikker en zijn vriendjes).

Velthuijs, Max
Frog in love / Max Velthuijs; [transl. from the German after the original Dutch edition by Anthea Bell]. London: Andersen Press, [1999]. [32] p.
First English ed.: 1989.
Transl. of: Was ist los, Frosch. 1990.
First Dutch ed.: Kikker is verliefd. 1989.

Verburg, Heleen
Fathers & eggs; Cinders / Heleen Verburg; transl. [from the Dutch] by Rina Vergano; introd.: Peter de Graef].
Amsterdam: International Theatre & Film Books, 2000. 112 p. (Theatre in translation)
Transl. of: Vaders en eieren. 1996, and: Assepoes. 1997.

Verhaeghe, Paul
Love in a time of loneliness: three essays on drives and desires / Paul Verhaeghe. New York: Other Press, 1999.
Transl. of: Liefde in tijden van eenzaamheid: drie verhandelingen over drift en verlangen. 1998.

Verhofstadt-Deneve, Lene
Theory and practice of action and drama techniques: developmental psychotherapy from an existential-dialectical viewpoint / Lene Verhofstadt-Deneve; [transl. from the Dutch].
Philadelphia, Pa: Jessica Kingsley Publishers, 1999.
Transl. of: Zelfreflectie en persoonsontwikkeling: een handboek voor ontwikkelingsgerichte psychotherapie. 2nd rev. and augm. ed. 1994.
First Dutch ed. publ. as: Persoon, ontwikkeling en psychodrama: een existentieel-dialectische visie. 1998.

Verhoog, Jeroen
75 years Organon: 1923-1998 / by Jeroen Verhoog; [research & manuscript Hans Warmerdam ... et al.; transl. from the Dutch STV Translations].
Oss: Organon; Noordwijk: Aan Zee, 1998. 120 p.
Transl. of: 75 jaar Organon: 1923-1998. 1998.

Vermeiren, Korneel
Praying with Benedict: prayer in the rule of St Benedict / Korneel Vermeiren; transl. [from the Dutch] by Richard Yeo. London: Darton Longman & Todd, 1999. 112 p.
Transl. of: Bidden met Benedictus: het gebed in de regel van Sint Benedictus. 1980. (Monastieke cahiers; 16).

Vos, Ida
The key is lost / Ida Vos; transl. [from the Dutch] by Terese Edelstein. New York: Morrow Junior Books, 2000.
Transl. of: De sleutel is gebroken. 1996.

Vree, Wilbert van
Meetings, manners and civilization: the development of modern meeting behaviour / Wilbert van Vree; transl. [from the Dutch] by Kathleen Bell. London [etc.]: Leicester University Press, cop. 1999. XIII, 370 p.
Transl. of: Nederland als vergaderland. 1994.

Vuijsje, Herman
The politically correct Netherlands: since the 1960s / Herman Vuijsje; transl. [from the Dutch] by Mark Hooker. Westport, CT: Greenwood Press, 2000 (Contributions to the study of world history; no. 76)
Transl. of: Correct: weldenkend Nederland sinds de jaren zestig. 1997.

Waaijman, Kees
The mystical space of Carmel: a commentary on the Carmelite rule / by Kees Waaijman; transl. [from the Dutch] by John Vriend. Leuven: Peeters, 1999. VI, 279 p. (The fiery arrow collection; 1)
Transl. of: De mystieke ruimte van de Karmel. 1995.

Wandering
Wandering the wharves: a historical walk through Utrecht city / composed by Margriet Hoogendoorn and Henk Denneman; photogr. by Rem Laan; transl. [from the Dutch] by Emilin Lap. Utrecht: Stichting De Plantage, 2000. 47 p.
Transl. of: Zwerven tussen Dom en werven: een historische wandeling door Utrecht. 1999.

Wang, Lulu
The lily theater: a novel of modern China / Lulu Wang; transl. from the Dutch by Hester Velmans. 1st ed. New York [etc.]: Nan A. Talese, 2000. 434 p.
Transl. and adapt. of: Het lelietheater. 1997.
Other ed.: London: Little Brown, 2000, and: [Rydalmere, NSW]: Sceptre, 2000.

Werkhoven, Henk
The international guide to New Age music / Henk Werkhoven; [senior ed.: Bob Nirkind; ed. by Lester Strong; advisor and collab.: Suzanne Doucet; transl. from the Dutch Galen Yates Beach ... et al.; introd. Steven Halpen]. 1st pr. New York: Billboard Books, 1998. IX, 236 p. + CD
Transl. of: De New Age muziekencyclopedie: de belangrijkste musici: de beste muziek: met uitgebreide discografieën! 1997.

Wesseling, H.L.
Soldier and warrior: French attitudes toward the army and war on the eve of the First World War / H.L. Wesseling; transl. [from the Dutch] by Arnold J. Pomerans.
Westport, CT: Greenwood Press, 2000. XIII, 248 p. (Contributions in military studies; no. 187)
Transl. of: Soldaat en krijger: Franse opvattingen over leger en oorlog, 1905-1914. 1969. Thesis Leiden.

Wessels, Anton
"A kind of bible": Vincent van Gogh as evangelist / Anton Wessels; [transl. from the Dutch by John Bowden].

London: SCM, cop. 2000.
152 p.
Transl. of: "Een soort bijbel": Vincent van Gogh als evangelist. 1990.

Westerbaan, Wim
Peacecommunities in a war zone: an experiment: experiences of an international observer in Urabá, Colombia / Wim Westerbaan; [transl. from the Dutch Robert van den Aker ... et al.; photogr. Lucas Silva; ill. Walter Laan; drawings Anja Lund; ed. Erik Laan].
[Oegstgeest]: Centraal Missie Commissariaat; Brussels: Pax Christi International; Utrecht: Pax Christi Netherlands [distr.], 1999. 54 p.
Transl. of: redesgemeenschappen in oorlogsgebied. 1998.

Wetering, Janwillem van de
The streetbird / Janwillem van de Wetering. [Repr.].
New York: Soho, 2000.
279 p. (Soho crime).
First American ed.: New York: Putnam, 1983.
Based on the first Dutch ed.: De straatvogel, 1982.

Witte, Els
Language and politics: the Belgian case study in a historical perspective / Els Witte and Harry Van Velthoven; [transl. from the Dutch]. Bruxelles: VUB University Press, cop. 1999.
239 p. (Balans; 12)
Transl. of: Taal en politiek: de Belgische casus in een historisch perspectief. 1998.
(Balans; 12).

Woerden, Henk van
A mouthful of glass / Henk van Woerden; transl. [from the Dutch] and ed. by Dan Jacobson. London: Granta, 2000. 192 p.
Transl. of: Een mond vol glas. 1998. Partly earlier publ. in: Granta, no. 69.

Working
Working conditions, safety and environment: an integrated approach in the Groningen University

Hospital / [ed. Wout Sorgdrager; final ed. Ada Bolhuis; photogr. Antoinette Borchert; transl. from the Dutch]. Groningen: AZG, 1998. 56 p. (AZG management reports; 5)
Transl. of: Arbo, veiligheid en milieu: een integrale aanpak in het AZG. 1998. (AZG managementcahiers; 5).

Worldwide
Worldwide banking, ABN AMRO Bank 1824-1999 / ed. by Joh. de Vries, Wim Vroom, Ton de Graaf; [transl. from the Dutch Maarten Ultee ... et al.; text ed. Ton de Graaf ... et al.; ill. ed. Ton de Graaf ... et al.; photogr. Bert Verhoeff ... et al.]. Amsterdam: ABN AMRO Bank, 1999. 608 p.
Publ. on the occasion of the 175 years anniversary of the ABN AMRO Bank.
Transl. of: Wereldwijd bankieren, ABN AMRO 1824-1999.
1999.

Ypeij, Annelou
Producing against poverty: female and male micro-entrepreneurs in Lima, Peru / Annelou Ypeij; transl. [from the Dutch] by Peter Mason. Amsterdam: Amsterdam University Press, cop. 2000.
VIII, 163 p.
Transl. of: Overleven, ondernemen: vrouwelijke en mannelijke micro-producenten in Lima, Peru. 1995.
Thesis Utrecht.

Zevenhuizen, A.
Erosion and weathering / [written by: A. Zevenhuizen; transl. from the Dutch by K.M.M. Hudson-Brazenall]. 1st ed. London [etc.]: New Holland, 1998. 78 p. 32 cm. (Natural phenomena)
Transl. of: Erosie en verwering. 1997. (Natuur in beweging).

Zoeter, Titia
Dynamism with a future: 125 years Louis Nagel / Titia Zoeter; [transl. from the Dutch by Woord voor Woord].

Noordwijk: Uitgeverij aan Zee, cop. 1998. 63 p.
Publ. on the occasion of the 125 years anniversary of Louis Nagel B.V.
Transl. of: Dynamiek met toekomst: 125 jaar Louis Nagel. 1998.

Contributors

Kader Abdolah (1954-)
Writer
Boekbinderstraat 36,
8043 AT Zwolle,
The Netherlands

Dirk van Assche (1955-)
Editorial secretary
Ons Erfdeel
Murissonstraat 260,
8930 Rekkem, Belgium

Saskia Bak (1964-)
Deputy Curator of the Fries Museum, Leeuwarden
Radesingel 14 B,
9711 EJ Groningen,
The Netherlands

Michel Bakker (1958-)
Advisor and researcher for the conservation of monuments, history of architecture and archeology
Sportparklaan 19,
2103 VR Heemstede,
The Netherlands

Jan Berkouwer (1947-)
Professor of Economics (University of Stettin) / Lecturer in Economics and Law (Holland College, Diemen)
Kerkweg 83,
2825 NA Berkenwoude,
The Netherlands

Daniël Bilterejst (1962-)
Professor of Film, Televison and Cultural Media Studies (University of Ghent)
Doylijkstraat 69,
1701 Dilbeek, Belgium

Rudolf Boehm (1927-)
Emeritus Professor of Philosophy
(University of Ghent)
Visserij 90,

Editor:
Dutch Book in Translation
Koninklijke Bibliotheek
The Hague
The Netherlands

9000 Ghent, Belgium

Kurt de Boodt (1969-)
Editor *Het Kunstenpaleis - Le Palais des Beaux-Arts*
Blokstraat 9,
2800 Mechelen, Belgium

José Boyens
Art critic
Hogewaldseweg 33,
6562 KR Groesbeek,
The Netherlands

Anton Claessens (1936-)
Member of the editorial board *Ons Erfdeel*
Honkersven 29,
2440 Geel, Belgium

Dieter de Clercq (1974-)
Architect / Researcher (Catholic University of Leuven)
Meersstraat 139,
9000 Ghent, Belgium

Jozef Deleu (1937-)
Chief editor / Managing director
'Stichting Ons Erfdeel'
Murissonstraat 260,
8930 Rekkem, Belgium

Dirk van Delft
Journalist *NRC Handelsblad*
Kalvermarkt 5,
2312 LL Leiden,
The Netherlands

Paul Demets (1966-)
Literary critic / Teacher
Kasteelstraat 56,
9870 Olsene, Belgium

Luc Devoldere (1956-)
Deputy editor
'Stichting Ons Erfdeel'
Murissonstraat 260,
8930 Rekkem, Belgium

Elsbeth Etty (1951-)
Editor NRC Handelsblad
Prinsengracht 4,
1015 DV Amsterdam,
The Netherlands

Rob van Ginkel (1955-)
Lecturer in Sociology and
Anthropology (University
of Amsterdam)
Groene Jagerstraat 9,
1551 ES Westzaan,
The Netherlands

Arnold Heumakers
Writer
Brouwersgracht 45,
1015 GB Amsterdam,
The Netherlands

Martha Hollander (1959-)
Assistant Professor of Art
History
(New College, Hofstra
University)
New College, 130 Hofstra
University,
Hempstead NY 11549, USA

Marc Hooghe (1964-)
Lecturer in Sociology
(University Institute
Antwerp) / FWO Researcher
Breendonkstraat 24,
9000 Ghent, Belgium

Rita Ingram Givens
Writer / Teacher
1396 18th Avenue,
San Francisco, CA 94122,
USA

Moses Isegawa (1963-)
Writer
c /o De Bezige Bij,
Van Mierveldstraat 1-3,
1017 DW Amsterdam,
The Netherlands

Yves Knockaert (1954-)
Lecturer in the History and
Aesthetics of Musicology
(Lemmens Institute,
Leuven)
Vaarstraat 51 A / 14,
3000 Leuven, Belgium

Dana Linssen (1966-)
Film critic NRC
Handelsblad /
Chief Editor Filmkrant
Prins Bernhardlaan 5,
3722 AE Bilthoven,
The Netherlands

John Mace
EU civil servant (retired)

Duisburgsesteenweg 39,
3080 Tervuren, Belgium

Erik Martens (1962-)
Film critic
Mellinetplein 1,
2600 Berchem, Belgium

Filip Matthijs (1966-)
Editorial secretary The Low
Countries
Murissonstraat 260,
8930 Rekkem, Belgium

Jos Nijhof (1952-)
Theatre critic / Teacher
Berkenkade 14,
2351 NB Leiderdorp,
The Netherlands

Wim de Poorter (1939-)
Film critic / Teacher
Rijselstraat 280 B,
8200 Bruges, Belgium

Cyrille Offermans (1945-)
Literary critic / Writer
Tersteeglaan 112,
6133 WT Sittard,
The Netherlands

Anil Ramdas (1958-)
Writer
c /o De Bezige Bij,
Van Mierveldstraat 1-3,
1017 DW Amsterdam,
The Netherlands

Mark Derez
Archivist (Catholic
University of Leuven)
Mgr. Ladeuzeplein 21,
3000 Leuven, Belgium

Marc Reynebeau (1956-)
Editor Knack
Hofbouwlaan 5,
9000 Ghent, Belgium

Filip Rogiers (1966-)
Journalist Knack
E. Demolderlaan 46,
1030 Schaarbeek, Belgium

Marc Ruyters (1952-)
Editor De Financieel-
Economische Tijd /
Art critic
Koning Albertlei 15,
2650 Edegem, Belgium

Reinier Salverda (1948-)
Professor of Dutch
Language and Literature
(University of London)
University College London,
Gower Street,

London WC1E 6 BT, United
Kingdom

Désirée Schyns (1959-)
Lecturer
(Erasmushogeschool,
Ghent)
Burgstraat 83 E,
9000 Ghent, Belgium

Rudi Tambuyser (1972-)
Teacher / Singer / Music
critic
Nationalestraat 79 / 2,
2000 Antwerp, Belgium

Lauran Toorians (1958-)
Writer
Kasteellaan 2,
5175 BD Loon op Zand,
The Netherlands

Hans Vanacker (1960-)
Editorial Secretary
Septentrion
Murissonstraat 260,
8930 Rekkem, Belgium

Koen Vergeer (1962-)
Literary critic / Writer

Abel Tasmanstraat 63,
3531 GT Utrecht,
The Netherlands

Bart Vervaeck (1958-)
Lecturer in Dutch Literature
and Literary Theory (Free
University of Brussels)
Kapelseweg 162,
2811 Leest, Belgium

Marjoleine de Vos (1957-)
Editor NRC Handelsblad
Frans van Mierisstraat 106,
1071 SB Amsterdam,
The Netherlands

Jan W. de Vries (1937-)
Emeritus Professor of
Modern Linguistics
(University of Leiden)
3e Poellaan 40,
2161 DN Lisse,
The Netherlands

Jeroen Vullings (1962-)
Editor Vrij Nederland
Lorentzplein 23,
2012 HH Haarlem,
The Netherlands

Translators

Gregory Ball (B)

Pleuke Boyce (CA)

Alex Brotherton (NL)

Sheila M. Dale (UK)

Derek Denné (NL)

Lindsay Edwards (UK)

Chris Emery (UK)

Jane Fenoulhet (UK)

Nancy Forest-Flier (NL)

Tanis Guest (UK)

Yvette Mead (NL)

Elizabeth Mollison (NL)

Alison Mouthaan-Gwillim
(B)

Sonja Prescod (UK)

Ina Rilke (NL)

Julian Ross (UK)

Paul Vincent (UK)

Diane L. Webb (NL)

ADVISOR ON ENGLISH
USAGE

Tanis Guest (UK)

As well as the yearbook *The Low Countries*, the Flemish-Netherlands foundation 'Stichting Ons Erfdeel' publishes a number of books covering various aspects of the culture of Flanders and the Netherlands.

O. Vandeputte / P. Vincent / T. Hermans
Dutch. The Language of Twenty Million Dutch and Flemish People.
Illustrated; 64 pp.

J.A. Kossmann-Putto & E.H. Kossmann
The Low Countries. History of the Northern and Southern Netherlands.
Illustrated; 64 pp.

Jaap Goedegebuure & Anne Marie Musschoot
Contemporary Fiction of the Low Countries.
Illustrated and with translated extracts from 15 novels; 128 pp.

Hugo Brems & Ad Zuiderent
Contemporary Poetry of the Low Countries.
With 52 translated poems; 112 pp.

Ludo Bekkers & Elly Stegeman
Contemporary Painting of the Low Countries.
Illustrated in four colour printing; 128 pp.

Elly Stegeman & Marc Ruyters
Contemporary Sculptors of the Low Countries.
Illustrated in four colour printing; 128 pp.

Hans Ibelings & Francis Strauven
Contemporary Architects of the Low Countries.
Illustrated in four colour printing; 128 pp.

Between 1993 and 2000 the first eight issues of the yearbook *The Low Countries* were published.